WORLDS APART

NEW IMMIGRANT VOICES

BY

MILLY CHARON

CORMORANT BOOKS

The author and publisher want to express their gratitude for funding assistance from The Secretary of State, Directorate of Multiculturalism, The Canada Council and the Ontario Arts Council.

The views expressed herein do not necessarily reflect the position or policy of the Government of Canada.

Cover photograph of the Netherland Ambassador Dr. J.H. Van Roijin greeting Dutch immigrants as their ship docks in Montreal, Quebec, in June, 1947. Courtesy of the National Archives of Canada. Photo by George Hunter of the National Film Board Collection.

Published by Cormorant Books, RR 1, Dunvegan, Ontario K0C 1J0. Printed by Hignell Printing Limited in Winnipeg, Manitoba.

Printed and bound in Canada.

Canadian Cataloguing in Publication Data

Main entry under title:

Worlds apart : new immigrant voices

Bibliography: p.
ISBN 0-920953-11-5

1. Immigrants—Canada—Biography. 2. Canada—Emmigration and immigration—History—20th century.
I. Charon, Milly, date

FC104.W67 1989   304.8'71'00922   C89-090191-0
Fl035.AlW67 1989

This book is dedicated to:

the visible minorities whose resettlement
and integration have been slower, more difficult
and which require more
understanding, patience and assistance;

my daughter Stacey Janett
who understood my anguish
and led me back on the path to the fulfillment of my dream—
completing my education and using it to write
about immigrants and ethnic people of Canada;

the special friends whose patient understanding
of my creative isolation was of great support.

CONTENTS

PREFACE

Before I had finished the compilation of Volume I of *Between Two Worlds—The Canadian Immigrant Experience,* I realized I had barely scratched the surface of the subject. There were so many other immigrants and first-generation children of different ethnic groups whose stories of their lands of origin and their resettlement in Canada demanded to be told. In addition, I felt that I was recording a statement of some importance by asking immigrants for their reactions to the process of integration—how to survive the immigrant experience and thrive, despite it. Their struggle for self-identification and adjustment might prove beneficial to those who would come after, along a path already travelled. I also encouraged, and even instigated discussions on controversial subjects which concern immigrants, hoping that government ministries and agencies would take heed and make some changes to improve the lot of the newcomer. And most important of all, I yearned for an end to the prejudice, bigotry and racism that have plagued our country for so many generations.

Idealistic? Perhaps, but I have great faith in Canada and her people.

In the course of my work—interviews, research, lecture engagements and organizational activities—I came across many people whose displacement and resettlement in Canada had not occurred without emotional and economical hardship. While I have chafed at restrictions, and, on occasion, even felt acute frustration at my inability to help, I have never walked away from anyone with a problem. Sometimes all it required were a few phone calls, some letters, or a calling-in of promised favours. At other times, it meant giving advice on where to go, whom to see, or how to go about putting a foot into a slightly open door. Doors somehow seemed to slam more often on immigrants than on established Canadians of second and third generations.

The visible minorities have suffered most. For that reason,

I have dedicated this volume to them—a small gesture, perhaps, but a sincere one.

Our once vast world has shrunk to a global village. More and more waves of third-world immigrants are being cast up, like the recent boatloads of Sri Lankans, on our shores. If we look around us, we can see there are more conflicts and civil strife in third-world countries, where minorities are all to often the scape-goats in political power plays.

As a result, we can expect to see the face of Canada changing to a palette of infinitely interesting hues. Our national emblem, the maple leaf, is perhaps the most fitting of all symbols, for when it changes its solid green shades of spring and summer to the vivid and vibrant tones of autumn, it reflects in its maturity the colour spectrum of our pluralistic Canadian society. In its mixture of red, golds, yellows, olives and brown tones, we can see Canada's visible minorities as a kaleidoscope image—varied, colourful and ever-changing.

Perhaps we should see the monochromatic red of the maple leaf on our national flag with the inner eye that interprets the subtleties of a surface uniformity in the truer and more representa-tive colours of our emerging society.

My *modus operandi* has been similar to that adopted for Volume I. Because of my desire to retain a style of diversity, reflecting our ethnocultural society, I have collected articles, short stories, essays, interviews and personal testimonials. Original manuscripts have not only been edited, but have had much re-searched material added in order to make them more interesting and to provide the readers with background knowledge of geo-graphical location and historical events. While some stories are collaborations between myself and authors, as well as newspaper articles, the majority have attempted to retain the speech patterns of most of my interviewees, although in a number of cases where they had only the barest of language skills, I found myself com-pelled to revise the vocabulary and syntax.

I offer this volume whole-heartedly to the people of Can-ada, in the hope that it will promote understanding among the many ethnic and visible minorities, and that one day we may all benefit from the many cultures in Canada and, in the process, discover that racism has finally disappeared from our pluralistic society.

ACKNOWLEDGEMENTS

In the two and a half years since I began working on Volume II of *Between Two Worlds, The Canadian Immigrant Experience,* I have researched a great deal of material both to augment and complement the stories I taped and those which were sent to me. In addition, every date, place and even certain statements made in the course of the interviews I conducted, had to be verified and noted. To better understand the situations, and even traumas, my immigrant interviewees had endured, I searched for documentaries, histories, and recorded events in clipping files. It was a massive piece of labour, and truly one of love.

But I could not have done it unaided, and so, I would like to thank those resource people who have contributed services, material or advice to assist me with the project. Among those were: Dr. Julius Pfeiffer, PhD; Dr. Simon Messing, PhD; Dr. Patricia Morley, PhD; Henry Rosenthal; Paula Draper, PhD; Ann Morton, Assistant Keeper, Search Department, Public Records Office in Surrey, England; Norma King of the British Consulate-General, Montreal; Antonietta Martuccio; Joe Vacirca; Luisa Frazzetto; Dominique Bertrand; A.J. Yaremovich; Stan Cytrynbaum; Harry Blank; Lily Tasso; Reverend Pranas Gaida; Eddie Hazen; C.D. Minni; Miodrag Brkic; Leo Zarins and Managing Editor Mel Morris of *The Gazette* (Montreal), who gave me unfailing support and access to the newspaper's clipping and photography files.

My gratitude goes to those who sent immigrants with stories to me: Harriet Saalheimer, Dolores Rosen, Bernard Spector, Jan Valenta, Donna Mosel, Sam Charon, Zaven Degirmen, and others whose suggestions, unfortunately, did not materialize into interviews.

I would also like to extend my sincere thanks to the special people in the Audio-Visual Department at Concordia University for photographic services, repairs to malfunctioning tape recorders and many other kindnesses. Without the help of Director Mark

Schofield, Winston Cross and his staff, and others, I would not have been able to honour my commitments. In particular, I wish to record my appreciation to Bernard Queenan, former Director of the Audio-Visual Department for his extraordinary assistance and encouragement in meeting my deadlines. A very special thank you goes to Clara Paradisis, whose word-processing skills in putting the final manuscript on diskette, left me in awe.

I am grateful to *Maclean's* newsmagazine and *Canadian Jewish News* for permission to use excerpts from printed articles, and to the Lithuanian weeklies, particularily to *Teviskes Ziburai* and its editor Reverend Pranas Gaida, and to John Kudukis for their help and donated research material on the history of the Lithuanian people. I would also like to thank the *Hamilton Spectator, Toronto Star, Ottawa Citizen, Winnipeg Free Press, Calgary Herald, Lethbridge Herald, Vancouver Sun,* as well as other newspapers that aided me in locating at least seven of the Lithuanians whose photograph appeared on the cover of my first book.

My appreciation and apologies to those friends whom I have neglected socially during those years of intense work. I hope I have been forgiven.

Last but not least, I would like to extend my gratitude to those who contributed portions of their lives in this volume, and to the Secretary of State, Directorate of Multiculturalism, without whose generous assistance, the writing and publication of this book would not have been possible.

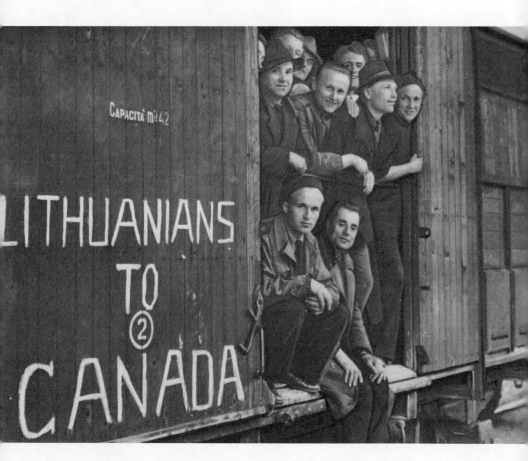

BOXCAR

by
John K. Kudukis
and Milly Charon

In September, 1939 when Adolf Hitler's armoured columns began to roll all over Europe, they bulldozed everything before them. Ahead of the German attackers fled entire communities, uprooted and terrified, moving in any direction that appeared to promise survival. Behind them came the conquerors, heartless and inhuman, gathering and sorting the survivors into units of slave labour or uniformed cannon-fodder.

After the war, the Allied Powers were faced with the task of resettling the hundreds of thousands of victims who had been so brutally dislocated by the savagery of military necessity or political expediency. These homeless human beings, stranded like debris tossed up on foreign shores, were known as DPs—Displaced Persons.

By March 23, 1948, a contingent of hundreds of such stateless wanderers from the Baltic countries had been gathered from various Displaced-Persons camps, and sent by boxcar to the Italian town of Collegno. They had been waiting for years while Allied governments debated which countries would accept how many of these unfortunate exiles.

And so it was that John K. Kudukis found himself in one of the groups milling around awaiting orders to climb into one the boxcars which had been provided for the lucky ones accepted by Canada. They were to be transported to Genoa where a ship waited at anchor to carry them to a new life overseas.

Kudukis fingered a piece of chalk in his pocket. Suddenly he had an idea. He strode over to one of the two boxcars assigned to the Lithuanian group and with bold, heavy strokes wrote on the rough boards: "Lithuanians—To Canada". With that simple action, Kudukis earned a place in history for himself and his group, for when the men climbed into the boxcars a few minutes later, crowding at the doorway before departure, an unidentified photographer snapped their picture.

It was to appear in the Montreal Star on April 8, 1948, over the cutline: "The photograph depicts part of a group of 860 Baltic and Balkan nationals brought in from camps in the British and American zones of Germany for resettlement in Canada. The group is moving under the International Refugee Organization's programme, which has, by this time, settled more than 12,000 displaced persons alone."

Thirty-five years later, Milly Charon, author and editor of *Between Two Worlds—The Canadian Immigrant Experience,* came across the photograph in the *Gazette* (Montreal) archives, where she had been seeking a suitable picture to illustrate the cover of her book. Her curiosity was piqued. The faces haunted her, and she felt she had to know who the men were and what had happened to them. She had twenty-five copies of the photograph developed and sent them to newspapers in twenty-five Canadian cities with the query: "Where are they now?", along with the request to contact her at the address indicated in an explanatory paragraph accompanying the photograph.

Letters began pouring in several weeks later from Lithuanians who had arrived in that group or in other immigrant resettlements.

However, she was unprepared when she answered the phone on a Sunday morning in late May, 1984 and heard: "How did you get my picture in the paper?"

"Which one are you?" she countered with a gasp.

"I'm the one who wrote the chalk message on the boxcar!"

The search had both ended and begun with John Kudukis. Through his help and that of Aleksas Paulius, another of the men framed in the doorway of the boxcar in the photograph, as well as with the assistance of editor Reverend Pranas Gaida of the Canadian-Lithuanian newspaper *Teviskes Ziburiai,* most of the men were identified. Several were seriously ill and therefore, not available for interviews. A few had died. Kudukis and Paulius were to provide most of the information for the story which follows.

* * * *

John Kudukis was born in March, 1914 in the small town of Kvetkai, Lithuania. His family lived just outside the town where his father, a farmer, owned some land. John Kudukis' early childhood memories included episodes from the later days of World War 1.

"In 1919, Russian Bolsheviks occupied our part of Lithuania," he recalled, "and it was during this period that Lithuanian Freedom Fighters were attempting to free our country. Russian Bolsheviks overran our farm and trampled our garden. When my father protested, they drew their guns. Had the neighbours not intervened, he would certainly have lost his life."

By 1920, the Freedom Fighters had formed a strong organization, which evolved into the Lithuanian Regular Army. Kudukis' two older brothers had joined them, and for almost two years they fought to free Lithuania of both the Bolsheviks and any Germans who had remained behind as settlers. At the same time, they were fighting against the Poles, who had taken over the eastern part of Lithuania, the Vilnius-Suvalkai region. Poland appealed to the League of Nations to intervene and settle the matter. Their decision was to remove a portion of Lithuania and hand it over officially to Poland, thus establishing a new frontier. Poland remained in occupation of this territory until Germany attacked in September, 1939.

The Russian counter-offensive in 1941 drove the Poles out of this region. Although the Russians restored the lands previously declared to be Polish to the Lithuanians, the results were equally sad, for the little Baltic country, along with Latvia and Estonia, lost its independence and became a Russian satellite.

"With the Russian takeover, the Lithuanian government was dissolved," explained Kudukis. "Officials were dismissed, some arrested and jailed, while others fled abroad. A number of people were deported to Siberia, my father among them. He was arrested on June 13, 1941 by the KGB Secret Police and sent to Siberia. I never saw him, or heard from him again. The Lithuanian Army was disbanded, and all its personnel were drafted into the Russian Army.

"In February, 1940, after the Russians had returned the city of Vilnius and other territory to Lithuania, I came to the city and

19

found employment in the Municipal Collector's Department offices. Standing in a crowd on the street that June, I witnessed the Russian Army marching triumphantly through the streets of Vilnius. Only members ot the Communist Party met the Russians with joy. For the other Lithuanians it was a sad sight, and from that day on a period of uncertainty and fear began."

No one knew when his turn would come. Some people were arrested, some simply disappeared from their homes at night, while others were picked up in the streets during the day by Russian Security officers. Many of the people were jailed, some were put to death, and others deported to Soviet labour camps.

Frightened that a similar fate awaited him, Kudukis left his job and kept moving in Vilnius and the area surrounding the city, never staying long in one place. Finally he hid out for two months in a bunkhouse hidden deep in the forest, living with fourteen men and women who were also on the run.

"By June 22, 1941, Germany was at war with Russia and early on the fateful Sunday morning, German planes flew over Vilnius and dropped loads of bombs. At noon we heard the Lithuanian National Anthem on the radio and learned that we had fallen into the hands of yet another conqueror."

Lithuanian rebel bands joined forces to fight against the Russians with the forlorn hope that Germany, in return, would grant them their independence. The Russians were viewed as the worse of the two invaders. However, as the German front pushed ever eastward, the Third Reich made it obvious it had its own system, no better than that of the Russians.

"We were asked to fight for a new Europe," Kudikis said. "Many of us fled. I was captured by German officials, put into uniform and sent to the front near Leningrad to fight against the Russians. I knew I had to get out of there. Both the Russians and Germans used manpower from captured countries to fight one another. The Balts were trapped in the middle, as usual."

Kudukis made contact with Lithuanian officers working at the German Army Headquarters. They agreed to help him get leave and obtained some official papers with a German stamp which would enable him to get train reservations, and the assistance necessary to return to Lithuania for two weeks.

"Before I left, however, I spent a month learning to forge

the German Major's signature. With the exception of one Lithuanian officer, I didn't tell anyone that I intended to desert. When I presented the German Army Transport officer with my fake documents, with the forged signature, he approved my pass immediately.

"I had no trouble travelling the first hundred miles to the check point at Luga, Russia. Here we were questioned by German Army Security Police. I was sweating with fear that they would discover my documents were forged. Fortunately, the officer checking the papers was an older man and not overly suspicious. He didn't notice anything amiss. He passed me through, although he asked why I did not have a train reservation number. I explained that our battalion was recently formed, and as yet we did not have a special reservation number.

"He told me that I couldn't continue on that train but would have to go to the Red Cross hotel and sleep there overnight. He wrote out a permit for this and told me I could take the first train next day."

Needless to say, Kudukis did not sleep much that night, worrying what might happen to him in the morning. At six a.m. he went back to the station and boarded the train without incident.

"I was able to get back home to my wife and one-year-old daughter, and we packed up and returned to the area where I was born. My wife and I both found jobs, as we had friends in the Lithuanian Police Force in that district. They saved me from the German authorities who were looking for me as a deserter in 1943."

The Russian Front began pushing westward, and a number of families, including the Kudukises, piled into a truck and headed for a safer place close to the German border.

"On the trip, two policemen, one German and the other Lithuanian, turned up and confiscated the truck. The police ordered some farmers who had transportation to take us to the nearest railway station, where we discovered many others in the same frightening plight. The German authorities quickly surrounded the Lithuanians, separating the men from their families. Single women under fifty years of age were left with the men, and the entire group of singles were taken to the Front to dig trenches. When we got there, the battle lines had started moving forward again, overrunning the spot where we were to dig. A number of us turned and ran for the railway station about twenty miles away with the intention of travelling as far west as we could."

But when the Lithuanians arrived at the station from which they had originally left, they discovered that their families had already been shipped out to Vienna in Austria. Kudukis knew he had to get there quickly, but the train system was in a state of chaos as priority was being given to troop movements to and from the Eastern Front. Allied air raids in 1943 on vital railway arteries had also thrown the entire transportation system into confusion. The Russians were on Germany's doorstep, and everyone was fleeing before the steady advance.

"Finally, a number of us managed to find a train going to Vienna by way of Czechoslovakia, a trip that was to take us over two days. At each stop along the way, we were questioned by German police, and had to explain why we were making the trip. Fortunately we had provided ourselves with false documents which indicated we had been sent to work in Vienna. We were hoping to find our families there.

"There were difficulties along the way, and when we finally arrived and made inquiries, we were informed our families had been sent to Pragersko, southeast of Maribor in Yugoslavia. It took us another two days to get there, but we found them."

Kudukis and his companions discovered their wives and relatives had been transported to work in industrial centres serving the German war effort. Under German supervision, armaments manufacturers were building a huge aluminum factory complex, and Kudukis and his group were forced to work on the construction. However, the Allies were well-informed about the potential importance of the plant, for bombers proceeded to demolish it. Twice a day, air raids halted production, and the workers had to take refuge in underground shelters located about a quarter of a mile from the factory and labour camp.

"Luckily no bombs dropped on our camp, and we felt the reason for this may have been the fact there was a concentration camp nearby, containing Yugoslavian families of Freedom fighters who were battling the Germans. The Allies did not wish to harm them. But we didn't have it all that easy. Often at night we had to go to a shelter closer to our camp for protection because the Yugoslavian Freedom Fighters were sniping at our camp.

"It took a week of steady bombing to destroy the factory. The Germans abandoned the construction and transferred our work-unit to another assignment. However, once the camp was disbanded, we were forced to go to the nearest village for food. We had no trouble with the villagers who were very kind to us, once they discovered that we weren't Germans. Some of the Lithuanian families had small children, and the villagers sold us milk, fruit and vegetables for the youngsters, and of course, booze for us."

Once more the Lithuanians were on the move, like gypsies, directed to the German relocation office in Innsbruck, Austria. On the way there, word was relayed that the town of Innsbruck had been badly bombed, and the train could not continue to its destination. Many of the men got off at stops along the way and looked for jobs. Kudukis, in the same situation as the others, was unable to find work, but was advised to go to Kufstein on the Bavarian border.

"Once I arrived there with my family, I was hired as an electrician in a sawmill. The owner, an old Austrian industrialist, was very good to me. He gave me an apartment, and helped me get food and clothing permits from the city. My employer was a very understanding man who realized how badly I felt about the loss of my country, and he wanted to hire me permanently. However, I remained there only until the end of the war in 1945."

By this time Displaced Persons' Camps were being organized in Kufstein by the United Nations in order to relocate those who had sought refuge there. Most could not be repatriated to countries now in Soviet hands. Kudukis registered at one of the camps and moved there, remaining until the Allies transferred Tyrol to the French-Occupied Zone. Then he moved to the town of Bad Worishofen in Bavaria, with the permission of the Occupation Authorities. He waited for several years before his big chance came.

"In December, 1947, we received news that those wishing to go to Canada to work in the gold mines were to travel to Munich and register at the Funk Caserne. A group of us went and found the Canadian Commission Office. After I passed a medical examination and answered some questions about my political affiliations, my application was accepted. With others, I was told to go back to the camp at Bad Worishofen and wait there until we received word to return to Munich, from where we would travel by train to get a ship at an Italian port.

"On March 10, 1948 a large group of Lithuanians set out in boxcars heading for Naples, but the train halted in Kufstein, where we waited impatiently for two days. Sent back to Munich, we were told the ship had left Naples for Genoa on the north-western coast of Italy. Two days later we arrived at Collegno, where the entire group was placed in a Jewish Transfer Camp to wait until March 23rd."

And that was when John Kudukis made his mark on history with a piece of chalk.

By 9:30 p.m. he was Passenger Number 476 on a ship bound for Halifax, Canada, with hundreds of other single male and female emigrants. The ship had been an army transport vessel, and the cabin area had been rebuilt to form one huge dormitory. About 160 men, separated from the women at the other end of the ship, were crowded into the forward section. There were no families aboard. Children and spouses would be sent for after contract conditions had been worked out.

"The voyage was rough, and for about three days most of the passengers were seasick. The men spent most of the time in their three-tiered bunks.

"March 28, 1948 was Easter Sunday, and the entire Lithuanian group joined together to celebrate the holiday by singing hymns, as there was no priest on board to say Mass for us. We sighted Halifax five days later, and by two in the afternoon, officials on the ship began checking our documents and separating us into groups bound for different destinations.

"Awakened early the next morning, we had breakfast, and then thanked the crew for the good care they had taken of us. When we left the ship, we went through Canadian Immigration and Customs where our documents and luggage were inspected. Immediately after, we were put on a train for Kirkland Lake, Ontario, where we arrived on April 5th. Staff from the Lakeshore Mining Company met us and found us temporary accommodation in the town. The next day we reported to the Company offices for our assignments.

"I was given a day shift and started work at 5,200 feet below ground level in a gold mine. It was claustrophobic for someone like me who had never done this type of work before, and it was so very hot that I felt I was in hell. I had never even seen an underground mine, as mining in Lithuania was all on the open pit system."

After a few days almost a mile underground, Kudukis was in such a state of nerves that he went to the offices to ask the management if they could put him on a higher level, or on the surface. It they couldn't do this, he asked to be repatriated to Germany. His terror was obvious. When he reported for work the next morning, he had no idea what to expect. To his surprise he was sent down to the 450 foot level, where it was so cold and windy that icicles hung from the ceilings and walls. He was totally unprepared for the change.

"I almost froze, but my partner Mike, an older immigrant from Czechoslovakia, saved my life by giving me his sweater. Despite the cold, I was greatly relieved to work at this level and stayed there until August, 1949, when I moved to Mount Brydges, Ontario, to work on farms harvesting tobacco. It was hard work and a big change from the mines, but very pleasant working outdoors. When the crop was sold the following spring, I moved to St. Catharines and found employment in the machine shop of General Motors."

And then began a period of movement, as Kudukis followed job openings in Niagara Falls and then London, Ontario, where he worked for eleven years for General Motors, until he resigned in 1963.

"I decided to quit, as there were too many layoffs and I waited around to be recalled to work. When I found a job with the London Public Library Board of the Eldon House Museum, I remained there until I retired in 1979. I was happy at my last job, and it was the best time of my life."

Kudukis had applied for Canadian citizenship, and on September 8, 1955, he becan a full-fledged Canadian citizen. It was a memorable day in his life, he said. "I felt as if I had been born again, and was equal to other Canadians in this great country of opportunity. I was proud of my citizenship.

"There were a few moments of unhappiness or dissatisfaction when I had first come to London, because when I walked the streets with friends, speaking our own language, we would hear some Canadians saying: 'Damn DP's! Why don't they go back to

Germany?' These pejorative remarks hurt, but it was worse when I was working in the gold mines. Canadians thought we were taking their jobs away from them. And there was more. After our contracts had expired, some of us decided to stay on longer, and we started buying houses with a small down-payment. The Canadians wondered where we got the money to buy the houses because they had lived here all their lives and still didn't own a house. They thought we must have robbed someone or done something equally dishonest.

"In general, Canada was good to me, and I hope I was good for Canada. Over the years we would hear Canadians complaining about low wages, but we ignored it. We just wanted to make a living so that we could stand on our own two feet and be independent of any welfare or government assistance. The people we heard complaining then are still complaining today. They should go to Russia and see what conditions are like there. Perhaps they would realize how well off they are here. The ordinary people in Russia have so little, and even their thinking is monitored by the system. There is no such thing as freedom of any kind—not in religion, speech, thought, travel or political choice. You have to live under the Russian yoke to find out what it is like.

"Canadians don't seem to realize why the Russians build walls around themselves. It is because they are afraid the world will see what kind of system they really have. Russians are forbidden to talk to outsiders or vice versa, for the Russians might realize under what terrible conditions they live, and that it is so much better in the Western world. They would all want to leave for a better life outside.

"I have many things to thank Canada for—a good life in a democracy where I enjoy freedom of religion and speech. No one spies on us as to what church we attend, or where we are going. To this day, I have never regretted coming to Canada. Perhaps if I had known as much about this country when I first came, I might have done certain things differently and better, but every one makes mistakes. All in all, there are many opportunities for a good future, and I only hope and pray that Canadians realize this."

A SMALL CRIME*

by
Jerry Wexler

When he was nine years old, he was brought to the door by a policeman who kept one hand on his arm as if to stop him from running away. He had been caught writing with a crayon on a wall of the subway station, and his parents were expected to discipline him.

The rest of the day, he stayed in his room, waiting for his father to come home from the shirt factory. A slap on the face, he thought, perhaps that's all I'll get. And maybe no allowance for the coming week. Still, he could not help but be apprehensive.

At five-thirty, he heard the front door open. His mother was talking to his father. They talked for a long time, much longer than he felt was necessary. Then the family ate supper. He was not invited and he felt that his punishment had already started. This saddened him greatly because he enjoyed eating supper with his father and telling him about the day's adventures. He tried to pass the time by reading through his comic books, but he was anxious and could not follow one through from beginning to end.

At seven o'clock, he heard the television come on as the family sat down in the living room. Every so often someone changed a channel. By eight-thirty night had fallen, and he felt more alone than he had ever been at any time in his life. He looked out into the garden behind his room. He could see the outline of the young tree his grandfather had planted a month before. It was beginning to sprout leaves, and he tried to decide how many it would have that summer. He decided on fifteen. That knowledge made him feel better. By nine o'clock he was feeling drowsy and had lain down on his bed.

* First published in the *Montreal Review*, Spring/Summer, 1979 and in *The Bequest and Other Stories*, Véhicule Press, 1984.

Shortly after, his father came into his room and sat down on the bed. The boy sat up, putting his feet over the side of the bed. His father looked at him, then turned away clasping his hands together. They were sitting side by side. The boy looked down at the floor the whole time.

"I remember when I left Romania," his father said, "I went to the train station in my town and had to sit in a special section for people who were emigrating from the country. There were many other people sitting there, and I remember how funny it was that we all looked the same with our best clothes and old suitcases almost bursting with clothing. But what I remember most of all were the walls. It seemed that every person who had ever sat in that part of the railway station had written on the wall, his name, his home town and the new place to which he was going. I spent a long time reading all the names on the wall. Many towns were represented, and I even recognized the names of many people with whom I had once been friends. And so you know what I did? I took out my pen, found a clear space on the wall and wrote my own name, my home town and the date.

But you see, I did not write on the wall out of mischief. It was my own way of saying, *this is who I am—now I am ending an old life and starting a new one.* Perhaps one day you will have the same reason. But as long as times are good, and we are welcome here, there are other and better ways of letting the world know who you are."

He put his hand on the boy's shoulder as if to say, 'Don't worry, everything is all right.' Then he rose slowly and said: "Be good to your mother and me and leave the walls alone." Then he left the room.

The boy lay back on his bed. Ordinarily it took him only two or three minutes to fall asleep. That night he lay awake for almost half an hour.

THE CONVERSION

by
Linda Ghan

Daddy dropped us off at the gate of the school.

"Can't you come, too?" Zelda asked.

"Nope." He pinched her cheek.

We watched the red car drive away. Then we looked at the school. It was the biggest building we had ever seen. It was big and brick and square, and there were a million kids swarming all over its steps and neatly mown lawn. The closer you got to it, the more prairie sky it ate up.

Suddenly a boy with blond hair and blue eyes floated into focus.

"Who are you?" the boy demanded. He was looking right at me.

"Leah Hoffer."

"I bet you're farm kids."

"We are not. We lived in the store."

"Oh, yeah? Where?"

"In Hoffer."

He didn't say anything. I thought he was finished. Then he asked, "How come you have the same name as the town you come from?"

"I don't know."

"Because," Miriam explained, (she always knew more because she was older), "Our grandfather was the first farmer there."

"How come I never heard of it?" He was looking at me again.

"Hoffer isn't as big as Weyburn," Zelda volunteered. Zelda was the youngest. She never knew when to keep quiet.

"So what?" I said, turning on her.

"How big is it?" the boy asked.

"It only has two elevators. And it doesn't have a bakery," Zelda answered.

"I bet it doesn't have a skating rink, or a comic-book store either," he sneered.

I hated him.

After school, Daddy was waiting to meet us in our red car. Daddy said it squeaked so we could hear him coming. He was smiling. "Well, are you smarter today than you were yesterday?"

"No," Zelda said, climbing into the car. She slammed the door.

"I met a boy today..." I started to say.

"You did?" Daddy teased. "You're only nine years old. You're too young to meet boys."

"Daddy!"

He listened respectfully.

"I met him, too," Zelda piped up.

"Boy, you sure did," I said.

"All I said was that Hoffer only had two elevators."

"Yeah," and then he said, 'I bet it doesn't have a skating rink or a comic book store, either.'"

"He's a silly boy," Daddy assured us. "Hoffer is even better than Weyburn. Ask him if he knows a place where you can get an ice-cream cone and a letter and a new pair of shoes all in the same store, and a comic book besides. You didn't have to go inside a dark, old building to go skating, either. Did he ever go skating with his Mommy and Daddy in the moonlight?"

"If Daddy went to school, too, he could tell that boy," Zelda said.

We turned into the peace and chaos of our yard. It was a new yard. We had just moved our house on it, and where the new road was, the prairie grass was chewed up. We had left the store behind. There wasn't even a tree or any kingbirds yet, just a yellow, two-storey farmhouse on the flat prairie against a soft, evening sky.

"How did you like your first day of school?" Mom asked when we came in for supper. We had been helping Daddy decide where the new trees should go.

"Awful," Zelda answered. "Can I have two potatoes?"

"Not unless you tell me why it was awful."

Zelda put down her fork.

"I wanted to find Miriam and Leah at recess, and a girl in my room told me that the big kids never talk to the little kids, so I couldn't go." Her brown eyes widened under her straight, black bangs. "Why can't we all be in the same room like we used to be in Hoffer?"

"Yeah," I agreed.

"But then you wouldn't have different teachers," Mom pointed out. "Isn't that more fun?"

"No, it's boring," Miriam said. "When you're finished your work, you can't listen to the teacher giving the other kids their lessons."

"And do you know what?" Zelda continued. "I wanted to play baseball at noon hour, and they wouldn't let me. That girl told me girls don't play baseball in Weyburn. And do you know what else? We were playing Pom-pom pull-away and we weren't even finished when the bell rang and we had to go in anyway."

Mom gave her another potato.

"Why did we move here?" Zelda demanded. She stabbed her potato with her fork. It fell apart.

Mom changed the subject.

"Who wants dessert?"

Later, Zelda and Miriam and I had a discussion in bed. Mom and Daddy were downstairs listening to "Voices of the Stars" on the CBC on our pink, crackly radio. "Maybe Daddy will make lots of money so we can move back," I suggested.

"I don't think so," Miriam said. "I heard Mom and Daddy talking, and they said it was the fifties and little towns in Saskatchewan were a thing of the past."

"Gee," Zelda said. She sounded like she was going to cry. Mom came up the stairs to kiss us good night.

"People in Hoffer didn't have much money." she explained. "If they don't have much, the storekeeper doesn't have much. And nowadays, most people don't like to live in small towns."

"I do," Zelda piped up.

"I know, but when children get bigger, they don't. And their parents like to go to cities like Weyburn where they can get things in different stores. They think it's cheaper."

"Is Daddy going to have lots of different stores?"

"No." Zelda always made Mom laugh. "We're going to have a trailer court,where people can come and park their trailers and live. That's why we aren't living in the city."

The boy with the blond hair and the blue eyes met me at the gate the next morning. He was in my room. His name was Bobby. He was the smartest boy in grade four.

"My Dad says you're Jewish."

He said it sort of funny.

"So what?"

"My Dad says there are seventeen churches in this city, and your family had to be Jewish. He says Jews are always trying to be different."

"You tell him he's different," Daddy advised that night. "All the Jews are the same as each other. In Hoffer, there is only one synagogue for everybody. Weyburn is all mixed up. They need seventeen different churches because there are seventeen different kinds of Christians. What could be more different than that?"

Miriam had brought home an interesting fact, too.

"Do you know what? Mr. Brown was showing us ratios. Do you know what he told us? He said the ratio..." She jumped up from the table to get a pen and a piece of paper. "He said the ratio of Protestant to Catholic to Jewish in Weyburn is 333.2:133.3:1. What does that mean?"

"It means that there are more of them than us," Daddy said. He looked at us. He didn't say anything for a minute. "It looks as though my girls are going to be real smart this year. What did you learn today, Zelda?"

Zelda looked up from her plate. "Mrs. Mortenson says we're not going to heaven."

"What's heaven?" he asked.

"It's the place where Jesus lives," Zelda explained.

"Who's Jesus?" Daddy asked.

"I don't know. His birthday is at Christmas time. Mrs. Mortenson says his mother could ride a donkey."

"What's a donkey?" Daddy asked.

"Syd!" Mom said.

Soon, I wasn't the only one who had met a boy. Miriam met Gordon. He was nicer than Bobby. He met her downtown on

Saturday afternoon and took her to a cowboy movie. He even bought her a box of Cracker-Jacks. Miriam brought the prize home for Zelda.

"Gordon goes to our church," Bobby told me on Monday.

"So what?" I said.

"His father isn't going to let him go out with a Jewish girl."

"How do you know?"

"Because my Dad is the minister, and he told Gordon's Dad. I heard him."

"Doesn't Jesus like it?" we asked Mom that night.

"I don't think Jesus knows anything about it," Mom said. "There are a lot of people in this town who think they know a lot better than Him."

"Jesus probably knows that my girls are too young for boys," Daddy said. He pinched Miriam's cheek.

"Daddy!" Miriam said.

"Tomorrow we're going to Regina for the High Holidays. You won't be going to school," Mom told us.

When we got back to school after the High Holidays, we discovered that there had been school anyway.

"How come?" I asked Mom.

"Because no one in Weyburn is Jewish. It isn't their holiday."

"But in Hoffer, when we had High Holidays, school closed."

"That was because your teacher was Jewish, dear, and because almost everybody in the school was Jewish."

"Donnie and Stevie weren't."

"I know, but they couldn't stay in school by themselves."

"But when it was their holiday, we got a holiday, too."

Mom sighed as if she was getting tired. "That's because the government says that all schools are supposed to close on Christian holidays."

"If school closes on their holidays, why doesn't it close on ours?"

"Do you remember that ratio Miriam's teacher showed her?" Daddy interjected. "I think it has something to do with that."

It was a clear, cold, blue sky winter day, the kind when the snow crunches when you walk on it...the kind that makes you happy school is over.

We ran down the steps towards Daddy's smile. "What's your hurry?"

"Guess what!" I said.

"What?"

"Mrs. Bauer says all Jews are rich and intelligent."

"Yuh," Daddy nodded in matter-of-fact agreement. "We're rich. We just don't have any money."

We rattled off. There was a large, white cloud with blue tints in its hair. It looked just like Mrs. Bauer.

We turned into the yard. We had lots to do before dark. Daddy had flooded a skating rink for us; Mom was teaching us how to make an igloo.

Eventually, instead of snow, there were crocuses and lots of places to get water in your boots, and then frogs in the ditches beside the railroad tracks, and, finally, wild strawberries and wild roses where the puddles used to be.

But soon there was no time to pay any attention to the strawberries and the roses.

Everybody was coming to help Daddy decide about his trailer court: people from the Power Company, and the Telephone Company, and the Highway Department, and the City Council. Everybody was worried about where the trailers should go and how many of them there should be and how far from the highway they should be. The City Council was worried that maybe Daddy didn't need a trailer court at all. Everybody had to come lots of times, even on Sundays on their way home from church. Bobby's father had come the most. (Mom said that Bobby's father was a very busy man; besides being a minister, he was in charge of the only factory in Weyburn and he was even on the City Council.) One Sunday, even Bobby came.

On Monday, Bobby got to school before me.

"My Dad says your Dad is never going to have his trailer court."

"He is so!"

"He is not! Mrs. Anderson is in our church and her farm is across from you, and she said that your water is poisoned. She said her dog drank some of it, and he died."

"That's funny," Daddy said that night. He didn't laugh. "We drink that water every day. So does your dog."

Mom decided that while all those people were deciding whether Daddy needed a trailer court, she might as well be a school teacher again.

"Your mother can't be a teacher," Bobby said. "Jewish teachers don't know how to teach Christian kids. That's what Dad says. Besides, your mother only taught in a one-room school before. City schools are different. Every room has lots of kids in the same grades, and country schools have a whole bunch of different grades. Your Mom wouldn't know what to do probably."

When I asked Mom if Bobby was right, she almost banged into the living-room door with everybody's bean soup.

"Esther!" Daddy said to her. "Watch what you are doing!"

Mom laughed so hard she started to cry. Then she left the room for a rest. Daddy finished making supper. He was a very good cook. He always let us eat whatever we wanted whenever we wanted. Usually, we ate dessert first.

Bobby was waiting for me at the gate again.

"My Dad says Jews aren't so smart. If they were so smart, they wouldn't be looking for a job in a factory."

Bobby thought I wouldn't know who he was talking about.

"He's not looking for a job in your Dad's factory. He's going to have a trailer court."

"Oh, no, he isn't. He can't. Your water kills people!"

"That's a lie!"

"Well, anyway, Weyburn won't need your trailer court. That's what Dad said. Weyburn is going to buy some of our church land and make their own trailer court. Then it won't need yours."

At supper time, I asked Daddy if it was true that Weyburn didn't need two trailer courts.

"What?" Mom said.

"Can I have another glass of apple juice?" Zelda asked.

Mom handed Zelda a jar of pickles.

After that, she was all mixed up, and we each got two pieces of apple pie for dessert, and she didn't even tell me I had to eat the crust.

"Your Dad's going to be working with all those high school drop-outs," Bobby told me the next day.

I asked Mrs. Bauer what a high school drop-out was. She told me I didn't have to worry about it because Jews were never high school drop-outs. They all went to university and after that they were doctors. Sometimes even Jewish girls were doctors, but usually they married doctors instead.

"Yuh, just like me and your mother," Daddy said. "When I was your age, I was a barber in a railroad station in Russia. Jews didn't go to school to drop out of. Your Mrs. Bauer doesn't know her history so good."

One day, a pair of work boots, brown, with round, practical toes and invincible heels stationed themselves beside the kitchen door. They were very serious, unsmiling boots. We didn't feel much like giggling when they were around.

"Do you think you three can walk home?" Daddy asked us. We were having a family council. All the important family decision were made at the family council.

"Sure," Miriam said. "Two miles isn't far. Kids don't get enough exercise nowadays."

"I won't be home," Mom reminded us. "I'm going to be teaching music lessons. Daddy won't be here, either. He'll be at the factory. You'll have to take care of yourselves until I get back. I'll leave supper for you in the oven. Miriam, I'll give you a key. Do you think you can manage not to fight until I get back?"

We nodded solemnly.

It wasn't much fun coming out of school after that. We missed the squeaky red car waiting for us at the gate, and we missed Daddy's smile teasing the corners of his mouth as he asked, "Well, are you smarter today than you were yesterday?"

"Look at that," Miriam said, balancing on the railroad track. "There are two hundred people down below watching to see if I cross this tightrope safely. And there isn't even a net!" She fell off.

We stalked through the cat-tails along the river bank. Two thousand Indians lurked on the other side. If even one blade of the river grasses rustled, we could never hope to see the welcoming light of our fortress again.

At last, the fortress loomed ahead, strangely dark.

We didn't see much of the captain of the fortress any more. Sometimes, late at night, after we were supposed to be asleep, the crunch of the car tires on the gravel, the protest of the car door, would waken us. Very carefully, quietly, we would approach the stairs. Almost always, even before the first step had creaked, there would be a conspiratorial whisper. "What are you three doing up?"

Then we would all have milk and toast and peanut butter and Daddy would find out how much smarter we were. Finally, Mom would appear. "Shouldn't my brown-eyed girls be in bed?" she would ask. The thud of Daddy's boots as they fell beside their bed ended the day.

But usually we had to look beside the kitchen door to see if the boots were back.

Pretty soon, we noticed that there was something different about those boots.

"Mom," Zelda finally demanded one morning. "What's wrong with Daddy's boots?"

"Nothing," Mom answered. She sounded surprised. "They're old, that's all. Everything gets old. Don't your shoes get old?"

We looked down at our shoes. They didn't look old. Just scrumfy, like shoes that take you exploring over prairie are supposed to look. We looked back at those boots huddled against the kitchen door.

"They're broken," Zelda insisted. "They can't go outside. They have to stay inside, where it's warm."

More and more now, Daddy was starting to resemble the drawing Bobby had shown me of a stork wearing argyles. Mom thought it was fine for storks, but not for Daddy.

"Don't you want me slim and elegant?" Daddy asked.

"Don't make jokes with me, Mr. Hoffer. I'm not one of your kids."

When Mom called him Mr. Hoffer, she meant business.

"What's wrong with chicken soup?" Daddy asked. "My mother gave us chicken soup twice a week every week, and we never got sick."

"Your father died when he was sixty-eight."

"Good. I've got thirteen good years left."

Then she got really angry.

"If you don't go to the doctor, I'll kill you."

"Ach, don't be silly."

If he was feeling better, on a day off, for instance, he fought back with more spirit. The smile would pull at the corners of his mouth.

"You've been holding out on me, Mrs. Hoffer. Where did you get the money for the funeral?"

Sometimes he didn't fight at all. He just asked a question. "Who's going to pay the doctor bills?"

Bobby supplied information faithfully.

"My Dad says your Dad is too old to work in a factory. Dad says Jews don't even belong in factories."

I kicked Bobby in the shins. Then I sat on him.

When I came out of school that day, Miriam and Zelda were waiting on the steps. I was late because I had sat on Bobby.

Just then, the red car came squeaking to a halt. We bounced down the steps.

But at the gate, we stopped.

"What's wrong?" Daddy called.

"Is this another day off?" Miriam asked. We approached the car slowly, and got into the back. Daddy's boots were lying on the floor.

"I'm a lucky man. From now on, I have all my days off."

"How come?"

"Well, when you're an old man like me, things change. You're not too old to eat, but you're too old to work."

We rattled off. There was a cloud with blue tints in its hair that looked just like Mrs. Bauer.

"Guess what!" Zelda said "Mrs. Bauer says that all Jews are cultured." By now we were moving up and getting each other's teachers.

"How come?" Daddy asked with interest.

"We all play the piano."

"Is that right? Me, too? What a lucky man! Do you mean I'm rich, and intelligent, and cultured? But if I'm so smart..."

He deliberated.

We turned into the yard. The house looked lonely in the midst of the hard, white snowdrifts. It would be a long time before we would be able to look for any frogs or strawberries.

"Well." He stopped the car. He didn't get out rightaway. "I guess I'm not Jewish."

THE DILEMMA OF MULTICULTURALISM

by
Glenn W. Bradley

Language and nationality are current issues in today's society. In view of the laws and general social outlook in Quebec, one has to realize that to survive here, one must "become French". Many of the language problems exist today because the younger generation did not want to learn to speak French, perhaps because of their parents who may have been immigrants and wished to keep the old ways and mother-tongue dominant.

I grew up under the new age of political reform in Quebec. The social phenomenon of the Quiet Revolution and Le Front de Libération du Québec were part of my childhood surroundings. These events played a part in the rise of the supremacy of the French language in Quebec.

My parents witnessed these social reforms and decided that if I was to have a future in Quebec, I would have to learn to speak French.

They could have rebelled in their own way. They could have brought me up with all the Scottish traditions they had been raised with. However, teatime, the clans, and Robert Burns were not to play a part in my childhood education.

My family roots are deep in Scottish soil. My parents and all my ancestors were born in Scotland. My parents decided to leave their homeland in the late 1950s. At that time, Quebec was looking for skilled workers.

My father, who had been an engineer on merchant ships sailing out of Scottish ports, decided that Quebec would be the ideal place in Canada where his skills would land him a job without too much difficulty.

Quebec City was my parents' first stop, but when they realized that Montreal was the industrial centre of the province, they moved to St. Michel, a suburb.

My father worked in the oil refineries in the east end of Montreal and continued to do so even after the family moved to Duvernay, a predominately French-Canadian sector of the city of Laval. They chose Duvernay deliberately because they realized that the children they were planning to have one day would be able to learn French by association with the other people in the area.

During my early school days in the late 1960s, my father had decided that the shift work in the refineries would interfere with his responsibilities as a parent. Education was booming in Quebec, and the need for technical teachers was great. My father capitalized on this and easily landed a job with the Protestant School Board of Greater Montreal as a metalwork teacher for Monklands High School in Notre Dame de Grace. At the time, my mother was the vice-principal of Laval Highcliff Elementary School which I would attend.

Because both my parents were involved in education at different levels, it made them realize that if their offspring were to flourish in this country, they would need a good education.

In the late sixties and seventies, the Laval school started testing its programme of bilingual classes for elementary school children. Highcliff was chosen as the test school, and a group of students who were considered above average would take their classes in French.

I was lucky to participate in that programme.

My interest in the French language actually had started almost from the moment I could talk coherently. Living in a French neighbourhood meant that whenever you went out into the street, nine times out of ten, the other children were speaking what I thought was a strange language.

Little did I know that "ballon-chasseur" was dodgeball and that "cache-cache" meant hide-and-go-seek. From then on I was determined to learn what they were saying so I wouldn't be at a disadvantage when playing with them.

Oddly enough, this decision, made when I was five years old, would dominate the rest of my life.

Since English instruction in the French school system left much to be desired, and I was already starting to learn French, I decided that I would play ambassador. Just as an ambassador is a liaison in another country, my role would be liaison between the two languages.

Imagine my surprise when I confronted the children in the street with my first garbled speech in French! My strained "Bonjour, je m'appelle..." was returned with "Maudit Bloke", a reference to the somewhat square-headedness of the English population. Chalk one up for French-Canadian nationalism, I guess!

Good old Scottish stubbornness, or whatever you want to call it, made me decide to beat them at their own game. I excelled in my French studies through bilingual and immersion programmes, to a degree where my knowledge of the language and grammar was perhaps better than that of the French children themselves.

Unfortunately, the responses I received had gone from one extreme to another. Although I got along with the other children, I was never really accepted by them. I finally discovered the reason why. French-Canadians hated the French from France almost as much as the English. My French accent was almost like that of the people French-Canadians called "Les Snobbes".

By the time I was thirteen, I realized that "French-Canadian" was a proper language and a culture all of its own. I decided to treat what I had already learned as a separate language and discover exactly what "French-Canadian" was and is.

In my final years of high school, I delved into dozens of written novels; the works of Savard, Thériault and Vallières, the plays of Tremblay and Gélinas, and the poetry of Vigneault and Nelligan. From these pieces written by prominent French-Canadian authors, I was able to obtain a good grasp of the emergence of the French-Canadian culture in Quebec.

It was interesting to witness the transition in myself. I was so involved with these studies that a few of my high school buddies started calling me "Frenchie".

I graduated from high school feeling very comfortable with my knowledge of "French-Canadian". As strange as it may sound, perhaps I had too much knowledge.

Just before heading off to Carleton University to study Communications, something in my brain snapped. I began thinking I was French-Canadian. I did everything to convince myself that I was. I had become a staunch Parti-Quebecois supporter. I even cried when René Lévesque lost the Sovereignty-Association vote. I defended everything that was considered French-Canadian.

At Carleton I was elected president of the Francophone Club.

My plan for assimilation might have worked except for two things—my name and my ancestors.

Once again my wise parents from the "old country" came to my rescue. They were able to grind into my thick skull that should the situation in Quebec worsen, my name alone would make me stand out like a sore thumb.

For most people it might have been too late to change, but at eighteen I began learning about my own cultural history—the glory of the Scottish clans and all the benefits that Quebec and Canada enjoy today because of Scottish immigrants.

Robert Bruce, Mary Queen of Scots, and the poet Robert Burns are well-known names in Scottish history, but what of those who immigrated to Canada and gave so much of their time and efforts to build this country?

Lord Selkirk, a Scottish philanthropist and colonizer, was responsible for bringing immigrants to Prince Edward Island. They later spread to Nova Scotia and established a colony there. Selkirk opened the West with his settlements in the Red River Valley in Manitoba.

Scottish immigrants were instrumental in the establishment of the fur trade in Canada and played the greatest part in the foundations of education in this country.

Early Scottish settlers placed top priority on education. The first non-sectarian school for higher education in Nova Scotia, Pictou Academy, was founded by a Scot. Dalhousie University, McGill University in Montreal, the University of Toronto, Queen's, St. Francis Xavier and the University of New Brunswick all owe their establishment to Scots.

Sir Alexander Mackenzie, trader and explorer, discovered the Mackenzie River and was the first white man to cross the northern part of the American continent to the Pacific Ocean. Simpson and MacTavish are other names synonymous with the building of our country. Alexander Mackenzie, a Scot, was Prime Minister of Canada between 1873 and 1878.

In addition, Scotsmen and Canadians of Scottish origin have played formidable roles in communications and journalism. There has been George Brown, founder of the *Globe*; William Lyon Mackenzie, founder and editor of the *Colonial Advocate*, and one of the leaders of the 1837 Rebellion; John Neilson, editor of the *Quebec Gazette*; John Dougall, both father and son, of the *Montreal Witness* and Hugh Graham, Lord Atholstan, of the *Montreal Star*.

Suddenly a new dimension was added to my research for cultural identity. I realized that I was neither Scottish nor French-Canadian. Talk about an identity crisis! Because Canada is not the melting-pot that characterizes the United States, there is really no distinct Canadian culture. Therefore, I didn't consider myself to be Canadian. I was a mixture, a part of three great nationalities.

After much deliberation I decided that the only way out of this dilemma was to combine the best parts of all three nations. To become a part of the French-Canadian culture, to be accepted as an equal, I needed more of the expressions in daily use.

To accomplish this I spent the summer of 1981 working in a French children's camp. That summer was the turning point in my life. I not only picked up the oral requirements but also a large group of French-Canadian friends.

I learned more about Scottish culture by reading books and poetry by Scottish authors, as well as the stories of the clans. I joined a curling club to get a taste of a Scottish sport and social gathering.

In order to become more of a Canadian, I relaxed my hardline views on independence for Quebec. I now try to picture Canada as a whole and am more sympathetic to the feeling of the people in other provinces.

I thought I was all set—I had satisfied my goals and those of my parents. The one thing I had forgotten to consider was my friends.

Each group of friends I had made in the past few years had accepted me in the way I related to them. I was the one who had adjusted easily to each group by simply changing my frame of mind and attitude to what each group was interested in and expected of me.

I went partying with my French-Canadian friends, bar-hopping with my Anglophone high-school buddies and was involved in intellectual stimulation with my university associates. Each world was different, yet I fitted easily into each one. What I had failed to consider was the interaction between the groups.

I soon discovered through trial and error that my old high-school friends would not be accepted by my university buddies;

nor would my English friends be accepted by my French-Canadian friends and vice versa.

This created a situation which is similar to the problems of Quebec society today. Because of my personal experience, I feel the French-Canadians and the English-Canadians will never associate unless some concessions are made by both sides. We will always run into people of both cultures who will refuse to speak the other's language. There is animosity even within each cultural group— animosity caused by intellectual, social and economic differences.

If only we could learn from one another, if we would be willing to mingle, we could absorb a great deal by association. With understanding comes acceptance. Unfortunately the situation may not be resolved in my lifetime. To keep the peace, the cultures may have to remain apart.

I don't favour apartheid in the South African sense, where one culture is discriminated against on economic, social, political and colour levels. I do believe, however, that many cultures can co-exist in one province as long as there is agreement on the equal value of each.

My plight is understandable. I enjoy the knowledge of many worlds, yet to keep harmony among them, I have to keep them separate. Therefore, in a sense, I am trapped in the middle of all three groups.

Because I can't combine all these worlds, despite the fact that each has so much to offer, I have to spend an equal amount of time in all of them.

Although it is satisfying to experience the diversity, you can't give 100 per cent of what you have to share and at the same time receive 100 per cent of what everyone else has to offer. The basic explanation for someone in this dilemma is that you can be acquainted with many, but totally involved with none.

It is another way of explaining and learning to live with loneliness.

LOOKING BACK

by
Milly Charon
from an interview with Aussie Whiting

Once a week the dilapidated train with its old-fashioned compart-
ments chugged up from the coast of New South Wales, Australia,
through Kelly's Gully. Along the way, it picked up and dropped off
sheep, cattle and passengers.

Hiding in the shadows at the small station of Kelly's Gully,
eleven-year-old Colin Francis 'Aussie' Whiting waited impatiently
for the train to arrive. It was night, and in his hand he clutched a
paper bag containing a chunk of bread and a bottle of water. Aussie
was running away from home—a home where he had known
nothing but verbal and physical abuse.

He had been born when his natural mother was only
fourteen years old, and she tried to conceal her relationship by
passing herself off as his older sister. Coincidentally, her mother
had been pregnant at the same time and had had her own son three
days after Aussie's birth. Aussie grew up with his 'twin' brother.
Eventually his mother married, but her husband killed her brother
in a bar-room brawl in the Australian Outback, and Aussie's
mother ran off when her husband was charged with manslaughter.
The boy was left with his grandmother, and although she claimed
he was her son, he was known as the 'little bastard' in the family.
Staunchly Catholic, she felt the disgrace of an illegitimate child had
brought down divine retribution on their heads, and the family
proceeded to blame Aussie for everything that went wrong in their
lives.

As a child in the Outback, Aussie's bleak life consisted of
hunting rabbits and kangaroos interspersed with short periods of
schooling. Whatever wasn't used was shipped to England to be

53

used for processing as foodstuffs, while kangaroo skins were sold for leather and fur. Aussie learned early in life how to be tough. His 'twin' brother was not as strong as Aussie and another brother was blind. Aussie would lead the blind boy on horseback to school, but the other children would steer the boy into barbed-wire fences or guide him toward holes in the ground so that he would stumble and fall. Aussie fought angrily, even savagely, for his brothers and developed into a tough and tricky brawler with survival skills that were to save his life many times in the future.

He wondered that night at Kelly's Gully station what kind of future he would have. He had known nothing but rejection up to then. At last he heard the eerie whistle of the train, still miles away. When it huffed finally to a stop at a siding where some cattle and sheep were unloaded, Aussie walked over, opened a compartment and climbed up. There was a water dispenser on the wall and he hunkered down under it to make himself as inconspicuous as possible.

The train arrived in Newcastle late the following day and Aussie alighted. He didn't know what to do or where to go. In desperation he hid under a building near the docks and slept there that night. He was awakened by rowdy, drunken sailors staggering back to their ship. Although he was frightened, Aussie watched them clamber up the gangplank. He waited until there was silence and sneaked onto the ship, stealing noiselessly down the passageway, where he found a place to hide—a rope locker. The ship's movement lulled him to sleep and before dawn, noises on deck awakened him. He heard orders being shouted, the bustle of casting off and hatches battened down. By dawn the anchor had been raised, and the ship moved slowly away from the dock. Aussie was trapped inside the hold in the rope locker with no food or water.

* * * *

"When the hatch was closed, I had no idea how long I would be locked up, or where the ship was going. It was four days and nights later, when the ship was off New Zealand, that I was discovered and let out. I was terrified and hungry. Another day without food and water, and I'm sure I would have been dead. I was immediately nicknamed 'The Stowaway'. Because I was short and looked about nine years old, the Captain wouldn't believe I was really eleven. He couldn't send a message back to Australia about me because it was the early forties and the world was at war. The ship had to observe radio silence, and the only message permitted was an SOS if the ship was sinking. As it zig-zagged its way across the Pacific, the ship changed course repeatedly to avoid encounter with enemy surface raiders or submarines. There was a general alarm when the look-out in the crow's nest reported sighting an un-identified warship on the horizon.

"The Captain sent for me and said, 'If we are sunk and taken prisoner or killed, no one will ever know where you went to.'

"I shrugged. 'Well, there's nothing to be done about it.'

"We reached Panama safely, and because I had no papers I was a suspect alien when soldiers in charge of security boarded our ship. Our Captain burst into laughter when one of the American officers said: 'You know, he could be a spy.'

" 'He's just a kid from the Outback. He's never been out of the bush', chuckled the captain.

"Nonetheless, I was taken off the ship and transported by night in a covered army truck to the other end of the Canal Zone, which was bristling with gun batteries, cruisers, destroyers and se-curity systems. I knew if anyone made a false move, he'd be blown away. The Canal was vital to the Americans, for it controlled entry and exit from both oceans. Of course, the Americans took no chances even though I was only eleven, but I had a great time looking in wonder at the different guns and rifles they carried. They gave me gum to chew and were really nice to me. It was then a message was wired to my relatives in Kelly's Gully that I was safe, but I don't think anyone there cared about me anyhow.

"American MPs with armbands accompanied me to the Caribbean Sea shore at the Canal's entrance, and they put me on a PT boat to rejoin my ship which sailed to Aruba in the Dutch West Indies. We arrived about four in the morning, and the harbour was dark with no lights showing on the ships moored there. The next day I transferred to another ship as a deckboy, and we sailed off to Brooklyn on a gasoline tanker, sailing empty in ballast, instead of fueled, to the Navy Yards where deck structure was to be welded onto the ship to load Lightnings, twin-fuselaged fighter planes. Again I was taken off for security reasons...the Americans just didn't trust me...and I was taken to Ellis Island and kept there for about eight days while the welding and loading went on. The ship then sailed up the Delaware to Marcus Hook where thousands of tonnes of high-octane gasoline were pumped into specially constructed holds. A few hours before the ship was due to sail, soldiers drove me to where the ship had dropped anchor, and an armed guard put me on the ship. It was so heavy with fuel and vital war material that it sat very low in the water. There were about eight to ten planes on deck, all sealed with waterproofing so no seawater could damage them and so we couldn't sneak a look at them.

"We set sail for Britain in a convoy of 125 ships. Many times when the waves were rough, water washed across the decks. En route, twenty-five ships were torpedoed by enemy submarines. Some of the ships were loaded with ammunition and blew up when they were hit. One night just before dark, a ship not far from us got it. The blast almost lifted our ship out of the water. I ran out on deck thinking we had been torpedoed, ready to jump into the ocean. We always had our lifejackets on—we lived in them—or we would never have made it over the rail in time. We called the jackets our parachutes. If we went up in a blast, we'd come down in them and float. No one knew who would get it first or next. Sonar was primitive in those days and not very effective in picking up the submarine wolf-packs lying in ambush.

"Our ship reached Scotland safely and after we dropped anchor on the River Clyde, the crew left the ship, and rode by train to Liverpool, where I joined the Merchant Marine and was placed on another ship. We sailed to Maracaibo where we loaded up with oil and returned to England. I worked on four different tankers on four successive voyages that were suicide runs. You never knew if you were going to make it back, but I was young and I didn't care. The sailors on the ship protected me, and they taught me all kinds of things—tying knots, painting, swabbing decks, chipping rust....

"We had eleven guns on those ships, one sixteen-pounder and one three-inch anti-aircraft gun, machine guns and revolvers. I never did find out what the revolvers were for...I guess to shoot the enemy in the head if they tried to board. I was trained to use those guns, but not all that well. Up to then, I didn't realize the tragedy of war, until I saw people dying around me. A plane would dive at us and start shooting, and we would never see the enemy, only a black head in the cockpit. And that was all I saw, the day my friend Ray, who was only twelve-and-a-half, and I were in the gun-pit working an anti-aircraft gun. A German plane dived at us, spraying bullets. My crew-mate was killed, and I got shot in the legs. I almost lost my life. The bullets cut my friend in half and spattered him all over the gunpit. The splinters hit me, and his blood and mine were mixed together. I thought I was finished. My gun wasn't even firing when it happened. I was so scared that I hadn't even switched the gun on. Although the other ships were shooting at the plane, it got away. None of us was trained properly. The gunners were from the Army and had been posted to the ships to instruct us in the use of weapons. We received a quick course, too quick. Someone would be sent up to the crow's nest to watch for subs or planes and when one was spotted, there was a yell from up top. Sometimes we didn't know if it was one of ours or the enemy's. There were lots of deadly mistakes made. The Americans were real good at blowing up their own.

"It was a rough war. I was in North Africa when the British, the Americans and the Germans bombed the same place. I was all along the coast of North Africa and Italy, through the Straits of Messina during the war and also at the invasion of Normandy, where we unloaded supplies and war material, and brought back wounded soldiers. Many of them were so badly shot up they died on the way back. By then I was more realistic about death. It was staring me right in the face. I was covered with the blood of others. I saw people, their arms and legs blown off, blood running out of them. That's when I realized what war really meant.

"Liverpool was my home base, a tough town. Most of the crew came from Liverpool, and after my first trip as a stowaway, I kind of shipped out of Liverpool for the rest of my sailing career. Other tough places were Glasgow, in Scotland, and parts of some of the Caribbean Islands such as the Dominican Republic. The officers put up a notice that we were at the most syphilitic island in the world, and they warned us to be careful with the girls. The minute the gangplank went down there were about fifty women waiting at the foot. I was kind of cute in those days—just a kid of about seventeen or eighteen—and when I walked down the gangway, two girls grabbed me, one on each side, and they were fighting over me in Spanish. I couldn't understand a word. I said I was going for a haircut, and one of them sent her brother with me to watch so no one else would get me. I was so scared I wouldn't do anything, but five of the officers caught what they told us to watch for on the island. I laughed over that. They were warning us, but they were the bad boys who got caught.

"Living at sea wasn't easy in those days. We didn't even have sheets and pillows. We had rations—a little can of condensed milk every two weeks, with a little sugar and tea, and we had to hide it or have it stolen by one of our mates. My wages at the beginning were only nine dollars a month, so you had to do a little cargo-stealing to survive. In those days they didn't batten down the hatches like they do in the container ships of today. In case the ship sank, the hatches would float around, and you could grab one and maybe save yourself if you were lucky...like wet rats clinging to the flotsam. So unsealed holds gave us a chance to get in there at night and plunder the cargo.

"I remember a trip down to Abadan on the Persian Gulf, when we stole some good suiting material and sold it. I took the padding out of my bunk mattress and stuffed in the stolen cloth until we reached the Gulf. When we anchored, I tried to sell it to two guys who had come aboard, but they were too foxy for me. They put down a deposit on the sale, but then grabbed the goods, slung them over the side into a little boat, and took off. I had less than half the value of the material and couldn't even report them.

"One night I left England on a ship, and at two bells I was called to duty on the night watch. A full moon was hanging in the sky, and an officer said there was someone up the mast. So I went up on deck to try and get the person down. I didn't know who it was because the crew was all new, and I didn't know any of them. A man, laughing strangely, and shirtless, slid down the main mast and went right for me. He was off his rocker from the moon, I'm sure, so I grabbed him, got him down to his cabin and locked him in. The rest of the voyage took nine months, but for the duration of the trip we would have to lock him up the day before the full moon so he wouldn't do anything bad to hurt himself or anyone else.

"One guy went crazy, and said he was steering the ship with his mind. I was called up to take his place at the wheel. He threatened to kill me many times. One day he jumped overboard and drowned. We didn't even stop to pick him up.

"You could be sleeping in a cabin with a guy whose guts you hated. I had a big fight with a Welshman and had to share a cabin with him. I slept with one eye open. One trip there were some Africans working as firemen. One of these guys was in the galley one night and accused me of stealing some books. I didn't know what he was talking about. He walked out and I sat down. Suddenly I glanced up, and there he was, standing with an open razor and threatening to cut off my head if I didn't give him back his books. I slowly inched my way over to where the kitchen knives were kept, grabbed a big chopper and threatened him with it. He left. I never reported the incident, but I was scared the rest of that trip that I would lose my head. Whenever I passed his cabin, I would hunker down so he couldn't stick his hand out with a razor and slash me. Nothing happened, but we did have a cook disappear one bad night. He was a terrible cook, and someone must have got rid of him and tossed him overboard, I'm sure. I didn't think the ocean was that rough for him to have fallen overboard...but he disappeared. The food improved.

"On one of my stopovers in England I got caught stealing cargo and selling dirty postcards. Who could live on nine dollars a month? I was arrested by Scotland Yard and detained for a couple of months. They thought I was part of a big smuggling ring, but when they finally realized their mistake, they let me go.

"I had been at sea for twelve years by then and was twenty-three years old. I had managed to get myself engaged to a girl who was emigrating to America. I wanted to go there and marry her. So I stowed away on a ship I thought was heading for New York. It ended up going to Halifax first. I spent nine days on the ship without getting caught and living on Cadbury's chocolate bars. When the ship docked, I sneaked off it at night. Because a guard was stationed at the foot of the gangplank, I slid down a rope to avoid being stopped and questioned. I hitchhiked across Canada to Vancouver, planning to stow away on a ship there and go back home to Australia. I really didn't intend to come to Canada or stay here. When my stowaway plan didn't work, I started eastward and stopped in Toronto, thinking of cutting across to Wisconsin where the girl lived. I found a part-time job on a ship preparing it for spring, but when I wasn't paid I couldn't pay my rent for the small room I lived in. I found a blank cheque somewhere, filled it out for more than what I owed and gave it to the landlord. The cash he gave me as change paid for my fare at the bus depot. I took the first bus heading out...to Montreal. If it had been going some place else in Canada, I might be living there instead.

"When I arrived in Montreal, I was tough, really tough. I had come out of Liverpool, a real mean city, and when I hit the streets of Montreal, I was starving. I didn't have a job. I slept under buildings, bumming a quarter here and there on the streets. I would go up to St. Alexander Street where the old Salvation Army used to be, and I would sit through a hymn-singing service just to get a bowl of soup and some bread. Then I'd go to sleep under some building on Lagauchetière Street with all the bums and rubbies. Occasionally I got picked up by the police for vagrancy or for loitering, but I would be released the next day. They didn't keep me in jail. They would say I looked too young. I'd tell them I was looking for a job, which I was, and they let me out, but the older guys would be locked up for a month.

"While I was living down there on skid row, I applied for a job at a store that sold lamps. There must have been five thousand of them in the place, and a man wanted me to dust them. I started working on them, and the boss came in and said, 'Who's that?'

"'Oh, that's the new guy we just hired.'

"'I don't like him. Get rid of him.'

"So he gave me half a day's pay and threw me out.

"I went back to bumming quarters in Victoria Square and sleeping under buildings. I had no clothes, no money, nothing, just what was on my back. I used to wash in the street, take my shirt off and wash it in a fountain and run up and down the street at night, trying to dry my clothes in the wind. I had no socks and no underwear, just a shirt, pants and shoes. When I managed to bum an extra quarter or two, I would go to Leo's flophouse on St. Dominique Street and live with the bums. It was 1951, and I was really suffering.

"And then I tied up with a couple of guys from Verdun who offered me a job driving a car. One was called Moose and the other, Pepsi. The job entailed driving a getaway car while they robbed banks. They said they'd pay me a couple of hundred dollars a job, which seemed like a fortune to me. I had had such a hard time finding work and owned nothing but the clothes on my back. I probably didn't smell too good either when I went looking for a job. Where could I bathe? So I said okay, and we climbed into a car which must have been stolen, because there was no key and we had to cross the wires to start it. We drove to a bank where I stopped with the motor running. The two guys came running out and away we went. On one occasion a cop chased us, but we got away. We turned left and he turned right for some reason I could never figure out. But after that I thought we had had a close call and I wanted out. One of the men handed me a gun the next day, and I asked if it was empty. It was a .38. He said, yes. So I pulled the trigger and the gun went off in my hand, missing my fingers by a hair. I had powder burns. The bullet hit the dashboard, ricocheted off it and hit me in the stomach. Scared me to death, but I was lucky to be wearing a heavy overcoat. I wasn't hurt. And that was the end of my bank-robbing career. I went back to bumming.

"My next job was in Griffintown, in Point St. Charles, delivering ice with a horse and cart. The man I was working with made me carry the biggest and heaviest slabs of ice to the upper floor, while he took the smaller pieces to ground-level flats. I finally got so mad, I deliberately let a big block of ice slip down my back and go bouncing down the stairs. It did a lot of damage, and the owners made him pay for it. I quit.

"But while I was working in the Point, three men made fun of me because I was wearing old-fashioned clothes, with wide pants. They called me a DP and jumped on me and started pounding me. I took all three on and beat the hell out of them. They were so surprised they became my friends. They respected my toughness, and we've been friends ever since.

"And talk about exploiting immigrants... I found a job working for a rich family in Westmount. They had a seventeen-room house and they had me do all kinds of odd jobs—sweeping floors, clearing garbage, anything. All they gave me was fifty cents a day. It was just enough to pay for a night in the flophouse. I didn't own a pair of socks, and winter and summer I walked around sweating or freezing my feet in my old shoes.

"One day the owner and the lady of the house drove up while I was sweeping out the garbage. They didn't move or come in until the dust had died down. They wouldn't breathe it, but it was okay for me to inhale it for an hour while I was cleaning. Then they got out of the car and had me carry in all the groceries. I couldn't even afford to eat on the money they paid me, but I got even. Before I quit, I pinched a pair of socks to wear and some golf clubs which I sold for food. I was so close to starving that I would go into a restaurant, watch people eating and when they got up and left, I'd slide into their seats and eat whatever was left on their plates. It was the only way I could survive.

"One day I saw an ad for a typewriter repairman and applied. They asked me if I had any experience and I said, yes, that I had worked at it for a year. So they gave me a list of names and I went over there, bluffed my way through it, got the secretaries to hold this, turn that and wiped off the keys. There must have been complaints, because on the following jobs the boss sent another repairman with me to see what I was doing. I lasted three days before I got fired.

"By now I was desperate. I decided I wanted to become a photographer. I'd been fascinated with cameras since I was a kid, but I had no money for cameras and equipment. So I broke into a camera store and stole some cameras. I still feel bad about it, and five years later I went back to see the owner of the store to talk to him, to explain and offer him money to pay for what I had taken. I had given him a lot of trouble. He refused the money I offered. He told me he would have been happier if I had taken the new cameras that were insured, instead of the ones in for repairs because he had a lot of trouble replacing them, and they hadn't been insured. He was an astute, educated, McGill graduate, and he told me I was worth the investment. By then I had become well known as a news photographer. But getting to be good wasn't easy. I would go to the *Gazette* and bug them every day. 'I have a picture for you,' I'd say. But they weren't interested. They would chase me out if I bothered them too much. You see, I wanted them to develop the shot for me. I wasn't sure how good the photo was, and I figured it would be a great way of finding out how I was doing. I really bugged them to death. And one day they did give me a job. It was the biggest break I ever had in my life...and I certainly worked hard for them. It opened up a whole new world.

"The job of press photographer has changed radically over

the years. It has a lot to do with new methods of communication. I don't like to think about it, but papers are dying. One of the problems is the trade unions. They are very strict about you finishing a shift and then going to do other work. You can't and if you do, there's a complaint. And papers are much smaller and don't use as many photographs. I always think of the old stereotype of a photographer in a James Cagney film where the photographer is carrying a big camera with a big flash and lots of wires, is plugged in and get excited, starts running down the aisle, forgets he's plugged in and strangles himself.

"But for me those early years covering hockey games were equally dangerous. You didn't strangle on wire, but there was no plexiglass around the ice at the Forum so you could get hit regularly with the puck or a stick. This was in the days of Kenny Reardon and those guys who slammed up on the boards, knocking over everyone, especially the photographer. Who cared about the photographer? One of the things we had to have was a hard head. And we had to be aggressive if we wanted to be good. Many a time I tried to get a good picture and pushed my way through a crowd of spectators. There was always someone who would start a fight with me, thinking I was just trying to shove ahead of him. I was there to get a good picture, and if someone got in my way, I just ran over him. I had quite a few people grab me from the back.

"At the beginning I worked for Gazette Photo which was a commercial subsidiary and supplied the *Gazette* with pictures. It was more of a commercial studio than a news photography division. I was there in the '50s, '60s, '70s, and '80s, over thirty years. You name it, I covered it. I was put on news, sports, and the paper did weddings every Saturday, which I hated.

"I remember once when the *Gazette* sent me out to do a wedding—something I had never done in my life—a lady said to me: 'So you're the professional wedding photographer from the *Gazette*?'

"I said, 'No, I've never done a wedding.'

"She almost died. I walked into her house, pushed her furniture all around, ruffled up her rugs, got on a chair right under the priest, looked up his nose, and when I saw the lady waving at me, I waved back at her. She was telling me to get off the altar. She said she wanted a picture over here, and I said I wanted one over there. While we were arguing, someone threw confetti all over me, and she said, 'You can leave.'

"I didn't complete the wedding, and the lady called the *Gazette* to ask: 'Who was that lousy photographer you sent to my daughter's wedding?' She didn't know who was answering her phone call.

"'It was me, Madame. Can I help you?'

"I got fired right on the spot. Actually I was fired eleven times while I was at the *Gazette*, but I never left. Sometimes I got a raise. But those weddings were funny and aggravating. I remember one in the Town of Mount Royal that was supposed to be a small one, but when I got there I found two hundred people. I had been covering a fire all Friday night and was exhausted. It was Saturday, and I had had no sleep. I sat down at the back of the church and while the wedding was going on, I fell asleep. The bride and groom came up the aisle, smiling and waving and looking gorgeous, and there I was snoring away. They had to wake me up, go down the aisle and walk it again. But that was nothing. I took back all the photos to the *Gazette* to develop. We had just bought a new machine that was supposed to print and develop photos in four minutes. I put the film in and was waiting for it, when I heard a funny noise inside. The machine ate up the film so there were no wedding pictures. The *Gazette* was sued for that.

"I was always in trouble. That was my last wedding. Two weddings messed up, they said. No more.

"Taking pictures, you see, is something more than just clicking a camera and getting the event on a negative. It's a big project, capturing a moment in life where it starts and where it ends. And what I like about the business is that there's always something different. You don't know from day to day what you are going to do.

"When my best picture 'Brute Force' was shot, the one that won all kinds of awards, it happened this way. The sports editor told me to go out to the University of Montreal. About five inches of rain had fallen that day, and it was still coming down.

"'You got to be kidding,' I said.

" 'Go!' he ordered.

"So I went, although I was sure the game would be cancelled. When I arrived, the game had already started, with five or six inches of mud and water swamping the field. The lights were glaring down on one side of the field, and I ran up and down in the mud, trying to shoot as many pictures as possible, even though I was convinced it was a waste. I lost my shoe in the mud and while I was hunting for it, I nearly got knocked over by a couple of New Zealanders racing for the ball. It was the worst day I had ever spent.

"On my return to the *Gazette*, the editor took a look at what I had taken after the negatives were developed, and he threw this particular picture into the wastebasket and printed a shot highlighting the mud, with the caption that it was an awful day for a game. The photo that he tossed out ended up by winning an award as best in its category in the world. When it won the prize, the *Gazette* printed the photograph in the paper with the line that their staffer had been singled out for a great professional honour by taking it.

"On another occasion, I took a picture of a Russian dancer and his wife, who were staying at the Meridien Hotel in Montreal. I asked her to put her head on his shoulder—a romantic pose—and they were so nice about it, smiling for the camera. Shortly afterwards, they went off to catch a flight to New York. Suddenly came the news that he had defected and left her sitting in the plane on the runway just before takeoff. Suddenly, my picture assumed a position of great importance, and I received phone calls from *Life*, *Time*, *Newsweek*, *Stern Magazine* in Germany and others. Everyone wanted the picture, but *Stern Magazine* wanted an exclusive. I said it would cost a thousand dollars. Fine, fine was the answer. I'm sure it would have been fine if I had asked for two thousand. An hour later I received a long-distance call from *Paris Match*. They wanted the photo and an exclusive. 'Sure, okay,' I agreed and asked for another thousand. So I had the same picture in two of the biggest magazines in Europe, and each publication thought it had the exclusive rights.

"But taking news pictures isn't all fun and games. At times it has bothered me that I was invading someone's privacy. I have stood there and seen young kids dying, mangled in the wreckage of their bikes, or seen people dead in the wet cement of a collapsed building project, being dragged out like dogs, or watched people burning to death. Sure, it's not nice, but someone has to record it. Many a time, I went home feeling sick to my stomach at what I'd seen happen to a child. Because I had a boy of my own at home, I'd come in, after he was asleep in his bed, and I'd go in and just stand there, looking at him while my thoughts were on the scene of some poor youngster smashed up on a street, and whose photo I had just taken. I had had to cover a lot of hit-and-runs, and there were times a mother would grab me, throw her arms around me and ask me for help, when I had come to take a picture that would only bring back all the memories of her child.

"One sad incident I will always remember happened in Ville Emard. Two young kids got into a refrigerator and suffocated. The boy was four, and his sister was five. It was close to dead-line, and I had to go out there and get a shot of the fridge. The parents were showing me photos of the dead kids as if they were still alive, and I had to be a little aggressive and keep asking to see the refrigerator which was in a next-door neighbour's basement, where the kids had been playing. We went over there, and the father got into an argument with the neighbour. They weren't friends any-more at that point, and while this was going on I got down on my knees and took pictures of the fridge, the door of which had been removed by the police. There were some clothes at the bottom of it. I raced back to make my deadline, and the paper received a lot of calls and letters criticizing the photo, and asking how the photographer could have been so cruel and insensitive. I had to do what I had been ordered. It was my job, and it cost me a lot in other ways. I was punched in the face so many times while trying to get a good shot that I stopped counting how often it had happened. My nose was broken, my eyes blackened, lips split, and my face doesn't look too good any more as a result.

"And insults....

"Years ago, I photographed W.H. Auden, one of the great-est poets in the English-speaking world, when he spoke before a packed audience of about 1,500 people at McGill University. Clanging and banging with equipment bags, I came down the aisle, dragging a chair to stand on. Because I had another assignment after that one, I couldn't sit for an hour and listen to Auden speak. I'm sure it would have been very nice, but my job was to get the shots and get out of there to the next job. So I stood on a chair and started clicking away. Auden got pretty mad, and everyone booed me. He made faces at me and asked what I was doing.

"'I'm trying to get a picture of you,' I answered.

"He made another face, and I snapped and took off up the aisle amidst the boos and hisses. The next day, the *Montreal Star* had a piece in it about a certain photographer from another newspaper who disrupted one of the greatest poets in the world. I know Auden was the greatest in his field, but I felt a bit proud of what I had taken despite the criticism. I had to get that shot.

"In my work, I had the pleasure of meeting some very special and important people—presidents, kings, queens—Eisenhower, Johnson, Queen Elizabeth, Princess Grace of Monaco, Prime Minister Trudeau, Terry Fox, and many others. I covered the Montreal World's Fair, Expo 1967, and I was in charge of 611 photographers at the 1976 Olympic Games. I met all the great political leaders, sportmen and athletes of the world, and even the not-so-great leaders. I have photographed and met gangsters, crooks, killers, rapists, people jumping up and down crying with happiness after winning millions of dollars in lotteries. I have recorded people dying in car accidents, motor-bike smash-ups, drownings, explosions, fires, plane crashes and people committing suicide with guns, knives or drugs. I've seen the results of drug overdoses by youngsters in their teens, and the tragedies among the teenagers is the worst, much of it happening because of social pressures. Kids want too much too soon, and are not prepared for it. They can't handle the stress. It hasn't been easy for me being exposed to all those things, but I realize that my early years of facing life's realities prepared me for it.

"I grew up in the Australian bush country among fighting, killing and surviving, and I went from one kind of killing to another. My mother was trying to kill me because her daughter's husband killed her favourite son, and somehow or other she managed to transfer the blame to me. And I went on to another killing scene. The war was a continuation of what I had been exposed to, only more so. Trying to survive those early years in Canada only strengthened my belief that this was what life was all about. I never knew there was a better side to life. And I'm still fighting to survive. After working all these years, winning all the awards there were to win in Canada, Europe and the United States, writing a book, *Cricket in Eastern Canada*, which sold ten thousand copies, here I am at my age without permanent work. I *have* to survive.

"But I sure learned an awful lot about life and people, discovering along the way that I don't hate people or dislike them. I'm just dubious about trusting them. I can't pin my faith on anyone any more. It's a sad situation, but I've found that people always want to know what you can do for them. I know that you don't have to be an individualist to be somebody, but I've always had to be different because I've always been on my own. And yet I could fit into a group because I am like a chameleon—green in the grass and brown on the branch. When I had to be with rich people, I never looked out of place, and when I was forced to live with bums on the sidewalks and sleep under buildings, I lived and looked like one. There's no question that I'm an individualist, but because of it, I know I've rubbed a lot of people the wrong way. Although I'm known and respected as a photographer in my professional life, I can't change although I know this has hurt me along the way. It has cost me jobs, even friendships. But I find people who really like me are truly real friends. They understand why I am what I am.

"The one thing I regret the most was my marriage breakup and the loss of my son. I married a beautiful lady and had a wonderful son, and I loved them both very much. I was responsible for the breakup, because I thought I had to be everywhere taking pictures, and I neglected my family. Thinking I was working for the future, I worked too hard and lost something in communication. When I look back on all the pictures I've taken, all the jobs I've had, all the laughs and all the pain, there is nothing in the world that hurt me more than losing my family. And naturally, in fighting to get my son back, I did the wrong thing again. I rode across Canada to the west on a train, watched and waited until the boy was alone in the backyard, and I grabbed him out of there. I jumped into a car and took off to where I'd hired a seaplane to stand by, on a river. I hid the car in a barn on a farm and took off, running across fields with my son under one arm and a suitcase under the other. I boarded the plane, flew to Vancouver and took a cab across the Rockies by night to Calgary at the cost of $700 in fares. I sat in the back seat holding my son and looking back at every automobile behind me, sure that one of them was a police car chasing me. My wife had a warrant out for my arrest in British Columbia. In Calgary, I boarded a flight to Montreal and finally when my wife phoned me at my home, she persuaded me to bring the boy back.

"'We'll all live together,' she promised. I loved her so much, I believed her, but when I arrived back there, she and her mother stole the boy and ran off with him. I couldn't find him, and that was when I decided to hang myself. Somewhere in Port Alberni, British Columbia, I bought a rope in a hardware store and went back to one of those dirty old rundown hotels where I had been staying, where just about everyone is drunk or on drugs. I tied the rope to the TV bracket up on the wall, looped the other end around my neck and jumped off the bed.

"Not only did the TV come down, but so did the wall, on top of me. I decided that was it. I was no good at killing myself. My neck was too thick.

"I was in bad shape out there, and eventually someone in Montreal contacted me, asking what the hell was I doing to myself with all my talent, and telling me to come back. So I returned to Montreal. I'd left the *Gazette,* and when I tried to get my job back, they refused. No one would hire me. I started working with the baseball and football teams, trying to rebuild my career and my life, but I just couldn't. While working for the Montreal Alouettes football team, I met Junior Ah You, a six-foot-three-inch Samoan, who played defensive end. We became friends and he asked me to accompany him and his family to Hawaii. I went, and while living with them as their guest on Oahu Island, I was baptized into the Mormon religion. They were staunch Mormons. I went to services at their church and studied at Brigham Young University where I took philosophy, religion and painting.

"This period was what I desperately needed to rebuild my soul. But fate dealt me another low card. I was struck down with spinal meningitis, which crippled me and left me with double vision. I spent five months in a Hawaiian hospital, and when I returned to Montreal, I was at the bottom of the ladder again. In a wheel chair for six months, I slept on the floor in a small room, living on almost nothing and nearly starving to death. No one would help me. I had to crawl on my hands and knees to cook something for myself in a kitchen, down a flight of stairs. You don't have friends when you're in trouble. I dropped to ninety pounds from two hundred, but I tried to fight my way back, and won. After five knee operations, I finally got back on my feet again and found a job at the

Sunday Express. Just as I was getting myself together, the paper folded, three and a half years after I joined it, and I was back to where I had started—at the bottom looking up.

"But I'm not giving up. I still think I'm lucky to have come to Canada even though I didn't start life here as honestly as I should have. Despite my problems, I got along pretty well with most people, and French Canadians were especially nice to me. They even apologized for not being able to speak English, and it's something they shouldn't have to apologize for. They're entitled to speak French just as I'm entitled to speak English.

"I know there has been antagonism between newcomers and established Anglophone and Francophone Canadians but there's another group, made up of Blacks, Orientals and Indians known as visible minorities, who have become targets of racism from all sides. Canada is supposed to be multicultural and ethnic-oriented, but I don't think it works. Part of the problem is that each nationality works in its own little sphere, instead of working together toward a common goal. Everybody's doing his own thing, instead of doing it together. That's what's hurting Canada.

"When I first arrived in 1951, Montreal was one of the most progressive cities in Canada. Montreal was heading for the status of a metropolis, and it ended up a small city. Toronto jumped ahead because people were leaving Quebec in the thousands as a result of the French-English animosity. If both communities could have worked together, they could have accomplished great things. We're all here in it together—English and French, ethnic, white, black, brown, red or yellow people trying to do the same thing—make a living, bring up our families in freedom, far away from wars and catastrophes, and contribute something to Canada.

"As far as contribution is concerned, one of the biggest wastes of human potential is the lack of participation in the Provincial and Municipal police forces by ethnics and visible minorities. Sure, there are a few token cops in those ethnic and visible-minority groups, but next to nothing when you consider the size of those multi-racial and multi-cultural communities. I've noticed that most Europeans seem to get along pretty well, because Europe is really such a small continent with so many countries near one another. There's a lot of interchange and intermarriage and it's not uncommon to meet people who speak three or four languages. I can't understand why there has to be such a division here. Why can't people get along?

"Now you take poor immigrants who come here. They put their trust not in the Lord, but in a lawyer or middleman who takes everything, and promises to get them into the country real easy. But there's no such thing. The dream many immigrants have of a land of milk and honey with gold-paved streets is just that—a dream. I think people put too much emphasis on money. I've worked all these years and don't have anything much, as far as money's concerned. Sure it's nice to get rich, but there's more to life than that. You have to have faith—in your religion, in other people, but most of all in yourself. Where some immigrants fail is that they expect everything should be given to them. And there are others who expect nothing and that way become something. I'm proud of these people. You see the Vietnamese immigrants working at convenience stores twenty-four hours a day, making less than a dollar an hour. They're lucky if they make a few dollars profit a day, yet they go home and sleep, and don't complain. And there are others here, who have so much more than that and aren't satisfied. Immigrants, however, will buckle down and do with less to survive despite ignorant and unfeeling criticism by established Canadians.

"I wasn't born here, but I love Canada. I always wanted to stay here, once I got used to it, and I feel I am a Quebecer, but I don't get much of a chance to show my love, because I'm English-speaking. If you don't speak French you aren't considered a Quebeçois, and this is terribly wrong because some of the ablest and most important Quebecers who built this province in the early days were English or at least English-speaking. They worked for it, they financed it and moulded it, but their descendants are packing up and leaving. It's a shame.

"Canada is one of the finest countries in the world, and a Canadian can travel everywhere and be respected. We may be known to the world as a mildly emotional people, which I don't think is much of a compliment, but I do think we're more emotional than we've been rated. We're more sincere, we're good fighters and are good at whatever we undertake. Canada is a fine nation, but living so close to the United States, Canadians get a lot of American problems rubbing off on them—crime, violence, drugs, media culture and soap operas on TV. What bothers me is that most of what we get on Canadian TV is American and violence-oriented. Another thing that bugs me is that whenever the President of the United States speaks on TV, everything else is pre-empted. Our own Prime Minister says something, and rarely at that, and hardly anyone listens. That's one thing that bothers me. We don't respect our leaders, and that's a great Canadian failing."

Everyone can look back at some point in his or her life and say, 'Oh, yeah, I could have done this differently; I shouldn't have done this or that.' When I look back, I realize the most important thing in my life was having my son, and if I hadn't come to Canada I wouldn't have had him. I may have produced a lot of great pictures, but the greatest thing I produced was a son. As far as winning every damn prize in the world goes, it doesn't mean a thing. Children are more important. But because I came from such a bad background and had been hungry and abused for so long, I decided I had to be somebody, and in trying to be number one in my profession, I lost everything that was important to me.

"Except for my son, I don't know how much I've contributed to Canada. I did my work as a news photographer. If I didn't come back with something, I couldn't keep my job and I wouldn't eat. I tried to do it better than the next guy so I could outdo other papers. I was always very competitive, but that's human nature. I tried to be good and decent after a very bad start, and I became a Canadian citizen. If there was ever a war, I would fight for this country, despite my age. I would be willing to give my life for it. But I still feel that the best thing I did was to have a son who may do something important for Canada...someday.

CANADA'S SHAME

by
Milly Charon
from an interview with Dr. and Mrs. James Hasegawa

March, 1941

A specific race of people are forced to register with the authorities. All adults and children over the age of sixteen have to fill out questionnaires listings names, address, age, sex, height, weight, marks of identification and occupation. Each person is fingerprinted and required to carry the registration card on his person at all times. The card has a photograph, thumb print and serial number of bearer.

December 7, 1941

Japan attacks Pearl Harbour.

Within two hours the government issues directives, and specific orders to branches of security are put into effect.

Shortly after, in thousands of homes, a knock on the door is the beginning of governmental security action. Police are waiting outside and without any warning whatsoever, they take away all able-bodied men between the ages of 18 and 45. Boys of 17 and under, women, children and grandparents are given one day to two weeks to prepare for pickup and delivery to distribution centres and from there to internment camps in the interior of the country. All possessions, except for 50 pounds of personal belongings, are to be left behind. These are subsequently confiscated and sold.

These "seize and disperse" tactics involve over 22,000 people of this race. The tactics are Gestapo-like in execution; the registration is similar to what the Nazis imposed on German and Austrian Jews in the 1930s; the confiscation and disposal of property, as well as the detention in camps are reminiscent of Hitlerian tactics in occupied Europe.
Where is this happening?
In British Columbia, Canada, the land of freedom and democracy.

Who are the people treated so shamefully?
Canadian citizens and Niseis, first-generation children of Japanese origin.

Who are the Gestapo-like police?
The RCMP, acting under orders from the federal government under the War Measures Act.

What is the War Measures Act? Does it grant these powers?
The War Measures Act, created in 1914, can do anything. It can be used as a club to bludgeon a peaceful race living on land they have bought and paid for, into detention and forced dispersion.

What does the Act say?
The exact wording in Part Two is:
"The Governor in Council may do and authorize such acts and things and make from time to time such orders and regulations, as he may by reason of the existence of real or apprehended war, invasion or insurrection, deem necessary or advisable for the security, defence, peace, order and welfare of Canada: and for greater certainty, but not so as to restrict the generality of the foregoing terms, it is hereby declared that the powers of the Governor in Council shall extend to all matters coming within the classes of subjects hereinafter enumerated, that is to say:

"Censorship and the control and suppression of publications, writings, maps, plans, photographs, communications and means of communications:
"Arrest, detention, exclusion and deportation;
"Control of the harbours, ports, and territorial waters of Canada and the movement of vessels;
"Transportation by land, air, water and the control of the transport of persons and things;
"Trading, exportation, importation, production and manufacture;
"Appropriation, control, forfeiture and the disposition of property and the use thereof."

And the Act is carried out with a vengeance.

Japanese-Canadian newspapers are shut down; all radios and short-wave radios are confiscated; all fishing vessels, including rowboats, are seized by the RCMP and given to the Custodian of Enemy Alien Property, an office created by an Order in Council on March 27, 1942. Under the watchful eye of the British Columbia Security Commission, headed by Austin Taylor, all citizens of Japanese origin are detained and relocated outside a 100-mile Canada Protective Zone away from the West Coast. Herded into cattle pens in Hastings Park, the exhibition grounds in the eastern end of Vancouver, the people are segregated, men separated from women and children, and guarded by armed soldiers. This act of displacement is seen as discrimination, for Canada has been at war with Germany and Italy since 1939 and not one Canadian of Italian or German origin is touched.

Millions of dollars in property and business are put into the custody of the B.C. Custodians, to be returned after the war. Not one penny of it is ever seen again. The people on the Commission, responsible for this heinous act of outright theft, are never prosecuted or brought to justice.

No reparations are made until forty-seven years have passed. After the war, over 4,000 Japanese are encouraged to return to Japan. The other 18,000 or more are scattered, dispersed like leaves, across the face of Canada.

* * * *

Dr. and Mrs. James (Helen) Hasegawa were children in Vancouver when Canada imposed this treatment on its Japanese-Canadian citizens. While James Hasegawa's memories are more emotional than bitter, the experience left lasting psychological scars.

J.H.:

My parents came to Canada in 1917, and I was born in Vancouver. I think I was ten or eleven when all this happened. My family had a very successful confectionery and restaurant business, and my father had just bought us the first radio and short-wave console we had ever owned.

The RCMP came without warning, like the Gestapo in Germany, and took my father away. They took our radio, and we never saw it again or any money for it. And, even worse, we had to give everything away. My father's business was sold for peanuts—$400—because people who knew the plight of the Japanese...their being relocated any day...were offering one cent on the dollar. They took advantage of us. That business was worth more than a hundred times the money we got for it.

It was a tremendous blow for us. One day we had a great business going and the next it was gone. With my father taken, my mother, older sister and brother had to make all the preparations to leave for the interior of British Columbia. There was no one to help us, no one to stop this collective madness. There were no cases of civil disobedience or riots...none. It happened so quickly. There was method to their madness. They took away all the able-bodied men, so who the hell was going to fight for us? The families were told to be ready for relocation, in anywhere from two days' to two weeks' time, and to be at such and such a place for pickup. We barely had time to pack, let alone organize against such injustice. It was easy for the government to round us up as a group while the Germans and Italians remained untouched. They were scattered all over the country, and we were in one area. It was also appearance. A Japanese Oriental is easily picked up, and as an ethnic group, we can be lumped together.

I've been told we all look alike to the white man.

H.H.: I was about six or seven years old and remember my father being taken away one day, and that was it. I really didn't understand what it was all about. I was the third of six girls. My mother had just given birth, and my father wasn't there. She must have had a hell of a time trying to manage, having to pack the few belongings we were allowed to take with us, and look after six children at the same time. My oldest sister was only nine. There were aunts, but they had their own problems with the evacuation as well.

J.H.: The worst thing was that an Order in Council had set up the Custodians of Enemy Alien Property and had given them the power to liquidate and dispose of our property. Most of us thought it was in safekeeping and that we would get it back after the war. But those people on the Custodian committee were a bunch of crooks. They stole everything and sold it to friends and relatives, or anyone, for a fraction of what it was worth. None of us ever had anything returned, and no reparations were made by either the federal or provincial government.

It had taken my family twenty-five years

to accumulate the material things we owned, and all that was left behind. It was one thing for the Custodians to take possession of the fishing boats, firearms, radios, properties etc., but it was another when people were forced to sell whatever they owned for peanuts because they couldn't take it with them.

Many families lost tremendous fortunes. The Kagetsu family lost over $20 million worth of land. They owned an island that was worth millions then, and ten or eleven years ago was worth $20 million. The head of the Custodians sold it to his nephew for $3,000.

When the Kagetsus moved to Toronto, a son became a lawyer so he would know enough about the law to fight the government on behalf of his family. He took the case to court a number of years ago, and it was quite a famous case. About eleven or twelve years ago, on W5 I believe, the two involved in the case were interviewed. The question was asked about the uncle having the right to sell the property to his nephew, among the other things they did. Of course, nothing happened as a result of this exposure. There was no conflict of interest charge, no punishment and no restitution.

To understand why all this happened, you have to go back years before the War Measures Act.

Most Canadians didn't know what was happening out in British Columbia. The government was silent about it for many years. They hushed it up because they were pressured into it by Caucasian groups in British Columbia, who resented the predominance of the Japanese in three main areas—the fishing, logging and market-gardening industries. At that time, the Japanese controlled most of these and owned millions of dollars worth of prime timber as well as the fishing fleets on the west coast.

These pressure groups sent a committee
to Ottawa and with their lies and bullshit, managed to convince the federal government that the
Japanese were dangerous people. They knew
damn well that once we were removed from the
coast, they could take over everything. And it has
been proven beyond a shadow of a doubt why the
Japanese were forced from the west coast in such
a despicable manner and relocated in the interior.
No one really suspected them of sabotage or espionage—there was not even one confirmed act of
it—that was just the excuse. But the government
believed all that baloney, that we were a potential
Fifth Column in the country. These lobbyists had
a tremendous influence through their Members of
Parliament, and once that War Measures Act was
passed, it was open season on the Japanese Canadians. What the Custodians did was sickening.

It was outright theft.

Today there are groups organizing in
Vancouver and Toronto in an effort to have the
federal government make reparations. But a lot of
people like me say: "To hell with it!". Making
reparations now is too late. The way I look at it, the
objective is to make sure that such a thing never
happens again. You want to blame someone?
Blame that archaic War Measures Act. It's the law
of the land, and under it the government has carte
blanche to do anything it wants.

Let's face it. There aren't too many people
left who suffered through that period. Our parents were the ones who bore the brunt of it. What
does a kid know? Our parents shielded us.

H.H.:   I remember everyone getting sick on the
ride in this rickety old bus that took us to Hastings
Park. There were kids throwing up from the
motion. The park was a huge and frightening
place.

J.H.:   The government used the park as a pooling centre. It was an amusement park like the Toronto exhibition grounds, with large buildings housing the exhibits. Into these buildings were packed thousands of people. The exhibits had been removed, and two-decker bunkbeds, thousands of them, row after row, were placed side by side, no more than three feet apart. Each family was assigned the number of beds according to its size. There were common showers and toilets down at the end of the stadium-sized room. There was absolutely no privacy.

H.H.   The dining room was in another building, and I remember my sister and me coming back on our own to our bunks because my mother hadn't finished eating. We opened the curtain around the bed on the bottom row, and strange faces stared up at us. We were so frightened we ran down the rows in terror. Originally the building had stalls for horses and cattle when the livestock shows were held, and the drains for the animals' urine were right there beside us and under us. They stank. I'll never forget that stench.

J.H.:   The floor was cold, damp concrete. We asked for extra blankets which we rarely got, and the only privacy we could manage was to string blankets along the side of the bunk from the top level down so at least those in the bottom were enclosed. All our personal possessions were shoved under the bottom bunk—all you had in the world, fifty pounds of it. And we had to be careful because people were stealing left and right.

The first people detained there were those from the fishing villages. They had to be removed from the coast because they were considered to be prime security risks. Some of these villagers spent as much as six months at Hastings Park, waiting for relocation. Those from Vancouver were the last to be detained at the centre. The farmers and fishermen came from as far as Prince Rupert and Skeena, hundreds of miles away, and they were dumped there like cattle, living out of a suitcase, to wait months until the internment camps in the interior were ready.

And who do you think was preparing these camps? The fathers and eighteen-years-and-up brothers who had been collected first and taken as cheap labour to build the most basic, Spartan lodgings for the families who would come after. The government called these men "road gangs", and they did all the construction. They built roads, cut timber, prepared the lumber for building, laid the pipes and put in the septic tanks, everything.

They were paid twenty-three to twenty-five cents an hour. As soon as a few homes were ready, families were notified and a trainload was sent up. At the beginning they were sending up people before the houses were finished, and many were packed into canvas tents for months, even in winter. It was like Siberia. There must have been some kind of outcry because the authorities began keeping people on the exhibition grounds for longer periods until the houses were ready.

We stayed in Hastings Park for only three or four weeks. I guess we were luckier than some of the others. Because we lived in Vancouver, we were the last to go. I met boys at Hastings who came from the northern coastal villages and spoke with a funny accent. They didn't talk English, only Japanese. They were anywhere from ten to seventeen years of age, and they had already established gangs when we city boys got there. They were tough and could beat the hell out of you. There was so much theft and fights, and we city kids had to protect ourselves by banding together, but we were outnumbered and I guess we were more civilized and less aggressive. I got beaten up plenty. I thought I was tough, but those walks to the bathrooms three hundred yards away and then over to the next wing and turn right were an experience. It was so damned impersonal. Half a mile of stalls and then a row of faucets for washing. As we walked by those bunkbeds, we never knew who was behind each blanket and who would reach out, grab us and beat the hell out of us. It was frightening.

H.H.: The washing area was just a wide, open room with faucets, and if you wanted to undress and wash all over, there was no privacy. It was worse for the girls and women because we were more shy and sensitive than the boys.

J.H.: Yes, it was more traumatic for the girls. My sister and her friends suffered terribly. All the men over eighteen were gone, and there were more women—mothers and daughters—than sons.

H.H.: I slept on the top bunk and would stand up and look around. From that height, it seemed all you could see for miles in either direction were bunkbeds, nothing else.

J.H.: We weren't allowed any radios, short-wave or otherwise, no cameras, newspapers, and of course, no firearms. We were kept totally ignorant of the outside world and the news of the war. When we finally were moved out to the internment camp in New Denver, B.C., we lived in a tent for a couple of months, but we were lucky because my father was a carpenter. Others weren't so fortunate. He was on the construction crew, so he was able to apply a little influence and ask to have a house prepared for his family. He would take us over to look at it as it was going up and say: "That's going to be our house."

But I know there were others who spent as much as eight or nine months in those frigid tents until the houses were ready. We moved in as soon as ours was finished.

H.H.:   We arrived just at the beginning of winter. It was bitterly cold, and there was frost on the ground. It was so cold in our tent that we slept fully dressed and in the morning, we would run over to the next tent to have breakfast. They had a kitchen in one tent and a dining area in another.

J.H.:   Once we got out there, we found a few people who were able to smuggle a radio in from one of the merchants in the village, so there was always a radio around. It was only a standard battery and not a short wave, so what was the use of having it? There were no stations out there, and the mountains surrounding us prevented any kind of reception. Other than the local village gossip paper, there were no newspapers, Japanese or otherwise. We were forbidden any communication with the outside world, even reading newspapers. Our isolation was total.

I think back and I realize our parents went through a great deal. As for me, I had a ball for four years. What did I know? Oh sure, we were deprived of many things that kids of other races and ethnic groups took for granted, but we had so much fun. We had schooling, swimming, baseball, and we could fish and hunt with bows and arrows.

There was skiing in the winter. A freshwater lake was just behind our house and the scenery was something. It was like Paradise.

The government set up a logging camp and a sawmill, where the men and some of the older boys worked, but the wages were nothing much, about twenty-five cents an hour. However, we lived in government-owned houses. There were just two rooms for five of us—a kitchen-family room and a bedroom where we all slept. Made of clapboard with tarpaper insulation, they were cold, but ingenious people like my father spent months insulating them properly, adding shingles and turning them into warm and nice-looking homes. My father even put a double floor down in our house so we would be warmer, and he added an extension on the back. Not everyone was this capable. Because we were in a logging camp, we could get all the supplies we wanted. Wood was plentiful, and he made everything himself—cutting, sawing, slicing, trimming and sanding the timber. He would hang it to dry from the rafters and with hand tools could make ten identical pieces without precision instruments.

H.H.:   New Denver was the first relocation centre I was in, and it was the prettiest place I ever saw. It was like a holiday resort, similar to parts of the Laurentians. The scenery was magnificent. When the water in the lake was still, it looked like glass and mirrored the mountains with their snow-capped tops.

My father had picked a house not far from Jim's family, but we didn't know each other then. My father, who was in his early forties, joined up with others of his age group and formed a league. They set up a baseball diamond not far from the house.

We were there for over four years, and then were moved to another camp called Tashme, way out in the sticks. It was just a little village cupped in the heart of the mountains. You couldn't get out anywhere but on the one road they had brought us in on.

J.H.:   My father fixed our house up into something that was beautiful—almost luxurious. We spent weeks digging up the ground to put in pipes for the plumbing and a septic tank, and then suddenly everything changed.

The war was nearing its close, and the International Red Cross intervened and sent people up to see us. They must have told the government to do something about us, and we were informed we would be given the chance to return to Japan or be relocated east of British Columbia and Alberta. We wouldn't be allowed to remain where we were. I guess we would have reminded them too much of what they had done to us, and we might have asked for our property back if we stayed in the province.

We had to make a decision. Those who chose to stay were sent to another camp, and those who were going back to Japan were shuffled off somewhere else. It was a tremendous upheaval. After three or four years of having to adjust and establish some sort of makeshift home, we suddenly were being uprooted again. We had to give up our little house and were sent off to another centre. There was nothing much there. My father had decided to go back to Japan, but my sister fought tooth and nail to stay in Canada, even if it meant being dispersed eastward.

When I think about it, I really don't know how my parents felt about this whole traumatic experience. Their biggest concern had been survival and something for us kids to look forward to. They hadn't worried too much about themselves. They wanted us to amount to something and hoped that one day the country would accept us and not treat us the way they had been treated. And although they had been paid slave-labour wages, lived in cramped quarters and didn't know what the future held, they still hung on. Even though they had been made to feel like dirt, deep inside they must have realized that our future was here. They didn't talk about the suffering, but I knew it was there. They just kept working and kept their mouths shut.

My father really couldn't go back to Japan even if he wanted to. Everything he had accumulated was gone, and to go back as a pauper would have made him the laughingstock of his village.

I'm sure he would have been run out of it by the scorn of the villagers. It was a matter of losing face, and for a Japanese this is the most important thing in his character. Maybe that is why more Japanese didn't go back. After thirty or forty years they had nothing to show for their labour and would have been asked: "What the hell did you do in Canada for so long?"

For us there was another situation as well. I had three brothers and two sisters who had been sent back to Japan before the war when they were five years old. An uncle was taking care of them, and my father sent money to pay for their education. I was in the process of being shipped back when the war broke out. My father had intended to go back to Japan one day when the kids were educated. Three of the boys went to war on the Japanese side; one was killed and two were living. One sister is still alive. We were like two separate families on each side of the ocean. How could my father go back penniless after the war and face his family? For him it was a disgrace. Those who did return had wealthy families, but those who were proud and couldn't take humiliation stayed in Canada.

And so, to expedite things, the two groups were separated. We went to a village called Rose-berry, a dump about three miles away. And we had to commute back those three miles every day to attend high school in New Denver. We lived in a tiny shack for a year and a half.

H.H.:   I guess we were sent to Tashme because my father decided to go back to Japan. He wasn't sure what he wanted to do. He had no money to go anywhere else, but I remember him saying he would go anywhere in Canada at government expense. That was how we moved from one place to the next. From Tashme we went to a relocation centre called Transconna near Winnipeg, just for a few months, and then we were packed up and moved to Angler, Ontario, in the northern Lake Superior region. It was here that German military prisoners had been interned. Winter was coming, and it was bitterly cold and windy. We were put in the old army barracks formerly occupied by the PoWs. I remember the barbed wire and watchtowers. For a youngster it was a scary place, and we wondered why we were there. What had we done? Some of us wandered through the barracks, looking at all those old pin-up pictures on the walls and the paper scattered all over the floor. We even went through the graveyard where prisoners who had died were buried far from home. We were never given any expenses or money to live on, but we did get our transportation paid to wherever we wanted to go. From Angler we came to Farnham. With the final destination reached we were on our own.

J.H.:   The relocation centre at Farnham, Quebec, was the old army barracks of the military base. We stayed for three or four weeks before moving to Montreal and out of government hands. My father had come to the city six months earlier so he could establish himself and prepare for us. He got a job as a carpenter, and when he had enough to rent an apartment, he called for us at Farnham to join him.

He wasn't bitter or angry about what happened, but he would say: "You have to do this, or that. You have to become somebody so you don't get pushed around by the damned Anglophones and white people. As long as your hair is black, your face yellow and your eyes slanting, you're going to get picked on, no matter what." That's what he told us. He said we should become professionals and not work for someone else for years and when the time came for promotion, we would be passed over. He said to go into business like the Jewish people, and no one could push us around. "Be your own boss," he said, and for that alone I am happy. I am a professional because with the temper I had then, I would have been fired right off the bat. I don't keep my mouth shut too long. If I don't like something, I say so.

H.H.: I don't feel our experiences were as devastating as those who survived the European concentration camps. I believe it was worse for our parents. I never heard mine talk about it, probably because it was too painful. In a few years all those who went through this will be dead, and these memories, this history, will be lost.

If I put myself in their place and had to go through that now, perhaps it would be worse for me. Materially we are so much better off now than we were then. We had a small rented house with the bare necessities, but I suppose there were many who lost more. My parents never grumbled. They always said it was fate. They just kept right on working, and when we arrived at Farnham, my father was ill for a couple of years, and my mother became the breadwinner. She used to work from 3 p.m. to 11 p.m. every day and look after a house and six kids. How she did it is beyond me, and today she is still active, teaching flower arranging. My father is still alive, but he isn't well.

J.H.: Instead of going back to school, we had to go to work right away, but I went to night school. My father gave me no choice. You have to work, he said. There were four of us working to make ends meet. We didn't have a penny in our pockets at the time. Apartments were very hard to find, and you had to pay an owner "key money", $200 just to sign the lease and get the keys for a $65-a-month apartment. My father had to borrow money from a relative in order to pay it. It was plain robbery, but there was lots of this going on.

We lived in the Syrian-and-Italian-immigrant area in the northern part of the city. A lot of the Japanese ended up on Colonial Avenue, De Bullion and Prince Arthur Streets.

After I had been working for eight years in a factory making smoking accessories at thirty-five cents an hour and trying to finish night school, my father said, "You can't stay in a factory all your life. You have to better yourself." So I looked in the "Help Wanted" in the paper. There were all kinds of jobs available, shipping clerks, etc., and I figured because I had gone to night school and was already taking first-year university courses, I might have a good chance getting a job. I would get an interview over the phone, but when they took a look at my eyes and colour, there was no job.

Another area that was shocking for discriminating was housing. When my wife and I first got married, I was interning for a year and she was working at the Montreal General Hospital. I went looking for accommodations in the area. Helen would answer ads advertising vacant apartments, but when she knocked on the door and the landlady saw her, she was told the apartment had been rented. After this happened a number of times, I got suspicious and called back to ask if the apartment had been rented.

"No," was the answer.

"Then how come you said it was, when someone was just there to rent it?"

Do you know what the answer was?

"I have nothing against Chinks and Japs, but the other tenants might object."

That was the most common excuse...not their prejudice, just someone else's. Sorry buster, you're out of luck!

We were shocked. I wasn't a bum. I was a dentist. I had graduated from McGill and I couldn't believe what was going on.

H.H.:   There were and still are a lot of small,

narrow-minded people around, sick people. I had never experienced this before.

J.H.:   And it happened in restaurants as well. You were automatically taken to a table near the kitchen, and a number of times when we made reservations at a restaurant under my name, we got there to find there were no reservations. My name had been crossed off, and the table given to someone else. It happened too many times, and so to avoid embarrassing my kids and having them feel humiliated, I made reservations under the name of Dr. James. I didn't want any hassles. You should have seen the looks on their faces when my name was called and I was asked, "You're Dr. James?"

      "Yes," I answered and I laughed. I know it was a sneaky way of doing it, but we had to. If I was alone, I would have made a scene, but I didn't want to humiliate my family.

H.H.:   Our eldest is now twenty-five, but as a child, he never thought he was different because we protected him from situations. He thinks of himself as pure Canadian, and when we tell him he is Japanese, he doesn't believe us.

J.H.:   And I tell him, "If anyone asks what you are, say you are Canadian." That's how he grew up. But it is amazing how prejudiced people are. It happens everywhere, even in department stores. I once had an incident at Simpson's and cut up my credit card in front of the clerk and told him where to put it. The next day I got a call from the manager, and I told him there were a bunch of bigots in his store.

      For a long time, I had an inferiority complex and it was reinforced by the period I spent in night classes in the years after the war. Most of the students were ex-servicemen studying on free government-education programmes. During recess the conversation centred on their war experiences where the guys had served. The talk was invariably about Nazis and Japs, and I wanted to dig a hole in the ground and lie there. I was waiting for someone to turn on me and say, "You dirty Jap". For many years I carried this stigma of inferiority and just cringed, waiting for the put-down. I used to think about those lousy, sneaky Japs who had bombed Pearl Harbour and caused us so much pain and anguish over here. It took me almost twenty-five years to get this out of my system. It wasn't until I went back to Japan for a month in 1970 on a church-sponsored trip that I met my two brothers and sister for the first time. Before this visit, I had always felt like a second-class citizen even though I tried twice as hard at school, was a successful professional and had a family of bright achievers. I always felt insecure. Always at the back of my mind was the thought that I was a Jap. Maybe it goes back to the way we were treated during World War II. I spent a month over there and was exposed to so much history, a two-thousand-year-old culture, incredible craftsmanship and the quality of work produced. I saw how industrious the people were, and when I landed back in Toronto, I felt ten feet high.

Ever since then, I haven't looked back. I told myself the heritage I come from is more than anything here. All we hear about is French Canada and its heritage. It's nothing compared to the age and quality of mine, and I'm made to feel inferior? So now I walk around with my head up. No one is going to push me around any more. Going back to my roots did it. It gave me pride. You have to do this, and I am encouraging my children to return to their roots. I am proud, no longer ashamed that I am a Japanese Canadian. I have two thousand years of heritage to prove I come from good stock.

I guess I owe a lot to my parents. My

mother was always happy. She worked until she was sixty-seven years old and never complained about the money we didn't have. I know there were many who were bitter and said if it wasn't for the Goddamn war, we'd be this or that, or have this or the other, but my parents never talked about material things that were taken from us during those years. But when I turned forty-one, I said to my wife: "You know, my father was this age when he was taken away overnight to a camp and lost everything he owned." I asked my wife, "What would you do if the RCMP came here now and took everything I've worked my ass off for for twenty years and shipped us all off to a camp?" And before she could answer, I said, "I'm not like my father. I would fight like hell, kill myself or end up in a nuthouse."

When you look at it that way, all I can say is that my parents were better people than I am. I wouldn't take it. I would raise hell, and I would have a hard time hiding the anger and bitterness from my children. But I guess I was luckier than most. I know of many families who are bitter, and when I look at them, I realize they were just average people who might have amounted to something if the war hadn't interrupted their lives.

On the other hand, and you'll hear this from others, the evacuation did do some good. It broke up and scattered the Japanese ghettos in Western Canada across the east. The Japanese now had to integrate and find acceptance in whichever area they were dropped. Before the war, the only place the Japanese frequented was either Little Tokyo in Vancouver, or the fishing and farming areas along the coast in B.C. People could go through an entire generation without speaking a word of English. That's why my parents never learned it. They didn't need it in the ghettos. You could get along because everything was in Japanese. Even the baseball games were played in Japanese.

The War Measures Act destroyed all this, and we had to start all over again. There were some things in B.C. that were so prejudicial they should have been smashed. Did you know that up until 1941, no Canadian of Japanese extraction was allowed to enter university in B.C.? Some of the children of wealthier families came out east and attended University of Toronto to become doctors, dentists or lawyers. Others went to the United States, studied there and came back to B.C. as practising members of the medical and legal professions. Anyone of Oriental extraction had to face this discrimination in B.C., and I know that Jews had the same thing done to them at McGill. I remember when I was going to Sir George Williams College at night, I saw open pieces of literature arranging ski-weekends in the Laurentians, and it was clearly marked: "Christians only—no Jews allowed". I was shocked, but I knew that treatment so well and being Japanese out on the west coast, you think you are the only race prejudice is aimed at. That was only thirty-eight years ago. It's not such a long time.

Now I know that the tremendous number of successful Japanese within the last thirty or thirty-five years or so was the result of our dispersion across the country away from the racism in B.C. That accelerated the assimilation of the Japanese Canadians into Canadian society. If not for that, there would still be a hell of a big Little Tokyo in Vancouver. The dispersion helped us better ourselves, especially the second and third generation, much more quickly than if we had stayed there unmolested. There are reasons for our split-personality behaviour. I've made this statement publicly several times and I will say it again. The biggest problem is that we are hyphenated Canadians. This has been eliminated in the States. You're just plain American, but here you have French-Canadian, English-Canadian, Italian-Canadian, whatever. Ever since former Prime Minister Trudeau said we would be bilingual, English- and French-Canadians, the concept has gone haywire. What kind of crap is this? We're all Canadians. We were born here. I think it is stupid that we see ourselves as hyphenated. The WASP thinks he's the only true Canadian and so does the Quebecois. The rest of us are split in the middle. I don't want to change my roots, but every time I go through Customs or Immigration, returning to the country, I am asked: "How long have you been in Canada?" It is natural to ask us because our colour is different and our first language was Japanese.

Remember when the DPs were coming from Europe after the war? After one year they were accepted as Canadians and as for me, I still get: "When did you come here?" I still have this problem and I don't think I will ever get over it...the colour and the different eyes. At one time I was overly sensitive.

Maybe I still am, but I don't make waves anymore. I just figure a guy doesn't know any better. Anytime someone calls me a Jap and asks how long I've been here, I don't get upset any more. I make a joke out of it.

Other races have the same problem. You have Blacks trying to find acceptance here. I have heard people say that some of their best friends are Blacks or Jews—providing they don't marry their kids. For social things, that's fine, but for anything closer, no way. Colour rules you out.

We're not socialites and we keep to ourselves. Our life centres around our kids, and we don't give a damn if we don't get invited here or there. That never even occurred to us that it might

be prejudice. Maybe people don't like us personally. Over the last twenty years we have lived
here, come to think of it, a number of families have
never once invited us to their homes. Life is too
short to think about those things any more. At one
time I used to resent it, but now I feel that if a
person is prejudiced, he's the loser. Some of the
nicest people we have met have been non-Japa-
nese and non-Christian.

However, prejudice, bigotry and racism
have caused many people to repudiate their ethnic
backgrounds. I asked one of my patients who had
changed his name why he had done it, and he
answered there was no way he was going to get to
the top with that Ukrainian name.

About twelve years ago, I saw an article in
a newspaper about a judge in an Ontario court.
He made a statement that he received many requests every year from Canadians who wanted to
change their names from Greenberg to Green,
Rosenberg to Ross, or Kowalavich and Rozinski to
something more Anglo-Saxon. The judge asked
these people why, and the answer was always the
same. None of them wanted any discrimination
aimed at them or their families. The judge said that
with one stroke of the pen he could eliminate all
the prejudices people practise on each other, but
on the other hand, he felt so sorry for people of
coloured races—yellow, black and red. No matter
how many came to change their names, none
could ever lose their identity because of their
colour.

The sad part was the implicit truth in his
remarks. In our class I remember several Lithuanian, Polish and Ukrainian guys who went to
court for a name change. I found it shocking that
people would give up their family names out of
fear. They all figured they would go farther with
an Anglo-Saxon name. I know a dentist of Ukrain-

ian ethnic background who said most of his patients had singled him out because he spoke their language, but he found it difficult to work with his own ethnic community. I know it has its advantages because you get a ready-made clientele who feel more comfortable being able to communicate with you. But this guy wanted a much more ungraded practice—maybe more WASPs, whatever.

But one thing common to all immigrants and first generation is the need to achieve. The parents work their ass off, and they expect better and greater things of their children. I have a lot of ethnics in my practice, and they are so bloody proud of their kids. They are Czechs, Slovaks, Hungarians and other ethnics, and their whole goal is to make sure their kids don't ever have to work in sweatshop factories. You should hear them talk about their university-graduate children. They are all leaders in whatever they do.

I guess I'm no different, but I also stress that material things aren't the most important. I tell my kids they have to be independent, and they must contribute to society. And if they have to compete to accomplish what they want, they must do their best to get the most satisfaction out of their accomplishments. One of my kids is a dentist and another is in medicine at McGill. A third son is a McGill science student, and my only daughter, who had 95 per cent in high school, has been accepted into medicine at McGill University. She is also an athlete like her brothers. They love school and have a strong sense of achievement. That's the most common factor you find in immigrants and their kids—this sense of achievement.

Maybe it's the result of what they had to go through, whether it was economic hardships, prejudice, racism or genocide. And today we hear that prejudice is manifesting itself again, and whenever there is economic hardship, a group will always be picked on and blamed for the country's woes. But if there is one thing I would like to do, it is to make sure that what was done to us, never happens again to any ethnic group. How it can be accomplished is something I don't know.

Do you know that when the Constitutional arguments for human rights were being debated in Ottawa, a group of Japanese Canadians went out there to present a brief on what a lack of clearly defined rights can inflict on people? After that brief was presented, the panel had tears in their eyes. They all stood up and applauded, and yet they didn't give a damn about the content of the brief. They didn't say that the War Measures Act should never be permitted such wide-sweeping powers again, and they didn't say that people should never be put into internment camps again. They didn't deplore the loss of all our property and material goods. Even with the new Constitution, we still aren't protected. Who is to say it won't happen again? We discovered that after so many years of silence and suffering, screaming your head off doesn't accomplish anything. Our two biggest champions were Barry Broadfoot and Pierre Berton who wrote and spoke openly about the injustice perpetrated against the Japanese Canadians on the black day the War Measures Act was used as a weapon against us.

As Japanese Canadians, we're a minority, but with all the minorities in Canada, surely it is time we developed a mutual respect for one another and stopped the racism and discrimination in this country!

Editor's Note: The following editorial by Kasey Oyama, *Asian Leader* Newspaper's editor, is a 1986-up-to-date summary of the Japanese Canadian community's struggle for justice and redress of property and money confiscated during their internment forty-five years ago.

The issue of providing compensation for Japanese Canadians who suffered heavy losses as a result of their mistreatment remains unresolved as of this date (1986) due to the inability of Japanese Canadians to have the government start negotiations. The current impasse between the federal government and the National Association of Japanese-Canadians, representing most of the 45,000 people of Japanese descent in Canada, in the matter of providing compensation for wartime injustices to Japanese-Canadian victims results from the unwillingness or the inability of Multiculturalism Minister Otto Jelinek to shift from his announced position of imposing a unilateral settlement of not more than ten million dollars to settle the redress question. The amount named by the Japanese Canadians as a basis for negotiations is twenty-five thousand dollars to each of the estimated 10,000 survivors plus fifty million dollars toward a community fund.

It should be stressed that the amounts mentioned are not necessarily the monetary goals that Japanese Canadians have set up for themselves. They believe it is necessary, above all, to establish the fact that the losses sustained were not trivial amounts, that they represent a large part of the community's assets, and in fact, almost all of what the poorer people possessed, apart from their dreams of the future which were also destroyed. This fact, the claimants hope to establish.

The amount claimed as basis for negotiations is based in turn on a study completed in May, 1986 by Price Waterhouse to determine direct losses in income and possessions sustained by Japanese Canadians, expressed in 1986 dollars. Undeterminable losses such as psychological stress, as well as certain other factors, like accumulated interest or punitive considerations, are not included.

The Price Waterhouse study arrives at a total loss figure of $433 million. Japanese Canadians' claims come to a total of about $300 million.

The delay in the talks on compensations is blamed by the

government on the Japanese Canadians representatives for not making concrete proposals. It is believed, however, that while much data is available to back up the claim for losses, the Japanese-Canadian group was waiting for the completion of the Price Waterhouse investigations which would be both impartial and credible.

A splinter group of Japanese Canadians representing a relatively small number, for the most part, of elderly conservative elements calling themselves by various names, have made separate representations to the federal government, leading Mr. Jelinek to believe he was dealing with a number of different groups among Japanese Canadians.

A meeting of Japanese-Canadian representatives with Mr. Jelinek in Ottawa recently resulted in a stand-off with Mr. Jelinek apparently unwilling to shift from his previously announced position of establishing a fund not exceeding ten million dollars for the benefit of all ethnics to fight discrimination. This amount was to be considered token compensation for the Japanese-Canadian losses.

Mr. Jelinek's zeal in trying to safeguard the drain on the government treasury is commendable. However, it is equally important to safeguard a nation's honour as well as to uphold justice.

Mr. Jelinek has advanced several reasons to back up his refusal to negotiate. He says there isn't enough money to compensate for all the wrongs committed. He says the burden of redress would fall on many taxpayers who were unborn when the wrongs were committed. He says the Japanese-Canadian organization headed by Mr. Art Miki is not truly representative of all Japanese Canadians. He says the community would take it as an insult to be offered money as compensation.

We believe Mr. Jelinek is too astute to believe all the arguments he has presented.

A little investigation will clarify the fact that the National Association of Japanese Canadians is the only representative group of those of Japanese descent in Canada. As in any group, there are dissidents, and in the current case, spokesmen claiming to represent some section of Japanese Canadians are either misguided or are merely voicing sour grapes because they, as erstwhile leaders, find themselves outside the mainstream of the redress movement.

The proof of this statement is in the fact that all who claim to represent Japanese Canadians are agreed on all of the basic issues in the redress campaign—that there should be a government apology; that there should be a modification to government's extraordinary powers which would allow similar injustices to happen again, and that there should be monetary compensation to the victims.

The difference is only in the amount of the compensation to be claimed and how this amount is to be distributed. While there may be differences of opinion as to the amount of the compensation to be sought, for anyone to suggest to the government that Japanese Canadians would consider it an insult to be offered money is sacrificing his credibility.

To imply, as Mr. Jelinek does, that past debts should not be visited on taxpayers who did not incur them requires little comment. This would be a most extraordinary world were that to be the case, even in the matter of national debts piled up for future generations to be responsible for. For those interested, the point was discussed on February 15, 1986, in a speech by former justice of the British Columbia Supreme Court, Mr. Thomas Berger, who stated:

"Nothing in our history demonstrates so well the necessity to constantly be aware of our attitude toward racial minorities, and the wisdom of entrenching in the Constitution our belief that racial measures are wrong, and of providing legal safeguards that will protect racial minorities against such measures. And nothing illustrates so well the necessity of providing redress—not only for the Japanese Canadians, but also for the good—and the good name—of the nation itself.

"Redress means compensation. Of course, there must be an acknowledgment by Parliament of past wrongs. But there must be compensation, too. An acknowledgment without compensation does not redress. If compensation for the survivors of internment during the Second World War will not help, then high-sounding language will not either.

"The Minister, the Honourable Otto Jelinek, has rejected the idea of compensation for survivors. But to talk of wrongs beyond monetary calculation is misleading. It is true we cannot give back the lost years. We cannot restore lost property. But compensation is possible: that's how we make good the losses suffered in personal injury cases including the loss of loved ones; we do it also in cases of wrongful imprisonment. Why imply that it is beneath the dignity of Japanese Canadians for them to seek compensation? Does this mean that the greater the loss, the graver the assault on the people's freedom, the more inappropriate it is to compensate them?

"There is nothing to prevent the Government of Canada from sitting down and negotiating compensation with the Japanese Canadians. This is not just something that should be done because the Americans may decide to do it. This is a Canadian responsibility. The Minister, however, has acted in such a way as to convert what could and should be an act of atonement into just another tawdry item in Ottawa's partisan ritual.

"The issue ought to be non-partisan. In May 1984, Mr. Brian Mulroney, at that time Leader of the Opposition, speaking of the Japanese Canadians said:

'I feel very strongly that Canadian citizens whose rights were abused and violated and trampled upon should be compensated.'"

"Not only Mr. Mulroney, but also Mr. Turner and Mr. Broadbent have made statements supporting the principle of compensation for the Japanese Canadians. Let them work out a resolution and present it to Parliament, committing the Government of Canada to negotiations."

On the matter of redress, the ball is now in the court of Prime Minister Brian Mulroney.   (June, 1986)

On September 22, 1988, more than 46 years after their uprooting and relocation during the Second World War, Japanese Canadians received a formal apology and a $300-million settlement from the Canadian government. On Parliament Hill at the official signing ceremony, Art Miki, president of the National Association of Japanese Canadians called the redress a landmark for his people and for human rights.

AN ISOLATED LITTLE UNIT

by
Nick Auf der Maur*

Growing up Swiss in downtown Montreal entailed some confusion. Well, perhaps not confusion, but certainly a slight feeling that we didn't quite fit. We weren't like the English and French, and we weren't like the other immigrant groups either, the Irish, the Poles, the Ukrainians, the Italians, the Jews, the Blacks and all the other myriads of people who make up Montreal.

The difference was that there was always plenty of the others to form ethnic associations, to have their own churches, annual national days or holiday fetes and dances where they could wear their funny outfits—all those things that immigrant groups cling to, in order to maintain their sense of identity. No, I had the feeling our Swiss family was an isolated little unit, a little island in a sea of lots of 'others'...a bit like Switzerland itself.

I was born on Shuter Street, now called Aylmer Street, where my family had a basement janitor's apartment. But we moved from there shortly after I was born, and my first memories are from Colonial Street, just east of St. Lawrence Boulevard in the heart of immigrant Montreal.

The only other Swiss I remember during that period was the Baumgartner family on Jeanne Mance Street. There were a few Swiss fellows, associates of my father in his weird business schemes, who used to drop by the house or who, in later years, I used to meet while they sat around Toe Blake's or in the Royal Tavern on Guy Street with my father discussing more business schemes.

Ours was a staunch Catholic family, and that also led to some confusion in my mind. Because of our education, I always thought, while growing up, the great division in the world was between Catholics and Protestants. The English-French Division

* Reproduced with permission of the author from newspaper columns (1981-85), courtesy of *The Gazette*, Montreal.

didn't occur to me until much later in my life.

In the 1930s, when the time came for my eldest sister to start school, my mother did the natural thing and marched her off to the closest Catholic school. But there the nuns wouldn't take her, because my mother spoke French with an accent and we had a funny immigrant name. So my sister was directed to an English Catholic school. The fact that my mother's French was much better than her English didn't matter.

So I grew up thinking the world was divided up between Catholics, most of whom spoke French, and Protestants, most of whom spoke English. How we came to be speaking English was always a bit of a mystery to me. In addition, there were lots of Jews in our neighbourhood. Where they fitted into the "Great Divide" was another minor mystery, but because they went to Protestant school, I tended to think they were something like Methodists or Baptists or whatever flavours the English Protestants came in.

This is not to suggest that these matters of confusion led to any major identity crisis. On the contrary, they helped solidify my sense of identity as a Montrealer, a Quebecer and a Canadian as I grew up. At various points in my life, I was able to feel a strong kinship to French Canadians, because of religion and other cultural affinities; to English Canadians because of language; to immigrants because that's what we were, albeit from a small group. And, of course, that sense of not fitting has long since dissipated. However, my sense of being Swiss is as strong as it ever was, and it was my mother and others like her who passed on that sense of identity, that set of values.

She isn't Jewish, but my mother has the classic traits of what is commonly called a "Jewish mother". Here I am over forty, and she still calls to wake me up to make sure I get to work on time. "You may lose your job if you don't show you appreciate it," she says. She still shows up at my door and insists on puttering around my house, complaining that the plants aren't properly watered, the refrigerator is either too full or too empty, and, "Here is some cheese and sausage that was on sale at the store. Eat it, it's good for you."

Fifteen or more years she's been telling me that. She's close to eight-four and still tireless and no doubt will be telling me the same things fifteen years from now. And despite my complaints about interference and nagging, I'll always appreciate my mother's concern and love.

Her name is Thérèse, and she came here in 1928 with my father just in time to catch the crash of Wall Street and the terrible effect of the Depression. She brought with her a fervent Swiss patriotism and a passion for everything that is poor, peasant and Catholic (an ecumenist, she'll embrace a cause on behalf of anything that has two out of those three).

Back in 1968, our whole family decided to go back to visit Switzerland together. My mother arrived at the airport with her own bags, plus a collection of other baggage. When my own bag only registered eleven kilograms on the check-in scale, she rummaged around and gave me a cardboard box, a bunch of aluminium pots tied together and a lawn chair. These items brought my luggage up to the weight limit.

Why we had to take all that stuff to Switzerland was beyond me, but my mother was adamant that we weren't going to waste any cargo space.

So my two sisters, my father and mother and I flew off to Switzerland loaded down like war refugees fleeing with our meagre possessions.

A few years later, I was flying to Italy on my honeymoon. Before we left for the airport, my mother showed up with a big suitcase filled with old clothes. The suitcase was labelled: "For the poor of Rome, care of the Pope."

"Ma, I don't want to drag around a huge old suitcase," I told my mother. "We're travelling light because we don't want to be weighed down. Besides, we're not going to Rome."

"Well," she instructed, "just take the suitcase to the Milan train station. Leave it sitting somewhere in public and when somebody steals it, it will probably be because they're poor. So it will be delivered."

Once I embarked on a tour of the Soviet Union. My mother loaded me down with individually packed plastic shopping bags, stuffed into my luggage. Each contained items like old jeans, shirts, socks and underwear that she had acquired at rummage sales. She gave me about twenty of these bags and told me to give them to deserving people.

"Leave some of them in church pews, or even a synagogue," she said. "I want some believers to get a little present."

So in Kiev and Leningrad and Moscow, I went on these little side trips, dropping off plastic bags on buses, in churches and just giving them to old ladies selling flowers on the street. It was as though we were operating our own foreign-aid programme.

My mother is a very practical person who believes in practising her Roman Catholic virtue of charity.

I remember her calling me up to tell me of a telegram she had sent to British Prime Minister Margaret Thatcher, concerning Bobby Sands and "the plight of the Irish Catholics". She has been upset about the Irish question ever since the Catholic civil rights movement started up over twenty years ago. She used to send her heroine Bernadette Devlin five dollars a month to help with the cause.

One morning she phoned and, as usual, started chatting about the news.

"Hey, Ma," I asked, perhaps a trifle uncharitably, "did you see where Bernadette Devlin had an illegitimate child?"

"Yes," she replied with a glow of pride. "Isn't she marvelous? She's almost a saint."

"But," I countered, "it was an illegitimate baby."

"Yes," she said. "She's so good. A young Catholic girl who refused to have an abortion."

She upped her stipend to ten dollars a month.

A couple of years ago, she was back in her home town of Sachseln in the Canton of Unterwalden, which, together with Uri and Schwyz were the three cantons to form the Swiss Confederation in 1292. She was there on her fifteenth or so annual visit to see her sister Ida and the rest of the family.

"I may not be here much longer," my mother always says.

During the visit, she was praying in the church that contains the tomb of St. Nicholas von Flue, Switzerland's patron saint and mine. Nicholas (not to be confused with the Eastern Santa Claus St. Nick) had been a soldier-statesman before becoming a hermit-saint in the fifteenth century. My mother had often told me the rambling story of how St. Nicholas managed to avert a civil war between the peasants and city cantons following a successful war against the Burgundian king, Charles the Bold.

As she was praying there, it suddenly occurred to her that St. Nicholas was the perfect one to intervene and bring peace to

Ireland. She caught a flight to Belfast and then called some Protestant pastor, whom she had once seen on TV and who seemed reasonable. She told him she was an emissary from St. Nicholas or some such thing.

The pastor came around and had tea. He arranged for her to meet the Protestant Bishop. She then arranged for all of them to have tea with the Roman Catholic Cardinal. At this meeting, my mother unveiled her peace plan, which I vaguely understand had something to do with an ecumenical plea to St. Nicholas.

The pastor's son was acting as a chauffeur and on the way back to the hotel, he made some anti-Pope remark. There was an altercation, and she hit him on the head with her handbag. In the end my mother distributed all her St. Nicholas literature in Catholic parishes.

But that didn't stop her.

For a month and a half after she heard that Pope John was planning a visit to Switzerland and Sachseln in June 1981, my mother tried to get me to write something about it.

"The whole federal council [Swiss Cabinet], composed of five Protestants and two Catholics, has asked to meet with the Pope," she explained. "It's the 500th anniversary of the Treaty of Stans in 1481, which prevented the civil war.

"There's a road in Switzerland built by Polish refugees in 1948 to mark the canonization that year of St. Nicholas. Everything fits together."

Ummm....

My father, on the other hand, has a style where an invitation sounds a bit like an order. Some time ago over the phone, he said: "We have to go the army today. The president of the Schweizer Kaese Institut is going to be there."

By "the army", he meant the officers' mess of the 3rd Field Engineers' Regiment at the Hillside armory in Westmount. Now when a Swiss is told "the president of the Kaese Institut" (the Swiss Cheese Association) is going to be on hand, it's an order. In Switzerland the president of the Institute is a big cheese, indeed.

So I hustled over to the officers' mess, where the president turned out to be Urs Marty, an old card-playing buddy of my father's and a longtime city resident. The way my father had put it

I had expected to meet the head of the whole "ball of wax" from Switzerland.

Urs, a nice friendly fellow, had just become the local representative for the Swiss Cheese Association, naturally to promote the sale of cheese from Switzerland. But there is a quota on Swiss cheese imports to Canada of 90 metric tonnes annually. The quota is always filled and the cheese all sold. So there really wasn't much Urs could do for sales. But that's a digression. The point was the army and our regular luncheons at the mess. Urs was there to tell us of the connection between the army and Swiss cheese.

Take those typical little Swiss cheese rounds, the ones that are divided into triangles and packaged in aluminium foil that you can never get all off, so there is always a small piece of foil that gets stuck in a loose dental filling. The package was developed for the Swiss Army in the First World War, so the boys up on border patrol in the mountains could have a handy snack.

At any rate, my father Severn, my brother Frank and I are on-and-off regular attenders of mess luncheons at the 3rd Field Engineering Regiment. And when I mention it to people, they are always somewhat perplexed.

"But the Swiss are so peaceful," they say. "They're not militaristic."

Ha! The Swiss have a concept of "armed neutrality" which means they are armed to the teeth, so their neighbours respect Swiss independence and don't fool around. The Israeli Army was modelled after the Swiss concept of a citizens' army.

Anyhow, we Auf der Maurs all have distinguished military records. In high school, I was a member of the Grenadier Guards cadet corps, (it was compulsory) and I spent several summers at Camp Farnham. Then I became a Sapper (private) in the 3rd Field Reserve and rose through the ranks to become Lance-Corporal. My brother graduated from Royal Military College and went on to become Captain and Adjutant (third in command) of the 3rd Field. So you see how I got roped into that.

But my father is the real war hero. He did his service in the Swiss Army during the First World War and was doing border guard duty just near the lines separating French and German forces.

One day while he was marching up and down in the woods

with his comrade, defending Swiss sovereignty, he looked up and saw what appeared to be an entire French regiment attacking. Being Swiss and pragmatic, my father and the other soldier ran like hell. But the French were too fast, and they soon overtook my father...and then passed him.

It was only then that my father realized the French soldiers were fed up with the war and were deserting to a safe neutral haven. So my father raised his rifle and ordered: "Halt! Thrown down your weapons and put up your hands."

And so, my father and his colleague marched the whole bunch, about a hundred and fifty, he recalled, into town where he received a hero's welcome. And every now and then, we retire to the officers' mess in Westmount and tell old soldiers' stories and reminisce about our respective military careers.

Like almost all immigrants, Joseph Severn Auf der Maur came to Canada because of a dream—mining, and the lure of the Canadian wild. Armed with his civil engineering degree and his self-taught knowledge of geology, he, and my mother, came to Montreal from Switzerland in 1928.

"The Alps," he used to tell me, "they're beautiful. But they're all granite, no minerals. Canada was the place to be, a place for the future where we wanted to have our family."

He landed his first job with the City of Montreal as a surveyor, and later engineer. He worked on such projects as the reservoir at Dr. Penfield and Pine Avenues, the Cartierville Bridge and Highway 11 leading to the Laurentians. But the Depression hit a year after they got here, and by 1931 the city laid off foreigners first.

"Swiss timing wasn't my strength," he often joked.

As it turned out, that was the last job he ever held as an employee. As the Depression ravaged the country, my father saw it as an opportunity to develop his passion for geology and prospecting. He prospected in parts of Ontario and Quebec, mostly in the Saguenay region, especially in Charlevoix county.

In the thirties, he managed to develop some mineral claims near Sault Ste. Marie, extracting high-grade copper concentrate and selling it to Noranda, as many small-time prospectors did then. The little money he made from that he ploughed into developing some claims in Charlevoix, where he had discovered a complex platinum

111

and rare metal ores.

When I was a kid, I used to visit the mining camp, spending many summers and a few winters there. It looked like a mining camp as seen in western films, remarkably like the photographs of gold-rush miners. There were rough-hewn log cabins, men dressed in those old-fashioned breeches, rifles in hand, wearing floppy hats and suspenders.

He built roads and bridges through the bush, a small smelter, a charcoal plant, a hydro-electric plant, and sold lumber to meet his payroll.

I grew up with Saguenay Mining and Smelting Company, Quebec North Mines, Marlowe Mines and all my father's dreams of developing the bush, as he called it. Our home and his office were always strewn with rocks and ore samples.

There were perhaps thousands of prospectors in Canada then, very few of whom ever got rich, but all of whom helped build this country and this province. My father would sometimes come home and show us pictures of a lake. "That's Lake Thaïs," he'd say. "I named it after your sister." All of us in the family had lakes and streams in the Saguenay area first charted by my father named after us. They're still on the maps.

Very often I felt my father was more romantic than practical. "Any day now," was his favourite expression. His platinum mining dreams were never quite fulfilled, but he loved his life as a prospector, seeing himself as a combination of explorer and entrepreneur. That kind of risk-taking and dreaming often meant financial hardship for the family.

As a kid I used to listen to him and his friend Frank J. Gagné talk of the company they formed to build a subway in Montreal, of plans to construct heliports and other great schemes. He had a remarkable collection of friends—Damon Runyon characters— from horse players to cooks to lawyers to mechanics to mining promoters. I could never figure out what some of the others did for a living.

We'd sit around Toe Blake's Tavern, and my father would pull out a note from Albert Einstein, who taught him physics at Zurich Polytechnic, and with whom he maintained a postcard-small note correspondence. Or he'd tell of playing cards at the Syrian Club on Jean Talon Street, where he had played cards with

Alexander Kerensky, the man the Bolsheviks overthrew.

He came to live with me and look after my two cats in 1983 when he was over eighty-four years old. Aside from mining, my father's other passion was animals. On Sundays, my brother Frank would come over with the two family dogs. They'd run up to my father's bedroom, jump on his bed and happily wake him up. But that first Sunday in July, 1984, he didn't wake up.

We held a service for him at Mary Queen of the World Cathedral. For some reason, he always preferred French churches. And around noon we gathered at the Alpenhaus Restaurant where he had spent many happy evenings playing cards with his friends.

And with some of my columns in the Gazette and this reminiscence, we'll always remember a proud Swiss who chose Canada and did his best to help build it.

* * * *

Every summer, Europe and Africa and just about everywhere, I suppose, are awash with North Americans out to discover their roots. In little town halls in Normandy, there is a steady stream of French Canadians looking up old birth and parish records, trying to trace ancestors who were among the first immigrants to arrive in Canada. For some it's a compelling search; for others merely curiosity, but for whatever reason, most of us at one time or another go back to discover our roots.

Last summer, I decided it was time to show my daughter from whence we came. So we, along with my mother and joined by my two sisters, went to visit relatives and the towns my parents left in the 1920s.

My father came from Schwyz, a little town off the big lake that Lucerne sits on. That town, which is the capital of the canton by the same name, gave Switzerland its name—Schweiz in Swiss German. The Swiss flag comes from the canton's white-cross emblem.

As do many Europeans, both my mother's and father's family keep family trees—my mother's goes back several hundred years, while the Auf der Maur's goes back to the year 958 or thereabouts. Schwyz was a walled town, and the first Auf der Maur

113

(which means "on the wall") ran a tavern in the town wall. (Whenever I go into a bar and have a drink, I can validly claim to be maintaining 1,000 years of family tradition.)

Today, Schwyz is a quiet little place that express trains zip through and, among other industries, boasts the Victorinox factory that makes Swiss Army knives.

My mother's home town Sachseln, whose chief claim to fame is that Switzerland's patron saint St. Nicholas von Flue is buried there, also is the home of Birkemuesli, the original Swiss crunchy granola factory.

Most early Swiss history occurred in that area of central Switzerland. It is the locale of William Tell and Heidi and the various battles where the Swiss were beating off the Austrians or Burgundians or Napoleon. When they were at peace, they sent off mercenary troops to fight for just about every crowned head of Europe.

So, when we arrived at Zurich airport, we headed off to Sachseln, a story-book Swiss village, nestled in a lake valley surrounded by beautiful mountains. My mother's family were farmers—peasants, in the vernacular, and they made cheese.

In the summer, they take the cows up to the high mountain valleys while the lower pastures are used to produce hay for winter feeding. They've been doing this for over 1,000 years, but lately some farmers have increased the use of commercial grain feed. As a result of the cows' change of diet, the holes in some Swiss cheeses are coming out smaller, and the Swiss cheese industry is alarmed. Research teams are looking into how to keep the holes big.

Anyway, one of my cousins operates a small herd in the old manner, and we trudged up to his mountain valley cabin just a couple of hundred feet below the peaks. After an exhausting climb up steep, twisting cow trails, we discovered that my cousin's son and all the other young farmers go up on trail motorbikes.

We spent a day and night there, making cheese and butter, taking in the scenery and breathing mountain air. We also made the obligatory visits to cemeteries in our two home towns, paying our respects to the relatives who had passed away since our last visits.

All in all, it was a tranquil, unhurried visit. There's something soothing and reassuring about visiting the earth and houses of one's ancestors, trying to visualize them and imagining what they had thought. I found myself wondering what would have happened if my parents had elected to stay there and I had been born there.

The peculiar thing is that I get a sense of wholeness from it, but at the same time realize how different I, as a Canadian, am from them. The genes are the same, but the different environment and mentality have moulded a Montreal city boy rather than a peasant or small-town Swiss.

I'm happy it turned out the way it did. But my attachment to the land of my parents makes me feel I can enjoy the best of both worlds.

BABA*

by
Ray Serwylo

There she sat, a sagging heap of chest and arms. With the smallest movement, protruding blue veins squirmed silently in the elephant legs and work-worn hands. On her belly, her great maternal breasts, like bottom-filled sacks, finally found a resting place. The dead mass of hair, recently posed by her daughter-in-law, lay on her head. Baba often had her hair set by Karen, always for events she had been only incidentally invited to. But this day was to be unlike any of those others. Today, the family was gathering because of her.

"Seventy years—to the day!—she's been here," Karen frowned, wrapping and unwrapping the telephone cord about her fingers. "She still can't speak more than twenty words to me."

Baba had landed in Swan River, and that, or rather the corridor which stretched from the farm to Winnipeg, was Canada to her. A four-hour drive—and Baba never really understood how a country could be much larger. From her home town in Ukraine, such a lengthy drive in any direction would have meant passports and armed guards. Though hazed by years and miles, a vision of her father after he had tried to sneak across the western border convulsed Baba in her seat.

Baba had now lived in the city for the last ten years. "Ivan asks her at least once a week to move in with us—God, how we fight about that!" Karen's lips were drawn tight. She stared at the back of the old lady's head, watching it bob forward. "I'll give her credit for that, though. She's never accepted. I told her: 'Baba, you're doing the right thing. You've got a nice home of your own.'"

Baba lived in the North End, close to the parish church. Those were her two patches of Ukraine. The house smelled of her home village, the walls continually giving back the odors they stole

* First published in *Student/Etudiant* and *Pierian Spring*.

117

from countless numbers of *pyrohy*.* And St. Sofia, the second Ukrainian church founded in the city, was a pioneer that was soon to be either renovated or destroyed, depending on who told the story. Along with five or six other matriarchs who had no place to go, Baba spent all her mornings in the empty nave. It was their morning ritual; they didn't have to waste their time sending children off to school or brushing their own toothless gums. Baba smiled when she opened her eyes. She saw her son's wedding picture sitting on the television in front of her. He had been married in St. Sofia's.

But, between church and home, Baba had to travel through foreign land. Down MacGregor Street, east on Selkirk Avenue, and two blocks north on Main. On the way back she would make stops for her bread, milk and fruit.

"No, she still has a bit of a garden in the backyard—you know, carrots and onions, tomatoes. She rarely has to buy vegetables. She even brings us some...The chickens?!" Karen laughed. "God, no! She had to get rid of them a long time ago. Mrs. Weimar reported her...you know, the one who lives across the lane. Yes, she did...can't really blame her...that's right, the Department of Health. Poor guy...Ivan had to go down and help him explain it to her. She never understands what's going on."

Baba now got her eggs from a Mennonite farmer. Every Tuesday he would park his truck in front of Mrs. Weimar's place, and it would stay there the entire morning.

During the shopping strolls, Baba used to rest at the Prince George Hotel, but no longer. She used to love her two drafts quickly washing down her parched throat with one toss, even before she took off her babushka. Dragged down so suddenly, the head of the liquid would lie ravished on the insides of the entire glass. The second beer lasted longer, and the white velvety head gradually melted into the cool golden ale. Baba never bought more than two beers—sixty cents was her limit. Yet it was no longer worth it. Three years ago, a shirtless drunk was flung into her table, and knocked unconscious.

"Listen to this," Karen laughed, switching the phone to her other ear. "Baba said...she said she never went back because...just listen...because the bartender wouldn't replace the two beers that

* dumplings

got spilled! Can you believe that?"

The extra sixty cents Baba saved now went to the Church. Every Monday night, she and Mrs. Svarich played Bingo—a quarter a card and the extra dime to phone Karen when it was all over.

Baba stretched her hands to the edge of the arm rests. She thought how stupid that was—phoning was a waste of time and money! If it wasn't for Mrs. Svarich's bad legs, Baba would certainly have walked home.

"Look, Josie, every single Monday night I'd come there at eleven o'clock, and sit and wait in the damn car—just sit and wait until she finally decided to waddle out of that bingo hall. That Special-Any-Two-Across-Twenty-Dollar-Jackpot or whatever you call it was the last straw. I'm not her chauffeur! I just couldn't wait any longer."

Baba had wanted to walk home, but Mrs. Svarich insisted that she phone. She even offered to pay for the call from her winnings that night. Baba laughed to herself, remembering how Svarich always farted whenever she yelled out 'Bingo!' It was one of the hazards of her winning. Ivan finally picked them up.

The vertical hold had slipped ten minutes ago, yet Baba still stared at the floating image continually rising anew on the television screen. Against her wrinkled cheek she now pressed a darkly spotted wad of tissue. The sore bled where she had picked it. Her son had not been unlucky, she thought. There were pretty Ukrainian girls back on the farm, but not one would have been a better wife for Ivan. But better daughters-in-law? Without Ivan, Baba had no one to talk to. Karen didn't understand her, and if she had had the language, she didn't have the patience. She felt it was enough to do Baba's hair.

"Let me tell you, Josie, it's no picnic. I just hate touching those crusty strands of hair."

"*Nu, neechoho,*" sighed Baba. And she was right—it didn't matter. As long as her Ivan was happy. Her life no longer mattered. Baba tried to find a dry spot on the Kleenex, to blot her streaked cheek. She was getting tired of waiting for her son. He should have been home from work by now. The party for Baba was his idea. Baba began to doze off, letting her hand fall from her face. Her chin sank slowly onto her chest. She dreamt of the rusted freight boat, bringing her and her lover across to the new country. Pain grimaced her face, and she jerked it up. A drop slid from her jaw onto her sequined collar. Still not here, she murmured. Baba's head now rolled to the side, and wedged itself into the corner of the chair. Her useless veins seemed still and dark, snow blue. The old hands and feet had stopped aching, anaesthetized by cold.

"Okay, I've got to go, Josie." Karen jumped up and smoothed down her slacks. "Maybe she wants something. I'll call you tomorrow...Sure, I'll tell her...but you could do it yourself next weekend...She's not going anywhere. And she's still as strong as a horse...you'll see...she'll outlive us all."

Karen began clattering the dishes onto the supper table. In the living room all was quiet. Images no longer flitted up and down the television screen, but remained fixed. The porch door at the back slapped shut, and Karen went to meet her husband. The old lady's head hung to one side, and the waxen hair, so recently set by Karen, stared like a clump of icy lead.

ENTRY REFUSED

by
Milly Charon
from an interview with Zaven Degirmen

Zaven Degirmen was sixteen-and-a-half years old, when he arrived with his widowed mother and older brother in Montreal, Quebec, as tourists on September 2, 1970. The child of an Armenian family, he was born in Turkey, a country where political unrest is a common condition.

Zaven and his family had fled not only from a harsh military regime, but also from compulsory military service and Turkey's abysmal treatment of its minorities. His grandparents had survived the Armenian Holocaust in 1915, when more than three-and-a-half million men, women and children had been brutally massacred by the Turks.

The teenager had seen many cases of savagery during his early years in Istanbul, his birthplace, but he was totally unprepared for what he encountered on his arrival in Montreal. Unaware that he had come at a politically crucial period during the October Crisis of 1970, Zaven was shocked to see police haul people out of a house, and a few weeks later witnessed a frightening scene after martial law had been declared in Quebec. He saw army vehicles and armed soldiers everywhere, and on Dorchester Boulevard watched some people lying on the sidewalk while soldiers pointed guns at them. A short distance away, a civilian was being beaten up by soldiers.

These events left Zaven in a state of terror. News of Quebec's Front de Libération (FLQ) crisis had not filtered to Turkey, and he did not understand what was happening. He knew only that he and his family had fled from this type of situation in Turkey to a land of peace and order, and suddenly they were face to face with terror again. In Turkey it had been expected, but not in Canada. Unable to speak English or French, the Degirmens, like many other tourists seeking immigrant status, could not comprehend why the province had turned into an armed camp, why people were fighting one another, and why Zaven was stopped before entering an elevator on his way to the Immigration offices, and a security guard searched him and rifled through the contents of his briefcase.

It was many years before Zaven was able to come to grips with the traumas of his early years in his own country, and those he survived in his country of adoption—Canada.

* * * *

Zaven Degirmen had been born in May, 1953 at a critical time in Turkey's political history. In 1950, the Democratic Party, founded four years earlier, had won 396 seats out of 487 in the national elections. Under Prime Minister Adnan Menderes, the Democrats had pledged to promote the economy with minimal state interference, and the next three years saw a noticeable economic growth due to exceptional harvests. However, when the wheat crop successively failed for the two following years, Turkey was forced to import much-needed grain. Because of a shortage of foreign exchange, industry was handicapped in its purchase of necessary materials and parts. Although the Democratic Party won the elections in 1954, inflation rose, and when government policy was criticized by the Opposition and the public, the government retaliated with repression, especially against other political parties—The Republican People's Party and the National Party.*

Newspaper presses in Ankara were confiscated; laws passed in 1954 imposed heavy fines on journalists who dared to criticize the law of the State; further laws in 1956 restricted the liberty of civil servants, including university professors and teachers, and members within the party itself, who dared to criticize the severity of the regime, were expelled. Public meetings were limited and monitored. The Opposition's verbal attacks became more vociferous, as it accused the Democratic Party of unconstitutional behaviour, and there was fear of open revolt.

By 1959, evidence of a conspiracy to topple the government was uncovered. The economy had worsened, and housing and employment problems had almost destroyed the country's faith in democracy. In April, 1960, the government ordered the army to

124

investigate the Republican People's Party, an act which sparked student protests.*

Martial law was declared on May 3, 1960. Political reforms were demanded of the government, and were refused. On May 7, a coup deposed the Democratic Party, and its leaders were imprisoned. After the formation of a National Unity Committee of thirty-eight members to prepare a new constitution, a series of purges took place. Dismissals and forced retirements were only the beginning. Many former members of The Democratic Party were brought to trial, and 464 out of 601 were found guilty of corruption and high treason. Menderes and two other ministers were executed, and twelve others had death sentences commuted to life imprisonment.*

The next five years were periods of instability, as the uncertain situation spawned two army coups in 1962 and 1963, both of which were foiled. For the next twenty years, the suffering economy and suspended social development of Turkey were to present untold hardships to most of its low and middle-income earners. As a result, emigration became the only solution for residents to escape impossible living conditions.*

* * * *

At a very early age, Zaven knew the difference between a good and bad social climate.

"Every minority group feels isolated at the best of times, but when there is a revolution there is more fear. And these years were not only producing a political revolution, but a social revolution as well," he reflected.

After a year at a regular public school had failed to control his mischievous and rambunctious nature, Zaven had been placed in a private boarding-school, where discipline was rigid. He was attracted to engineering and showed an aptitude for drawing blueprints. When the Turkish Government passed a law in 1967 which nities and freedom their families enjoyed in the New World.

"So we decided to go, even though we had been warned we would be turned back by Canadian Immigration if we said we had the intention of staying in Canada. We came as tourists, and not much later, the law was changed forbidding application for landed immigrant status from within the country.

"We left at a time when there was labour unrest in Turkey, and military jeeps, trucks and tanks were everywhere. To leave Istanbul, we had to cross over a huge drawbridge that was heavily guarded. The spans had been raised to allow a ship to pass and every moment we waited, we became more nervous. What if someone was watching us? What if someone had informed on us that we were leaving to avoid military service and were taking money out of the country? We would have been in very serious trouble had we been caught. Until we boarded the KLM flight in Istanbul and left Turkish airspace, we were shaking in fear."

It was a rainy day when the three people arrived at Dorval Airport in Montreal. Zaven had expected to find himself in a space-age country and discovered that the airport was much smaller than the one he had left from. He searched in the crowd, after passing through Immigration, for his friends' relatives who had promised to meet them and help them settle in.

"My brother spoke a little French, and I asked him to go up to the other level and make an announcement that we had arrived, so that we could be picked more easily out of the crowd. As he left, I heard someone behind me say in Turkish, 'Look, there's a Tarzan.' In Turkish, this expression means a person who doesn't know anything...someone who eats hay. I turned and there were our friends' relatives, whose remark I had overheard. I kept my mouth shut and didn't comment on the slur."

The Degirmen family were taken to a basement apartment on Birnam Street in Park Extension. Zaven was shocked to see that the streets and buildings all looked the same. In Turkey every house had been different. That first night he noticed that he could hear people snoring and doing other things next door. The walls were paper-thin.

"Next day was miserably rainy, and my brother and I went out to buy some cigarettes. We got lost. We hadn't noted the number of the house, and they all looked the same in the rain. By the time we retraced our footsteps, we were very disappointed at what we had seen. We didn't come expecting to find money in the street, but what we did expect were different people and different mentalities, different houses and cars like those we had seen in movies. We had been told that Montreal streets were clean, and we discovered that Park Extension was a dirty, stinking place—and still is."

Like many illegal immigrants, the two teenagers worked without labour permits for two years to keep from starving. Once they received their work cards, Zaven toiled for nineteen dollars a week at an optical company that ground lenses. His brother earned sixteen dollars a week at a car-wash. Zaven's impression was that the Armenian community did little to help its members. He and his family were totally isolated. They could not even see the street from the basement windows of their tiny, damp flat. They had no friends, and no money saved, because the five thousand dollars they had brought with them evaporated on food, on the purchase of winter clothes and on beds and bedding. They had no way of knowing that there were places where they could get help. They went to church, hoping help would come from God, or from some kind members of the congregation. They were ignored. The one person they were in touch with was their lawyer, an older man, who had been recommended to them.

"It was a bad period. We would get letters from home and cry because we missed everything and everybody. The letters were our only links with the past. Although we met some people in the Armenian community, one thing kept us from getting involved with them...money. We had none. Young people go to movies, to restaurants, taverns—something impossible for us. We couldn't afford it. The few people who showed any sympathy did so out of pity. If there were a few overtures of friendship, we drew back, because we were afraid people would talk about us and our status. In addition, my mother had this old-fashioned idea that if she visited any married ladyfriends, people might think she was chasing their husbands. I guess she didn't know any better. She had married at fourteen, had had tuberculosis, recovered, gave birth to my brother at twenty, survived a World War and a civil war, and by thirty-four was a widow. She had traumas, and they had their effect on us. She hung on to us more tightly and passed some of her and our lawyer who discussed the case, didn't understand why we were refused, either. We were so ignorant of procedures. We would sign anything without knowing what we were getting into. When the officials laughed, they could have been laughing at us for our foolishness, or out of good or bad humour. All I knew then was to say 'Merci', nothing more, and leave the room. No one explained anything, and to this day, I'm not quite sure why we were turned down so many times. I thought perhaps the FLQ crisis may have made everyone paranoid, and perhaps we were thought to be spies. Maybe it was because we hadn't served our military service in Turkey. And it seemed that the authorities didn't like our reporting to the Immigration offices accompanied by a lawyer. We had to. We didn't know the language or the law, and even if immigrants buy a Civil or Criminal Code law book, they still can't interpret what is written in it and how many ways it can be interpreted. Only a lawyer can figure it out. We didn't even know what our lawyer was arguing about with the officials, yet the lawyer said that either my brother learned the language in three months and defended his case, or he would have to leave the country. I didn't get the same ultimatum because I was only seventeen. But that poor brother of mine went to classes and sat in front of a TV screen with earphones on his head so as not to disturb us late into the night, and all he did was study non-stop.

"When we tried to get an extension to stay, either the lawyer forgot, or neglected to attend to the matter, and it cost us five hundred dollars. We had to pay his fees, and it was frustrating going back and forth not knowing what our fate would be. Finally we made out our papers on our own, because we figured that at the rates our lawyer was charging, it would cost us thousands of dollars and years of pestering him to get things moving. At least he was there when we needed him at the Immigration offices, but his assistance was very expensive, something we couldn't afford. It was then I realized that lawyers are not always necessary. What an immigrant needs is a good interpreter, if he doesn't know the language, to know what is going on because Immigration officals often treat people like idiots. They are insulting, just by the way they look at you, as if you are a piece of dirt under the rug. And even if the officer is unsure of regulations and runs back and forth to his superior to ask what kind of forms to use, he still has the power to deny your right to seek landed status in Canada."

While his case was under appeal and Zaven was battling to be admitted, he tried to improve his working conditions and salary. He ended up in a lens-grinding factory again, but earning sixty dollars a week, a better salary than the previous one. At the same time, he took courses at night in optics and tried to learn two languages.

After two years of regular visits to Immigration, Zaven's persistence finally paid off, and the family was granted landed immigrant status. But on the work front, Zaven was frustrated and upset. It hadn't taken him long to discover that he could not advance to a higher position because his foreman refused to explain more intricate techniques of operation.

"My supervisor was afraid I would take away his job. Maybe it was true, maybe not, but I had to get ahead, and finally switched to another company in the east end of the city. From there I went to Baril Opticians on Drummond Street, and it was the biggest and most progressive step in my life. I had contact with the public, could practise my language skills, and Mr. Baril, God bless his soul, gave me so much responsibility and kindness that I developed a sense of self-confidence and self-esteem, something I had not had up to then."

Zaven was put in control of five stores, hiring, firing, communicating with the public and dealing with representatives of other companies. Mr. Baril made him feel his opinion was important, and Zaven showed his loyalty, out of appreciation.

"He made me feel that I counted. To this day I appreciate what he did for me, and I learned a lot from him. When he sold the company and moved to the States, I was very sorry. He and a Mr. Gaffney were exceptionally good to me. They even came to my wedding and were like family. These are people I will admire all my life."

Through an unusual combination of circumstances, Zaven became involved in community affairs, social work, immigration and interpreting. Someone he was working with at the Armenian Community Centre suffered a heart attack. Zaven rushed the man to the hospital, and the attending doctors praised Zaven for his speed, and for his expertise in handling the long list of information required on hospital forms.

"That was how I became involved with other people's suffering, with people who had little knowledge of the language and the country. I was lucky I had learned the language through working with people at the optical companies where I trained, and

I had been a student in Turkey. I had a friend, a French journalist, who later moved to France, who would talk to me in his broken English while I answered him in fractured French. This was how we each learned one another's working language. And as a result of the hospital incident, the Armenian Community Ambulance Service called me in, to help people who were ill and needed help getting to the hospital, and assistance communicating with those who didn't understand Armenian. I was the liaison between patients, doctors and nurses."

Before long, Zaven was asked to serve as a translator. A women he had met at the Armenian Youth Organization suggested he apply to government Immigration offices because so many minorities were coming from the Middle East. Zaven's ability to speak Turkish, Armenian, English and French would be useful. And it was his own frustrating experiences with the bureaucratic maze at Immigration that made Zaven decide to help others.

"I'm still here because I fought this kind of treatment, because I refused to take 'no' as an answer. But how many can do this? That was why I got involved in helping prospective immigrants."

Zaven began working at Mirabel and Dorval Airports as well as at Immigration centres. What disturbed him the most were the faces—frightened faces of people terrified of being deported or jailed. He knew this fear, for he had felt it himself, and it gave him a greater compassion for the unfortunates lining up at Canada's doors, pleading for entry.

"Today, if I were given a thousand dollars a day, I wouldn't go back to work there. The insults, the initimidation and harassment these immigrants are subjected to, is more than enough to scare people away. What I would like to see is someone play the undercover role of an immigrant and expose what is going on at Immigration centres. Ottawa doesn't know what is happening in the provinces, and no one reports these civil servants who give immigration services such a bad reputation by taking advantage of the situation. If I were given a chance, do you know how many I would turn in for investigation? I'm not saying that they are all crooks, but many play God, when they are just clerks taking down information to relay to Ottawa. They should not have the authority to play with people's futures—with human lives. The decisions should come from Ottawa. With computer networks in use, all this processing could be handled in a month, using modems to Ottawa. Teams should be created to handle the backlogs with the Minister having the last word on policies, rather than some petty official.

"I was talking to Kerop Bedoukian just before he died, who was personally responsible for helping 2,500 Armenian refugees emigrate to Canada after the Armenian Holocaust. He told me it was not the Minister who decided the fate of the refugees. He said it was a power-group in Ottawa who decided. I find that absurd. That is a government Minister's job. Only when a case receives unusual publicity does the Minister take notice. I feel newcomers should be assured of direct contact with the Immigration Minister."

To prove his point, Zaven mentioned a few cases. When he had lived in Canada a number of years, and after he had received his citizenship in 1978, Zaven's future wife, whom he had known as a child in Turkey, came on a visit. She was able to come as a tourist in 1980, but the rules in force at the time stated that she had to apply for landed immigrant status outside Canada. Even if she married in Canada, she would still have to leave the country to apply. Zaven took her to Longueuil Immigration Centre to fill out her application.

"The official asked all kinds of absurd questions, which, of course, she couldn't answer because she didn't speak English or French. I had to translate.

"'Why did you come here?' she asked her.

"I answered that she had come to visit and we had just gotten married.

"'Couldn't you have found someone already here to marry?' came the question.

"I looked at the official, a woman, and laughed. 'Well, you weren't available at the time.'

"She didn't laugh. She looked like ice.

"This kept going on and on, over and over, and then came medical difficulties. Blood samples were required, and they took blood six times. They told me that any person who has been here for three months and has non-immigrant status has to pass a medical examination.

"However, someone at the lab mixed up the blood samples,

131

and suddenly I received a call from Immigration, saying that my wife was to go to the Royal Victoria Hospital immediately. Why? I asked. They had found syphilis. I should tell you that this is the greatest possible insult there is to a person from my country, especially a woman. It is a terrible condemnation. I couldn't even tell my wife what I had been told. I said it was some kind of virus whose name I didn't know in Turkish.

"The doctor at the hospital laughed uproariously. My wife was still a virgin. How could they make such a stupid mistake? So we went back and everything was straightened out, but it took such a long time. We had to go back every three months or so. I would have to get permission from my boss to take my wife to Immigration, until finally in exasperation I said to the woman officer: "Listen, lady, it takes only a week for people to get to the moon, and we've been coming here for two years now.

"Her answer was: 'In order to get to the moon, they worked twenty years to make it possible.'

"When my wife's sister came to visit us some time later, she was held at Dorval Airport by Immigration officials. My wife and I went to pick her up, but she had had some difficulty with her airline connection in Europe and had missed her plane. Instead of coming directly to Montreal, she had been rerouted via Chicago.

"An Immigration officer called my wife and me into the office, and when I told him the woman he was holding was my sister-in-law, he looked at me slyly and said: 'Are you going to find somebody for her, so she'll stay here?'

"I just looked at him, but I had the gut-feeling that he couldn't do anything to me because by then I was a Canadian citizen. If he were to get nasty, I would give as good as I got. So I smiled and asked, 'Do you know anybody here who would like to marry her?'

"He looked at her again and asked, 'Are these both sisters?'

"'Yes, they are.'

"'They don't look alike.'

"I held up my hand. 'Do my fingers look alike?'

"'No,' he admitted. 'You're very quick.'

"'I'm also a Canadian.' He got even.

"'Give me your identification,' he demanded.

"I had to prove the woman with me was my wife, that I was

a citizen, but what infuriated me was that he had no right to ask for *my* identification papers. I wasn't travelling; my sister-in-law was. I said I didn't have any papers with me, and, indeed, I didn't. However, what frightened me about the system was that he took my name, went next door and returned, saying...'You entered Canada on September 2, 1970...you got married on this and this date...your wife was accepted on this date'...he droned on, and he had everything about us down on paper. I was thinking, shockingly enough, that Big Brother was watching. Everyone's life is on file. Who would have thought we were coming to a police state?

"But you don't know how good it felt for the first time in my life to be able to talk back to government officials, to the authorities. That's what Canadian citizenship did for me. I could fight back, and it made me feel like a human being and not an animal cowering inside myself."

A period of enlightenment was beginning for Zaven. He started noticing things and hearing remarks that he had ignored or shrugged off before. Only, this time, he didn't turn away in frustration. He began to speak up. He advised new immigrants on how to integrate more quickly and more easily. He explained that they should get involved with French and English-speaking Canadians and not isolate themselves sitting at home, feeling sorry about everything. "Get active," he told them. "It's your duty to learn languages and communicate."

"This inability to communicate and the resulting isolation are the two main reasons why immigrants suffer from depression. I still have it periodically, to this day. Do you know that to be able to talk to a girl, other than an Armenian, was a big triumph for me when I first arrived in Canada? I couldn't even pronounce names like Ruth and Claudette. I know of many people who left Canada, and returned to their own countries because they couldn't take the loneliness here—the lack of communication—and were unable to get into any kind of business. Most of the people I knew were merchants, and the red tape of permits, leases, licenses, and other papers intimidated them so much that they were afraid to even make the attempt to sort it out. Some even believed that if they screamed at their kids or smacked them, the kids would pick up the phone, call the police and have them jailed."

Zaven also discovered that prejudice and racism existed,

and were difficult to combat. He felt he had been insulted many times. He heard *"Maudit immigrant"* at work or *"Deporté"* and *"Tiens, un autre deporté..."* in French and English. The language was different, but the meaning was always the same. When he had first heard remarks about DPs, he hadn't reacted. In Turkey his minority group had been called "heathens" for centuries. So he figured that if Turks could name-call, so could Canadians. However, one incident on Bay Street in Toronto shook him up.

"There were three cars in three lanes, two of them heading in one direction, and the third in the opposite direction. Beside me on my left was a Sikh driver in a turban, and diagonally was a Caucasian, all of us stopped and waiting for the red light to change. The white guy rolled his window down and spat in the Sikh's direction as we went by when the light changed to green. Something clicked in my head. What is this, I asked myself? It's like the racial tension in the Southern United States between the blacks and whites. It can't be happening in Canada. I couldn't take it. I was so upset, I left the city the same day. This kind of treatment of any minority has to be stopped. The public must be educated, and it has to start early, in the schools. I have seen so much of it in Turkey. Is there any difference here?

"Canadians whose parents or grandparents once were immigrants must learn to understand what newcomers are enduring, even if it means going back to their roots to find out. Every immigrant who comes here contributes something—either by paying taxes, or opening a store or other business, or employing fellow Canadians, or having children. There appears to be a lack of communication between immigrants and established Canadians. And politicians seem to forget we exist, except at election time when ethnics are wooed for their votes. Politicians show up, make all kinds of promises to the minority groups and when the election is over, the orators go back to Parliament Hill or the National Assembly, and forget the minorities completely.

"I remember some member of former Premier Lévesque's Cabinet coming to an Armenian organization and donating some money in memory of the Armenian genocide, in order to get votes. He didn't give a damn what happened to the Armenians then or now, and if he had been asked where the country was located, he wouldn't have been able to answer. Immigrants, unfortunately, fall for this brown-nosing, because they don't know any better. They know little or nothing about the voting process, yet they make heroes out of politicians who come offering gifts at election time. Immigrants are so happy to be noticed by someone important that they don't see the reason for the sudden visits.

"And this is what I try to explain to new immigrants. I tell them to read papers, listen to the radio, watch TV and not to just one side. I feel that newcomers should learn the political systems in Canada and how to choose candidates, how to vote. Immigrants must be represented in municipal, provincial and federal affairs. They should get involved with other minority groups. Often ethnics will be loyal to representatives of their own backgrounds, voting for them even if they aren't capable politicians. Newcomers feel comfortable with their own. An ethnic representative will understand their problems."

Zaven would like to see some changes in the way people are treated at Immigration centres. In his capacity as a registered interpreter, he realized that many who translate are not accurate in explaining questions or answers. Often the real meaning is lost in the translation.

"For example, when I was at the Immigration centre with my sister-in-law, I explained the situation and my role in it. The officer ordered me out of the office, saying he needed a real interpreter, because I was talking with my emotions as a relative. I could understand that, but I noticed that when I tried to say something which the official interpreter relayed to the officer, it came out as something else, and not what I had really said.

"When I translate for immigrants, I always repeat everything to make sure it hasn't changed through one stage of relay. There is a great difference in the questions: 'Why did you come to Canada?' and 'Why did you choose Canada?' If my mother hadn't chosen Canada I wouldn't have come here. I know of others who chose it, too, but are waiting for years to get a definite 'yes' or 'no' to their plea for political asylum. I could talk at length about refugees waiting for such a long time to be accepted or turned away—living with the fear one finds on Death Row—execution next day, next month or next year. It's like dying slowly, and not knowing when it will happen. The indecision is agonizing."

Zaven accompanied a woman with two children to Immigration. Her husband had been shot in her homeland. When the daughter applied for entry to a Canadian University, she was turned away because she had no papers. Zaven found it difficult to understand how people can be expected to put their documents in order when fleeing for their lives. He feels it is even worse for women with children.

"Just what does Canada want of these people? Most of them aren't asking for charity or welfare. I wouldn't like to see my sister-in-law on welfare. She's young; she can work. So give her papers so she can work, instead of sitting and doing nothing. And contrary to what the public says about immigrants taking jobs from Canadians, the newcomers create work and income. It's a two-way process. I may have taken a job that a Canadian relinquished when I was hired, but my taxes pay for his welfare cheque if he doesn't get another job."

Zaven believes that the Immigration Department should keep track of immigrants, once they have been admitted. There should be some reports on their progress, failures, accomplishments, health and education for at least five years after they have been processed. This system would prevent immigrants from falling into the welfare system which destroys the incentive to work. It would also be a means of helping those immigrants who are isolated, depressed, or unable to cope with poor health or adjustment to a new way of life.

"There are some street-smart immigrants who will exploit the welfare system," he admits. "Push them to work. Canada needs money, manpower and new businesses."

Zaven says there should be more programmes for ethnics on radio and TV, where immigrants could listen to music and hear the language of their homelands. He points out that there are programmes for Italians, Greeks, Spaniards and Chinese, but Turks, for instance, are reluctant to participate in radio broadcasts because they are afraid of Armenian and Greek harassment.

"The old wounds from the Armenian Holocaust, and the enmity between Turks and Armenians and Greeks, are still very deep. Turks in Canada keep a very low profile because they are afraid of retribution from the Armenians. At one time, the Turks had a soccer club here in Quebec, and some of the team members were beaten up by Armenians who are violently anti-Turkish.

Because of the increase in confrontations, the club was disbanded.

"One night the Turkish community had a Ball to which everyone was invited. Unfortunately, there was a bomb-threat and everybody ran out of there in fear. I'm not saying that what the Turks did in the early 1900s was right, but for God's sake, don't brainwash kids from succeeding generations to continue this hatred in another country. This is happening in Armenian and Greek schools. We have to learn to live together here, without hating one another. It doesn't mean we have to forget our history, but we must stop propagating the hatred imported from our countries of origin. Look at what was done to the Jews for two thousand years. Turks have as much right to live here as Armenians and Greeks."

Zaven agrees that political assassinations in this country are rare, and that our political leaders walk around in crowds without bullet-proof vests and with just a few guards. Yet Canada, a relatively safe and free country, permits demonstrations and violence by one minority, directed at another. He cites assassination attempts against Turks in this country; one attempt succeeded and another failed. However, an innocent Canadian was killed. Iranian and Iraqi students clashed at Concordia University in Montreal and were responsible for considerable property damage in a Canadian institution of higher learning. Sikhs and Indians have been waging a vendetta in Canada against one another, a vendetta which originated in India. The downing of an Air India jet in 1985, returning to India from Canada, was blamed on terrorists, but it has not been determined who they were. Hundreds of innocent lives were lost.

"Why does the public have to suffer? Why does Canada permit these things to go on? The Canadian Government should simply say: 'You have a grievance against people from your homeland? Go solve it in your land of origin. We don't need it here. This is a peaceful country. When you come here, you start fresh. Let's keep it that way!'

"This admonition has nothing to do with the Constitution or personal liberty. It deals with peace of mind for the public, which should not have to suffer the imported hatreds of immigrants who are looking for a better life in Canada. An Act or Bill would be helpful in prohibiting one ethnic group from maligning another on the basis of old-country feuds. Freedom of speech is one

137

thing; verbal abuse, promoting hatred, racism and physical attacks is another.

"If I had the chance to do it all over again, I would still come to Canada, but first I would learn all the aspects of life here, and most of all, the language. I would start to work at it in my homeland. It is so much more difficult when one is already here and must work night and day to survive. There is very little time as earning money for food and lodging comes first.

"But now that I am established, I realize that Canada gave me a sense of freedom which I know I wouldn't have found in Turkey—freedom to pack a case and leave the country, all on the same day, without hustling clandestinely to buy foreign currency or going to the military police for permission to leave. I can go from here to Vancouver or Halifax, and no one will stop me or ask where I am going. Nobody would even care. I could get involved in political affairs and could express my feelings, as I am doing now, without the fear I would be locked away, or shot.

"You can live like a king here if you so desire, and as long as you don't interfere with someone else's right to exist, you can do as you please. Whether you fail or succeed in business is entirely in your own hands.

"Canada, for me, is a country that I often see in the abstract, strange at times, yet warm despite the cold winters—a country of paradoxes. I could talk about them for the rest of my life."

ILLEGAL

by
Milly Charon
from an interview with Carlos Rodriguez

It was the kind of street you might find yourself running down in a nightmare. Part of a rough neighbourhood in South Bronx, New York City, its sidewalks and road were littered with garbage that had been uncollected for months. The limp bodies of several dead cats lay near the brick walls of an empty dilapidated tenement. Further along, the rotting corpse of a long-dead dog added its putrefying odour to the refuse. Rats scuttled about unafraid. The windowpanes in the buildings on both sides of the street were broken or missing, the empty rectangles staring hopelessly at the prospect of imminent demolition. Derelicts and drug adddicts lay on the sidewalk or in doorways, unconscious to the world around them.

Every night, twenty-one-year-old Carlos Rodriguez gingerly picked his way through this scene like a sleepwalker and passed along the street again when he returned to his squalid little room before daybreak. His job at a bakery four blocks from the subway forced him to walk in terror every night. It was a street that even the police avoided.

When Rodriguez saw a drunk with his ear cut off, lying in a pool of blood one evening, he reacted instinctively. He had to protect himself in case he was attacked. He asked a few casual questions at the bakery, and one of the employees directed him to a man who had a .22-caliber handgun with a supply of bullets. Rodriguez bought the gun for twenty dollars. He didn't know until much later that the gun had been stolen from the stockroom of a small-weapons factory by one of the employees. Rodriguez didn't realize that he needed a permit to carry a gun. Each day he carried the loaded pistol to and from work, stuffed into a paper bag with his

141

lunch.

Had the authorities known that he was an illegal immigrant from Uruguay and carried a weapon, the twenty-one-year-old would have been in serious trouble. Rodriguez was not a criminal. He was a victim—a victim of a social, economic and family disorder that left him with an emotional disability—an anger that would erupt one day and almost destroy him. Because his country was not at war, he could not claim refugee status; however, Rodriguez *was* a refugee fleeing from an emotional war whose unseen scars had forced him to seek sanctuary in another country. It would take years before he made peace with himself.

* * * *

I was born in Barcelona, Spain in 1946. My father was a travelling salesman, a peddler who lived by his wits on the shady deals he transacted. He took great pride in saying he worked for himself, because he believed that working for another person was a shame—something to be avoided at any price. Although I was born seven years after the end of the Spanish Civil War, the country still had not recuperated from the ravages of war. I had heard from people who had lived through it and the post-war period that the starving population had eaten barn rats to survive, and potato and banana peels had been sold as food. Germany and Italy had used Spain as a testing-ground for the weapons to be employed in a war that had been shaping since the early thirties. When World War II broke out on September 1, 1939, Spain remained neutral; she had been broken by a civil war which had ended only six months before.

From several sources, I learned that my father had managed to avoid military service between 1936 and 1939 by buying his way out of it. Somehow he acquired a disability card and used it to good advantage. He had never learned to drive, yet he was able to get around, using a driver at the wheel of a car that materialized almost out of nowhere—a car which took him from villages to towns where my father would sell anything. He could sell sand to Bedouins. He used every selling trick in the book as well as inventing a few of his own. He even set up shills in the crowds that gathered to entice people to buy his wares, when he turned on the loudspeakers rigged to his car.

Thus he was able to eat in good restaurants when others were starving, have a quantity of good clothes when most of the population went ragged, and avoid military service. This apparently successful image was how he impressed my mother. She was a simple, good woman from Valencia with a provincial, small-town mentality. She came from a family of unusual closeness and devotion, whereas my father had been on bad terms with his own relatives for years. No one liked him and he had no friends. He had a way of alienating everyone, but he snared her after a determined courtship and they married and moved to Barcelona.

However, marriage didn't stop him from travelling around the country. He took her with him and when he heard reports of an economic boom in the Canary Islands, he moved there and stayed a few years. My sister was born there and shortly after, my father tired of island life and returned to Spain.

I think he felt Spain was too small for him and that marriage was too constricting, for he suddenly decided to go to Brazil where he had heard things were good, and money was readily available. I was about four or five when he convinced my mother he had to go to the New World, where he would remain for two years. He returned to visit for a month and went back to Brazil. After another two years, he convinced himself that Uruguay's economy was better and he could use his mother tongue instead of the Portuguese spoken in Brazil.

By the time he returned to collect us, I was already nine years old. He arranged for our sea passage to Montevideo, and for me the prospect of emigration to Uruguay was a great adventure. I was excited to be quitting school and leaving Spain for something new. None of my friends had a father who had been to South America.

When I look back on it now, that was the turning-point in my life. I had been alone with my mother and sister for a long time, and it had been the happiest period of my life up to then. But when my father came for us, everything turned sour. We moved almost immediately after everything had been packed into trunks and crates.

However, it was only when we were on the ship that I

became fully aware of my father's terrible temper. We had been accustomed to eating at home because my mother never had enough money to take us to restaurants. The food on the ship was different from what we had had, and we didn't like it. My father went into a towering rage, blamed my mother for bringing us up poorly and there was terrible argument in the ship's dining salon. My mother was seasick and couldn't handle the situation. He got into an argument with a steward and became verbally abusive, yelling at the top of his lungs. He dragged us out with him, and I was crying, terrified that he would be thrown overboard or killed, and here I had just gotten together with him after so many years. I could never really figure out what was the reason for it all, probably because he always treated us children as nuisances and never explained anything. Now I realize that maybe he was just too impatient with anyone who wasn't as quick-witted as himself.

When we arrived in Uruguay, we didn't have a place of our own, and one of his friends took us in. Limited to one room, the four of us stayed there for a month. My father couldn't stop complaining. He was a disciplinarian, and I wasn't allowed to do anything. If I did something, I was scolded for doing it, and if I didn't do anything, the reprimand was that I should have done it. His sarcasm, bitterness and verbal abuse escalated to the point where I wondered why my mother hadn't simply refused to go with him and remained in Spain with my sister and me, where all of us could have had some peace and quiet without him. Finally he rented an apartment for us near the river and we moved in. He set up a table on a busy street and began selling things there. However, this street-trading without a permit was illegal and every once in a while, the police would come and pick him up. The whole way of life frightened me.

Meanwhile I was enrolled in school, but I had a difficult time integrating because the local accent and idiom were very strange to me. I spoke Castilian, a different type of Spanish from that spoken in Uruguay. Of course, people looked down their noses at me. I felt like an outcast until I adapted and changed my way of speaking. The immigrant, as is usually the case, was looked down on, and a pejorative expression I heard often enough was *Gallego*, a term applied to people from Galicia, a poor province in Spain. However, because most immigrants leave Spain for economic reasons, no matter what part of the country they are from, the term *Gallego* is thrown at them the minute they set foot in South America. Anyone with a foreign accent was labelled *Gallego*, and there was an implied stigma to the word. It denoted someone who was ignorant and clumsy. It was years before I realized how much that hated term affected me. But that wasn't the only injustice. If immigrants worked hard and opened shops or food stores after years of pinching pennies and saving, the native-born inhabitants scorned and boycotted them because they themselves had not been able to accomplish as much.

It was not a pleasant environment for a sensitive child. But if things were hard outside, they were worse at home. One of my father's friends told him he chastised his own son with a leather belt, so the next time I did something he thought was wrong, he used this method of punishment. My mother would have to treat me for bruises and weals after one of his beatings. Several times he locked me in the washroom for about a month-and-a-half in the summer because I did something of which he disapproved. It was stifling in there, and the door was locked from the outside, so I couldn't get out. I was permitted out only to eat and when someone needed to use the washroom. He didn't do it during the school year because questions would have been raised about my absence, but on weekends, back I went. To keep myself from going mad, I took to hiding books behind the water heater in the washroom. I was about twelve or thirteen and went through collections of books I had borrowed. I loved every minute of it. I read translations of books by Rafael Sabatini, Jack London, Steinbeck—anything I could get my hands on—even the Reader's Digest. It got to the point where I looked forward to being locked in so that I could read. I was adapting to an unbearable situation because I wasn't strong enough to fight him physically, emotionally or mentally.

He was even harder on my mother. There weren't any supermarkets in those days, and the one small store across the street sold food at a little more than at the market. My mother had to walk a kilometre and back to buy food every two days at a market where farmers came to sell their produce. We had a decrepit old fridge, and food didn't keep very well in it. Milk was only good for a day. To make matters worse, my father kept her short of housekeeping money. She was thrifty anyway and didn't waste it. However, going to the market meant she had to carry everything herself because my father didn't consider a cart necessary. It would have cost money. So I would walk the distance to meet her and take the bags, resting along the way when the load became too heavy. It was agony for her because she had a problem with her feet. Although the doctor had told her she needed special made-to-measure shoes, my father wouldn't spend a hundred pesos on a pair of shoes for her. Her needs were not important.

To all this misery was added an isolation impossible to describe. We had no family and no friends in Uruguay. All my father wanted to do was make money, and he had no time for anyone. We never celebrated Christmas, birthdays, festivals or other holidays. At a certain point in his life, he should have realized that having children and a wife wouldn't solve his problems or make him fit into community life. When he couldn't run away from himself any more, he ran to another country and unconsciously set out to make our lives as impossible as he could through deprivation and abusive discipline. My mother was too weak to cope with it, something I resented inside and always had trouble dealing with. She was afraid to talk back and afraid to leave him. There were times he wouldn't speak to her for months at a stretch. It was another of his quirks. If he got angry, silence was a weapon of abuse. When I was born, he was so pleased I was a boy that he took me to see his mother whom he had not spoken to in years. That was how the silence was broken. He had a demon inside him and argued with everyone.

At one point my mother, in desperation, went secretly to the Spanish Consulate to be repatriated to Spain. Everything was ready for her to leave, but she changed her mind and decided to stay with him.

All these family insecurities, as well as the uprooting from a safe place with my mother and sister in Spain, left me with a deep psychological trauma that I still haven't overcome to this day. I grew up with anger.

There may have been some kids like me who found refuge in school, but even that was denied me. Someone told my father that the public schools were bad, so he put me into a private Catholic school, where discipline was as emotionally destructive as what I endured at home. One of the priests even called me *Gallego* in front of the class.

And there was a priest who liked young boys. When I went to confession, he appeared to be very kind. Because I had never known any kindness in life from anyone but my mother, I was taken in by it. But when he began to kiss and caress me and I heard other children saying things about him, I refused to go back and went to another priest. I was learning about life the hard way.

Because I was an immigrant and the educational system and language were different, I had been put back in school and lost a few years. Finally, when I left private school, I entered a public secondary school where I spent four years. It was difficult for me to study because I had to work with my father after school, selling things. He had obtained a permit, the only one on the block, and it was amazing how he had made a success out of a venture as small as a card-table set up on a main avenue. But although we were better off materially, he was still miserly with my mother. When a friend jokingly said he gave his wife only so much, and he named a sum less than what my mother received, my father cut her money down even more. By the time he learned his friend had been kidding, we were close to starvation, living on a diet of potatoes.

It was worse in the summer. We lived near the water and everyone was sunning or swimming while I had to go downtown to stand on the sidewalk, breathing in the fumes from cars and buses to sell things from that table. As a result I developed a sort of allergy to society—to people who were shopping downtown while I was working. I was so tired and felt a contempt for the public. To me they were petty and stupid. I became hostile to anything and anyone involved with fashion or jewelry. I associated that with my slave status. That feeling was intensified by the escapist literature I was reading—swashbuckling tales of adventure, of people who were independent masters of their lives, globe-trotters, explorers, hunters of big game in Africa. I felt my life was despicable because it collided with my fantasy world of books. I was torn by this constant frustration of not having lived my childhood, not being able to play like other kids, not having any friends, not having money or time to go to the movies. Despite the passage of many years, this frustration is still inside me.

In 1964 when I finished high school, my father was off and running again. He had money by then and decided to return to

Spain. My mother was ecstatic. She had never wanted to emigrate in the first place, and had lived a life of hardship for so many years. My sister and I, however, had made a few friends in Uruguay, so we had mixed feelings about the move. Because I had never accepted my uprooting from the country of my birth, I readapted to Spain very quickly. But now I had to work for someone else and didn't like it. Half the day I worked with my father who bought a stall at a market, and the other half of the day I worked somewhere else. It was the same thing all over again. My father was barely making enough to survive and after a year of this, he decided to take us all back to Uruguay.

It was terrible for my mother. She had just returned to the closeness of her family ties and suddenly he was off again. He had criticized her family very harshly and had forbidden her to see them. She had to visit them behind his back. She must have spent months crying. My sister and I were happy, but when we reached Uruguay I realized I would have to go through another integration process. I saw Montevideo as a little town.

I knew I had to get away from my father, and at the age of seventeen wanted to take a trip to Manaus in Brazil. Although he finally gave me the authorization, which I needed as a minor, he refused to give me any money and I didn't go. But the good thing that came out of it was that I realized later I wasn't prepared for this kind of life. I was ignorant and naive because I had been isolated from other children and lived only in a world of adventure books and adults, whose world I didn't understand and despised.

I saw life only from my father's narrow point of view. I had not gone through the normal process of growing up—maturing morally, emotionally and sexually. I may have been above average intellectually, but my knowledge in other areas was limited. I had lived a life of isolation, conditioned by a form of brainwashing imposed on me by a rigid disciplinarian. I remember thinking there were two people I wanted to see dead—a priest, who was a real inquisitor, beating us across our knuckles with a heavy ruler and doing other cruel things, and my father. I was young then and repressed it all to survive, until I remembered it just recently. I saw my mother as a suffering saint.

My sister was even more repressed than I. When she was fifteen, a boy walked her home from school one day. My father saw them, went downstairs in fury and he hit the boy, right out on the street. At the top of his lungs he yelled that he would kill the boy if he ever went near my sister again. The boy hadn't done anything wrong.

When my father learned that a volunteer organization concerned with the well-being of children like us had set up neighbourhood classes in sex education, he went there and forcibly removed my sister from the class. He said: "Those things you learn by yourself. They are not taught." He said such things were done only in America and repeated this expression many times in describing the New World. "America has food without taste, men without honour and women without shame."

That was when I started going with Raquel. She was a very nice girl who appeared very sensuous to someone like me who had no knowledge of such things. I almost saw our relationship as a perversion because my mind had been influenced so much by my parents. When my girl friend got pregnant, I realized I was not ready for marriage, much less for parenthood that could have been avoided. I had the emotions and sexual understanding of a fifteen-year-old. Half of what was in my head, planted there by my father, was barely sane. The other half, which I concocted from my own ignorance, was just as wrong.

And so I gave Raquel money for an abortion. Although Uruguay was a small country, society was very progressive and women were more liberated. People had a way of looking openly at sexuality as a natural thing. Abortions were easy to obtain, and there was no secret about it. Raquel took the money and left, but once at the clinic, she decided not to go through with it and came home.

She didn't tell me what had happened. Later when she began to show, she said the woman had fooled her. I felt responsible and married her, and my son was born a month later.

The marriage didn't last a year. It was a nightmare neither one of us could handle. When she tried to kill me with a knife, I knew she was driven to it and I really couldn't blame her. The only way out was for me to leave.

I decided to go to New York to earn money there—at least $4,000 to buy part of a taxi or bus—that is, one sixteenth or one thirty-second of one, because that was the only way you could be a taxi driver in Uruguay. You had to own part of the vehicle. I figured if I worked like hell the way I had done all my life, I could go back to Uruguay with all my problems solved.

In the seven months I lived in New York illegally, I caught North American fever—freedom fever. I grew to love the city because it taught me about people, about the world, about the things I had missed in life. But so many things shocked me. I was spellbound watching women reading newspapers in the subway. When a woman held open a door for me because my arms were full of groceries, tears came to my eyes at her kindness. There was such a difference in people's attitudes. The thought that people who were not related to me were performing little acts of courtesy was unbelievable. I would stare at people a lot, and suddenly it all began to make sense—it was teammates, teamwork, all building together toward the future.

I found a job as a doorman in Queens during the day and at night worked in a bakery in the worst part of the Bronx. I was so frightened I would walk down the middle of that terrible street going to and from work. I worked a double shift, saving money and getting sick and rundown every week from eating stale food to pinch pennies. Suddenly I realized I was doing the same thing as my father. I hadn't seen it until I began living it—the whole immigrant experience. I kept to a tight budget, spending a little on myself and sending money to my wife and child. Before I bought the gun for protection, I took driving lessons and got a licence in order to buy a car for one hundred dollars, so I wouldn't have to walk down that street unprotected twice a day. Soon after, I found the car on blocks—the wheels had been stolen. I dipped into my hard-earned savings and replaced them.

Although I needed a lot of other things badly, I splurged and bought myself an old TV. It was the only recreation I had ever had in my life. I spent my free time in front of it. I laughed myself silly at a programme called *The Addams Family*, and it taught me English. I even found TV advertising fascinating.

I felt I was living an adventure while I was in New York. I was glad to be alive. But I made the mistake of going back before I had earned enough money because Raquel kept writing to me to come back. When I left, I was crying like a child as I watched the skyline of New York disappear. For me it was the end of liberty and the end of a learning experience I desperately needed.

I went back to Uruguay with my two thousand dollars, but it slowly melted away. Things got worse with my wife. There was no work and no money. One day, after so many years of mounting despair, I asked myself what was I doing there. I had to get back to Paradise. I applied for a visa, and it was denied. The American authorities compared the questionnaire with the one I had filled out before, and said I had lied. The reason there were discrepancies was that the first time I didn't feel some things were important, so I left them out. The second time I wrote more. It was enough to disqualify me.

So I had a choice between Australia and Canada. I went to see someone at a travel agency and asked for advice. He told me to go to Montreal, Canada, probably because it had a Latin background. He said he had sent many people there.

I trusted him blindly. I just wanted to get away from Uruguay. I had changed as a person. I was anti-system, anti-conformist, anti-everything at that point. Although I was supposed to fly to Montreal, I was planning to leave the plane during the stop-over in New York, and run back to my Paradise where no one could find me. But things had changed in New York in 1970 without my knowledge. Immigration procedures had been tightened. I missed the Air Canada flight to Montreal because the plane from Montevideo arrived too late for the connection. The next flight I could book was five or six hours later.

A policeman was assigned to watch me, and I was forced to stay with him. Perhaps they suspected that I had planned to slip out of the airport and disappear somewhere in New York. The officer didn't feel like sitting around the airport for hours, and he took me with him while he did his errands. He went to pick up radios and walkie-talkies for his station. I was stuck with him.

He was very curt, didn't talk much, only what was necessary. When he said he had to eat, I went, too. I had to go to the washroom, and he went with me. He wasn't going to let me escape that way. But I did learn something from him. I discovered French fries. In my previous seven-months' stay in New York, I had never tasted them. And where I had only Spanish before, I now spoke some English. After we finished eating, he took me back to the airport to wait some more and while we were sitting there, he fell asleep. I could have escaped, but he had my passport in his inside pocket. I could have gone without it, just the same. There are people who have been illegal for many years, and no one can find them. Had I been a criminal, I probably would have walked out. But I wasn't. I had to wake the officer half an hour before, so I wouldn't miss my plane. He felt bad about falling asleep. He insisted on going inside the plane with me, gave my passport to the steward and told him not to give it to me until the plane was airborne.

So you can say I arrived in Canada on the wrong footing because of my failure to get back to New York. I was upset and tired, and when the announcement on Air Canada's P.A. system came on in French, I sat up in astonishment. French! What is this? I thought. It took me so long to learn a little English and now there's a new language to worry about. What kind of travel agent was that guy in Montevideo to send me where French is spoken?

I didn't have trouble getting past Immigration here. In 1970 you didn't need a visa to enter Canada. I was given a month to stay. It was April 1, a funny day to start a new life, and still winter. Some Uruguayans had given me the address of a rooming house in Montreal. Run by a Spanish woman, the place was barely adequate, but I had a room and meals for fifteen dollars a week. Despite my problems I was happy. I managed to find a job within a month. On the same day I went to Immigration Offices on Dorchester Boulevard to renew my visa. I noticed a sign in a restaurant's window which offered work to a dishwasher. I took it and for thirty-five dollars a week, I not only washed dishes but delivered food. By the end of fourteen months I was up to forty-five dollars a week plus tips. I worked six days a week, from seven in the morning until five in the afternoon. I didn't complain about the salary because I didn't even have a labour permit. The owner was Romanian, and he was very good to me. The rest of the staff were Greek. We were all immigrants.

However, you can imagine how terrified I was when the staff told me some of the Immigration officers came for lunch there and when the restaurant was busy, I would fill in serving them. Even if it wasn't my function, I had to oblige. I noticed that my boss appeared to be very friendly, even influential with the officers, so finally one day I opened up and confessed that I was working illegally. He offered to help me. And that is why I am so grateful to that man to this day. He's dead now, but he gave me a job and introduced me to an Immigration officer who told me what to do. He made an appointment for me to see him. First the officer renewed my visitor's permit and then told me how to go about becoming a landed immigrant. I was terrified of being deported. I brought him all the documents requested, and he wrote down all my qualifications. He showed me how to fill out the forms and what to write. He was surprised that I knew how to write in English. Many immigrants don't. At that time the points system was in use, and he added up all the points and said I had enough to qualify as an immigrant.

I'll never forget that scene. The officer was an elderly man, a French Canadian, and his name was Hamel. I have often wondered if he is still alive today. After that he continued to come to the restaurant to eat. He saw me there, yet I felt uncomfortable and tried to stay as far from him as possible. For me it was paradoxical to have been illegal and to be working in front of an Immigration officer who knew what I was and what I had been doing. It didn't make sense to me, and I felt uncomfortable for him, too.

That was how I became a landed immigrant in Canada and once I acquired my status, my boss raised my pay to fifty-five dollars, plus tips. Despite the small salary, I managed, for money went farther in those days. I lived in a rundown rooming house, unable to afford anything better and slowly adapted to Canada and the new ways. I sent some money home to my wife and bought myself a small scooter-like bicycle, a radio and a record player. After being so deprived all my life, I suddenly felt rich. I met a girl and we lived together for a few years. She wanted to get married and pushed me to get a divorce. I told her I wasn't ready to remarry yet and have children. She agreed to wait and one morning she told me she was pregnant. She had stopped taking the pill without telling me. I asked her what she was going to do.

She decided to have the baby. We weren't married, and I didn't have the courage, the self-respect or the wisdom to realize that a child who is unwanted will always feel rejected. Here it was happening to me all over again.

She had the child, and everything went wrong. We separated but reunited after I got a divorce from my wife. When my first child with her was about three years old, we were married, had a daughter, lived together for two years and then separated again. It was an unstable situation. I was seeing a psychologist, and my wife and I attended therapy sessions to help solve our marital problems. Yet I felt trapped in a situation because of my own inadequacies and I did what most men do. I cheated on her for a year, and she found out. I didn't even try to keep it from her. I think I wanted her to know. Although we finally reached a point where we were getting back together again, it was a game of push and pull. She decided she wasn't ready, and I suspected she was seeing someone else.

And so, I did what is common in South America and the United States. I followed her and saw her with another man. When I confronted her, she told me he was just a friend. I believed her but followed her home one day and spied on them through the window. She was in bed with him. I don't know what came over me. I must have been temporarily insane. I still had the key from the time we had lived together, and I stole in and assaulted the man. I broke his arm. Bad enough, but I was mad enough to kill him.

That was the end for me. I had to go to the hospital because I was in such a state that I couldn't even drive. Admitted overnight for sedation and released the next day, I would take over a month to accept the fact that my marriage was finished. It was a year before I realized we were truly separated. I had been through a lot of therapy with her and had come a long way in understanding my behaviour, but obviously not enough after what I had done.

Her lover went to the police, brought charges against me and sued me. I had to go to criminal court, where I was declared guilty with extenuating circumstances. However, the judge said I would not have a record, and the two-hundred-dollar fine was waived. I still had a civil court case to cope with, but when I went into personal bankruptcy, I was no longer liable for damages demanded in the suit.

My psychologist explained that in my rage I could have torn the man to pieces with my hands. All that anger from my abusive childhood had built up into a terrible fury. It could have been anyone who might have triggered the explosion. A year before, when a man insulted me, I kicked in his car door. All the deprivation, humiliation and brutality I had suffered and swallowed stayed inside. This time I couldn't keeep it in any longer, and it exploded. I had been a walking emotional time-bomb.

It took a lot of therapy for me to start picking up the pieces. In a way, it could have affected my ability to stay at the same job for too long. Being an immigrant also means taking jobs that aren't satisfactory. After my first job as a dishwasher, I went from a sandwich man in a Decarie Boulevard restaurant to a kitchen at a motel. At the same time I worked as a part-time waiter in Old Montreal during the mid-day luncheon rush. From there I worked as a waiter and jack-of-all-trades at an Italian restaurant on Notre Dame Street. While I was there I learned about an opening at Murray Hill Limousine Service and in the taxi industry. I applied for a licence, got one and drove a cab. I made two dollars on my first day on the road. That lasted two months and when I applied for a job as a chauffeur, I worked for two years driving a limousine.

I went back to night school and at the same time met a man who had a taxi permit. He let me rent his car and the permit and finally sold me his car. I worked fourteen hours a day, seven days a week, to pay off the one thousand dollars it cost me a month for the car. And I finished my high school education, breezing through it in no time. When I was done, I sold the taxi.

When I saw a Greyhound Bus ad for drivers, I applied. Out of eight hundred people, I was one of eight accepted. That salary of four hundred dollars to six hundred a week in American funds was astronomical to me. I worked for a year, taking the Montreal run to New York and back three times a week, but the shift work was very tiring and I couldn't take it.

I went from a four-year stint at Nordair as a traffic agent to a real estate agent. I didn't like that either. It was always a question of money—the insecurity of not having it. Somewhere I associated freedom with having money. I was trying to prove something to my family, expecially to my father, that I could do the same thing as he did—earn good money and save it.

Six months after I left the real estate business, I opened up my own business. I would buy used furniture, refinish it and then sell it and make a profit. But it was hard on my back lugging the stuff. I opened a store selling used furniture and antiques. Suddenly I realized I was imitating my father again. I was becoming so rude to customers that I closed up and declared bankruptcy. I took a good look at myself and what I had to do with my life. I wanted to study, start reading and writing again. But first, I went down to Cuba for a few months to return to sunshine, warmth, to be with people and learn how to communicate again.

All these emotional disturbances and traumas in my life created so much anguish that to this day I don't know whether I have contributed very much to Canada. But I do feel that Canada gave me a great deal. I discovered myself here and have learned to recognize and accept myself. By gaining confidence with each new job, I was able to move upward, improving my skills and at the same time I was able to see a psychologist for counselling on how to sort out my life. I doubt if I could have done it in another country. What might be considered a contribution to Canada is that I did it here, that I have known people here whom I love, that my children are Canadian and that I am teaching others English and Spanish at a college.

Although I have lived here over sixteen years, I have lived the equivalent of a complete lifetime, due to the intensity of my experiences. Now I am seeing solutions and analysing situations. I know there are very good things about Canada, such as personal security and the mixture of cultures. People generally are pleasant and one can communicate on different levels. There is an openness and willingness on the part of the government to be on your side, to respect your rights. I know that if I wanted to buy a house in Westmount, I could do it if I put my mind to it. If I wanted a fancy car, I could get that, too, but I don't want it. If I want to study, I can. I feel Canadian because I can do anything I want. I'm not limited. I can use all the possibilities, all the advantages Canada offers.

If there was anything I would criticize, it's the Canadian attitude, mentality and often mediocrity. The latter is probably the result of lack of motivation—a form of apathy. Most Canadians are conformists. They follow one road and won't deviate from it. If you don't want to eat popcorn at the movies, people think there is something wrong with you. If you don't drink coffee, they can't understand why.

I could criticize Canada as a capitalistic society, where the bottom eighty per cent of the people work for the top twenty per cent, but Communism isn't better. The solution isn't in politics. The worst I could say about the country is the Canadian winter. I suffered for thirteen years or more, and I decided a few years ago I was not going to suffer through another winter. From now on I go south. If I had a chance to do it all over again, I'd probably go to Australia, only because of the weather. I hate the outdoors in Canada's winters. Because I worked so hard as a child, I missed the warmth of the countries I lived in and I have to travel to warm places.

As far as racism and prejudice are concerned, they're still around, and immigrants will always be targets. When I worked for a short while at a place called Café St. Jacques in downtown Montreal, there were some French Canadians who called me *importé* and would make faces at me because of my accent, or stop talking to me. It was a while before I realized there are some who are very kind and will give you their home if you ask them. Racists are extremists, and it doesn't go by nationality. Racism is a characteristic found in certain types of individuals.

Because many immigrants feel badly about leaving their countries, they have difficulty adapting and criticize their new environment. And because they don't adapt, they don't live fully. What has kept me from living fully is my personal problem and that has nothing to do with Canada. I'm not saying that an immigrant has to submit totally and forget his roots and customs. No, he should remember them, but he should leave behind his prejudices, his pettiness and misconceptions. An immigrant should learn the language well and try to mix with local people. He should study, get an education, go on to university, if he wishes, and try to enjoy Canada on all levels. Canada is not only work and money. There are other things, some of which are more important than money.

The educational system here is excellent, and an immigrant can learn something without expense. He can go to lectures for nothing. He can follow the entertainment section in newspapers and attend free performances in all the arts. An immigrant should try to write, to read, try to get involved in other activities—social, cultural and political—anything, but get involved. Only then can he understand what Canada is about. This is what most immigrants lack—a sense of involvement. Many don't adapt because of this lack, and they become bitter in their isolation.

And as far as established Canadians are concerned, they should not be so quick to condemn and criticize the differences in people from other countries. Perhaps the immigrant knows something the Canadian is unaware of. He hears a different drummer. Canadians should attempt to learn something of the newcomer's customs and traditions to better understand his behaviour. And the same goes for immigrants. They have to understand why Canadians behave the way they do. It may not be acceptable, but at least understandable.

People come here for many reasons. Some are trying to improve their economic conditions or better their education. Others are fleeing harsh military regimes. A few are looking for adventure and most want peace of mind. One way of finding the latter is to get something to love—places or people. For me it is Mount Royal Park. It could be something else for another person. And if an immigrant could look at Canada as a whole and not a part of something, he would see the country as a landscape of many colours.

It bothers me when I see immigrants becoming bitter about Canada. I hear some say they are working ten to twelve hours a day, seven days a week to earn and save $20,000 or more so they can go back to their homeland and buy land, property or a business. This is an illusion, this going back. There is no time like the present to make it, and no other place than this country which allows an immigrant the chance to make it. And to do that, a new immigrant should live freely and intensely in order to see, do and feel everything of the Canadian experience.

INTEGRATION

by
Taimi Hindmarch

It was almost Christmas and on the family farm in Central Finland, Lempi Lauttamaki was milking the cows in the barn. Her twelve-year-old brother Lauri was helping her. He sensed she was troubled and finally asked what was bothering her. Lempi put her arms around him and made him promise not to tell. That year of 1912 was to be a very special one for Lempi, for Hemming (Hemmi) Julius Kekalinen, the neighbour's son, was coming over to ask her father's permission to marry her. She knew Hemmi had plans to go to Canada, and she wanted so much to marry him and go with him to the New World.

Three years previously, Hemmi's twenty-one-year-old brother Emil Aleksius Kekalinen had left his birthplace in Multi, Finland, to emigrate to the west coast of Canada, where one of his cousins had participated in the Sointula (Harmony) experiment in communal life on Malcolm Island in the Queen Charlotte Strait. This movement in British Columbia had developed into a famous Finnish settlement in North America—a utopian socialist commune—where immigrants of Finnish origin, scattered all over Canada and United States, had decided to return to farming.

Another cousin owned a farm at Port Hammond in the lower Fraser Valley, where other Finns were also established on the land. Using Webster's Corners, a nearby Finnish settlement, as headquarters, Emil had found employment in the logging camps. Because he found it difficult to spell Kekalinen in English, he shortened his name to Aho, the last three letters of the name of his parents' farm—*Kekalisenaho* (Kekalinen's Meadow)—in Finland.

And so, Hemmi and Lempi were looking forward to joining family members, and hoping their emigration and settlement would not be difficult. However, Lempi was very nervous. She

161

was afraid her father would think she was too young to marry at eighteen and go so far away from her homeland. Lauri wondered if he would have time to slip into the recessed space behind the big corner fireplace in the living room and eavesdrop on the discussion between his father and Hemmi.

He managed to conceal himself without difficulty and, peeping out from behind the rough stones, he saw Soloman Lauttamaki looking up over his glasses at his tall, prospective son-in-law. Solomon did not want to lose Lempi, who was an asset to him in managing the big farm. At thirteen, she had taken charge of the younger children when his wife died. Soloman had remarried, but Lempi did not get along with his second wife. To keep the peace in his household, he thought that perhaps it would be a good idea to give Lempi her share of her mother's estate and let her go. And so, he gave his consent to the marriage.

At twenty-two years of age, Hemmi was a big man, mature and strong, certain he could make a good life for himself and his sweetheart in Canada. Because they had both witnessed the sad, tearful farewell parties given to others who had emigrated, Hemmi and Lempi decided that, outside of the immediate family, they would keep their plans of departure for Canada a close secret.

The banns were announced and posted in the parish church in the rural village of Multia, and on March 3, 1913, the two young people were married there. That evening a wedding party of over a hundred guests crowded the roomy Lauttamaki farmhouse, where the festivities lasted until dawn.

Sometime before midnight, the young couple slipped away and were driven by horse and sled to the train station at Keuruu, about twenty kilometres away. They boarded a train which took them to Hanko, a port on the Gulf of Finland, from which they sailed to England on the first leg of the voyage across the Atlantic to Halifax, and then westward to British Columbia.

They arrived at Webster's Corners in the Fraser Valley after a six-week journey. Their emigration to this particular part of Canada was decided by the fact that many other Finns, including family members, had settled there. Emil had already been notified by letter that the newlyweds were en route, and he traveled from Vancouver Island to pick them up and bring them back to Sidney. His girl friend, Alma Nujala, took charge of Lempi, while Emil took

Hemmi, whose name had been changed to Aho, with him to work in a logging camp. Alma arranged a job for Lempi, packing cigarettes and cigars in the Winch tobacco factory in Sidney. A year later, the four of them moved to Nanaimo, where the women continued working for a branch of the tobacco company. The men returned to their logging camp and later found employment close to Nanaimo.

In 1915, Emil and Alma married. At the same time, Hemmi decided to work in the Nanaimo coal mines so he would not have to leave Lempi alone for weeks and months at a time. Hired as a contract digger, he did well, and the two moved into a cabin in a coal-miner's backyard in the south-end of Nanaimo, while Emil and Alma moved away to a small farm just north of Ladysmith.

In that little coal-miner's cabin, their first daughter Taimi was born on July 16, 1916. Nine months later, her parents bought a four-room house on Nicol Street in Nanaimo, where her sister Helen was born four years later. In that humble house, the two sisters grew up. Lempi died of cancer in it in 1928, and Hemmi lived there until two years before his death in 1959.

Taimi cherished the memories of those early years and recorded them to be shared with her children and grandchildren.

* * * *

My mind is full of happy memories, from childhood on, of picnics in the summer and family dinners during the winter. We were close as a family, and all of us pitched in to work on Emil's and Alma's farm whenever there was work to be done.

Growing up in an Anglo-Saxon working-class neighbourhood, my sister and I picked up the language and values of our peers. Their opinions of what was, or appeared to be, right or wrong carried some weight although we ignored, or tried to, the neighbours' disapproval. When bobbed hair became popular in the mid-twenties, it became a source of censure where we were concerned because Lempi (we called our parents, aunts and uncles by their first names) took us to the barber shop to get a professional haircut of this new style. I had a shingle, layered only at the back, and my sister had a boy's bob which was layered all around the head. Our pious fundamentalist neighbours quoted chapter and verse from the Bible as they lectured us about hair being a woman's crowning glory. It took all the pleasure out of getting a professional haircut instead of the amateur trims Lempi or Hemmi gave us periodically. Because Lempi liked the advantages of short hair, she kept ours fashionably short, even though our neighbours continued to disapprove.

Though we did not live in a Finnish community, which would have given us the support during our assimilation into the Canadian mosaic, we did have contact with the Finnish communities within a fifteen-mile radius from where we lived. There was Chase River, a group of three or four-acre farms about two miles away, with a Finn Hall, and ten miles away there was the North Oyster and Cedar district with larger farms. Then at the top of the hill in Ladysmith, about fourteen miles away, was a group of Finns large enough to support two Finn Halls—one White for the Nationalists, and one Red for the mixture of Socialists and Communists.

We had not been influenced by the different groups, perhaps because we had lived outside the Finn communities, and so, we attended affairs at all three halls where we heard recitations from the *Kalevala*, the Finnish epic poem, as well as songs and plays about the Russian Revolution which had resulted in Finland's establishment as a Republic, free of her Duchy status under the control of the Czars.

In our home and that of our uncle, as well as in those of other Finns, there was an emphasis on Finnish national values in the children's development. But the neighbourhood children were with us for most of those vulnerable, formative years. In our daily tussles on the street and in the empty lot across the road, Helen and I learned to defend ourselves verbally whenever we were at odds with other children.

I remember talking through the fence when I was about two years old with our Scottish neighbours' children.

"What's your name?" asked Cilia and Jack McArthur.

"Taimi."

"What's your mother's name?"

"Lempi."

For a number of years after, I was called "Taimi Limpy". I would protest, but it seemed the entire McArthur clan (there were ten children) would remind me that I had said my mother's name was Lempi. I would agree and try to explain that it was my mother's Christian name. It didn't help. Mrs. McArthur called my parents Mr. and Mrs. Lempi for a good few years until she learned from someone with more authority, probably my dad, that our surname was Aho. That Aho name didn't bother me because I already had my name of Taimi to contend with, but my sister still has many unpleasant memories of being called Helen Yoo-Hoo, Helen A-ho, Ah-ha, A-hol and many more variations. She wished many times that it could have been Smith, Brown or Jones. I recall wishing at some early period of my life that my parents had been able to take my maternal grandmother's name of Sandelin. There were so many Finns whose names ended with *Maki* which means "hill" in English. Many had kept only the *Maki* ending as a surname, while others had changed it to Hill. With so many of these names in use in Finnish communities, my mother's maiden name of Lauttamaki did not appeal to me as an alternative to Aho. Not that I had any choice.

On my first day of school, my teacher Miss Case suggested it would be much simpler for everyone concerned if I used my second name of Esther instead of Taimi. I wouldn't agree. I have vivid memories of my six-foot-one-inch father bending down and saying I could be Taimi at home and use Esther as my school name. I wanted so much to agree, because I felt Esther was, and is, a beautiful name, but I could just hear two of the neighbourhood children, Billy Hudson and Jack McArthur, who were enrolling that year, jeering: "Yah, yah, had to change your name to get into school!" So I adamantly refused, and Miss Case graciously enrolled me, and called me Taimi.

When I was three or four, I noticed another cultural difference—the curiosity the Anglo-Saxons had about the human body. The words "bare naked", spoken in whispers had a mystique and allure to all my playmates. When I commented that I had seen my parents naked, they called me a liar and demanded proof that I had. Quite innocently I informed them that we were all naked in the sauna, and besides, I helped my mother wash my father's back every day when he came home from the coal pit. There were no washrooms in the Canadian Colliery mines in those days.

Some subtle division of "them" and "us" occurred in my

mind, probably because I did not like the insistence on details about nakedness. Though I hated being called a liar, as I was many times, about other differences in viewpoints and our way of life, I shut my detractors up by firmly declaring that they did not know what a sauna was and therefore, they knew nothing about being really clean.

To this day I have many lovely memories of going to the big, old, smoke sauna on Emil and Alma's farm. Both families went together, including my paternal grandfather, whom Emil and Hemmi had arranged to bring out from Finland in 1924 at the age of sixty-four.

An older brother Justus had contracted, according to Finnish tradition, to look after Vanha Papa in return for legal control of the family farm. Unfortunately, Justus was ill and had over a dozen children whom he could barely feed, and so Vanha Papa's care was taken over by family in Canada. On the land, many Finns still follow this custom of *Kaupe Kirje,* a legal contract whereby the master of the household divides his assets among his offspring, assigning the bulk of the estate to the son, who undertakes to supply lodging, food, clothing and a proper burial for his parents. The change of the head of the household usually occurs when the master is in his fifties, and it is his decision when this change will occur. When I visited Finland in 1964, my uncle Lauri, who was sixty-four, informed me that my twenty-six-year-old cousin Reijo was the *isanta* or head of the household.

As the first child of immigrants, I had more family influence than my Anglo-Saxon friends. I was continually explaining to my parents the customs of my playmates and their parents, from my point of view. At times my parents challenged and even reprimanded me, but on the whole, they listened and questioned me for more information. I was also the family interpreter. Whenever pedlars came to the door, I translated for my mother, and became quite adept at politely refusing to buy anything or attempting to tone down the bargaining process as my mother haggled over the price. At times it embarrassed me, and to this day I cannot bargain.

On one occasion when I was eight years old, I learned I didn't know everything. We had chickens in a corner of our back yard, and my mother gave me some fresh eggs to exchange for a tin of peas and a tin of lye at a nearby grocer's. I argued with her that "lie" mean *valehtella*. Lempi insisted that she needed lye, so I went reluctantly to the grocer who welcomed the fresh eggs, gave me the peas and listened patiently when I said, "A tin of 'lie'—my mother doesn't seem to understand that 'lie' can't be bought in tins."

His answer: "Aye, lass, but it can. This is a different kind of lye," was the beginning of my realization that some words which sounded the same had different meanings. I began to differentiate between homonyms. When I was given the words "pane" and "pain" in a grade-three class during spelling period, I had a flash of insight. Previously I had puzzled about how a window could have a pain.

The disagreements between us and kids of other nationalities continued. In some altercation with our neighbours' visiting cousin, I was called a "Dirty Hun". I yelled, "We're not dirty. You can eat off our steps, but you can't say that about yours!" After my verbal riposte behind the safety of our back fence, I ran inside to tell my dad about it, and to ask him what a "Hun" was. *He* certainly knew that some of their fathers still signed their names with an "X" because they couldn't write their names, let alone read. Eventually I learned that "dirty" had many connotations.

School was a pleasant experience, but I soon realized from grades one to four at the South Ward and Middle Ward Schools that I was mediocre in all sports activities such as football. However, I was a top pupil in class. When I moved up to the Central School, I found myself in a heterogeneous social group. I still continued to lead the class in rank each month, but now I was in contact with a new-to-me breed of girl. The merchants' and white-collar workers' children had more extensive vocabularies, and while most were friendly, some girls looked down on coal-miners' kids. I was too busy making friends to feel the digs, but in retrospect I realize some of my friends with Czech, Slavic or Italian names were more sensitive to the negative comments.

In grade six I was assigned to a double desk. My seat partner was Annie Hynek, a very attractive olive-skinned girl of Czech origin. Curious about her surname, I asked her what its national origin was. Her comment startled me. "My sister's skin is as fair as yours."

In grade seven, I was embarrassed for a classmate called

Angelo, who was loudly berated by the teacher, and told not to eat garlic during lunchtime because it was not fair to those who sat around him.

I was fortunate in always being sensibly and adequately clothed. My mother sewed and had an innate sense for combining current style with quality material. Somehow, from my parents peasant background I learned to value common sense. At no time did I feel inferior or superior in dress, although my sister definitely had an inferiority complex where clothes were concerned. Her apparel seemed to me to be as good as anyone else's, but I know that those teen years could be awkward for most kids and could be worse for those who had reason to feel inadequate in any way. Living in the south end of Nanaimo had prepared me, so I could feel good about myself and good about the strengths and weaknesses of my peers. No, I couldn't run as fast as Cilia, nor sing as well as she did, but I excelled academically. My neighbourhood friends shared their homes and church with me and in addition, I had my home, my uncle's home and the Finnish community for warmth, love and much variety of living experiences.

My parents enjoyed their new home and became Canadian citizens as soon as they could. Lempi was homesick at times and reminisced about friends and relatives in Multia. She wrote many letters and sent snapshots Hemmi had taken with our box camera. Hemmi was happy and commented on many occasions on the freedom he had found in Canada. As a child in Finland, he had been taught to bow to everyone. Here he had the respect of his fellow workers, who called him Harry. He was among the last of the contract diggers and always had miners hoping he would select them as partners.

He participated in the Finnish community's affairs, mostly as a member of the general public, and joined others at picnics and social functions. He was treasurer of the United Finnish Brothers, Chase River Chapter, for many years. As a representative of this group, he traveled to Astoria, Oregon, and Seattle, Washington, on many occasions. He certainly was proud to be a Canadian and happy to be recognized as a good and loyal employee. Although he could have visited Finland, he never did. He always maintained that he wanted to keep his memories of Multia intact, without the distraction of the changes he had missed over the years. Had Lempi lived, he probably would have visited more than once.

In 1964, I returned to my roots in Finland, to meet my mother's brother, two of her sisters, and many cousins in Multia. I returned in 1973 to renew our friendship, and I shall go again. I have traced my roots back over two hundred years on both sides of my family, through male and female lines of descent in the Lutheran Church records—a meticulous documentation of births, deaths and marriages.

We have always been grateful for what Canada has done for our family. Both my sister and I graduated from Provincial Normal School in Victoria, and became teachers. In 1968, I graduated from the University of British Columbia with a Bachelor of Education Degree.

Emil and Alma's son, Aaro, graduated from the University of British Columbia and received his PhD from Stanford in 1954. He became head of Dynasty Explorations and founder of the Anvil Mines in the Yukon. Forty per cent of the Yukon's economy comes from the mining industry and from the mines Aaro was instrumental in developing. Mount Aho was named in his honour, and on top of the mountain, Aaro placed a memorial to his immigrant parents, Emil and Alma Aho (Kekalinen), who made the family's most significant contribution to the Canadian mosaic by emigrating to this country and working hard to build it up.

EVACUEE

by
Milly Charon and Patricia Thompson
from an interview with Patricia Thompson,
and a newspaper article by the interviewee,
courtesy of *The Gazette* (Montreal)

To the eye of the casual observer, the scene at any one of the mainline railway stations in London, England, during the month of September, 1939, appeared to be an episode from a twentieth-century version of the Children's Crusade. As far as the eye could see, were straggling lines of children, many carrying small valises, and all of them tagged with clearly marked names and destinations. A gas mask in a small, square cardboard case hung from a strap around each child's neck. It was supplied by the British government which had organized a civilian evacuation plan as early as 1934, in order to reduce casualty figures in the event of enemy bombing.

Three successive waves of evacuation between September, 1939, and June, 1944, would move over four million women, children and disabled adults to relative safety by billeting them in remote country areas away from obvious danger zones in major population centres.* A separate plan to send large numbers of children overseas was aborted after the *City of Benares*, a ship loaded with refugees and evacuees, was sunk on September 17, 1940. Although the War Cabinet was unable to provide convoy escort and could no longer approve the official evacuation scheme of children to Canada, Australia, South Africa, New Zealand and the United States, nonetheless many parents made private arrangements. About 2,664 children were already overseas before officials

* Richard M. Titmuss, *Problems Of Social Policy, History Of The Second World War*, HMSO and Longmans, 1950. Reproduced with the permission of the Controller of Her Majesty's Stationery Office.

171

halted the British plan, and 11,000 evacuees left the country by private arrangements.

In most cases, this uprooting from family and friends would prove to have a devastating effect on the emotional well-being of the young evacuees—an effect that could not have been foreseen in 1939. Many children saw their parents' desire for safety as a form of rejection. They felt betrayed, unable to understand that the deadly rain of destruction and death falling from the skies during bombing raids and later, V2-rocket attacks, would level entire areas. The psychological effects of maternal deprivation were not to be examined and analyzed until years after the war. In some cases, children from poor neighbourhoods were billeted in middle and upper-class homes. Others from middle-class families were placed in environments inferior to those they had come from. There is no doubt a number of children were exploited or abused, and that the allowance the government provided for their room and board was shamefully misused.

When the authorities judged it safe for the children to return, they did not take into account that there would be a second wave of evacuation traumas. There were cases where children came back to a bombed-out house or to a mother living with a stranger claiming to be their new father. Many children had been orphaned, losing a mother to the enemy bombs and a father in active service. A few children were abandoned. Some lost the comfortable middle-class life they remembered, and returned to crowded slum conditions. They found almost alien environments—perhaps previous neglect had suddenly turned to over-indulgence and attention—the result of parental guilt for earlier deprivations.*

The emotional damage was impossible to assess immediately after the war. Years later it was to surface, as the children who survived the evacuation experience began to speak and write about their insecurities and fears with the insights of growing maturity and the hindsights of remembered experience.

* * * *

* *Ibid.*

172

On July 4, 1970, a group of people were having dinner at a restaurant in Knowlton, Quebec. They were Mrs. and the late John Glassco, Patricia Thompson and her escort the late John Richmond. While the other three discussed literary works, Patricia half-listened, her mind in the past, haunted by sad memories. Her father had died a month earlier. Suddenly her eyes filled with tears. She put her hands to her face to hide her distress, but the tears trickled through her fingers.

Richmond remarked coolly: "You shouldn't cry in public. You're British."

Embarrassed, Patricia fished in her purse for a handkerchief. John Glassco, a look of consternation on his face, stared at the other man in amazement, but made no comment.

Five months were to elapse before Patricia realized Glassco had understood and had been moved. A poem dedicated to Patricia arrived in the mail. Her anguish had been immortalized.

On Patricia, Weeping*

Patricia wept. And all the gods, dismayed
At Grief's assault on this their loveliest maid,
Covered their faces—as she covered hers
With slender fingers (O chaste officers)
And sobbed. Aghast, they saw the early reign
Of suffering liquidated in the rain
Flowing from one small heart grown overfull,
And Sorrow's self change and grow beautiful.

John Glassco—from *Buffy*

Christmas 1970   In memory, Auberge du Relais
                                   Knowlton.
                                   July 4, 1970.

*Courtesy of Mrs. John Glassco, used with the permission of William Toye for the Estate of John Glassco.

* * * *

"Britain was at war when I was a toddler.* Like thousands of kids born at that time, I was totally unaware I was living in the middle of a Holocaust. It wasn't until I grew older that I realized my life was in daily danger. When I did discover England was at war with Germany, I thought this state of affairs was normal because I had known nothing else.

"I knew that somewhere across the sea were some bad people called Germans who wanted to invade England. And people at home were always listening intently to the wireless. These Germans wore hobnailed boots and steel helmets and looked very fierce. I knew, because I had seen them on the newsreels whenever I went to the cinema. Anyway, I knew they weren't my friends.

"Every morning I crossed a bridge on my way to school in London. At the end of the bridge was a swastika scrawled on a wall. Along with a host of other children, I'd spit at it in the most spiteful way, almost frightening myself. I knew the sign signified something close to the devil, something hateful. But when I crossed the bridge alone, coming face to face with the swastika, I'd run past it, not even bothering to spit. I feared an evil hand might spring out of the wall and grab me.

"At school I often fell asleep in the classroom after a sleepless night because of air raids. I was never scolded by the teacher. Instead, I was carried out of the class into a small room, specially prepared for war-weary kids like myself. I usually felt ashamed, but I really couldn't help it.

"Sometimes the bell rang during class, signalling we were in danger, or announcing a drill as a rehearsal for an enemy attack. We'd dash out of the class and clatter down the stairs to the school shelter. If we were in the playground when the alarm went off, we had to throw ourselves onto the ground immediately, lying perfectly still, in order to escape shrapnel or debris flying about if a bomb burst nearby. Eyes tightly closed, my head cradled in my hands, I'd wait in frightened anticipation for dropping bombs, expecting to die. As the seconds passed, I'd listen to the droning of

*The following material (from pages 155-161 inclusive) originally appeared in The Gazette (Montreal), November 10, 1979.

enemy planes. Sometimes there were only nerve-wracking silences. We had to learn to act quickly, not to panic in an emergency. Schools were often destroyed during the nightly bombing raids. But there were times when the Germans attacked in the day, their bombs killing children having their school lunch. And so, we couldn't take chances. Our teachers definitely didn't. They prepared us for the worst that could happen.

"Like most wartime kids, I was given a daily dose of cod-liver oil and malt, topped off with some watery milk. I loved the malt but detested the rest. This concoction was intended to combat-malnutrition because of the shortage of food. Chocolate and oranges were things we dreamed about but rarely saw. When we did, they were a real treat.

"Apart from the lack of food, there was another side of war—lice. Perhaps because of the crowded conditions in the communal shelters and the bombed areas, lice menaced both children and adults. At school we were regularly deloused. It was a humiliating experience that most kids wanted to forget. A vile-smelling chemical liquid was poured over their heads or their hair was shorn off.

"Chewing gum was a mania with most of the youngsters. It was about the only thing that seemed permanent. Like the children following the Pied Piper, we'd trail after American servicemen, pestering them wherever they went, shouting out: "You got any gum, chum?" A piece of chewing gum dangled in front of us was enough to make us commit even treason, if necessary, to get it. We'd exchange all sorts of things with each other for gum: cigarette cards, marbles, penknives, ribbon, even a headless doll—our most valuable possessions. We'd often transfer one piece of gum from one child's mouth to another's until it was utterly tasteless. Gum chewing was deplored by our teachers and completely forbidden. Anyone caught was severely reprimanded, but we were hooked. Even punishment was a small price to pay for the delight we got from chewing gum.

"As a Londoner, like thousands of other people, I suffered the nightly air raids. I'd snuggle down into my bed, hoping to get some sleep and dream about rabbits. Yes, I really loved rabbits, having read *Bre'r Rabbit*, a favourite childhood book. I'd imagine myself visiting them in their burrow, having tea. I'd be even so kind as to do the washing up. Too often, jolting me out of these reveries was a siren wailing in my ear. I'd jump out of bed and fumble for my slippers. In the blackout, I'd grope my way to the Anderson shelter half-buried in the back garden.

"Decamping in the middle of the night was something of an art, and most people in England became quite adept at these manoeuvres. As soon as the siren went off, the whole household would awake, scrambling for their lives. Sometimes I didn't have time to get to the garden shelter, so I'd throw myself under the dining-room table. Lying in the dark, I'd clutch my gas mask, anxiously listening to droning death-threats above us.

"The shelter, shaped like a galvanized metal igloo, was usually damp, musty and cold. Spiders and cobwebs were every-where, even though it was regularly used. I often felt claustropho-bic, and the sound of the German bombers filled me with terror. If we expected to be up all night, cocoa would be made before going into the shelter to warm us, and we took along lighted candles, to dispel the dark during those nightly ordeals.

"After the 'All Clear', I'd stumble out of the shelter usually shivering from the cold night air. Sometimes the moon lighting up the garden created an eerie atmosphere. A huge silver barrage balloon, shimmering in the moonlight, was always there floating impassively, as though hanging by a thread in the sky. It almost seemed human, like an old man tired of war. I'd look up, and searchlight beams would still be dancing across the sky. I'd feel strangely disturbed by the idea that German airplanes had previously been circling among the clouds trying to destroy us. Picking up bits of shrapnel around the garden, I'd wonder why people wanted to kill each other. It was such a silly way to pass the time, I'd think, returning to my bed. I pretended it was a bad dream.

"On one occasion I suddenly lost a slipper during one of those swift nocturnal flights. Because our garden shelter was in poor condition, we had been heading for a big communal one on the other side of the bridge. Breaking away from my family, I turned and ran back to the bridge where I had lost my slipper. My sister Maisie dashed after me and caught me, dragging me by the hand to the shelter. It was a lucky escape because the bridge was hit by a bomb. I practically fell into the shelter, crying because of my lost slipper, not realizing that had I not been prevented from returning,

I would have been killed. That night a block of flats nearby was hit, and most of the people living there were casualties.

"One Christmas morning I awoke to find myself covered in glass. During the night my bedroom windows had been blown in by a bomb explosion. The few toys I had were stolen by someone who had sneaked in while I slept. It was a dismal Christmas.

"Bombed sites became our playgrounds. Away from the grown-ups, we'd create our own little fantasy-world substitutes. Somehow we'd try to put order into our otherwise chaotic lives. We'd build small playhouses out of bricks picked up from the charred ruins. Sometimes the walls would be as tall as we were, and we'd top them off with a tin roof. If some kid found a kettle or even a battered saucepan, we'd attempt to make some cocoa which somebody had discovered in one of the ruined houses around the site.

"In our family, my sister Maisie was the most tragically affected by the war. She was a young wife whose husband Jimmy was in the Royal Air Force. He was a handsome man, over six feet tall, with hair as black as a raven. Whenever he came home on leave, he loved surprising her. Instead of coming through the front door, he'd climb through one of the bedroom windows. Sometimes I spotted him first. Still wearing his RAF uniform, he'd put a finger to his lips, silencing me. I'd giggle with delight as he stole into the kitchen where my sister was usually to be found, and give her a loving embrace. He adored her. I'd run around him, begging for attention, which I usually got. His arrival always changed our previously drab lives to something exciting. While my sister was preparing a meal, he'd play hide-and-seek with me. I always found him. I'd jump up and down with such joy, my voice echoing throughout the house: 'I've found him...I've found him'. These moments were the happiest of my early childhood. He was my hero.

"Clutching a teddy bear he had brought me, I went with my sister finally to the station to see him off when his leave was up. Pinned to his uniform jacket was a small pair of baby's booties my sister had knitted for their first child, a daughter. They were his good-luck charm which he always wore on missions. As the train began pulling out, he leaned out of the window and waved good-bye. As if gripped by some feeling of foreboding, as soon as the train was out of sight, I suddenly threw myself down on the dirty platform, crying hysterically. It was the last time I saw him.

"A few weeks later, the police arrived at our house with the fateful telegram. I remember following my sister to the door, and watching her open and read it. From the shock on her face, I knew it was bad news. She immediately began to shake, her whole body shattered by this flimsy piece of paper. Holding her baby daughter, she suddenly turned pale, and I thought she was going to faint. She called out to the elderly couple living upstairs in their flat and asked them if they would mind taking care of the two children until she got back. I watched her being driven off in a police car.

"While my sister was gone, the couple looked after us. Sitting on the edge of the sofa, I began crying, sensing something was wrong. Looking around the room, I began staring at a horrific painting of a First World War battle scene of dying horses and men. Eventually, the monotonous ticking of the clock sent me to sleep.

"It seemed an eternity before I saw my sister again. When I did, I learned the devastating news that her husband, whom I adored, had died in her arms. He was twenty-five years old. He'd been hit by bullets from an enemy plane's machine guns on his way back from a raid in Germany. He managed to nurse his plane back to England where it crash-landed. He held on to life long enough to see his beautiful wife for the last time. My sister was grief-stricken. I was inconsolable. As a widow of twenty-two, she was left with one child and was pregnant with another which he would never see.

"As the bombing escalated and became even more dangerous, I suddenly had to leave London as an evacuee. I was sad to be separated from my sister who had given me the parental love I needed since my mother died when I was three. I seldom saw my father, who was in the Home Guard.

"In an English village, I became an evacuee along with other kids. I was placed for one year with a miner and his wife. The Frosts had a daughter Beryl, who was about eight years older than I and had ginger-coloured hair. Their house was untidy and dark, a layer of coal dust showing on the dingy curtains and on the peeling wallpaper. Through the window I could see birds trapped in snares, in the garden, some still twitching as they lay dying.

"The following day I went to school and during the lunch break, I ate my sandwiches of white bread and cooking lard in the cloakroom. They made me feel like vomiting, so I chewed the crusts and tossed the rest under the large chest used for the children's galoshes. Then I went outside to the school playground and began to outline a hopscotch on the gravel with a twig. No sooner had I finished than the other children encircled me and stamped out the lines. They called me a filthy foreigner because of my London accent. Suddenly a heavy-set girl punched me and dragged me to the ground by my hair while the others proceeded to kick me all over. When they had finally finished with me, I had two black eyes.

"A few weeks later, the class teacher indignantly asked who had thrown bread under the chest in the cloakroom, which had been invaded by a colony of mice. When I didn't say anything, she stormed across the room, dragging me by the collar to the front of the class. She scratched the nape of my neck so hard it began to bleed. As she hysterically accused me of being the culprit, since no one else ate doorstep-sized sandwiches with suet filling, her spit sprayed my face. Afterwards she slapped me across the face and thumped me violently in the back. Through my tears I could see the children deriding me because the teacher had implied that my sandwiches signified I was a social misfit and not the type one welcomes into the family circle. When I tried to hit back, she quickly threw me out of the class. It was hours before I dared go back to the Frost house.

"Things were no better there. Once Mrs. Frost became enraged because I revealed to a neighbour that I had no pyjamas after I had been ordered to bed as a punishment. She grabbed my hair and pulled me down the stairs. As my back hit each step, I felt sharp pain shooting along my spine. In the living room she abused me even more, finally boxing my right ear which began to bleed. When I cried, she threw me out into the cold, dressed only in a little woolen vest that came just a few inches below my waist. I was almost frozen when I was finally allowed in.

"The following week I was hired out as cheap labour, forced to pick potatoes in the bitter cold for two shillings and six-pence. A lorry picked me up at dawn, and inadequately dressed as I was, I worked in the cold of the early morning, occasionally losing my shoe in the mud, running after the tractor unearthing potatoes. The money I earned was taken from me and transferred to Mrs. Frost's pocket.

"Whenever the miner's wife went to the market, she locked

me in. I was forbidden to play with my school friends. She also stole money my sister sent her for my welfare, as well as my pocket money. Instead of decent food, I lived mostly on bread and cooking fat, a diet which I found so repulsive that I preferred to go hungry rather than force it down.

"My situation was by no means an isolated one. Mrs. Frost made me listen to an announcement she had heard on an earlier newscast. There was a report that a young evacuee had been tied to a bed and been beaten to death. I was threatened the same thing would happen to me. I heard of two brothers, both evacuees, who were living in the area with a man who beat them regularly with his heavy leather belt. They finally fled and hid out as fugitives in the neighbourhood, feeding themselves by raiding chicken coops and garden patches. They hid in barns or hay-ricks, sleeping where they could at night. Both boys were under ten years of age.

"And there were many other incidents of abuse—cases where young evacuees were used as skivvies by their newly found foster parents. I'm sure there were many children who were happy and well-cared for in their surrogate homes, but there were some, like myself, who were not so lucky.

"My sister was completely unaware of my deprived and desolate life, and the authorities must have been lax in checking on the well-being of many of the young evacuees. When my sister came to take me home, she was angry with the woman after discovering how poorly dressed I was. Pale and forlorn, almost on the verge of tears, I didn't believe escape was possible until I finally got into the taxi. As we drove away, my sister instantly took off my hat and threw it out of the window. She gave me a bar of chocolate, the first I'd seen since arriving in the village.

"The war was over. Holding my sister's hand, I walked home through the bomb-scarred streets. I sensed something was different about the street where I had previously played with so many wartime kids. One side of it had been completely destroyed. My sister told me some of my little friends had been killed. My eyes began to sting with tears. Heaven was on the other side of death, so I believed, and that's where my playmates were...with the angels.

"On the threshold of a new life without war, I was home at last!"

* * * *

"I had first heard of Canada when I had been at the village school. One wintry morning, the teacher called me to the front of the class and handed me a large box containing a light brown, woolen dressing gown with a golden-yellow collar. I was ecstatic. I didn't know that my gift was one of hundreds of parcels sent to wartime British children by Canadians. When I learned the origin of the parcel, Canada was a name I would remember.

"As I grew up in the aftermath of the war, I discovered London was full of surprises. My first glimpse of bananas hanging in a shop window was a revelation. My first pair of nylons was so precious that I kept them in an empty jar to protect them from snags. I found a job and when food and sweets were no longer rationed, chocolate became a weekly passion I satisfied each payday. As a shy and insecure teenager delighting in things I had never had before, I still cherished the symbol of Canada's generosity. That dressing gown, many sizes too small, continued to hang in my wardrobe. It was a constant reminder of a time when clothes had been a luxury. Canada and her gift became synonymous with love.

"After the war, I again heard many people speak with great affection about Canadians. It never occurred to me that one day I would work and live in Canada—the country that had left such a deep impression on me as a child. It was some time before I realized that more value was placed on ability than social pedigree in Canada.

"I chose to leave England because I was angry—angry about the spirit of dissatisfaction and apathy I found in the people. The system of class and privilege was something that upset me, too. Ordinary people like myself were forced to suffer discomfort and privation while those with titles and family connections moved ahead and looked down on us. Everything I saw disturbed me. I even found the content of most of the daily newspapers distasteful. They were, and still are, plastering pin-ups across their pages and raking up sex scandals—pornography for the masses. I often felt that daily doses of near-nudity were an insult to the intelligence and sensibility of readers.

"Because I had been born on the wrong side of the social

* *Ibid.*

and economic fence, I was supposed to accept this situation without questioning it. I longed for more stimulating contacts, but I had neither the money, the right address, nor the social background to move in more cultural directions. I tried to take foreign language classes after work to fill the need, but I finally realized that my problem was that I had a mind at war with my environment. To get off the social treadmill, I would have to change my way of life and leave England. I reached this decision after I overheard a talented young writer being told he would never get anywhere because he did not have an accent that would receive social approval. Traumatized, he began taking elocution lessons to learn acceptable diction.

"Another example of the daily snobbery encountered in many walks of life surfaced when I spoke to an English gentleman who wanted to buy some property in London. When I suggested a suitable place, not far off, with a lovely view of the Thames, he answered: 'I can't live there. It would mean I'd have to drive through a working-class area.'

"I was shocked. This remark was further proof of the caste system in England. After two world wars and after hundreds of thousands of Englishmen had died for freedom, England still had not abandoned her feudal ways. The class system produced a structure of second-class and third-class citizens subservient to a ruling class, although the post-war government was Socialist. I found the existing system snobbish and abhorrent, and it should have been dismantled years before. I could never understand how millions of people passively accepted a hereditary place in society and continued to accept an inferior style of living. It pained me to see so many people born into poverty offer no resistance to their lot, never struggling for anything better.

"Of course, there were some exceptions—people who possessed an incredible determination or talent to escape from their disadvantaged backgrounds. I decided I was going to be one of them. And I chose Canada because it appeared to be a country free of social prejudices. Although it was difficult for me to leave my family, I decided to emigrate to find a more meaningful existence. I wanted to embrace life, not retreat before it.

"Soon after, at a London railway station, I tearfully hugged my relatives. Just before the last goodbye, a sudden moment of panic seized me. I wanted to run out of the station and return home.

To prevent this from happening, I steeled myself, cutting short my farewells and boarded the train. I entered a compartment and settled myself. But the attempt to hide my feelings only heightened my stress during the final moment of departure. Somebody knocked on the window, and I turned to see my family waving goodbye. As the train pulled out of the station, I smiled back with tears trickling down my cheeks.

"When I reached Liverpool and made my way to the docks, the sight of the gigantic ship *Empress of Canada*, looming over the quay, made me feel more alone than ever. I was aware that I was beginning an adventure that would lead me to prosperity or poverty. On the quay, porters were busily struggling with mounds of luggage. There was something dramatic and emotional about the sight of a trans-Atlantic liner, carrying hundreds of human beings to a new country and a new life.

"Once aboard, I knew there was no turning back. I noticed people around me forming groups, as though searching for human contact. Eventually the ship became a floating island of committed exiles, as we swung away from the land and moved into the estuary leading to the high seas. I heard a Salvation Army Band strike up "Land of Hope and Glory", the music drifting from the pier across the widening strip of water.

"I was on my way.

"The voyage was uneventful, and a week later I caught my first glimpse of Montreal as the ship reached its destination on the St. Lawrence River. It was a sunless day, and a grey mist engulfed the ship as it neared land. I stood on the deck waiting to disembark. Most of the passengers were excited, but became tense as Immigration officials began checking our passposts. When I handed mine over, I was in a state of anxiety, expecting immediate deportation because of my limited funds. I had been permitted to take only $125 with me. England was going through a period of austerity, and monetary restrictions had been placed on immigrants and tourists leaving the country. Although I was convinced I would be turned away, nonetheless I was ready to battle for the right to enter the country.

"I had to convince a disbelieving Canadian Immigration official that I was quite capable of finding a job and that there was no chance I would fall into bad company or become a burden on the taxpayer, as his sceptical glance implied. The fact that no one was waiting for me on the dock didn't make things easier. I knew I was taking the biggest gamble of my life, and I had to brace myself for a letdown.

"Reluctantly, the Immigration official finally gave me a landing-pass and with it he handed me a piece of paper with a woman's name and address. It offered accommodations until I found my own apartment. Rather than take a chance of going there and not finding a vacancy, I decided to spend my first evening in Montreal at the YWCA on Dorchester Street. It was a restless night. I checked out early the next morning, stopped for some breakfast and took a taxi to the address I had been given by the official. It turned out to be a large family residence converted into a boarding-house, in the east of Montreal. Although it was in a poor neighbourhood, it wasn't unpleasant, with shade trees growing on either side of the street.

"The lady who owned the boardinghouse was Belgian, and she was a good cook. When she asked me for two weeks' rent in advance, I paid her for both food and lodging. I had very little money left. Fortunately, within forty-eight hours of my arrival I found a job working for a newspaper. And a good thing, too. By the time I received my first pay cheque, I had exactly one dollar left to my name.

"On the first evening at the boardinghouse, I sat at the dinner table with ten men. I was hungry, but I felt overwhelmed yet fascinated, eating with a lot of strangers. When the landlady appeared from the kitchen, redfaced and damp from the heat of her stove, I was relieved. Her presence helped lessen my embarrassment at being the only woman at the table. These strangers, hungrily tucking into their food, reminded me of the guests at a wedding feast in a Breughel painting. Their faces were weather-beaten and brown, glowing with health, probably from working in the open air. I listened to them speak and realized they were French, not Quebecois.

"I sat next to a seemingly sensitive young man named Jean-Claude from Brittany, who thought himself superior to his table companions. He kept himself aloof, eating slowly and sparingly. He appeared to lack the wholesomeness and vitality of the others. He was pale and slim, with light green eyes and curly brown hair.

"I didn't know then that I would eventually flee from the boardinghouse in fear of my life. Although I had never dated this man and we saw one another only at the dinner table, he began relentlessly pursuing me and kept asking me to marry him. When I spurned him, he put threatening letters under my door. A woman alone was definitely at a disadvantage in such an environment. As soon as I received my first pay cheque, I moved out. Somehow he discovered where I had gone and followed me. Several times on the street going to or coming from work, I would catch a glimpse of him half a block behind me. I lived in terror and moved again and again until I finally shook him off my trail. It was a poor beginning of a new life, but slowly things began to change.

"When I had first arrived in 1969, I was terribly shy with an ego the size of an undernourished gnat. The war years had left my nerves in bad shape, but the more accustomed I became to Canada, the less nervous I felt. I gained weight and felt relaxed, perhaps because there was no vestige of the British class-system to disturb my peace of mind. I met all kinds of people, including journalists, academics, writers and poets—people to whom I could relate. Montreal was throbbing with creative activity in those days, offering something I wanted to be a part of.

"The news of my father's death in a London hospital was the catalyst that precipitated a period of emotional devastation—a black depression—from which I was to emerge stronger and more determined than ever to succeed in my new country. I applied to Concordia as a mature student in 1979 and in five years earned a Bachelor of Arts and a teaching certificate while holding down a full-time job. But something was missing, and after sixteen years in Canada I realized there was something I had to do.

"I had to return to England. Although I had found Montreal one of the most beautiful and inspiring cities to live in, I always felt there was a weakness here. It was frustrating for me because I couldn't fulfill my potential as a writer. This is really the only reason I'm leaving the country. I feel only half of me is functioning. The other half is still spiritually rooted in England. I admit I actually found myself here. I discovered I could write, I met marvellous people and found that I was able to handle myself well in the academic environment. And I do love this city, because I've been accepted here for what I am, and not for where I come from or whom I know.

"Unfortunately I can't find writing outlets here with newspapers and magazines closing down at an alarming rate. There is a wider market in Britain—more papers and magazines. There are only two English-language daily newspapers here, and magazines operating out of other cities are really not interested in what is happening in Montreal. An anglophone non-fiction writer, especially a middle-aged one, is very restricted in Quebec.

"I'm sure I will have to go through a readaptation process again, but my return to England will be like the rediscovery of an old land. I know I've changed and so has England, but I'm looking forward to exploring a new scene. It is difficult for me to say that I'm going home, because Montreal has been my home for over sixteen years. I feel, instead, that I am returning to my roots, but I have left some options open. I'm a Canadian citizen now, and I want to keep my ties with Canada.

"I shall always remember the country that gave me such great warmth when I needed it the most. Some day I shall be back to visit, and until then, I have photographs and memories which will keep alight the love I feel for Canada."

MORE THAN ANYONE COULD ASK

by
Miodrag Brkic and Milly Charon

Babi Yar, Katyn, Lidice and Oradour-sur-Glane sound like part of a list of small towns in a gazetteer, but those who survived the Second World War and had lived in the vicinity of those places, know only too well what they represent. The more publicized and better documented crimes against humanity, perpetrated by the Hitlerian and Stalinist regimes, so overshadowed an atrocity in Yugoslavia in May, 1945, that, to this day, most people are ignorant about the annihilation of tens of thousands of Serbs and Slovenes in Kocevje, a small town in Slovenia, by Josip Broz-Tito and his Communists. For many years, Britain's role as an accessory to this act of horror was concealed, despite survivors' attempts to inform the West.

Miodrag Brkic was one of the lucky ones. His cousin, however, was not as fortunate. He died at Kocevje at the end of May with thousands of other Yugoslavs who had fled the country, only to be returned by the British Army to Tito...and death.

* * * *

Early in life, Miodrag Brkic discovered that war and political ideology had a way of splitting families. The eldest of three brothers, he was born on April 20, 1922, in Velika Krsna, a village in the Sumadija region in Yugoslavia. Fiercely independent and rebellious, Brkic did everything he was forbidden to do.

"You could say I was a devil when I was young," he said. "By the age of eleven, I had acquired an affinity for town life and decided to move to the city of Smederevo, where I had many relatives. I took my dog with me—a dog as tough as I. A year after

189

I arrived, my grandmother ordered me to move with her to another town, Mladenovac, because she felt I should learn a trade or continue my school education. She was convinced I was well on my way to becoming a bum."

Instead, Brkic moved in with another relative, who taught him to become a baker. Within five years, Brkic not only learned the trade but ended up as the town's strongest boy, fighting his way to dominance of his peer-group. However, there was a price to pay for his scrappy nature. His education was neglected. The only subjects he did well in were religion and mathematics. He barely passed the others. But he was ambitious. He was determined to open his own bakery shop and get married, and when he was seventeen and a half, he moved back to Smederevo to start his own business.

He had just arrived when World War II broke out on September 1, 1939.

"I had to return to Mladenovac, because all the men of fighting age, including my father and uncle, were called up for service. As the oldest son in the family, all responsibility fell onto my shoulders, and I had to take over the operation of my uncle's bakery.

"Before he left us, my father gave me instructions on how to care for the family, and he told me to be a good man in case he did not survive the war. From then on, I forgot what it meant to be young; my youth was lost forever."

Although Brkic was working at his uncle's shop and taking care of the family, he was not exempted from war duty for long. He was inducted as a "volunteer" because cooks, bakers and similar skilled tradesmen were needed in the army.

On March 27, 1941, two days after Yugoslavia's Regency Government had signed a pact in Vienna pledging allegiance to the Axis, a group of Yugoslav Army officers, led by General Dusan Simovic, pulled off a coup d'état in Belgrade. They overthrew the Regency in favour of seventeen-year-old King Peter II and reversed the government's former policy. Because of the coup d'état, Hitler postponed his attack on Greece, scheduled for April 1, 1941, and in collaboration with Italy, Hungary and Bulgaria, launched a massive attack on both Yugoslavia and Greece on April 6, 1941.* It did

*Chronology of World War II, compiled by Christopher Argle, Marshall Cavendish Books, London, 1982, pp. 58-61.

not take long for Yugoslavia to capitulate on April 17 and pass under German military occupation. With the Royal Yugoslav Army defeated, Brkic returned to Velika Krsna, his birthplace, to look after his mother and brother.

However, nationalist movements of resistance were already forming, and one day word came that a Serbian Colonel named Draza Mihailovic had not surrendered to the Germans but had organized an army of freedom fighters from local village militiamen, or Cetnici. They came to be known as Cetniks and as early as 10, 1941, they began an open revolt against the Germans.

"I joined their cause. As one of the few people in the village who was an Anglophile, I made up my mind to keep myself informed of the global war picture, and I listened to the BBC from London every evening, despite the danger involved. Had I been caught, I would have been killed."

On June 4, 1941, Germany attacked the Soviet Union and only then did the Yugoslav Communists, led by Josip Broz-Tito, commit themselves to battling the occupation forces. Mihailovic, fighting for the monarchy, and Tito, fighting for revolutionary socialism, could not agree on a common programme of tactics. By November, 1941, the Cetniks and the Communist Partisans were at each other's throats, while fighting a common enemy—Germany.

"It was chaos. The Communist Partisans began killing Germans in different cities. In retaliation, the Germans issued and enforced a ruling that fifty Serbians would be killed for every German soldier injured, and one hundred Serbians shot for every soldier killed. If a German officer was assassinated, two hundred Serbs would die. There were no exceptions. I, myself, saw and heard terrible things about thousands of Serbs who lost their lives because of this type of retaliatory action. In Kraljevo and Kragujevac, a town close to my home, over two thousand people and then another six thousand students were massacred by the Germans as part of their vengeance programme. Pleas for mercy were ignored. The Germans said they had no time to waste in chasing petty bands of reactionaries."

One day in September, 1941, Brkic was listening to a Mr. Harrison speaking on the BBC. He called on the Serbs to rise up and die on the doorsteps of their enemies. He said that Serbs dying for the cause of resistance to the Nazis was like cutting grass—new blades would grow tall and strong in their place.

"Harrison closed by saying that when the masses of Serbs died fighting the Germans, the British people would erect a monument dedicated to us, inscribed with the words: 'Here lies the last Serb.' At first I was greatly inspired by these words.

"The next evening, the Serbian General Milan Nedic made a radio response to Mr. Harrison. My whole village listened intently. He said something like this: 'Mr. Harrison, please come to my country, and I will cut off your head. I want to see if another grows in its stead!'"

Brkic began to understand General Nedic's objectives by hearing more from him. Nedic was organizing a Volunteer Corps to combat the Communist Partisans, in order to prevent the hundred-for-one massacres that were taking place. The Germans agreed to allow him limited movement to hunt out the Partisans. Brkic found himself sympathizing with General Nedic. He thought it was better for a few Serbs to die rather than have a hundred innocent people massacred for one stupid German soldier.

"But then I realized that this was unlike any previous war in history. There were three levels of war. The Allies were fighting the Axis; the Communists were fighting the Capitalists and the Axis; and my countrymen were fighting each other. The ironic twist was that the Allies had the Communists and Capitalists combined—two opposite and opposing ideologies—after the Soviet Union joined the Allied cause. The Capitalists who believe the Communists had the same war objectives were totally fooled.

"Anyone who knows anything about Communism understands that it is a fiercer and more fanatical force than any Fascist threat, and I could never understand how Stalin called to the free world and was so well received."

At the end of 1941, Brkic moved back to Smederevo and remained there until the spring of 1944, when he went to Belgrade to learn radio-telegraphy. He was still a member of the Volunteer Corps. However, on October 12, 1944, he had to flee Serbia and retreated with other Volunteers to Slovenia in the mountains northwest of the country because Tito's Partisans were overpowering both the Cetniks and the Volunteer Corps. In the spring of 1945, while the Allies were struggling up the boot of Italy, Brkic and his groups were again in retreat, this time fleeing into Italy, as Tito's campaign escalated. Both the Cetniks and the Volunteers had been completely routed by Tito and his Partisans.

"A month later, in April, Italy was captured and when Germany surrendered in 1945, I was in Palmanova, Italy, which had been designated as a soldiers' camp for the Yugoslav military. I had to learn the language, and the best way to do that was to date an Italian girl. Shortly after, our camp was moved to Forli, Italy. This was a very crucial period for all of us 'emigrants'. England wanted to return us to Yugoslavia as political criminals, and Tito wanted to execute us. About 20,000 people, men, women and children, had fled to Austria ahead of the Communists. There were thousands of others in camps in Italy, and suddenly around the middle of May, 1945, England made a deal with the Soviet Union and Tito to ship back all nationals to their countries of origin."

The Yugoslavs in Austria were told they were being taken to Italy. Instead they were shipped to Tito. Those in Italy were moved again, many to Eboli in southern Calabria where there was a concentration of Yugoslavian soldiers' camps. At least 20,000 had escaped to Italy.

"At the time, I was a member of the elite Sumadija Division, and General Mihailovic was now my commander. What had happened was that the Volunteer Corps and the Cetniks had formally united in Slovenia to fight a common foe—Communism—in a last attempt to prevent the Communist takeover of our country. However, during this amalgamation, General Milan Nedic had been captured by the British, who handed him over to Tito to be executed without trial."

Luckily for many of the Yugoslavs in Italy, many of the British military were disgusted with what was happening, and sympathy for the plight of the refugees was growing rapidly amongst the British Army Corps. Brkic's regiment was given permanent guard duty in the army camp. When Field Marshal Lord Alexander of Tunis, Commander of the Allied Forces, discovered what had been happening, he ordered an immediate halt to the deportations.

"Soon after, we were sent to Germany by the British to be interviewed by a special commission under Brigadier Fitzroy Maclean. The commission would determine whether or not we would be returned to Yugoslavia for punishment. Over 100,000

Yugoslavs were sent back and executed in death camps, among them my cousin Dragoslav.

"King George VI of England somehow came through and negotiated an amnesty for the rest of us. I later learned that the Archibishop of Canterbury had played a large part in getting amnesty for us in 1947. We were freed and listed as Displaced Persons in the war documents. As a result, I got the chance to emigrate from my now lost homeland to England to work in the coal mines."

Brkic arrived at a time of national rejoicing, when Princess Elizabeth was marrying Prince Philip. After spending the first evening in a hotel, he was sent to Market Drayton in Shropshire to be shipped later to another destination. A doctor, who examined him, determined he wasn't fit to work in the coal mines. Instead he was sent to a farm in Yorkshire where he was to await further instructions. A farmer paid him sixteen shillings a day to pick carrots. In one week he made enough money to buy himself a good pair of shoes and pair of trousers.

"Finally I was assigned a place and moved to Shilton, near Oxford. When I arrived at the camp, I discovered there were many young ladies working on different farms as part of the Women's Land Army. I thought this would be a great time to learn English and promptly found a girl who was willing to teach me the language. I must say my instruction ended up being a lot of fun.

"I spend four years in England, my language ability improving by leaps and bounds. Early in 1951, someone told me of a large, rich and beautiful country called Canada. One day I made it my business to go to London and look for a Canadian Government office. I had no trouble in finding it and was well treated by the staff. When they asked what was my occupation and I said I was a qualified baker, they told me my trade was on the approved list for immigrants. I immediately applied for acceptance. It didn't take long before I received permission. I had managed to save enough money to pay for my boat fare, and I paid my own way across the Atlantic.

"I landed at Quebec City on June 2, 1951, and moved immediately to Montreal. I had been told Montreal was the Paris of North America. However, instead of finding streets paved with gold, I could not find a job. I had arrived with no money, and I spent the first seven days without any food whatsoever. I slept on park benches, and drank water from public drinking fountains. I remember how desperate I was. I tried eating grass and leaves in Westmount Park. I was starving, and my only thought was that if I had any money, I would go straight back to England."

Then Brkic's luck changed. He found a job as a baker's assistant at the Trymore Restaurant on the corner of Ste. Catherine and Peel Streets. He had a difficult time learning about Canadian tastes in food. He had never heard about tropical fruits, and didn't know what coconuts and pineapples were. Many times he almost lost his job because of his ignorance. However, he did not give up, and earned himself a few promotions.

"Shortly after, I met a Montreal-born girl of Ukrainian descent, and on January 20, 1952, we were married in the Russian Orthodox Church on Dorchester Boulevard. She helped me to get a job at the bake shop at St. Mary's Hospital, and a year and half later I left for a higher-paying job at Dominion Structural Steel. I received $1.25 an hour. The following year I became a spray painter and remained so for eleven years. When the firm went bankrupt, I found work as a baker at the Montreal General Hospital for four years.

"My wife Annie and I have a son who is now thirty years old and an electrical engineer. In 1973, after a long and terrible illness, Annie died of cancer. I remarried late in 1974 and with my French-Canadian wife, moved to Hamilton, Ontario, where I found a job as a nursing orderly in a hospital. Five years later we moved to Bramlea where my son found work with Northern Telecom. Now I work as a security guard for K-Mart's Head Office in Brampton."

Miodrag Brkic realized his dream of Canadian citizenship in 1957. He felt great pride in being a Canadian, for Canada had allowed him to immigrate and attain the freedom he had been longing for all his life.

"Canada permitted me to retain my human dignity and my hope in my fellow-man. This country gave me two lovely Canadian girls as wives, a son, and all I possess. For me this is more than anyone can ask.

"And in return, I feel that I have contributed something to Canada as well. I have brought up a son this country can be proud of. And don't forget, I have made two Canadian girls happy by marrying them and looking after them. I bought two houses in Montreal East, a total of ten flats, and repaired and maintained them well. My tenants have always been pleased to have me as their landlord. I have always paid my taxes—too many taxes—and am still paying them. Because I have great pride in self-sufficiency, I have always worked, regardless of low wages and lowly positions. I have never relied on government-support programmes on the grounds that I was too proud to take a low-paying job.

"In addition, I have never had any trouble assimilating into the Canadian way of life. I have made many friends here. Every member of my family is bilingual, something I approve of very strongly. I am also involved in a non-profit brotherhood organization for Canadian Slavs and I am president of the St. George South Slav Benevolent Association which has 150 members.

"I may have encountered a few bits of prejudice, but nothing I would consider abnormal. If my name had been Smith or Jones, then probably a few of the obstacles I came up against would never have happened.

"But if I had to do it all over again, I would still come to Canada without hesitation. Canada is the greatest country in the world today."

FREEDOM WITHOUT RESTRICTIONS

by
Milly Charon
from an interview with Anni Sebag Selinger

By May, 1967, there had developed an alarming buildup of Arab forces around the tiny, beleaguered State of Israel. United Arab Republic President Abdel Gamal Nasser of Egypt had demanded that the United Nations withdraw its 3,400-man peace-keeping army deployed in the Sinai Desert and in the Gaza Strip—an armed force that had served as a buffer between Egypt and Israel ever since Egypt's defeat in the Suez War of 1956.

Syria and Jordan, under Egyptian leadership, mobilized their troops on the north-eastern and eastern borders of Israel. As the world waited anxiously for the tension in the Middle East to decrease, Nasser announced his decision to blockade the Gulf of Aqaba at its entrance—the Strait of Tiran. This action effectively cut off Israel from its vital shipping route to the east, especially its oil supply from Iran.

The blockade was viewed as an act of war, and by June 3, the die was cast. The Israelis had been secretly mobilizing their military forces, and suddenly in a pre-dawn air raid on June 5, 1967, they struck, using surprise to counteract their lack of military presence. With an armed force of mainly civilians—71,000 regulars and 205,000 reservists—the Israelis faced the resources of fourteen Arab nations with a population of 110 million.

Radio and television reporting, and newspaper headlines around the world brought the startling news that Israel had launched its offensive, striking with devastating effect at several dozen Arab airbases in Egypt, Syria, Jordon, and Iraq. Of the Arab warplanes caught unawares on the ground during the first day of battle, 387 were destroyed.

199

Almost simultaneously, Israeli armour and mechanized infantry ripped into the Egyptian-held Gaza Strip, followed by concentrated thrust into the Sinai Desert. Although outnumbered by more than two to one, the Israeli divisions, supported by 900 tanks, smashed through, encircling the Egyptians and leaving a fourteen-mile-long trail of burnt-out wreckage—tanks, trucks, jeeps—and casualties and corpses.

Hailed as the briefest and most brilliantly executed war of the century, the victory was to produce a backlash of retaliation and revenge against Jews living in the Arab world. An exodus of frightened people began leaving, some heading for Israel, others seeking shores as far away as possible from the Middle East. Canada, specifically the Province of Quebec, was the chosen haven of those immigrants whose second language was French. About 25,000 from Morocco alone were to adopt Quebec as their new home.

* * * *

Anni Sebag Selinger had chosen June 5, 1967, as the date to leave Casablanca, Morocco, to visit Expo 67 and two brothers and a sister living in Montreal, who had emigrated a few years earlier when unrest in the North African Arab countries was already beginning to cause unease among small Jewish minorities.

Anni had been born in Meknes, near Rabat, Morocco, and after twenty years had moved with her family to Casablanca. But the prevailing mood of anxiety followed them to their new home.

On the morning after Anni's arrival in Montreal, she awoke to hear the radio announcing the outbreak of the Six Days' War between Egypt and Israel.

"I was shocked," she recalled. "We began to receive bad news from Morocco. People were leaving everything behind them, trying to escape the country. There was propaganda being broadcast that Jews were murdering Arabs, and as a result, Jews in Morocco were threatened by different Arab groups. Many Arabs identified Jews with Israelis, even though the Jews had been born or had grown up in countries outside of Israel. The argument used was that all Arabs were brothers, and Jews were the common enemy. People were hiding in their homes, afraid to leave. The military government closed the airport to prevent a mass exodus."

Soon after, King Hassan appeared on television and radio in an attempt to calm the Arab population. He said that Moroccan Jews had nothing to do with the Middle-East War and should not be harmed. He said they were loyal Moroccan citizens and were to be treated as such.

"I know of stories where people were concealed in their homes, afraid to go out, and their Arab friends brought them food and necessities until the paranoia diminished. I know of some Jews who fled the country, leaving all their possessions behind. Some returned after the crisis had passed, but it was after this time that the major Jewish exodus from Morocco began, much of it headed toward Canada. I myself didn't return. I was afraid. Instead, my sister and two brothers, who were already here, made plans to bring the rest of my family, brothers and parents, to safety in Canada."

At the time, it was possible to apply for landed immigrant status from within Canada. Anni went immediately to Immigration Offices and filled out application forms. The Quebec government appeared ready to accept this large group of immigrants, who spoke French, because their native country had been a colony under French administration for many years. Independence from Colonial rule had been achieved only in 1956.

Anni decided to stay in Canada, not only because of the situation in her homeland, but also because she liked what she saw here. "It was freedom. The moment I entered the country, I felt I had dropped a huge weight from my shoulders—the weight of restrictions in speech, thinking and expression. Finally I felt free, really and truly free. I could say anything I wanted; I could talk to anyone I pleased; I could do anything I felt like doing, and no one would stop me. I didn't feel frightened anymore and afraid that I would be arrested if I did something wrong, however unwittingly.

"Despite what people think, Morocco isn't a democracy. It's a police state. It may have the appearance of a democracy, but the police can arrest you anytime, without any excuse or explanation. We couldn't talk about Israel; we couldn't mention Jews or synagogues, and we couldn't criticize the Royal Family, the government or Arabs in general. Once a week we would listen secretly to the Voice of Israel. We turned the volume of the short-wave radio down very low so that no one outside the room could hear it. Because Israel was considered an enemy of the state, we would have been arrested if caught."

Another restriction imposed on Moroccan residents was a ban on their travelling directly to Israel as tourists. Arrangements had to be made for connecting flights in Europe and thence to Israel. The necessary visa had to be on a separate paper and not attached to the passport, so that there would remain no entry in the passport to show that the bearer had visited Israel. The Israelis knew about this situation and cooperated. They never entered official stamps in any documents carried by Moroccan Jews visiting their country.

"It was probably the same for Jewish citizens of other Arab lands. Had it not been done this way, we would not have been permitted to re-enter our own country with an Israeli stamp showing on the passport. All our movements required this clandestine process, so you can understand what I mean when I say I felt such freedom here because I could express myself without any restrictions.

"Except for this lack of freedom and the all-pervading fear, life had been pleasant and agreeable in Morocco. We had servants, spacious homes, a beautiful climate, and there were magnificent pools and beaches, a relaxed social life and all the amenities that go with the geographical location. There were lots of outdoor sports and year-round swimming because the winter was so short and so mild."

For the closely knit Jewish community, everyday life revolved around the social connections. Everyone knew everybody else.

"Whenever you went out, you were sure to meet many people you knew—on the street, in the cafés and at the cinemas. It was taken for granted that when you went shopping, you had to make time for chit-chat here and there, stop for a coffee during the errands, or for an aperitif and perhaps a walk or drive."

She admitted, however, that for most people in Morocco there was a general ignorance of what total freedom implied, because they had never been out of the country and seen conditions elsewhere. It had been taken for granted that all those restrictions were the normal way of life, and so many people managed to live fairly contented lives.

"Once I was here, I applied for a work permit, and after

three months, received one. Then I received landed immigrant status and became a citizen in 1970. My marrying a Canadian hastened the process.

"I had been a teacher in Morocco, so I continued teaching here for a few years. I taught French in an English school, and then worked as a volunteer in the community for several years. Then I went into office administration and finally opened my own business.

"In all the things I've done, I've been involved in the growth of the community. Anyone who works does give something. Teaching contributes to education, and office work contributes to the business community. Everyone is a productive component of the community and country.

"But more than anything, it's what Canada has given *me*. This country has given me a home and a feeling of comfort through this new sense of freedom, but freedom is like a double-faced coin. It is magnificent to feel that you are protected by the law when you live in this great democracy, but on the other hand, the judicial system allows people too much licence. That is why the crime rate is so high. People know that if they are caught, the penalty is not so severe. This is part of the price we pay for the system.

"Another thing I have received from Canada is a sense of grandeur because the country is so vast. The streets are spacious, the mountains are immense, the trees are big, the sky is unending, and everything is oversize. The feeling I have of Canada is of spaciousness, of size. The rivers are endless, the lakes are like small seas, and there is so much room to move around.

"If I had any criticism, it would be the pettiness of a few individuals. I know it isn't right to generalize, but there are people who are narrow-minded and not tolerant of anyone but their own kind. I have found generally that people are kind, helpful and sociable, but I've come across some bigotry. Because of my foreign French accent, so unlike the Quebecois one, I was told a few times to go back where I came from if I wasn't happy here. It was a rejection, pure and simple, caused by the xenophobia of a few members of the French-Canadian community. The first time it happened I had just arrived and was shocked to hear it. My sister explained the mentality of certain people, but it still bothered me.

"Since then I have been to Ottawa, Niagara Falls, Toronto, Vancouver and Quebec City. I've been in the United States and have never been treated badly. In fact, people who had heard my accent paid me a compliment and asked where I was from. When I told them, they became even more friendly and interested and wanted to know more about my birthplace. Everyone here seems to have a fascination for faraway places.

"As an immigrant, if I had any recommendation to give others on how to adjust, I would say: 'Be patient. It takes a while. There is no secret formula to adapting to another way of life, another culture, another climate. You have to learn to live in them. The best way to adjust is to live this new life to the fullest without resisting.'

"You can't say to yourself you've never done this before or you simply can't bring yourself to do that. That's a type of attitude that makes for unhappiness. Immerse yourself. If you come from a climate where you swam all year round and you find eight months of snow here, don't swim. Do something with the winter, like skiing or skating. Enjoy what is offered. Everything is good, hot or cold. It's just a matter of getting used to it. If you put an Inuit in Morocco, he'd hate it at first. The reverse is true of a Moroccan transplanted to Canada. I feel that since you can't change the culture to which you've immigrated, the only thing you can do is change your attitude. It comes with time. You can't push a button and say: 'Okay, tomorrow I'm going to adjust.'

"I have a pleasant life here. I love Canada, Quebec and Montreal. I like the people I've come across, but who knows if I might not have had the same feeling in another country?

"However, I must say that Canada must be one of the best democracies in the world. Maybe it's not perfect, but comparatively speaking, Canada is, for me, still superior to anything I've known. My family feels the same way. They're very happy, and life has improved tremendously for them.

"I feel my home is here now and when I travel, it's always good to come back here. When I return to Montreal and see the familiar streets, I feel warm inside, even if it is winter and cold. Everything is dear to me, for I've found something here that is so much better than what I had in North Africa."

Editor's Note: Anni Sebag Selinger died of cancer five years ago. This interview was arranged shortly before her death.

ENEMY ALIEN

by Milly Charon
from an interview with Dr. Julius Pfeiffer

With the escalation of the Nazi blitzkriegs in Europe from 1939 onwards, country after country fell to the Panzers. Thousands of refugees fled before the invading German armies to Britain and other countries. The British Government, suspicious of the German-speaking Austrians and German Jews thronging into their seaports, interned thirty thousand refugees as "enemy aliens".

And still they came in a deluge from war-torn Europe, until the internment centres were filled beyond their capacity. Camps on the Isle of Man, originally intended to hold prisoners of war, were crammed with the boatloads of refugees, now to be detained alongside enemy PoWs. The atmosphere of anxiety and crowded conditions amongst the refugees induced the senior British officer in charge, Lieutenant-Colonel S.W. Slatter, to issue a printed statement in German and English.

TO THE INTERNEES OF THE ISLE OF MAN

It is my wish that every man who enters internment on this island shall be assured that nothing avoidable will be done that might add to his discomfort or unhappiness.

It must be obvious to you all that a uniform code of discipline is essential if a community of men are to live together successfully. That code will be mine and will be obeyed. There is, however, a good reason for every order, and there will be no aggression. The officers and troops who are given charge of you are men of understanding. In any case, it is not a British characteristic to oppress the man who is powerless to retaliate, and you will find no one anxious to foster a spirit of enmity which, within the confines of an Internment Camp, can achieve nothing.

My duty is concerned with your security and discipline, but my interest goes beyond this. With the help of my Camp Commanders and their Staffs, I wish every permissible measure be taken that can relieve your internment of its irksomeness. This can only be done with your own co-operation—your own goodwill and orderly conduct. A man's internment is not regarded here as a reflection on his character. He is credited with being a man of good intent until he proves himself otherwise. If he should make the mistake of proving himself unworthy of this confidence, then the reaction on his own treatment (and inevitably that of his fellows) will be his personal responsibility.

There are amongst you men of widely divergent political views and religious beliefs. You will neither find favour nor encounter prejudice from us on this account. My advice to each one of you is to seek amongst yourselves as much ground as possible upon which you can find agreement, and thrust aside from your life here all that will lead to dissension and ill-will.

The measure of your co-operation and good behaviour will decide the measure of your privilege and the consideration shown for your welfare.

In all events, you are assured of justice.

S.W. Slatter
Lieutenant-Colonel
Commandant Isle of Man Internment Camps

1st June, 1940

The prevailing climate of public opinion in Britain during the spring of 1940 indicated a deep mistrust of German-speaking aliens, and latent anti-Semitic feelings toward the refugees. War hysteria had generated an escalating fear that the refugees were a potential Fifth Column in the country, and that if all were not bent on espionage, subversion and sabotage, certainly many were.

As the hysteria mounted in the home country, Britain

appealed to Canada and Australia to take some of their prisoners of war (PoWs) and refugees for detention. However, the British specifically referred to "dangerous men" in their request to Canada to accept custody of about seven thousand PoWs. Three thousand German prisoners of war had been collected, as well as two and a half thousand German civilians domiciled in Britain and suspected of subversive activities. However, bureaucratic bungling created a situation responsible for incarcerating innocent victims of Hitler's barbaric regime alongside their persecutors. Because there were insufficient "subversives" and PoWs to fill the four ships bound for Canada, the British Government made up the number by filling the vacant spaces with refugees.

Four ships—*Duchess of York, Arandora Star, Ettrick* and *Sobieski* left England between June 20, 1940, and July 4, 1940, packed with internees. The *Arandora Star*, torpedoed by a German submarine, never arrived. More than half of its twelve hundred passengers drowned, locked in the holds and unable to escape.

When the other ships finally touched port in Quebec, the authorities were amazed to see a line of teenagers, rabbinical students and a number of Catholic priests and seminarians, who had dared to denounce the Nazi regime, filing down the gangplank, instead of the dangerous enemy soldiers they were expecting. Thirty-five per cent of nearly 2,300 refugees admitted in July, 1940 were between sixteen and twenty years old.

Twenty-two camps had been set up for internees and prisoners of war in Canada. Camps in Quebec, Ontario, and one in New Brunswick absorbed the European refugees from the *Duchess of York, Ettrick* and *Sobieski*. The internees were to spend up to two and a half years in detention.

* * * *

Among the internees on the *Sobieski*, was Dr. Julius Pfeiffer, who had been born in Essen, Germany in 1907 and raised in Dusseldorf. As an Orthodox Jew, his religious beliefs immediately created problems for him when he attended a high school with an enrollment of predominately Catholic students.

"In observance of the Law, I wouldn't write or do class

work on Saturday, the Sabbath, when any labour was forbidden. Classes were conducted on Saturdays as well as on weekdays. Although the school was a good one, there was an undercurrent of definite anti-Semitism," he said.

However, Pfeiffer's commitment to learning overcame any obstacles in his path, and he graduated with top marks, which gave him immediate acceptance into law school.

"At eighteen, I registered at the University of Cologne, where I spent one year, and then transferred to the University of Munich, where I became involved in politics in the Students' Parliament. I was very much in the public eye. It was an uphill struggle because of the twenty students in the Parliament, eight were already firmly committed to the Nazi doctrine."

When Pfeiffer finished university in 1929, he returned to Cologne and passed the first of two bar exams. He received his PhD in law with distinction in 1931, and at the end of 1932 passed his second bar exams *Magna Cum Laude*. On the basis of his high standing in the top two per cent of graduates in the country, he was immediately accepted to the Bench as a judge.

On March 15, 1933, a month and a half after Hitler was elected Chancellor of Germany on January 30, 1933, Pfeiffer was in his courtroom, when a Nazi lawyer walked in with a Swastika pin in his lapel. Although the Nazi flag was already hanging outside the court building, Pfeiffer asked the lawyer to remove his pin. "In my court there are no political sides," he said.

"The lawyer looked at me threateningly and told me I should not have said that. My court recorder warned me the lawyer would make a lot of trouble for me."

Pfeiffer returned home in the mid-afternoon and told his mother what had happened.

"'You were awfully stupid,' she commented bluntly. 'You don't know what's going on in the country. There's a five-o'clock train to Amsterdam. You should be on it.'

"'How can I go, mother? I have to be at the tailor to try on a suit. I have things to do.'

"'You go at five o'clock,' she ordered.

"By evening I was in Amsterdam. On March 15, I had been a judge in a German court, and on March 16, I was just a bloody refugee."

Almost immediately, Pfeiffer volunteered his services to a refugee committee in Amsterdam. It did not take long for him to observe that the Dutch Jewish Congress was not taking political events in Germany very seriously. The Congress encouraged refugees to return to Germany and said the situation would "blow over".

"I didn't like that. I wasn't going back. Instead I made an application to the University of Amsterdam to register as a law student. Two weeks later, I received a letter from the Dean, refusing my request. Places had been reserved for Dutch citizens first. The country was afraid of being overrun by German Jewish refugees, and most European countries, particularily the smaller ones, suffered from this fear of domination by outsiders."

For Pfeiffer, the next seven years were like the "seven lean years" in the Bible. In 1936, he married an old friend with whom he had been in contact during his exile, and later became the father of two sons. He tried to get work, and when he couldn't, he set up his own business in hardware. He lived with a cousin, and conducted his affairs out of his small bedroom.

"The merchandise was under my bed, next to my bed, on top of my bed, next to the door. I had to get used to it. I had no personal life. During the day I walked with two suitcases to stores to sell my products and was told: 'We don't need anything today.' Many times I was rudely ordered to 'Get out!' Just a few years before, I had been a judge; people bowed to me and called me 'Sir'. Now, it was humiliating, but it was a good preparation for what was coming in the future.

"In a strange way, the German invasion of the Netherlands was a lucky stroke for me. It put an end to my struggles as a salesman or I might have stayed that way. I would not have been a success in business. I was inept. But I did learn one thing from it, and that was a system. My three months as a public prosecutor in Germany had taught me how to make order out of confusion...lessons I would never forget."

On May 10, 1940, Pfeiffer's exile in Amsterdam was abruptly terminated. He awoke to the sound of distant artillery bombardment, and turned on the radio to discover what was happening. The shock sent him to his files which he began cleaning out, discarding what he wouldn't need. His wife awoke and looked at him in amazement, convinced he had lost his mind. His first words were: "Let's go to England." At dawn he asked neighbours what was happening. No one knew. When he told them what he had heard, they laughed at his warnings. By the next day, the news reports confirmed the Germans were approaching rapidly.

"Tuesday, May 14, the radio announced the German Army would occupy Amsterdam the following day. The bulletin ended with the playing of the Dutch National Anthem. That was all. Holland had fallen."

The general belief was that the invaders would treat women and children with respect, and so the decision was taken for Pfeiffer to go ahead alone and find some haven where his family could join him afterwards.

In the streets, Pfeiffer could hear alarms ringing everywhere. It was just before 4 a.m. He grabbed his bicycle and in the darkness headed toward the harbour. There was enough light to see as he approached, for the oil tanks at the harbour's entry point were ablaze. He could see the glow of huge fires raging on the horizon in the direction of Rotterdam, which had been bombed. Pfeiffer's mind turned to his friends who had been unwilling to join him. They had felt Germany would•never dare to attack Western Europe. In fact, The Jewish Community Centre, at the first hint of invasion, had advised everyone to stay in Amsterdam and not go to IJmuiden Harbour about fifteen miles north-west of the city. No boats were permitted to leave.

"I succeeded in reaching IJmuiden on my bicycle. The heat and smell of the burning oil tanks added to the confusion. Thousands of people, mostly Jews, were gathered there, trying to escape. Later the harbour police intervened and practically forced everyone to leave the zone and return to Amsterdam. Those who were fortunate in leaving Holland that morning did so against the instructions of the authorities. I was lucky enough to board a small boat, the *Jonge Jochem*, which was filled to capacity with forty people. Two German-Jewish brothers, the Kaufmans who owned a big department store, had paid for the boat and refused to take any money from the many people who had joined the voyage.

"Just after five in the morning on a cloudless day, we were heading for the open sea. The main entrance of the harbour had been blocked by a large ocean steamer which had been sunk by the

Dutch Navy in order to prevent German U-boats from entering. We left the harbour by a second exit, one of the three boats to leave that morning, and later discovered ours was the only one to arrive safely. A second boat was captured by the Germans and all its passengers were placed in a concentration camp, while the third struck a mine. There were no survivors.

"At nine in the evening we arrived at the small fishing village of Lowestoft and were officially welcomed by the mayor. Then fate caught up with those of us who held German or Austrian passports. We were segregated from the rest of the boat's passengers, and taken to Pentonville Prison in London. While this was strictly contrary to the rules of the Hague Convention governing the treatment of civilian internees during wartime, we were told there was no other way of dealing with us. Thus, I concluded as a lawyer, that the conditions of the Articles of War are applicable only in times of peace."

Pfeiffer remained in Pentonville Prison for a full week. When he asked to be given "kosher" food, the Governor told him that the Chief Rabbi for London had given dispensation, and for that reason he could eat anything. He balked at eating unkosher food and as a special favour, one of the guards, sympathetic to his plight, arranged for him to be served potatoes cooked in their skins in a brand-new aluminium pot.

"A few days later, I was visited, at my request, by an Army Captain named Morin, who was the Jewish Chaplain of the prison. His first question was to ask me why I wanted a rabbi, when I was listed as Roman Catholic on the prison records. His amazement grew considerably when I asked him to get my phylacteries which had been impounded. Obviously such a request is an unusual one from a Catholic."

There were quite a few refugees from Holland and Belgium arriving daily at the prison. Some kind of communication among the men was necessary, and so, to compensate for the illegality of the confinement, the authorities allowed an 'open door' half-hour period daily, when the prisoners could mingle and discuss, even criticize their situation.

"When my phylacteries were returned, I passed them along, after my prayers, to my 'shipmate' Max Adler, whose cell was next to mine. A young man occupying a cell in the same wing but on the opposite side and one level lower saw us, and called up to ask if he could borrow them. I threw them quite a distance across the hall. They landed safely and were returned the same way. To this day, I still think of "The Case of the Flying Phylacteries" with amusement."

Pfeiffer had a cousin living in London, Professor Eugen Mittwoch, who had formerly been a lecturer at the Hildesheimer Seminary in Berlin and also *Ordinarius* for Semitic languages at the University of Berlin. When Pfeiffer requested permission to inform Mittwoch about his safe arrival in London, he was turned down by the authorities. It was the period of Dunkirk, and military censorship would not permit the conveyance of any messages. And so, it took more than three months for his wife and his parents to discover that he was alive and well.

A week later, he was transferred with a group of refugees to a transit centre at Kempton Park, near London, joining other civilian internees already there. They remained only a few weeks, and by mid-June were shipped to the internment camps on the Isle of Man.

"I was there only about two weeks. Whatever I had of value on my person had been impounded on my arrival in May. However, after the war when I wrote to England for my property, mainly a sum of money in Dutch gulden, I was fortunate to get the money back. My leather briefcase, which I had received as a Bar Mitzvah present, disappeared—probably stolen. I never saw it again."

Other internees were not so lucky. A British Commandant on the Isle of Man persuaded the two thousand or more prisoners that retention on their person of any valuables was unsafe. Everyone turned over his things to the officer. Shortly after, he vanished. It was years before he was found and courtmartialed.

On July 4, 1940, the *S.S. Sobieski* left Greenock, Scotland, with 548 prisoners of war and 982 internees, none of whom knew what the ship's destination was to be. Julius Pfeiffer was among the internees.

"The Atlantic crossing appeared uneventful. At one time we were told the armed ships in the convoy were trying out depth charges and that we should not be alarmed. Later we were informed that it had been the 'real thing' and not an exercise. A

German U-boat following our convoy had been sunk, and much later we heard that during that same period, the *Arandora Star*, carrying refugee-internees, had been sunk by a German submarine, and there had been very few survivors among the internees."

The *Sobieski* carried a different group of prisoners—German sailors. They seemed to take a perverse delight in tormenting the Jewish internees, who formed about fifty per cent of the ship's passengers. Arguments soon broke out, and the Captain, to maintain order, separated the PoWs from the internees. When the ship docked at Quebec City, the German sailors left the ship to be sent onward to camps in Ontario, where they would wait for the end of the war. Part of the Kitchener Group, as the Jewish internees were called, were to be shipped to Ile aux Noix and the rest to Little River, New Brunswick. To the Internees' dismay, the entire shipload of passengers were marched to a stadium on the outskirts of Three Rivers where they found the German sailors, with whom they had been thrown together on the *Sobieski*. When the sailors saw the Jewish group, they burst into song—an infamous piece in German which translates: 'When Jewish blood drops from the knife, we feel twice as good...'

Pfeiffer and his Kitchener Group were transported to the Little River camp, where they were to remain for a year. The existence of a 'kosher group' of internees, who refused to eat non-kosher food, had made the camp authorities realize that it would be convenient to put these refugees all together in one camp. Ile aux Noix was chosen. Thus the Jewish internees were transferred to Three Rivers for a month, only to be moved again to the internment camp at Ile aux Noix in June 1941, rejoining those 'kosher' internees from whom they had been separated more than a year before.

The 'kosher group' served to emphasize the ignorance of camp officials in not recognizing the difference between Jewish internees and enemy military PoWs. Initially, many of the camp officers and guards had thought that the black hats, beards and earlocks were a German espionage disguise. They were totally unaware of the different gradations of Jewish observance, from non-practising Jews to Conservatives; from Orthodox to Hassidic.*

The group of Jews who observed 'peculiar' customs and

* Courtesy of Rabbi Erwin Schild and *Canadian Jewish Historical Society Journal*, Spring 1981

rituals and demanded strange and even outrageous privileges, not only created confusion and bewilderment in the Canadian camp system, but it also reawakened a latent anti-Jewish prejudice.* A good deal of pejorative and even inflammatory remarks added to the already humiliating experience of being an enemy alien.

In an attempt to prove the authenticity of their religious and ethnic background, the ultra-Orthodox internees participated in a scheme which should have alerted the prison authorities to the error of their detention in a PoW camp. In a demonstration timed to coincide with the inspection by General Panet of Military District Number 4, the Orthodox Jews placed themselves around two large tables. Each man with beard, earlocks and religious books in front of him, stood facing the entrance.

"As the door opened, the sergeant barked: 'Ten-shun!' Everyone froze into the rigid military position, but the Hassidic Jews continued their bowing and bobbing," Pfeiffer recalled, a gleam in his eyes at the memory. "General Panet entered, red stripes on his pants, a red band around his cap, followed by a group of officers, sergeants, corporals and other military officials. The General stopped immediately, looked and looked again, continued on, stopped and looked back. Obviously we had made a big hit. I was in seventh heaven. Surely our release was now only a question of days!

"A few days later we received the answer. A parcel arrived, sent by Army Headquarters Number 4, and it was addressed to the 'Orthodox Group, Camp Three Rivers'. The parcel contained one thousand razor blades, first quality.

**"This was not the only time that the Orthodox Jewish outlook and military administration banged up against one another. Shortly before the High Holidays, 'one prisoner of war' herein designated as F., a former scholar of the Gateshead Yeshiva and today a well-known rabbi of the Lubavitcher Yeshiva in Montreal, was called to Major Razey's—the Commandant's—office. The Major looked very serious.

"'You are plotting to escape,' he accused, opening the conversation. 'This is a very serious offence. You may be moved to another camp for punishment.'

* *Ibid.*
** Courtesy of *Jewish Life Publications*, New York, July, 1973.

"'I?' answered F., 'impossible. I did not do anything against the rules.'

" 'Don't try denying it. We have proof. See, here is the letter you wrote, let's see, to a correspondent in Brooklyn—a cover address very likely.'

"And the Commandant read aloud: 'Dear Friend, do not wait any longer. Send me a "chauffeur"'.

"'See here, you have it very clear. You asked for a chauffeur.'

"Thereupon, in contrast to the seriousness of the charge, prisoner-of-war F. smiled broadly and explained: 'But Major, you read it wrong. We have High Holidays in a few weeks and I asked for a *shofar* and not a "chauffeur". Sir, you read it wrong.'

"And it took the intervention of the Vaad Hoir, the local Rabbinical Council in Montreal and the confirmation of the leaders of the Orthodox group to convince Major Razey that a *shofar* is not used for an escape attempt. A week later, F.'s letter to Brooklyn passed the censors without hindrance.*

"We were still astonished that we, as Jews of German or Austrian descent, who had fled our home countries, could for one minute be suspected of being Fifth Columnists. We tried everything to make the Canadian Government realize that we did not belong in the 'subversive' category. We drew up petitions documenting our past, stating our aversion to Nazism, citing our race, declaring our intention to go immediately to the United States, where nearly everybody in our group had close relatives. No one paid any attention."

Jack Resnic, who served during this period as a guard at the Trois-Rivières camp, was instrumental in alerting the Canadian Jewish community to the injustice of the internment of fellow Jews. He smuggled out a letter from one of the prisoners in his leggings and took it to the Canadian Jewish Congress in Montreal. Slowly, oh so slowly, after initial disbelief, the wheels started turning.

If relations between internees and camp security staff were strained at times, through misunderstanding of cultural and religious differences, conditions at the different camps scattered throughout Quebec, Ontario and New Brunswick were enough to increase the already high levels of emotional stress among the in-

* *Ibid.*

ternees because of their incarceration.

One of the dirtiest and ill-equipped of the camps was in Sherbrooke. It had been an old, filthy and decaying railway repair station, without any of the amenities necessary for the most Spartan of prisons—no beds, no showers and no toilets. When the prisoners first arrived, there was not even a kitchen, no cooking utensils and no plates or cutlery. Food was dumped on the floor in a pile because the building lacked tables. The internees slept on planks on the floor.

Galvanized into action by the disgraceful lack of facilities they were forced to endure, the refugees began building their quarters from scratch. They installed showers and toilets, cleaning and fixing the decrepit building in an effort to make it habitable. They slept in huge rooms with rows of bunkbeds. There was no privacy. They ran their own laundry, allotting tasks on an equal basis. A canteen was set up so that cigarettes and small toiletries could be purchased.

Prisoners were given a choice of how to spend their spare time. They could work, and could also attend classes instructed by other prisoners. The Sherbrooke camp developed an educational programme, using the talents and abilities of some of their highly educated, even brilliant inmates. Among them were musicians, artists, craftsmen and very eminent university professors who taught a variety of subjects. So high were the standards that many of the internees, when released eventually, went on to immediate acceptance into university, earning degrees with distinction.*

The camp at Little River, New Brunswick, had other limitations which created more hardship for the internees. When they were shipped out there after arrival in Canada, the camp was still in an unfinished, even primitive state, in the process of being hacked out of the mosquito-infested bush. Included in the group were men who were rabbis, or had been studying for the rabbinate, before displacement and dispersion by the British authorities. Now these bearded religious scholars became hewers of wood and drawers of water, as the prisoners pitched in to chop down trees and lug them to clearings for use in building a camp compound. Pails of water had to suffice for washing and drinking, until pipes

* Julia Maskoulis, "An Odd Way to Choose a Country", July 12, 1980, courtesy of *The Gazette* (Montreal).

could be laid and a simple plumbing system installed in the camp.

The mosquitoes were one of the worse problems the men had to endure. There were no screens to keep them out of the cabins once they had been built. Pfeiffer, during his sojourn there, had collected money and purchased textile screens as metal ones were unavailable. The result was that neither mosquitoes nor fresh air could get into the cabins. A complaint to the authorities about the situation met with the claim the money which must have been budgeted for proper screens, had been stolen.

However, for most, the worst deprivation was not only the loss of their freedom because of the suspicion that they were Nazi spies, but their isolation from the outside world. Radios and newspapers were forbidden, and the only news the refugees could get was what they wheedled out of the camp guards. A number of men were emotionally affected by the camp experience. They withdrew into themselves, pushed over the edge by the imprisonment and knowledge of the terrible events in Europe. All of them suffered traumatic family losses while they sat out the war, overwhelmed by pangs of guilt at their inability to communicate with the outside, or contribute something significant to the war effort. Depression was a common condition in the camps.

Release was slow in coming, although an uproar had already been created in the Press and the House of Commons in Britain, as a result of the sinking of the *Arandora Star* on July 2, 1940. From the releases, the British public learned for the first time that the internees who had been shipped out had been lumped in with prisoners of war, and that among the casualties were known anti-Nazi leaders and concentration-camp survivors. There was an outcry to stop the indiscriminate evacuation, and to review the cases of those in the process of transit and those already in Canada. Suddenly, citizens' committees joined in the investigation. The United Jewish Refugee and War Relief Agencies, the Canadian National Committee on Refugees and Victims of Political Persecution, the Canadian Jewish Congress, the Organization for Rehabilitation Through Training (ORT), and others, united as the Central Committee on Interned Refugees under Senator Cairine Wilson to do something about the situation.

At the same time, some of the men in several of the camps found other methods to get word to the outside. At the Sherbrooke camp, the internees befriended a guard, gave him gifts and liquor and persuaded him to bring his daughter to the camp after he boasted how beautiful she was. The guard was sympathetic to the internees' situation, and soon the daughter was carrying letters and gifts smuggled out of the camp. Letters went to influential people, including one to Lionel de Rothschild, a member of the banking family, who had connections in the British Government.

The wheels of bureaucracy began to turn a little more quickly, but for Pfeiffer, not quickly enough.

"There were some internees approaching their sixties and seventies, and youngsters who had been sixteen when they were first interned. The older ones felt it was their right to see freedom first, but, strangely enough, the youngsters were released first under a student scheme whereby they could complete their educations, while the older internees had to wait. In addition, we had both intellectuals and craftsmen in the camps, and the latter were released as factory workers and farmers, especially with the help of a training school financed by ORT.

"The intellectuals had to wait, but later achieved distinguished careers after release, and there are many professors in Canadian and American universities, not to mention other prestigious professions, who originally came to Canada labelled as 'prisoners of war' and later identified as enemy aliens. It took three years and more for Ottawa to reclassify them as 'Interned Refugees' (Friendly Aliens) from the United Kingdom. This group of less than a thousand men supplied Canada with a contingent of architects, artists, businessmen, chemists, dentists, engineers, economists, filmmakers, historians, journalists, lawyers, mathematicians, novelists, philosophers, professors, psychiatrists, researchers, religious leaders, sociologists, electronic media executives and even an impresario."

Pfeiffer's anger was directed towards what he felt was insufficient action by the Jewish organizations in pushing for the internees' release. The first and persistent answer to repeated requests by the internees was that the Jewish organizations were busy helping refugees stranded in Southern France and Spain to get to Canada, while those already in camps were safe from the Nazis. Pfeiffer found it hard to believe that Canadian Jewish Congress could not work on two cases simultaneously.

"It reminded me of the situation in Amsterdam in May, 1940, when the German Army was closing in on the city, and all the officials of the Dutch Jewish Congress were completly paralysed with fear, and in need of help, instead of offering it.

"What did arrive in answer to my entreaties for help was a beautiful chesterfield set for the reading room, and thirty to forty daily, weekly and monthly papers and magazines, to bring us up to date with outside events. Unfortunately for our spirits, the Jewish Congress felt compelled to inform us, who were hoping to be released within weeks, that the subscriptions for the reading material had been paid for two years.

"What the camp, and especially the reading room needed, was a good light. The electric power on Ile aux Noix was very poor. The light bulbs were very small and fixed directly below the very high ceiling. When I repeatedly asked for wiring so that the bulbs could be lowered a few feet, the answer I received from Congress was that electrical wiring was unattainable because of the war. Three days after my eventual release, I bought some at my own expense for two or three dollars and mailed it to the camp. Anyone who has spent a few years in a camp can readily understand the importance of being able to sit down after work, and have sufficient light to read a book or write a letter."

By Fall, 1942, Pfeiffer had been interned for more than two years. His depression was increasing, and more and more his thoughts were turning to the past—to his wife, his two young sons, and his parents from whom there had been no word since his flight from Amsterdam. Were they still alive? If not, where was their final resting place? His anguish deepened. Outside the camp, the colourful leaves were falling. It was his third autumn behind barbed wire, and the passing of the seasons reminded him of the passing of the years and the waste of his life in captivity.

He had been daydreaming during Saturday morning services, while the drone of voices washed over him. It was Yom Kippur, the holiest day of the year, and one line of the chant penetrated his preoccupation: "He who heals the sick and frees prisoners..." Suddenly a friend interrupted his train of thought, whispering in his ear: "A message just came from the Commandant's office. You are wanted there. Your release came through just now."

"I jumped up and bolted for the office. A few minutes later I was officially informed of my freedom, and a few days later a guard brought me to the railway station in St. John, Quebec, where I paid $1.25 for my ticket to Montreal. I thought ironically of the actual cost of my fare from Amsterdam to Montreal—only $1.25— but the hidden cost had been internment and the loss of my freedom and privacy for more than two years. But at least I was alive.

"My brother-in-law, Professor Dr. Shalom Weyl, and his wife, accompanied by her cousin, met me at Bonaventure Station. They had accomplished the impossible, obtaining my release by working quietly behind the scenes.

"Now came the second stage: where was my family and were they still alive? How could I locate them and get them over to Canada? Who would help me and who would help them?"

Meanwhile Pfeiffer had to find some means of support while the search for his family began. He had arrived in Montreal in September, 1942, and almost immediately found a job in an accountancy office, where both partners were immigrants. He received $52.50 a month while another employee was paid $140 a month for the same work. He felt exploited, nonetheless he remained there for nineteen months, taking night classes to re-educate himself. His PhD in law was useless in Canada. In April he moved to another firm, which he left at Christmas, 1944, to work as a bookkeeper and secretary in a textile factory.

"At the same time, I worked to get my degree as a chartered accountant. I applied for membership in the Accountancy Students' Society, and a month later was informed by letter that I had been refused. Why? Because I was an enemy alien. I was furious. I had been cleared and released from camp, but I was still considered an enemy alien. I had another problem. I had to write an exam at McGill University and was dismayed to discover it was scheduled for a Friday night from six p.m. to ten. I had never written on the Sabbath; my religion forbade it. It was a dilemma, and there was no way out. I had no choice but to write, but I finished it by eight-thirty p.m., before sundown, shaving an hour and a half off the four-hour exam. I scored ninety-seven per cent.

"That exam was the culmination of two years' work telescoped into one year. My third year's work ended with a mark of ninety-four per cent, making me eligible for a student's prize, but

I couldn't get it. My degrees taken elsewhere in Europe had never been recognized, and I was still considered an enemy alien. In frustration, I appealed to Saul Hayes, head of the Jewish Congress, and he called a Mr. Asher who was unable to help. Mr. Hayes said he couldn't do anything for me, telling me to return in six months.

"'You know, you must realize you are actually an enemy alien,' he said. 'There is a certain amount of xenophobia here.'

"'Mr. Hayes,' I answered. 'In Germany, it's called anti-Semitism.'

"And I left.

"I worked like hell in my exams, leading my class every year. One of my professors wrote 'A very good student' under my work. His name was Reginald Dawson, and he has been the Mayor of Town of Mount Royal for many years.

"My unchanged status still bothered me, and I finally appealed to Mrs. Dickson, the Secretary of the Chartered Accountants' Institute. I believe she was also on the Protestant School Board, and she apologized that I had not been deemed acceptable by the association.

"'Are you a Canadian Citizen?' she asked.

"'Yes. The status was granted retroactively from the time I arrived in Canada.'

"She said she would accept my application to present to the Board. A month later, she called to tell me it had been accepted for membership, and I could write my exam, a prerequisite for membership in the association, in three months."

Almost five years had elapsed since Julius Pfeiffer had been herded down the gangplank of the *Sobieski* as an internee in July, 1940. There was still no word of his family, his wife Flora and two sons, Fred and Robert. An agency in New York involved in tracing refugees wrote to Pfeiffer after he had addressed an inquiry to them. He was informed that it was more than likely his family had been sent to Bergen-Belsen. But there was no proof. The Red Cross staff told him he could send parcels to Bergen-Belsen. He put packages together during 1945, which were forwarded by the Red Cross, and still there was no word.

Shortly after Germany surrendered on May 8, 1945, the lists of survivors in the camps began coming through. Pfeiffer went every day to see if his family's name appeared on them. One day in June, there was a name and place: "Robert Pfeiffer, born in The

Hague, 28/7/37 found in Horst, near Venlo, Netherlands". His heart skipped a beat. Bobby was alive. But what of the others?

On June 25, 1945, Julius Pfeiffer's prayers were answered. A cable arrived with the message: "Two years Bergen-Belsen, survived. Back in Amsterdam. Your wife, Flora."

Two days later another cable arrived, this one from Sweden and sent by Pfeiffer's sister-in-law, who had survived Auschwitz, the notorious death camp. The cable contradicted the first one: "Wife and son probably not alive. No contact with Bobby."

Pfeiffer was shocked, but realized there must be some error. "It was a good thing I had received the other cable first, or I don't know what I would have done. And a few days after that, my friend Max Adler, my old 'shipmate' sent a cable: "Congratulations! Your wife and son Freddy found. Liberated in Germany and on the way back to Holland."

On February 12, 1946, after much correspondence, Flora Pfeiffer, nine-year-old Bobby and eight-year-old Freddy arrived at Windsor Station in Montreal, making history as some of the first post-war immigrants to Canada. The family was reunited after six years of separation. Pfeiffer's parents and father-in-law had not survived.

* * * *

"More than forty-five years have passed since Canada put me behind barbed wire and finally released me after over two years of incarceration. In return, Canada gave me citizenship and the same rights given to everyone else. They made no distinction. Except for those first two years, Canada treated me as a human being and I wasn't discriminated against. I found, however, that prejudice came from the Jewish community because we had come from Germany and were considered to be 'different'. Quite a few pejorative remarks were made, and many of the other German-Jewish men reinforced this realization of prejudice. The attitude in helping and accepting us was 'nothing is too much'. And that was precisely what happened. We received very little help, when we tried to adjust and integrate, once we were on the other side of the barbed wire. There were many of us who went back to England, but

972 of us remained, to make great contributions to Canada.

"I, too, have filled my place in society. I wrote a textbook in the German language on Canadian income-tax laws and I wrote for a German-Canadian paper on the subject of income tax, my specialty. I was very active in bringing money to Canada from Germany, in the form of restitution for those who had suffered so much at the hands of the Nazis. I never forgot what I had been through, and tried to help others who had problems as new immigrants

"If I had had a choice, I'm not sure I would have come to Canada. What happened to me was not my choosing, but I think if I could do it over again, I wouldn't come to Quebec, where two linguistic groups are fighting amongst themselves, and the others are caught in the middle. But this is happening all over the world—in Belgium, South Africa, India, Sri Lanka—and minority groups always seem to get it.

"If there was some advice I could give, it would be for the authorities to deal more leniently with immigrants. The law should be applied without hardship. Often, when immigrants have to fight to be accepted in this country, legal costs clean them out. If they lose, they are kicked out, and if they win, they are broke. Either way, they are the losers.

"I would also insist that information classfied as 'from secret sources' should not be used against an immigrant who is accused of some alleged crime. One case I have been involved with deals with a man born in Germany, who has a certificate stating he has no criminal record. Israel, another country where he resided, claims he has no criminal record there either, yet Canadian Immigration officials say he has a record and cannot remain in Canada. But they refuse to release the information as to the nature of the accusation. In a case of this kind, there should be access to information so that the accused can defend himself. This is not the first case of this type I have come across, and it is a grave injustice to anyone, not just to immigrants.

"If there was one thing I would like to do, it would be to demand the same thing as the Japanese Canadians are asking. Don't you think we deserve an apology for being placed behind barbed wire and forgotten for more than two and a half years? Shouldn't we hear something for being called 'Dirty Jews' and being insulted many times by soldiers of the Canadian Army guarding us? It isn't a case of remuneration as it is with the Japanese Canadians, whose possessions were confiscated and sold. This is a question of principle. I and all the others were victims of stupidity and bureaucratic bungling forty-six years ago.

"I would do anything to prevent this from happening again."

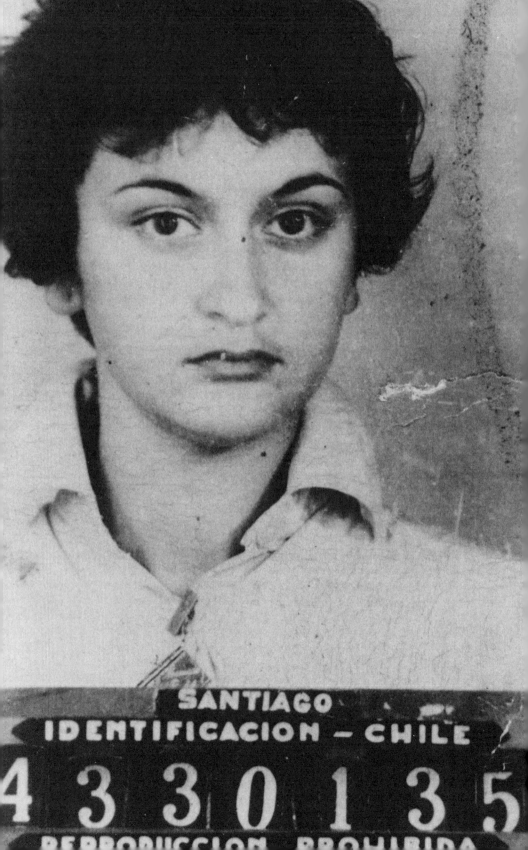

SANTIAGO
IDENTIFICACION - CHILE
4 3 3 0 1 3 5
REPRODUCCION PROHIBIDA

RECALLED TO LIFE*

by Milly Charon
from an interview with Anna Torranz

When the khaki-coloured jeep carrying four men in army uniforms pulled up in front of Anna Torranz's house in Santiago, Chile, she knew they were coming for her. The men climbed out of the vehicle and marched up the walk. Each had a sub-machine-gun in the crook of his arm.

Anna felt as if the sky had fallen on her head. She could not speak. Quickly, she gestured to her fifteen-year-old son to take his eight-year-old sister and two-year-old baby brother and run out the back door. They had discussed the possibility that she might be arrested, and her son was old enough to understand he might not see his mother again. But he obeyed instantly.

Anna's mind was in turmoil. She could think only that her children had escaped. She had heard of cases where a father was forced by soldiers to rape his daughter at gunpoint, and some mothers had been raped by soldiers while the children watched. She knew of a twelve-year-old girl who had been raped in front of her parents. Anna was too frightened to resist. The soldiers blindfolded her and forced her into the jeep.

They drove for hours. At one point they stopped the car, threw her out and threatened to kill her at the side of the road. Suddenly they pushed her back into the jeep and drove back to Santiago, where they deposited her inside a stadium-like building which had been used to hold country fairs and exhibitions. Now it was a military prison, holding thousands of political prisoners. Anna was to spend more than a month here, living on the edge of imminent death. During that period she had time to reflect on the events that had brought her to that traumatic point in her life.

A Tale of Two-Cities by Charles Dickens

* * * *

Anna had been born in Linares in Southern Chile in September, 1940. Her father's family had emigrated from Corsica, and her mother's family from Spain. One of nine children, Anna had always felt lonely and often neglected.

"I was a dreamer. I read a lot, seeking refuge in books. I devoured them. Because I was so sensitive, I had a tendency to withdraw into myself. It was a pattern in our family. My mother and sisters were very quiet and submissive, and my father and brothers were very 'macho' males. My father was a very strict man who demanded absolute obedience."

Because it was impossible to find employment in Linares, the family split up, the men moving north to Santiago to find jobs. One by one, the other children joined their father, and finally the entire family was reunited. But Anna's father did not live to see his family established. When Anna was fourteen, he died of lung cancer. He had chain-smoked most of his life.

The family was divided again. Three of the children lived with an older brother, and the younger ones remained with Anna's mother. It was a difficult period for all of them. Chile was not yet industrialized in the 1950s, and jobs were scarce. In order to help the family, Anna began to work at seventeen as a secretary.

"I had taken business courses at school, and I had learned to use a typewriter. I didn't earn much, but I gave it all to my mother to help feed us."

Like many Latin-American countries, Chile was undergoing political upheavals as it tried to break out of a rigid feudal system. Politically, Anna's family were Leftists, that is Socialists following social democracy. Although her father had been a militant Socialist, the children merely followed the party's ideology. They participated in meetings and rallies, and it was at a fund-collection rally for the Salvador Allende election campaign in 1957 that Anna met the man who would become her husband. Many young people were involved in these activities for they saw it as a way of establishing a new social and political order in Chile.

"It wasn't love at first sight," said Anna recalling the event. "We talked, we danced. His family was there and so was mine. I liked him, but real love came afterwards. We married two years later, in 1959. Meanwhile in those two years, Allende had lost the election; the Christian Democrats had united with the traditional Rightists or Conservatives to win, and Jorge Alessandri had become the new president. It was a blow to our party, but we continued to struggle for reform in a democratic fashion."

For the next five years, Anna immersed herself in family life. She had two children, and her husband was working as a maintenance supervisor for *Línea Aérea de Cobre (LADECO)*, the airline for the copper industry—the country's main source of income. But politics continued to dominate the Chilean scene and interest her family. In 1964, the Centre Right of Christian Democrats led by Eduardo Frei won the elections, effectively preventing the Socialists from taking power.

Eduardo Frei's platform was land reform. He promised to distribute Chile's irrigated land by 1970, a move that would benefit 100,000 families. For several hundred years, Chile's land had been owned by wealthy landowners who operated enormous holdings and exploited poor farm labourers. Huge areas of arable land were left untouched while thousands of peons went hungry. It was a pattern a powerful oligarchy had repeated many times in Latin-American countries.

However, even with American assistance from the private sector, and suspected backing from governmental agencies in the United States, Frei could not keep his promises. The laws he passed were never put into effect, and an underprivileged population looked to a new party and a new leader for liberation.

Anna saw the struggle as a multi-faceted power struggle based on greed. The political parties were being manipulated by different factions.

"On one hand, Frei and his Christian Democrats were supported by the Americans who feared a takeover of the copper mines controlled by American interests. The copper belonged to Chile, and using poorly paid, almost slave labour, Anaconda Copper, the American conglomerate, mined, shipped and sold the metal all over the world. Chile received only a tiny fraction of the profits.

"On the other hand, the Catholic Church, in conjunction with the Conservatives, was becoming increasingly militant and demanding better working conditions for farm workers and social reforms for the poor.

"The Socialists were another Party who were determined to correct the entire economic and power structure in Chile. Unfortunately they were considered to be Marxist extremists, a good enough excuse to prevent them from gaining power...and when they did, from keeping it.

"The best-entrenched group were the landowners, the oligarchy who held enough power to try to stop the unions, which were forming to prevent the exploitation of the workers and to demand better labour conditions.

"And then there was the army and the para-military police force which was used both by the oligarchy and whichever party it deemed worthy of support. Its loyalty could change with the circumstances."

For the poor and oppressed, and for the lower middle class, Salvador Allende appeared like a Messiah seeking social justice and equality for all. And by 1970, he had gathered such a loyal following that he was elected on September 4 with 36.3 per cent of the vote. The Conservatives had 34.9 per cent. He took power on November 4, 1970.*

One of Allende's first acts was to nationalize the Anaconda Copper installations in the country. It was a massive blow to the Americans. In retaliation, they began actively to undermine Allende's new regime, with the help of the CIA and the other Chilean political parties. A conspiracy was organized to assassinate General Rene Schneider, a Constitutionalist, in order to neutralize the Left. He was loyal to the people and to the new government, and had respected the results of the elections indicating the people's choice and political will. His refusal to cooperate in a *coup d'état* to topple the new government signed his death warrant.

"For the poor, however, Allende's new measures aroused a popular fervour and much joy. He began unprecedented social and health programmes. Rich or poor, every child was to receive a litre of milk a day in the schools. He initiated low-cost housing to replace the shacks inhabited by the poverty-stricken. Even the Church gave its approval. For the first time in history the masses

* Gabriel Smirnow. *The Revolution Disarmed*, Monthly Review Press, New York, 1979, p. 6. Copyright © Gabriel Smirnow, reprinted with permission of Monthy Review Foundation.

were not being ignored," Anna explained.

"But the oligarchy became furious when Allende started agrarian reforms. He confiscated land and gave unworked acres to the poor in order to rid the country of an outmoded feudal system. The wealthy landowners had cultivated only a fraction of these massive estates. Of course, the proprietors raised a ferocious resistance and began undeclared warfare, killing many of the peasants who had taken over land allotted to them.

"In a display of resistance, the Rightists killed a police lieutenant who was one of Allende's supporters, and this man became a martyr to the cause. The oligarchy began to agitate even more and found another way to harm the regime. It organized a movement to control food production and began to hoard food—tea, coffee, butter, sugar, flour, rice and potatoes—so there was a shortage. The landowners even dumped food into the sea to halt production and distribution. They wanted Allende blamed for the near-famine conditions that would follow. It would result in dissatisfaction with his administration."

The government was forced to intervene and take measures to stop the hoarding and dumping. Because of the shortages, a black market emerged and flourished, despite attempts to halt it. Prices escalated. Hoarders released supplies for astronomical sums. Allende introduced a rationing system and formed an organization to monitor the process. A special commission worked to help distribute food in a just and equitable fashion to the needy.

"It would have worked, except that the Rightists began a general strike, financed by CIA money. Truckers went on strike, so no food could be shipped around the country for distribution. Slowly the country was paralysed. Next the College of Physicians and Surgeons went on strike for an indefinite period. The walk-outs brought day-to-day life to a halt. In the universities, a movement began, which was called "Country and Freedom", opposing Marxists, Jews, workers and anyone hostile to the dominance of the rich elite. The children of the wealthy and the extreme Rightists worked energetically to bring down the Allende regime. It threatened their existence—their wealth and power."

Anna's entire family was deeply involved in the struggle. They distributed food and tried to minimize the breakdowns in distribution. Her uncle was president of the "Truckers' Syndicate" which continued to bring food down from the coast northwest of Santiago. It became a hazardous trip, for the Rightists spread nails on the roads to stop the trucks. Barricades were erected to slow down vehicles, and the drivers were pulled out, beaten or killed. Many of the trucks were pushed into ravines or driven off the roads over cliffs. Allende's opponents were determined to bring the country to its knees, if not by starvation, then by terrorism.

"There were demonstrations in the streets, and Allende spoke on the radio to the people, urging them to have confidence in the regime and declaring that together they would continue to fight for the rights of the people. He spoke frankly and directly, informing the masses of everything that was happening. The Rightists were trying to instigate a civil war—brother against brother, families split, and a country divided.

"Allende planned a referendum to be held on September 11, 1973. Fearful lest Allende address the people and win the referendum, the military and the Rightists, supported by the CIA, attacked the Moneda Palace the night before. General Augusto Pinochet, appointed by Allende as head of the army, betrayed the man who had trusted him. The night before the coup d'état, Pinochet cut all communication systems in the palace so Allende could not reach the provinces and call for help. The government was sealed off. The army moved tanks and military trucks into the centre of the city and surrounded the palace. Allende's supporters begged him to leave. They had no arms to protect him. He refused. They were willing to die for him, willing to be killed to protect the palace.

"There was one line of communication left, a radio frequency, and Allende went on the air for a last plea to his supporters. He said that treason and felony were trying to impose themselves on the country, but they would not succeed. He told the people not to allow themselves to be killed. He said he would not allow himself to be deposed. The enemy would have to pass over his dead body.

"An army deputation told him he could have a plane for his family and himself to leave the country. He refused. His last words were that all should fight for the return of social justice. He said he believed in the Chilean people, the country, the struggle and that one day, the doors of salvation would open to the free man.

234

"I never forgot what he said. He had so much faith in the working class. He was a country doctor and he loved the poor, sick and underprivileged. We were in despair. Everyone listening to him was crying. We could hear the bombardment. We lived near the army airbase and heard the planes flying over our house. The Moneda was bombed, and Allende was murdered with his loyal ministers and friends inside. The soldiers machine-gunned everyone."

Soon after, the reprisals began against Allende's followers. No one was exempt. Many people were denounced by jealous and spiteful neighbours. Leftists were arrested; Jews were detained because one of Allende's ministers had been Jewish; priests and nuns were picked up and imprisoned because their sympathy for the poor automatically gave them the stigma of "Leftists". Everyone was suspect.

Anna and her family were caught up in the wave of terror. Concentration camps were set up in the North. Denounced by a neighbour, one of Anna's brothers was arrested and detained in one of these camps and tortured physically and psychologically.

"Every night the guards would play a game to drive him crazy. They would stand him up for execution, blindfold him and shoot—into the air. When the guns went off, he expected to die. They did this night after night until he was a trembling wreck. They tortured him—electric shocks to different parts of his body. My other brother, also imprisoned, was placed with common criminals, not political prisoners, and there, too, they were tortured. A third brother was sentenced to be shot, but because he knew the captain of the firing squad, he was spared. Our entire family was imprisoned, and only because we were originally French were we able to get the French embassy to intervene and get most of us out of prison. Two brothers remained in jail for another year and a half. They were young, only eighteen or so at the time. My brother-in-law was interned, but because he was of Italian origin, the Italian embassy got him out.

"Women with young children, pregnant women and old women were thrown into jail. Women were giving birth in prison and their babies were taken from them, never to be seen again. Soliders and guards were raping women and young girls. Thousands of people disappeared, many dropped from helicopters over

235

the ocean. Never had the sharks feasted so well. A river which ran
through Santiago was full of naked corpses drifting out to sea. We
were so frightened. People were hiding everywhere, living in
terror, waiting to be picked up. Had the soldiers known I was
involved in the struggle, I would have been killed immediately."
    And now they had come for her.

* * * *

    Anna looked dazedly around her. There were thousands
of people in the stadium. The women had been separated from the
men, and she could see women with small children and babies
huddled in one large group. A number had been jammed into a
small enclosure, packed like sardines. The stadium was built like
a plane hangar—the roof peaking to its highest point at the centre.
The floor was hard, packed earth. The first day and night, Anna
was part of a crowd sleeping on the ground. No one was fed. By
the second day, she was separated from the others and put into one
of the stalls reserved for farm animals. There were five people in
each stall, and all conversation was forbidden. Guards watched
them constantly. A day and a half passed before food finally
appeared—a hunk of bread and tea or coffee.
    The following day, the questioning began. Anna heard her
name called on a loudspeaker, and a soldier came to take her to a
small room for interrogation.
    "'Do you belong to any organization?' asked a soldier.
    "'No.'
    "They didn't believe me. They wouldn't accept it. I had
worked for the government for the Junta Altísima Popular (JAP) in
the distribution of provisions. I had been responsible for distribut-
ing food to the people and was in charge of a sector. It had to be
done so the poor could be fed. They couldn't afford to buy on the
black market from which the upper classes were profiting."
    "The soldier continued. 'We know you were head of
distribution and that you were making money from it,' he accused.
'I want the names of all the people who worked under you.'
    "'I don't know any names,' I answered.
    "He hit me across the face, not just once, but many times.

But there were women who were beaten much more than me. They were the women who had been in charge of food distribution in the slum areas of the city. I saw and heard terrible things that will haunt me all my life. A woman of about forty was locked into a box for two months—a box built in such a way that she couldn't lie down, sit or stand. She died. There were people who were taken up in the air in helicopters and dropped.

"I saw young girls raped many times. Some were taken away and never seen again; some gave birth to babies, and the babies were removed from their mothers and vanished. Some infants were neglected and died not long after birth, and some were sold in other countries—Paraguay and Uruguay—or handed over to rich people who did not have children. It was an industry, a barbaric industry. Many mothers died, but to this day, some of those who survived and the grandmothers of these children are still hunting for their little ones. The mothers didn't die naturally. They were murdered and their bodies dropped into the sea. The 'Desaparecidos' will never be found.

"I wasn't questioned every day, but when I was, it usually took place two to three times daily. Sometimes a day or two would pass while they worked on other prisoners. It was psychological. You never knew when they were coming for you. They called me a Communist, a Socialist, and some other things I wouldn't repeat. Several times when I was in interrogation, my captors would bring in a woman and ask, 'Do you know this one? She's a Communist, isn't she?' To save her skin, the woman would agree to anything.

"I was there for little over a month. Meals were bad. We didn't get any breakfast. At noon it was a piece of bread with a bowl of soup. At night we were given beans or some noodles with nothing on them. Once in a while there were vegetables. After a while I lost track of time. I slipped into a depression under the strain of expecting to die at any moment. I was waiting to be called up and taken away to be killed somewhere far away. And the things I saw were just too much to bear."

When the soldiers came to take Anna from her animal stall more than a month later, she was convinced she was going to die. This time she was marched out of the stadium and put on a military bus at midnight. She sat huddled in a seat, too terrified to cry. The door slammed shut, and the bus drove off into the darkness.

"I was sure I was going to my death. Suddenly in the middle of nowhere, the bus squealed to a halt on a lonely country road. I was pulled to my feet and thrown out of the bus. I was very frightened. I was convinced they were going to shoot me right there. The bus started up, and I picked myself up and ran to hide in the bushes beside the road. When I was certain the soldiers were gone, I began to walk toward what I thought was the direction of the city.

"All I was wearing were the clothes I had on when I was arrested, and they were filthy. My hair was matted and unkempt. The only water we had in the stadium was a fountain the animals had been drinking from—nothing more than a trough. Everyone had tried to wash there, but it was impossible to stay clean. We didn't have any soap. I had no identification or money. Everything had been taken from me in prison. True, it had not been much, for we had not been permitted to bring anything with us when we were arrested. But any jewelry found on prisoners was confiscated by the soldiers.

"No cars passed on the road. It was very dark. There was a curfew in effect, and any civilians traveling during the night were in danger of being stopped and shot."

Anna stumbled along for about an hour and a half. Several times she tripped and fell. She was weak and very tired, and had to stop and sit by the roadside many times because she was dizzy. A few times she dozed off. Eventually a car came along, and she flagged it down.

"I told them I had lost my bag. I lied. I made up a story because I couldn't trust anyone. I asked to be taken as far as a public phone. I had no money, but it wasn't a pay phone. I called my mother and sister. My mother was old and didn't understand what was happening. I said I had no money and didn't know where I was. At that point, my brother took the receiver and I tried to explain where I was by describing the landmarks. It was a town not far from the city, and that was how they found me."

It was dangerous for Anna's brother to leave the house during curfew, but he came, driving without lights. She was standing in the middle of the road when she heard the car coming. Anna knew the tricks the solders used. They would release people just before curfew and then pick them up after curfew, knowing full well there was no time for them to get home. The soldiers considered it good sport to shoot them down in cold blood. She expected to be picked up by them. When the car stopped, Anna saw her brother-in-law driving his car and her brother beside him. She fell into her brother's arms in hysterics.

"We drove to my mother's house because I was certain the soldiers would be waiting for me to show up at my house, so they could arrest me and shoot me for violating curfew. I just broke down. I couldn't stop crying. I sat down and someone pushed a cup of tea into my hands. No one asked any questions. They saw how depressed I was. When they did speak, I began to cry harder than ever.

"As soon as my brother phoned my husband, my husband drove the kids over to my mother's house to see me. I stayed there for a day and then went into hiding at a friend's house. Later I discovered what had happened while I was imprisoned. My husband, who worked at the airport, was friendly with some engineers, some of whom had been former air force officers. One of these men had contacted a friend who was an army officer, when my husband asked them to find me. He didn't know where I had been taken or what I was charged with. The neighbours had told him what had happened when he came home the night I had been detained. From that moment on he was like a man obsessed. He had to find me and enlisted the aid of my family. They worked tirelessly to track me down, and the same day my husband discovered where I was held, he went to see the officers. He had done them many favours, and they returned them by setting the wheels in motion to get me out.

"One officer had moved up through the ranks when the government changed, and he was very powerful. Through his assistance my husband discovered that my papers—birth certificates, school and medical records, identification, labour permits—all had disappeared. Even my fingerprints and footprints taken at birth were gone. We realized that I had been on the death list, for this was how they prepared for people to vanish without a trace. Firstly, all records of their existence were wiped out so no inquiries would be made. There would be no way of tracing someone who had never been born, lived, gone to school, worked or married. Everything had been prepared for my disappearance. I had been that close to non-existence. My husband's friend who worked in the investigation office told him that even my dossier was gone— as if I had never been born."

This method of destroying records created havoc with the statistics compiled by humanitarian and human rights organizations, Anna pointed out. Because there was no proof of existence, many people did not even become statistics. The Amnesty International figures for "The Disappeared" were ridiculously low. Thousands were unaccounted for.

"The military made prisoners sign a paper acknowledging they had been released. The people were escorted out of the prison and a short time later were again picked up, and this time they disappeared for good," Anna explained. "When relatives and Amnesty International made inquiries, the paper was shown to prove that those being sought had, indeed, been set free. And, of course, the authorities knew nothing of their whereabouts. It happened all the time."

But the danger for Anna and her family was not yet over. In an attempt to protect his family, her husband went to a church run by the Oblate Fathers, many of whom were Canadian. Then he went to the Canadian embassy to file an application for permission to emigrate. He paid a visit to the United Nations office to try to get out of the country as soon as possible. The authorities found it difficult to believe that the government had gone to such lengths to liquidate people. They demanded proof of Anna's existence. An official at the United Nations made arrangements for an entire set of new documents, proving that Anna Torranz was a real person.

Meanwhile, Anna lived in fear that she would be arrested again. To avoid this, she had to be one step ahead of the police. She moved from one place to another, never staying too long at the same address. However, it was to be four years before the family could leave Chile. For Anna it was period of acute anxiety.

"We saw a lot of starving people begging in the streets. Children were dying of hunger before our eyes. The military had the right to enter and search any house for papers and arms, and they would brand the occupants as Communists or extremists and kill them. People were informing on neighbours. My brother and I found a bullet tossed into our garden. We thought it had been thrown there by a neighbour who disliked us. Had the military been informed and found the bullet, we would have been declared guilty of concealing weapons and punished.

"Fear breathed down our necks. It was everywhere. There was a constant smell in the air of burning paper coming from many houses, even in the summer. People were burning documents and books they felt might incriminate them. No matter how innocent the content, the books might have been misrepresented. Suddenly an entire world had collapsed and turned into a nightmare. My husband and I were in hiding; my brothers were in prison, and I cried constantly, unsure that I would ever see them again. Even the one weapon we had had for protection from thieves was gone. When the coup d'état took place, my husband went to an isolated spot where he dismantled the gun piece by piece and threw the parts away. To have it in his possession meant death if it was discovered."

The family's emigration permits arrived in 1976, three years after they had applied, but they waited another year before leaving. The feeling of abandoning the family was the main reason why Anna delayed. Her brothers were still in prison. What finally pushed them to a decision was learning that more of their friends had disappeared or had been killed. And so, on January 23, 1977, Anna, her husband and three children arrived in Montreal.

The family was placed in classes at a French orientation centre (COFI) to facilitate their integration into Quebec life. But Anna found among the Quebecois a discrimination based on language that left her dismayed.

"When we didn't speak French, people didn't like it. What did they expect, instant fluency? We were taught international French, which is not what you speak in Quebec. We had to learn expressions no one could understand, and when we mispronounced words or sentences, we would get 'Pardon, pardon?' And people would be angry with us. We were afraid to speak. We discovered that the Francophones were more racist than the Anglophones, probably because the Anglos are a minority themselves.

"For three years we lived in Longueuil, a predominantly French neighbourhood, and we definitely didn't have friendly neighbours. They treated us as if we weren't welcome there. If there was trouble amongst the kids on the street, it was always my son who got blamed, not the other children. We lived there for three

241

years before moving to the Snowdon district. Everyone knows us here, and all our neighbours are friendly."

Anna discovered there were other problems besides the language one. A former high school teacher of literature, she could not find work. It was seven months before she was hired as a chambermaid at the Four Seasons Hotel. It was back-breaking work, and she had trouble with her spine. Forced to quit after a year, she could only find work packaging pasta, "a mindless job". After a year of that, she polished fillings in a dental laboratory, but that didn't last. She took a a three-month course to learn soldering and worked in a factory soldering different types of electronic circuits. It was a good job, but she was laid off when business was slow.

She placed ads in newspapers, looking for work. "All I got were obscene phone calls," she recalled wryly. "I went back to school to study computer keypunching. I had been told there was a need for this kind of labour. But employers wanted people with experience. How could I get experience if no one would hire me?"

Again Anna went back to school, to study gerontology in order to work with the aged. She found a job as a sick-leave replacement at a CLSC, a local community service centre, but she was laid off when the person she had replaced returned to her job.

"I haven't been able to find steady work since I came to Canada. I even applied to the provincial Education Department for a permit to teach Spanish. I was told there already are too many unemployed teachers ahead of me, looking for work. I really think there is discrimination against older women seeking jobs, and yet people like me are needed in gerontology. I know because I worked as a volunteer when I was unemployed, helping elderly people, mainly from Spanish-speaking countries, who were isolated in their homes. Their children would go to work and leave them alone. They didn't speak either English or French, were worried about getting around and didn't trust anyone. They had to be taken to the doctor, dentist or shopping. They could speak only with their children, and because of the language barrier, they couldn't communicate with their grandchildren. It's a generation gap in the total sense.

"The entire immigrant ghetto around St. Lawrence Boulevard is full of poor people, but it is especially difficult for the old. It's very frustrating for me because all the effort made in that direction did not bear fruit. I visited many sick, old people, and they were so sad when I couldn't come back. Why isn't something being done for these aged immigrants?

"I'm always filling out job applications and I'm getting fed up because nothing ever happens. It has been like that for a long time now. My training is being wasted. And it is happening to many immigrants. Although my husband had a job at Canadair, he was laid off and can't find work either.

"I know there are agencies that are given grants by the government to find work for people. When I was working at the CLSC, I was hired through such an agency. But it was advantageous to the CLSC, because the people there could say there was no work and lay us off. In addition, they didn't have to give us vacation pay. I wasn't considered an employee. There was no protection and no social benefits because I wasn't under contract. And if you are handled by an agency, you get the minimum wage, and the difference is kept by the agency. I wonder if the government knows what the agencies are doing. Is that where our tax dollars go? Imagine all those big buildings where employees and secretaries are paid for administration, and most immigrants are forced to go there to ask for jobs. It would save the government a lot of money if these middlemen were eliminated. It's a great way to exploit people and get money for nothing."

Anna feels the government does not do enough for immigrants. Therefore, immigrants and ethnic groups should band together and form organizations to help people, without discriminating in any way. There should be open communication between different ethnic groups.

"We should not wait for the government to do this. We are the ones who are isolated and suffering. We know how it feels, so we have the understanding to help others. I'm sure many Anglophones would help because they are more friendly toward immigrants. There must be more communication between established Canadians and immigrants. Many immigrants have intellectual aptitudes, and they should be encouraged. Unfortunately the government sees only statistics and not individual cases. Many of the young people who emigrate suffer so much from isolation and alienation that they turn to alcohol, drugs or crime. The young are more susceptible to wrong influences, and they get depressed when they feel rejected by society. Many commit suicide. It's becoming an epidemic.

"And it doesn't help that the Quebecois don't want us. It shows up in the language situation. My husband wanted our children to start English school, because French is so close to Spanish it would be easy to learn later. They would have had no trouble with it. But they were forced into the French education system. We have nothing against the French language, but the way it is rammed down our throats is bad. We have no choice. French businesses won't hire us and when we go elsewhere, we hear English. If someone who speaks French can't find work in Quebec, he has to leave the province, but he won't get a job outside Quebec because he doesn't speak English. It's a no-win situation. It would make more sense to learn both languages from childhood on.

"My son took his education in French, yet when we made an application to the University of Montreal, McGill University and Concordia University, he was turned away by the University of Montreal. But Concordia and McGill accepted him. How do you explain that? The Quebecois come first even if the rest of us are citizens.

"As for myself, my courses in key punching and electronics were useless. Most of the technology is in English. Why don't they teach us English? When we are thrown on the labour market, our French technological terms are useless. I want to study English, but it will be impossible once I start working.

"But even with all the hard times and both of us out of work, I would still come here if I had to do it all over again. I am happy to raise my kids in a peaceful environment. It is easy to get a good education here. In my country only the very rich could get an education. It was denied to even the middle classes. Canada is a big country with many resources, even though there isn't enough work available to tap these resources.

"However, if there was one wish I could have, it would be to go back and witness the new upheavals in Chile. I would like to see a reversal of the events which took place there in the seventies. There is a chapter missing to that story. We still don't know how it will end."

RESISTANCE

by Milly Charon
from an interview with Lena Kraouse

The Montparnasse railway station, like others in Paris, was in a state of confusion on June 12, 1940. A week earlier, Germany had launched its invasion of France and was hammering its way toward the City of Lights. The Nazi armies were only a few miles from the northern outskirts. Panic-stricken passengers were pushing and shoving their way across the platforms before descending to the train level. The stairs were jammed. Clutching the few belongings they could carry, hundreds milled around in a frightened crowd. Parents were holding children in their arms or tugging at youngsters' hands lest they be lost or trampled in the rush for the last train.

Twenty-year-old Lena Voseur-Delacour and her mother had just pushed their way to the edge of the platform. Lena looked back and saw the iron grilles clang shut in front of her father who was remaining in the city in an attempt to straighten out his business commitments. His face was grey and haggard. She wondered if she would ever see him again. Lena's husband Georges Delacour, mobilized in 1939, less than a year after their marriage, had just returned to his unit after a six-month convalescence. While loading shells for transportation to the front lines on the German border, he had injured his back and had been sent home to recuperate. It had been very painful for Lena to say goodbye to both her husband and father before she, herself, left Paris with her mother.

The train ride westward was not a pleasant one. There were people packed between the cars, sitting on the couplings between the sections. Crowded into a compartment with her mother, Lena had one foot on the floor and the other on a man wounded in battle, lying beside others in the same condition. They were being evacuated from Paris. There was no place for Lena to put her feet, and each time she moved, the man groaned.

Madame Voseur and her husband Leon had agreed to meet, if possible, at the little town of Les Sables-d'Olonne, south-west of Nantes. Voseur went home to La Garenne, a suburb seven kilometres from Paris. That evening he wheeled an old bicycle onto the road and began pedalling westward. He overtook a curé fleeing on his bicycle and after exchanging a few words, they agreed to switch to secondary roads. The curé knew the main roads were blocked with refugee columns and military vehicles, which had been bombed and strafed by German aircraft. The Loire bridges already had German gun emplacements, while planes were bombarding the bridges and machine-gunning civilians to prevent them from crossing.

Ten days later, Leon Voseur was reunited with his wife and daughter. They knew that there would be terrible times ahead. France had surrendered. The Voseurs were fortunate in having kind friends to take them in and feed them for six months, but they were effectively cut off from information.

"We had no news of anything, and it was disturbing to see our soldiers fleeing before the advancing Germans," said Lena, looking back, years later, at the Occupation.

By November, 1940, the German Occupation authorities were allowing people to return to Paris. The Voseurs, like so many others, were crammed on a train heading eastward. Paris, the jewel of Europe, had lost her lustre. Food shortages created terrible hardships. People were starving. The Germans took everything they could lay their hands on. Stores were emptied, factories ransacked and private homes looted.

Lena watched one day as German soldiers moved magnificent furniture and desks from a building.

"It must have been an office warehouse that provided quality furnishings to Ministries and important people. The pieces were being loaded on trucks and carted away. We nicknamed the Germans "The Movers". Piece by piece, sector by sector, they stole everything beautiful or useful, and shipped it all to Germany. It was happening in every country they occupied."

Lena's husband, who had been taken prisoner fighting at La Rochelle in Charente while she was at Les Sables-d'Olonne, was released and permitted to return home. The Germans had no desire to support hundreds of thousands of disarmed French military prisoners. Delacour, grateful to be alive, returned to Paris and his old job at a bank.

He and Lena were in Paris about a year when the programme of purges and arrests began in earnest. Leon Voseur had realized that things would worsen and was prepared. The Nazis were already arresting Jews and shipping them out of the country. Voseur visited some friends he knew in the police prefecture and obtained false papers for his family. Because males were more easily identified by the Germans, he left for the free Unoccupied Zone to stay with Jewish friends while his wife and daughter remained behind.

"So, there I was, Jewish, with forged papers and stuck in Paris," said Lena shrugging her shoulders.

One day Lena was on her way to a restaurant at Place des Ternes where a few precious ration tickets and some money could still buy a meal. She took the Metro, and when she left the subway, she began climbing the stairs to the street. Suddenly she noticed people running toward her down the stairs. Fear was etched on their faces. Glancing up, she continued upward and saw burly men in leather coats at the top of the stairway, pulling people out of the crowd. She knew they were Germans, probably Gestapo, for she had seen others like them taking people away.

"I didn't know at the time they were snatching young people, wherever they found them, to send them to work as slaves in munition factories in Germany. I was afraid to go further. I saw more people with looks of terror on their faces, rushing back down the stairs to avoid being taken. I asked one of them what was happening, but I didn't catch the answer in the mad flight."

Because she didn't understand, Lena kept climbing. Waiting at the top stood the three leather-coated men, and they appeared to consider her not worth their attention. As she crossed the street, she saw they were marching a number of people to a truck at the curb. She walked for an hour or more doing some small errands and retraced her footsteps to the restaurant across the street from the Metro.

She sat down and ordered a hot cocoa. Barely ten minutes elapsed when she heard a commotion at the door and looked up.

The three Gestapo she had seen earlier had entered the restaurant.
They came straight to her table.

"Papers?" they demanded.

"No, why should I show you my papers?" she asked, stalling for time.

They asked again, this time menacingly.

She handed them over, and they said, "Follow us."

"No, I won't."

They seized her arms and took her by force, dragging her resisting from the restaurant. They pushed her into a black car and drove her to police headquarters at *Quai des Orfèvres* on Orfèvres. The interrogation began and continued until four in the morning.

"They must have thought I was a spy. They wanted to know why I wasn't working and said I had to work. I told them that if my parents could afford for me to stay at home, why should I work? That was why I was living at home."

The men informed her she was to be shipped out to work in a labour camp in Germany. Dismayed, Lena jumped from her chair and snatched the inkwell from the inspector's desk. She threw its contents into his face.

"He threw a blue rage, but I didn't stay to gloat. Before any of them could move I darted into the hall, ran into the waiting room at the end straight for a window. I jumped on the bench, opened the casements, prepared to jump from the second storey."

She heard a noise behind her. The men had been caught by surprise but reacted swiftly. Right on her heels, they sprang at her and dragged her back. She was handcuffed but continued squirming and struggling to get free. They hauled her downstairs, pushed her into a police van and drove her to a jail where there was a mixture of whores, crooks and petty criminals. She was kept there for eight days and then transported with others to Gare de l'Est where she was loaded onto a train heading for Germany.

Luckily the Germans did not know that Lena was Jewish or they would have sent her to a concentration camp. Instead she was sent to Krailburg-am-Tun, a little village about seventy kilometres west of Munich. When she asked how long she would be kept there, she was told "for the duration of the war". It was a disciplinary camp, they said, for people who had refused to cooperate with the German Forces. She arrived in 1942 and would remain there for two years.

But Lena was not ready to give up. She watched and waited, keeping track of activities in the camp. Her fellow prisoners were a mixed lot, Russian, Polish, Ukrainians and others.

"I never saw so many ethnics in one place. And just beside our camp was another, packed with more women—French, Czech, Estonian, Lithuanian and others I couldn't identify. The Germans had swept up everyone."

Against her will, Lena was assigned to a work-squad to make explosives with other prisoners in the barrack-like factory. Some of the women with her had been told the powder they would be handling was ground rice.

"I told them they were stupid, and that it was blasting powder they were working with and that rockets were being built in the factory. I told them it was unhealthy, even dangerous to breathe that stuff. I told the guards I wouldn't work with the powder, and I refused to go in there. I didn't want to catch a lung disease."

Lena was put in a camp cell. But that didn't have any effect on her rebellious nature.

"I gave them a hard time and didn't quit. It's a miracle they didn't shoot me. At times I still wonder about my nerve."

The prisoners lived in little barracks with straw roofs in the woods, four women per room, and were marched out daily in shifts to the factory hidden deep in the Bavarian forest. The factory complex extended over a range of about seven kilometres and held four separate compounds. The first section was involved in mixing powder and bagged it in fabric sacks. The second section was doing something secret that Lena was unable to discover, and the third was working on the most dangerous of all—other kinds of explosives. Later she was to discover that the fourth compound was building rockets to attack England. The entire operation was obviously important to the Nazi military supply machine.

But for Lena, the landscape held more attraction than the forced labour. Because she worked separately away from the other prisoners, she was not under constant surveillance. She would slip away and gather blueberries and blackberries in the forest instead of working. Flat on her stomach in the tall grass, she would stretch out and eat fruit.

251

"The guards didn't see me because the camp was such a huge complex, and the forest hid many activities. But one day, the elderly Obermeister, the head supervisor, caught me."

"'So,' he smirked, 'you like blackberries?'

"'Yes, it's better than your shitty work,' I answered defiantly.

"He laughed, but said nothing.

"I was marched back to work, and the poor dullard caught hell for being so easy on me. He returned to yell at me, to show how tough he was. We argued, and he made a move to grab my shoulder and hit me. I yelled, 'Hey, don't you touch me or I'll claw out your eyes.' He had red hair and a terrible temper, but he put down the shovel he was holding, and that was the end of the argument."

Lena's little acts of resistance continued, but there was one confrontation that left her shaken. Standing in line while waiting to get milk at the canteen, Lena was behind a Turkish woman who was known to be a collaborator and traitor.

"'Of course,' said Lena sarcastically, 'the Boches have to go first.'"

She was reported, and later in the day the Obermeister appeared with two Gestapo officers. Lena was not afraid of the Obermeister because she suspected he liked her nerve and her gutsy arguments with him. She knew his background. He had been an undercover Nazi sympathizer and Fifth Columnist planted at Lyon before the war. Because Lena's father had come from Lyon and knew many of the same people as the Obermeister, a strange bond developed between the two. Lena made it her business to pump him for information that might be useful later on. The Obermeister spoke perfect French and knew many of the Frenchmen in Lyon as well as documented information about their activities and lives. This system of gathering information years before the war simplified the German occupation of country after country.

Now, however, Lena knew the meaning of fear. It was one thing to spar with the Obermeister, another to tangle with the Gestapo.

One of the officers asked her about her remark.

"Boches, Boches, I said, so what?" she answered determined to brazen it out.

"It is an insult. It is not acceptable!" He glared at her.

"Listen, my father was in the First World War just like your Obermeister there—in the trenches. And when my father talked about those days to us kids, he would say, 'You could hear les Boches ten metres away. You could hear their messkits rattling.' It was as natural to call the enemy a name when talking about the other side as it was for you Germans to call the French soldiers 'Frogs'.

"The Obermeister shook his head in agreement. 'Of course, she is the daughter of a 1914 hero and picked up the name from her father. She meant no harm. It is a common expression from that period.'

"The Germans were more respectful of old war heroes," explained Lena. "I got out of that one, but I was lucky. I had already imagined myself being shipped off to a concentration camp. I went back to work, and later the Obermeister told me to try to be more careful with my tongue."

Life went on in the camp, and Lena continued to raise problems. Although she didn't belong to a specific Resistance group, she worked against the Germans, as many French people were doing. Outraged at Petain's Vichy Government and his collaboration with the Nazis, many ordinary men and women in their daily walks of life—merchants, accountants, secretaries, editors, bakers, doctors, teachers, engineers, maids and even housewives daily risked their lives, trying to save the honour of France. These were the real heroes and heroines, constant irritants and threats to the Germans in their active or subtle resistance.

Lena's room in the small barracks in the forest looked out on a barbed-wire fence. At intervals, where the wire grid ended, there was a crimped knot of wire. To leave the camp by the official exit, Lena would have had to go to the entrance where the camp police were stationed. She desperately wanted to go into the village but knew she would have been turned back by the camp guards and reported. Fraternization with the villagers was forbidden, and, of course, as a labour-camp prisoner, she had no papers. Everything she had had been confiscated by the Germans.

"I watched and waited for a chance, and one day when no one was around to see what I was doing at the fence, I picked at the joint in the wire until I had unravelled it in such a way that I could open and close it at will. With this unofficial back door, I began regular visits to the village about four kilometres away. I would go to the café in the inn, which was run by an old man and his daughter. She had studied at the Sorbonne in Paris. Although they were Germans, they liked the French and were not at all sympathetic to the Nazis. There were many people of that kind who disliked the Nazis, but had to keep their views to themselves or risk being thrown into a concentration camp."

The innkeeper's daughter had billeted prisoners of war, as the Germans wanted to disperse their captives through the German Reich. Part of the inn had been requisitioned as a regular prison unit. She would feed the men in the kitchen and spoil them with good food. The first time she saw Lena she invited her inside and introduced her to the prisoners there. To the twenty-two-year-old Frenchwoman, she was a sweet, kind person who cared about her charges. Lena was stuffed with home-made food each time she sneaked out of camp to visit the inn.

Lena's successes made her so bold that one morning she untied the wire, sneaked through the underbrush beside the road to the village and took the train from there to the city for the day. There were some volunteer workers who were given passes to leave the camp, but Lena was not one of these. At the Toging station on her way back, she noticed the police were checking people for passes, and she knew that papers would have to be shown on arrival at the village station. She was trapped.

"I had to get off the train. If I didn't, I was finished. Just before the station there was a bridge and a sharp turn where the train slowed down. I opened the door and jumped, rolling down the slope. When the train had passed, I bypassed the village and sneaked back into the camp without detection.

"On one of these excursions, I lost my way on a footpath in the forest and blundered into a small clearing where there were small wooden buildings. There were bars on the windows, and people with haunted, hungry-looking faces were staring out at me. I asked, 'Who are you? Why are you here?' but they didn't answer. Maybe they couldn't understand, but to the day I die, I will never forget the fear on their thin, bony faces. I was never able to discover who they were and why they were hidden out there in the forest and not locked in the camp."

Finally Lena's illicit excursions were discovered. She was

certain someone had informed on her. As she was returning from Toging and had made her usual jump from the train, the police were waiting for her at the bridge. She was arrested. In custody was another girl who had been picked up shortly before.

"Luckily for me, it was my same sour-puss foreman in the three-man group. He was talking to the other two guards, and I whispered to the girl: 'I'm not going back to work. See...over there is a trail. The minute I give the signal, we started running and don't stop.' We walked along as if nothing was amiss and then zip...we burst into a dash like crazy people. I was scratched by the bushes and thorns, and behind, old Sourpuss was running after us. I developed a stitch in my side and couldn't run anymore, but it was a long time before they caught up to me. They caught the other girl first. Sourpuss was so angry he grabbed us by our necks and shook us against each other. He was a big man. Breathless and red-faced, he was soaked with sweat, and his clothes were torn. I had heard that he had been an Olympic running champion who had been mobilized. So I was pretty proud of my performance."

Lena was marched back to the factory at eight that night and forced to work right through to make up for the lost day. Her shift was to end at three a.m., but it wasn't long before she stopped and walked away from her machine. The Obermeister was called.

"'You are not at your work,' he said coldly.

"'It's too late.'

"'We caught you, eh?' he gloated. 'You get back to work.'

"'Okay, but not for long, because tomorrow I'm escaping again.'

"I laughed in his face.

He smiled. "'Yah, and I'm going to Paris tomorrow. That's a Frenchwoman for you...always joking.'

"'Yes, and we'll meet in Berlin, because I'm going to be there when it's all over to see you all get it good.'

"He thought it was a big joke. However, when I returned to my room at about four that night, I knew I had to go quickly. One of my campmates had whispered that I was going to be shipped out to a concentration camp, probably Dachau, north-west of Munich, just because of what I had done."

Half an hour later, Lena was at the fence unravelling the barbed-wire knot again, and she fled into the night. She walked for hours avoiding the roads. Her absence was noticed by one of her roommates and by mid-morning the guards were out with tracking dogs, hunting for her in the forest.

She hid in a water-filled ditch, and the dogs missed her scent. She waited a few hours and then climbed out and followed a canal for seventeen kilometres through a forest and past a small village. Lena had no idea where the canal was leading her, for no boats plied the water. The war had affected all cargo transportation in the country. She reached the outskirts of the village and hid in the woods for two days, waiting for someone to pass. The last time she had eaten was three days earlier, just before she had been arrested near the bridge.

When a man walked by whistling 'Douce France', a PoW song, she knew he was French. She called to him and told him she had escaped from a labour camp.

"I told him I was starving and except for some berries, hadn't seen any food for three days. He said to stay there in hiding and he would be back with help. He came back with a French Major who had been a doctor in the army and was now treating released war prisoners. He brought food, but I had such a severe case of hiccups that I couldn't eat."

The two men asked Lena what she planned to do. When she said she didn't know, they suggested she hide deep in the forest until they could get forged identity papers for her. She found a spot in the heavy undergrowth where there was no path and settled down alone. Someone would bring her a bag of food each day and some blankets to use, and she remained in the woods for three months. Summer passed and the fall began, and Lena knew that she would not survive much longer. Winter was coming, and the cold would finish her off.

She appealed to her mentors. The Major knew of a Russian soldier hiding in a small shack on a nearby mountian. He asked the man to take Lena in for a short time until her papers were ready, but the soldier said it was impossible. He couldn't even make a fire for fear the Germans would see the smoke.

When the Major saw how precarious Lena's plight was, he pushed harder to procure her false papers so she could move freely from one area to another. The moment she had them, Lena left for Munich by train, where she would have to transfer to a train to

France.

"Unfortunately I didn't watch as carefully as I should have when I approached the train platform in Munich. A member of the Gestapo was standing there asking for passports. All I had was a permit, no passport. I was in real danger. I turned back and walked around the station and went back to the gate two or three times in an attempt to figure out some way of boarding the train. It had to be good because I had already been arrested several times, had been in a Paris prison and a cell in camp, and had a record. I had been forced to sign a paper on which was written that I was a volunteer and I was accepting deportation to Ravensbruck if I got into trouble again. Who in their right mind would accept deportation to a concentration camp?"

Lena was walking along the platform and suddenly noticed French prisoners boarding a train near the one she had wanted to take. There were no German guards there. At the entrance to the passenger car, three French officers were talking and did not notice Lena. The train was full of prisoners being repatriated to France.

"The train was asking me to take it. I slipped up the steps, sat down and stayed quiet. No one bothered me or asked anything. For an hour I sat in fear before the doors closed and we were off. When the train reached the countryside, a soldier asked me what I was doing there, and I told my story."

"'Now that you're here, stay here,' said one of the Frenchmen.

"I had no choice. The Germans had locked the train doors, and no one could get out until the train reached its destination, where the doors would be unlocked.

"The soldiers all had pink slips with their permits. Mine was mauve. At the border checkpoint, the Germans were waiting to unlock the doors of each car. The prisoners alighted, one car at a time, to prevent overcrowding. The border guards asked for their papers, looked them over and led them right back to the cars. One of the soldiers realized I would be stopped. He gave me a military jacket to drape around my shoulders.

"'You are going to get through,' he said.

"'It's no use. I won't make it.'

"He stopped me. "'Listen, you made it this far, and you will get off the train and you will pass. That's that!'

"I got off, hemmed in on all sides by the others so I would not be noticeable, and I made it. I can thank the Italians for that. To this day, I love Italians. Why? Because inside the station an Italian officer was sitting at a table, checking the permits. He was singing an aria from *Tosca*, and as he sang, he kept time with a rubber stamp slammed on each permit. He looked as if he didn't give a damn about the army, the war or what he was doing. I extended my militarily clad arm along with the others and no matter, pink, lilac, or mauve, he pounded that stamp down on my paper. The guard who put me back on the train didn't even wonder what I was doing there. I was just another faceless body in a military jacket getting into the coach."

After another hour, the train stopped at Mulhouse in Alsace. The French people of the town were there to welcome their repatriated soldiers with cake and fruit. The German locomotive with its German crew was removed, and a French locomotive and crew replaced them. And while this was being done, the people of the town made it an occasion. They shook hands with everyone and welcomed them back.

"And so, after another train ride, that was how I returned to Paris, but I could stay only two or three days to visit my parents. They had been hiding in Leblanc in the Unoccupied Zone, and remained there until 1943, when they returned to Paris. I knew I had to find a way out of Paris, because it was dangerous to stay. You could be denounced by anyone. My instincts proved right. I went out to do some errands and on my return, my father said the police from the Vichy government had been there. The landlady had denounced me. No one else knew I was there, but her.

"I discovered that while I had been in Germany, my father had been in jail. Like so many others, his only crime had been his travelling to the Atlantic coast without proper papers, when he was selling jewellery for his brother-in-law. But in prison he had made some friends who were released about the same time as he. My father contacted these people, and they came to get my mother and me. They took us to a place near Poitiers where we hid in the maternity ward of a hospital for eight days. From there the Underground moved us to an unoccupied apartment over a boutique that belonged to one of my father's customers in the town of Civray."

But Lena had no food card and when she went to the City

Hall to get one, the man in charge found it strange she lacked one. Lena had been told the man was a collaborator, and so she contacted the Resistance before she was reported and picked up. She had been told by the group to go to the umbrella saleslady selling her wares in front of the police station. She was a contact. The butcher and baker in the village had been warned that they were to be picked up and had also gone underground, using the same contact.

"She put me in touch with others, and on the day arranged for a group to leave and join the Maquis, the butcher, baker and I followed them with provisions. There were about thirty of us strung out in a straggling line, so it wouldn't look too suspicious. We had to pass in front of the police station. The Germans asked where we were going, and we said on a picnic. It was a good excuse to cover the provisions we were carrying. The guards didn't think it odd. They told us to have a good time. If they had known what we were up to, we would have been finished. We were carrying food to Resistance members, an act punishable by death."

But time was running out for many of the Resistance fighters. In April and May, 1944, their sabotage teams had halted production at the Bronzavia aircraft components plant and stopped work at the Timken ball-bearing factory, near Paris.*

A few weeks later their units damaged eight tanks and stole armoured cars from the Renault works on the outskirts of Paris. A day later, they hit the newly repaired Dunlop factory at Montluçon and then arranged a strike which shut down the Aubert and Duval steel works at Ancizes. The following day, 100,000 litres of acetone were sent up in smoke by the Resistance in the Lambiotte plant at Premery.*

The attacks continued: production of self-propelled guns at Lorraine-Dietrich works in Bagnères-de-Bigorre was halted; the CAM ball-bearing factory at Ivry-sur-Seine was raided; the hydro-electric station at Bussy was blown up four days later, and a sabotage operation in the *Arsénal National* at Tarbes stopped production of artillery pieces.*

Infuriated by these subversive activities, the Germans mounted an intensive campaign to round up those responsible. And in retaliation, deportation to labour and death camps was

*Chronology of World War II, Marshall Cavendish Books Ltd., London, 1982, pp. 153-156.

stepped up. At the same time, the Germans cut food supplies to the Occupied Zone. In the spring and summer of 1944, Paris was suffering severe shortages of food and medical supplies. Those who did not starve, or had escaped the sweeps of the Nazi dragnets, either remained in hiding or joined the Resistance. People huddled around their radios listening to the BBC and yearning for the end of the war. Famine sat like an invisible spectre on Paris's doorsteps. The city was starving; the population dropping like flies.

Meanwhile in Civray, the umbrella lady was in a particularly dangerous position—right in front of the German guards stationed at the gendarmerie. Lena was one of the Resistance couriers who passed on messages. One day when she was at the library, the librarian whispered, "There will be an attack by the Germans tonight. They are planning to clean out the group operating in this area."

Lena immediately took her urgent message to the umbrella lady, who jumped on her bicycle and alerted the Resistance group. When the Germans raided the hideout, no one was there.

"But," said Lena, "word must have got out somehow because the umbrella lady was arrested. Four or five days later, a plumber met me on the street and told me to leave quickly. The Germans knew I was responsible for the tip-off, and I was in trouble. But as it turned out, I didn't have time to escape because that night, the Germans moved out northward, ordered to abandon Civray. The Normandy landings had begun."

Many of the Resistance members had come out of hiding in support of the Normandy landings on June 6, 1944. Tables had been set up in the town square, and food prepared. Wine bottles were brought out of hiding places. Suddenly a member left on guard outside the town came running to warn everyone the Germans were heading their way. Everybody ran off in a panic. Lena had been eating breakfast in the restaurant facing the square when the first shots rang out. She ran to the window. Unknown to the townspeople, the Germans had set up gun emplacements in the hills and began strafing the town at a two-kilometre range. Terrified the little restaurant would be blown up, Lena ran out into the street.

"When I reached the corner, it looked as if it was raining bullets. There were holes all around me. I took cover in a garage doorway. It appeared that they could see me and were following me with bullets. So I ducked out and zigzagged, darting into one doorway after another and bent over, I kept my body as close to the ground as possible. I managed to continue home this way."

But then the Germans began to close in, moving down from the hills around the town. Once the Resistance fighters saw targets to aim at, they began retaliating. But the Frenchmen didn't stand a chance. They were outnumbered and were dropping one after the other. As each one fell, another member darted out to pick him up and run for cover. The medical staff from a private clinic, operating right under the noses of the Germans attended to those who had been shot.

"The Germans must have radioed for help because the next day a large reinforcement of soldiers arrived, and another battle broke out. We fled, four Resistance members, my mother, carrying my three-and-a-half-year-old cousin Bernard, left in her care, and myself.

"We jumped into a ditch flanking vegetable gardens and fields and hid there all day. Beyond the fields was a heavily wooded area. We could hear all kinds of sounds around us. The gunfire had not stopped. At one point several of us raised our heads slightly to peer out and saw an open convertible coming down the road. Inside were German officers with peaked caps. The car stopped right in front of our hiding-place.

"'That's it. We're finished,' I thought. The Maquis men and I burrowed deeper. At the bottom of the ditch was a large patch of poison ivy. We were trapped in it, unable to move. I hugged little Bernard close. He knew something was wrong. He looked at me and whispered, 'Are we going to die?'

"'Yes, I think so,' I answered, trying to stay calm.

"I put my hand over his mouth so he wouldn't cry out, but he pushed my fingers away and whispered, 'Will it hurt?' I held him closer.

"'Not very much, no.' He didn't move. We heard the Germans setting up a machine gun above us. The stream running through the ditch amplified sounds.

"'They've seen us. They're going to shoot us. That's it!'

"We said our farewells to each other and waited to die, cut to ribbons by machine-gun bullets."

261

But nothing happened. After an interval of silence, one of the men peered out. The Germans had packed up and left. Again they waited, but by 10 p.m. Lena became impatient.

"That's it. I'm not staying here any longer."

Several of the men didn't want to leave, but the others said they would try to rejoin the main group by a back route. There was still heavy artillery pounding away. A short while before, a shell had whistled past over their heads and exploded on contact.

So the small group sneaked back to the street where Lena lived over the boutique. En route they were joined by others. Lena peered around the corner of the street, and to her dismay saw a German post with a guard stationed opposite her small flat. The guard would march up the street, turn and then march back to his post. Lena suggested to her comrades that they hide at her place, but they would have to get in while the guard's back was turned on his patrol. She was the first to go, running quickly and quietly unlocking the door. She slipped inside, her heart pounding. And each time the guard began his monotonous march away from his post, one by one, all of the group made it to the doorway and inside.

"It was an incredible stroke of luck for us," Lena remembered. "Earlier that day there had been a battle on the street, and at least thirty people had been gunned down. One of the more recent arrivals to the group told me about it. The butcher, the baker and an eight-year-old boy were among those who were dead. And the man who had tipped me off had not been able to get back to the Maquis. He had been shot dead like a rabbit, coming out of his house."

The empty boutique below had once been a shoe shop, and about fifteen people were hidden upstairs, crammed into the attic above Lena's small flat. Those who had been in the ditch spent the night scratching themselves, trying to find some relief from the poison ivy they had touched.

The next morning the Germans were still there, and guards were posted up the street watching the road. A machine gun had been set up on the sidewalk in front of the boutique. About mid-morning they came to search the house. They found nothing in the abandoned boutique, and then they mounted to the second floor to see if there was an arms cache or any Maquis hidden there. One of the Resistance group saw a soldier carrying a tin of gasoline. He was ready to torch the building if something incriminating was found. Rumour had it that these soldiers had been responsible for setting the Oradour-sur Glane church on fire on June 10, 1944. As a warning to all towns involved in resistance work, the Nazi SS used Oradour as an example of retaliation. Rounding up the entire population—men, women and children—the SS had herded them into barns, garages and sheds around the square. Another large group of villagers was forced into the church. Without warning, the Germans had sprayed the tightly packed people with machine-gun and rifle fire. Then straw and wood faggots were thrown in, spread around and set on fire. That day the SS troops massacred 642 men, women and children at Oradour.

"And now these savages were staking out our hiding place. We were sure they would burn it down just to smoke us out. They were angry at the resistance they encountered in the villages. Not too long before, a group of critically wounded men, some of them Germans, had been found in a private clinic. Because the soldiers couldn't be moved, the clinic was left intact. Instead the SS troops killed all the villagers. More than two hundred civilians were killed. That type of infamy was typically Nazi.

"We kept silent, not daring to move, breathe or scratch. Finally convinced the building was deserted, the soldiers ignored the attic and clumped down the stairs. We tried to get some sleep. And while some of us tended to our poison-ivy rashes, a few men were left on guard duty. By morning the Germans had left the village, and the people were back on the streets. There were many dead to be buried."

The Maquis came back, as did another group—the Communist Party resisters, who called themselves the Franc-Tireurs et Partisans Français (FTPF Sharpshooters).

"'It's finished,' said the Maquis. 'Only we are left. We got rid of the Germans.'"

But one of the Maquis group resented the Communist Franc-Tireurs and warned them to get out and go elsewhere. The villagers didn't want the two groups there, or there would have been a pitched battle. Despite their common hatred of the German invaders, the politically oriented resistance groups, of which there were more than a dozen, squabbled amongst themselves like children in a school yard.

263

"The villagers dug a huge hole in which to dump the dead Germans," Lena remembered with distaste. "Our dead people were buried in the village cemetery. The woman who owned the house where I was hiding came to get me to participate in the burial of the Germans. Those who were left alive among the villagers lined up to spit on the bodies in the hole.

"I didn't think it was right. They were just soldiers like ours, blindly following orders. I remembered the fifty-five-year-old guard I had met some time before on a bridge. He had said, 'What the hell am I doing here at my age, fighting this dumb war, while my wife and kids are slaving away on the farm to give most of the crop away to feed the army? I haven't seen my kids in years.' The soldiers were like anyone else. They were forced to fight a war they hated. Not all of them were Nazis.

"One of the German officers who had been killed had a wooden leg, a souvenir of an earlier battle. The villagers were parading around with the leg, passing it from shoulder to shoulder. They had found a young, twenty-year-old wounded German in a wrecked car. His stomach had been slit from chest to groin, probably by one of the villagers. The umbrella lady, who had been released from prison, was straddling the hood of the car, hysterically screaming and forbidding anyone to give the dying youth any water.

"Her fist raised in the air, she shouted: 'Keep killing them! Kill them all!'

"The poor soldier was dying and crying for his mother. All around me people were doing terrible things to get even, and it horrified me. The Fifth-Columnist collaborator, who had asked why I didn't have a food card, was seized by a village firing squad and shot as part of the celebrations. But that one deserved it. He was responsible for so many people killed through his denunciations."

The war dragged on through 1944. In Italy the Allies struggling up the boot were pushing the Germans northward, foot by foot. The French Resistance continued its activities, each strike taking its toll on German resources.

Lena returned to Paris in January, 1945 and discovered that everything in the house had been stolen. She was certain it was the landlord because he had a key. Without any money or any means of support, she decided to join the army.

"I had to eat. I was rundown, anemic and sick because of the deprivations I had suffered and I needed treatment. Medical tests showed I was suffering from a lung problem aggravated by anemia, but the army found help for me. I had friends who took care of me while I recuperated, but I couldn't leave Paris until the end of May."

Lena's parents had returned to Paris to be with their daughter. Most of their friends had died either in the trains transporting them to labour camps or in the death camps. The reunion was short. As soon as X-rays showed Lena's lungs had cleared, she signed her final papers and was hired as a secretary attached to an Allied Military Occupation command. A few weeks later, a new posting order arrived, and she was sent to Berlin. Her outspoken prophecy when taunting the Obermeister had been realized. She would be in Berlin when it was all over.

"But unfortunately, France did not have its own zone at the time, and the British and Americans didn't want France muscling in," Lena recalled wryly. "So we got stuck at Baden-Baden. Naturally, with the typical disorganization of that period, nothing had been planned for us. We had no food. The Germans had stolen all the good wines from the wine cellars, even those from the Rothschild estates. But when the French arrived at Baden-Baden, lo and behold, they found huge stocks of stolen French wines and grabbed them back. They *did* belong to France. We installed ourselves in a home that had escaped the bombing and lived in a wine haze for a while to dull the hunger ache in our stomachs. And it got worse. We had to scavenge for food. There was a typhus epidemic raging in Berlin, and we had to get shots against the disease. We couldn't wait to leave."

Finally one morning orders came through to leave for Berlin. An old passenger plane picked up the group, which included a colonel, two information officers, three gendarmes and Lena, and flew them to Berlin via Strassburg. A French General was waiting to welcome them. Although the French zone had not yet been properly organized, a villa, at least, had been requisitioned for their use. The general, the colonel, and a small contingent of soldiers and staff were installed there.

"We had a PX canteen and had to eat in a big garage set up as a cafeteria. But to get there, I was accompanied by two soldiers with fixed bayonets. There were Russian soldiers in the zone, and they had no respect for property or women, German or otherwise. They were looting and raping, and many women had been violated. It was a while before things became more organized."

Lena had requisitioned a room near the Russian zone but didn't like it. She was afraid. Some drunk or crazy Russian had fired a gun in the direction of her lodging, and a bullet had plowed through the wall into the pillow on her bed. Luckily for Lena, she was elsewhere when it happened. She insisted on another billet. Her commanding officer wanted to know why she was moving out.

"'Hey, listen,' I said. 'You assigned me to a room on the edge of the Russian zone, me, a woman alone. If I don't get shot, I could get raped. This is no picnic.'

"And so, I settled in a villa where Hitler's architect Speer had lived with his wife and daughter. The architect's son had joined the German Werewolf movement which had been formed with other diehard Nazis to harass the occupiers. When Speer was questioned about his son's whereabouts, he hemmed and hawed. And sniping continued. Life was dangerous in Berlin at that time. If the Germans or Russians didn't get you, it was disease. With the typhus epidemic raging, I got sick and almost died."

Lena found conditions primitive in those days immediately after the collapse of the Third Reich. Berlin was almost deserted and in ruins, as the different Occupation forces eyed each other suspiciously. However, she was determined to see something of the city, instead of remaining locked away in the villa.

"Once, on a Sunday, a group of us went out to visit the Reichstag, or what was left of it. I have never seen a city in such a state. I still have a fragment of stone I picked up in the ruins. We lost ourselves in the damaged corridors up there, and at one place noticed a lump of greyish matter crawling with maggots. We knew it had been a soldier from the tattered uniform which was protruding from the heap. Our stomachs were churning. It seemed it took forever to find an exit. We went into a café to get some beer to compose ourselves, and there were corpses rotting in the basement. It was hot, and the smell was terrible. No matter where we went, we could not escape the devastations of war. We just looked at one another and shook our heads. We didn't feel comfortable. We bolted our drinks and left."

It was late June, 1945, and Lena began to enjoy her work, but it was a while before conditions improved. The French embassy, destroyed in the air raids, had not been rebuilt. Each of the Allies had its own zone and didn't check at all with the French. There was no contact except at the PX when the French group went to get food and supplies.

"Of course, the Americans got first choice, so by the time the French arrived, nothing much was left. Some of those Americans were wild, but a small number of the French occupying forces were worse. They behaved like savages, driving their jeeps up on the sidewalk and killing pedestrians. A French Captain was arrested and returned to Paris for raping two German women. Sure, they wanted revenge, but they were no better than the others who did the same thing. There was little law and order to stop them. It was a disgrace, and probably many of the commanders turned a blind eye.

"There were all kinds of parasites there, friends of friends, who were getting big salaries, and here we were just getting by on our soldiers' meagre wages. The word must have filtered back because one of the big French magazines sent a journalist up there to look into the corruption and do a story on it. But because I knew so much and had a reputation for being outspoken, I was confined to my room for two days so he couldn't get any information from me. Everyone else clammed up.

"Yes, it was a thoroughly bad period. The German underground kept sniping at the occupiers—American, Russian, British and French—and my colonel was recalled to France for selling his revolver to a member of the Werewolf movement. Suddenly I found myself without a boss."

And so, Lena was reassigned to the International Zone in the American sector. She attended conferences and worked regularly with interpreters. Each of the occupying Powers had its monthly conferences, and reports and paperwork had to be written on Berlin city management. She was installed with a British officer, a German secretary and a Russian officer in a large building where each Power had its own offices.

"Each officer had a secretary in the interpreters' pool. The Russians were the most difficult to get along with. When things finally straightened out fourteen months later, I returned to France, divorced my first husband and married a French army officer.

"Strange things were happening in France after the war. Through De Gaulle's peculiar foreign policies in dealing with outside nations, he stirred up much anger and criticism. Many people acknowledged how bad his policies were. They ruined France. And instead of reducing the power of the resident Communists and Socialists in France, De Gaulle actually planted them more firmly in French soil. There were KGB officers operating freely in France, coming and going as they pleased. It was a subject often criticized in my second husband's family, for his parents had been White Russians who had emigrated to France."

Emigration was at its highest during those years. Over two million people left the country to settle elsewhere. Taxes climbed to astronomical heights, the brunt of the burden falling on the professionals and business people.

"Many businesses failed for this reason. Every cent you earned was heavily taxed. The government took everything, and by 1968 the population was totally disenchanted with De Gaulle and wanted him out."

Lena and her family joined the lists of emigrés in 1968 and came to Canada, with the intention of using this country as a springboard to prepare eventually for emigration to the United States. When Lena learned her son would be inducted into the American Army and sent to Vietnam, she decided to remain in Canada. He entered university and by the time the Vietnam war had ended and he could move across the border, he had lost interest in the States. He preferred to finish his studies in Canada, and the family remained in Quebec. Lena's husband found a job at Canadian Vickers two days after his arrival, and her daughter became a computer programmer, eventually switching to real estate. Her son, who had initially wanted to become a dentist, went into chemistry and became director of a company.

But Lena found the adjustment hard. She had spent so many years of her life resisting Fascism and then Communism in her country that it became second nature to resist the latest changes in her new way of life. She could not adjust or feel she had given something to her new country.

"I wish I could have said I contributed something to Canada. Many other French immigrants who came to Quebec, settled here and opened businesses. Many educated Quebecers into the art of hotellerie business—good eating, and the drinking of good wines, which sets this province apart from the others. But young people contribute more. I was older when I came here, and older people don't adjust as easily as the young. I don't think Canada did anything for me; I've never been happy here. Too many things bothered me—the lack of education around me, the ignorant people I came across, the insatiable love of money and material things, and the selfishness I saw. My family felt that way, too. We probably would have been happier in France, and did go back several years ago, but were forced to return. It was just too expensive living in France. I'm going to wait a few years until the French Government changes and then try again," she says, with a determined look on her face.

The worst thing Lena hates about Canada is the climate. She can't stand it. France's climate is more temperate. Although she loves Canada's changes of season, she finds the opposites in summer and winter too extreme. To spend eight months of the year, locked in because of the weather, is more than she can bear. Every year, sometimes twice a year she returns to her country of origin. Her health has suffered in Canada, she says.

"I'm always sick here, and when I return to France, I'm fine. I'm used to eating fresh food, and everything here is shipped in from somewhere else, and the quality suffers. Animals are kept in barns here, eating dried and even mouldy hay for seven months of the year. They should be in pasture all year round to produce good milk and meat. I can't even drink milk here; it's like water."

Lena found much to deplore when she emigrated. She was dumbfounded at many of the customs and practices in Quebec, expecially prejudices against immigrants.

"And as for immigrants being accepted, you would have to change the mentality of Canadians to make things better for new-comers. But it is difficult to change them because their mentality is what makes their identity. There has been a lot of racism toward immigrants. It isn't only in their adjustment and integration in every-day life. Immigrants can't be a part of the government, not in politics or public services. Maybe their children will, but not the immigrant, no matter how educated or how intelligent he is. So what do you want an immigrant to do when he comes here? Serve as cheap labour? Some are lucky to make money, but not all. I have met many who see Canada as a place to make money and then take it back to their homeland to spend. They are quitters. There would be less quitters if more immigrants were interested in Canadian politics. But basically we are all quitters. My son won't stay, and most of the people we know will leave. They have been frightened too many times before in the lands of origin, and they are ready to go at the first sign of trouble. Can you blame them?

"And very often, an immigrant receives his citizenship papers and still is not regarded as a citizen. There are immigrants here who ask nothing but the chance to give of their knowledge and intelligence, and no one wants them. And only because they aren't Quebecois. And on the other hand, you have Quebecers who are lazy and incompetent, yet have incredible jobs with huge salaries, and they look down their noses at immigrants.

"And what irritates immigrants is that while the workplace is English, you have to speak French. Quebec is forcing kids to speak French, so they grow up to be unemployed. I am French but I still find that nonsense here with the French language ridiculous. Let them speak both languages. Use English and French at home, or wherever the situation demands it. Forbidding an international language like English is stupid. And what if you move to another province to look for work? What good is your unilingual Quebecer then? If Quebecers want to hear and speak only French here, English will be wiped out totally in this province. And as for the quality, who calls *joual* a language? My kids were never allowed to speak it. They'd get a slap. English or proper French, but none of that dialect—not in my house.

"Another thing that is wrong is for the Quebecois to blame the English for the province's problems. The priests did more harm to Quebec than the English ever did. The priests cut Quebec off from Europe after the French Revolution and to this day, the priests are still angry at France for losing The Hundred Years' War.

"When my son, who was at a college run by priests, had his boots stolen, I went to see the priest in charge to complain. When he realized I was from France, he said: 'You damn dirty French, you abandoned us.'

"I said it wasn't true; we lost the war. It was the bishops who cut Quebec off. They didn't want Quebec contaminated by the doctrines of the French Revolution—liberty, equality and fraternity. The priests kept the Quebecois submissive, using religion to control them more easily.

"As far as the immigrants and their relationships with other Quebecers are concerned, they don't get close, even with a mutual language and common ancestry. Immigrants make friends with other immigrants. Quebecers won't accept immigrants as friends. The Quebecois don't have any affection except for their own kind, their pay cheques and their beer. They are xenophobic and don't want to see people of other backgrounds. In many cases they won't even see their own families.

"We tried to make friends, but it didn't work and many other immigrants said the same thing. The Quebecois' existence and his *joie de vivre* revolves around life in restaurants and bars. They don't visit one another too much. What happens when there is no humanity is that there is no love for others, and no country can live without love. If there is no heart, you can't ask for help from anyone. Try, and see how long you wait. Or you get a 'Nice to see you, give me your phone number and I'll call you.' You can bet your life you will never hear from them.

"And that's probably why our hearts are still in France. We are Europeans. Even my son says we will be Europeans until we die. If I had to do it all over again, I wouldn't have come here. I would have stayed in France. If it wasn't for the political and economic situation there, no Frenchman would leave his beautiful land. We are proud of our heritage, but why isn't it acceptable here?"

FALASHA

by
Milly Charon
from an interview with Malka Abraham,
newspaper clippings from *The Boston Globe,*
The Gazette (Montreal), and *Canadian Jewish News;*
excerpts from *The Story of the Falashas*
by Dr. Simon D. Messing, and other sources

A slanting early morning rain drizzled down into the grey mist hovering over the city of Addis Ababa. It was the rainy season in Ethiopia. Figures huddled into dripping garments picked their way toward the prison. By 6 a.m. a few hundred people had already gathered. Hundreds more would continue to arrive over the next few hours. They carried bundles, pails or pots, and as the crowd grew in size, the lines in front of the rough grey walls lengthened like a stretching serpent, patiently waiting for the huge iron gates to open.

Falasha Malka Abraham waited in line, as she had waited every morning for three years, in baking sunshine or pouring rain, to bring food to her husband imprisoned seven years earlier. For the first four years prison food had been provided, but then government changes had created a new system under which families of prisoners had to feed their relatives, incarcerated for undetermined periods of time.

She did not know why he had been arrested or what he had done. When Emperor Haile Selassie had been deposed on September 12, 1974, the Provisional Military Administrative Council known as the Dergue had taken over the country. A Marxist-Leninist policy was adopted by the Dergue, and for the next three years there existed a period of terrorism and civil disobedience, as Monarchists, Liberals and revolutionary dissidents warred against the military government.

The President of the Dergue, General Teferi Benti, died on February 3, 1977, in an attempted coup against the Dergue itself, and a few months later neighbouring Somalia launched an invasion of south-eastern Ethiopia. One of the creators of the Dergue, Lieutenant-Colonel Mengistu Haile Mariam, took over as head of the military government, losing no time in accepting Soviet aid in quelling internal dissidents, halting the Somali invaders and recovering territories taken during the previous five years. Ethiopia now had an alliance with the Soviet bloc, and suddenly thousands of Soviet advisers appeared, to set up residence throughout the country. The population lived in fear, as arrests and imprisonment became everyday occurrences.

"There was usually a two-to-three-hour wait at the prison, so I had to get up very early in order to be back home before 8 a.m., to feed my three children, take them to school and then get to work at the clinic," Malka explained. "I prepared my husband's breakfast, lunch and supper and carried all the food in a simple pail. For so many years this was my existence—so much hardship, and no joy whatsoever. We had drifted apart before his imprisonment and although there was so little understanding between us, I still went to visit him, and for the last three years I waited every morning outside the gates for hours, in all kinds of weather, to bring him his food.

"I knew I could never marry another man, and when I finally told my husband that I was leaving the country to start a new life, he understood why. There was nothing we could offer each other, and I had to bring up the children myself."

Malka's life had not been an ordinary one. The tiny, beautiful woman had been born into hardship and service to her people—the Ethiopian Jews or Falashas known as Beta Israel. Among the oldest and most devout of Jewish sects, they had numbered approximately 20,000 to 25,000 in 1983, living among thirty million Coptic Christians, Moslems and others in Ethiopia.

According to Ethiopian legend, the Falashas had descended from Menelik I, the child of the union of the black Queen of Sheba and King Solomon, who ruled over Israel in the tenth century B.C. Some stories said that the Falashas' ancestors migrated to Ethiopia after the destruction of the Temple of Jerusalem by the Roman Emperor Titus in 70 A.D. Other sources said that these black Jews were descendants of the Tribe of Dan, one of the ten lost tribes of Israel, who had trekked southward from Egypt during the Exodus, in the thirteenth century B.C.

Falasha in Amharic means "stranger", "wanderer" or "one who owns no land". They have lived in the Begemdir, Tigre and Gonder provinces of Ethiopia for over 2,000 years and still keep kosher homes, practise circumcision rites and read the same chapters of the Torah as the rest of the world-wide Jewish communities. They celebrate all Jewish holidays except Chanukah and Purim because they were isolated from the two historical events which created the holidays.

* * * *

During the fifteenth century, there were accounts of Falasha wars against the Coptic Christian emperors, waged in the mountains of Abyssinia, and in the seventeenth century, when there were an estimated 250,000 Falashas, their final uprising against King Susneyos, a Christian Amharic King, was crushed.* Thenceforth the Falashas, their numbers decreasing each year, lived as second-class citizens without the right to own land.

Until the mid-eighteenth century, the Falashas had led such an isolated life that their very existence was considered to be mythical. Christian missionaries had read reports by explorer James Bruce about the Falashas. Bruce had travelled to Abyssinia in 1768. Missionary Samuel Gobat reached Gonder in 1830 and rediscovered the Beta Israel. However, civil wars forced him to leave, and it was more than twenty-five years before the missionaries returned. Inadvertently, their reports alerted the Jews of Europe that a lost tribe, practising the laws of Israel, had managed to survive thousands of years of isolation and were being converted to Christianity by the thousands.

The French-based Alliance Israélite Universelle was shocked into action. Famous Orientalist and Philologist Professor Joseph Halevy, sent to analyse the situation in Abyssinia, arrived

* Information on this and the following page is drawn from *The Story of the Falashas—"Black Jews" of Ethiopia*, by Simon Messing, Hamden, Conn., 1982, pp. 14-15, 16-18, 56-57, 60, 68.

in 1867 and tried to sponsor a young Falasha for rabbinical studies in Alexandria. The young man died before he could leave.

Halévy returned to Paris, and his lectures about the Falashas attracted the attention of one of his young students from Poland, Jacques Faitlovitch, who decided to dedicate his life to the Beta Israel.

Faitlovitch planned to help the Falashas bridge the time-and-culture gap through a programme of education. Schools were to be built, the first in Asmara, in Eritrea, and its graduates were to go out and teach others. His first student, teenaged Getye Yeremias, was entrusted to him by the boy's parents. In Asmara, Faitlovitch found another brilliant Falasha student, Taamrat Emmanuel, whose parents had been converted to Christianity. Faitlovitch reclaimed him from the Swedish Mission, and in 1905 enrolled his two pupils at the Ecole Normale in Auteuil, a Paris suburb.

When the young men returned several years later, clad in European clothes, and spoke about their education and experiences, other Falashas were eager to enroll their own children. Students were sent out to Switzerland, Germany, France and Jerusalem and they, in turn, were to educate and reclaim the Falashas from centuries of isolation. Several of these students later served in the government of Haile Selassie. Of these, Taamrat Emmanuel was probably the most distinguished.

Italy invaded Abyssinia in 1935, and when Mussolini's troops arrived at Addis Ababa, Taamrat had managed to accumulate rifles and ammunition to protect his Falashas, whose villages were being pillaged by wandering bands of defeated soldiers. However, in 1937, the Fascists instituted a manhunt to kill modern-educated Ethiopians who would oppose the invaders of their country. Taamrat was forced to flee for his life and he joined Faitlovitch in Jerusalem. Two years later Taamrat accompanied Haile Selassie into exile in London. In 1941 he returned with the Emperor to liberate Ethiopia and was appointed to rebuild the Foreign Ministry. Later Taamrat had a political disagreement with Haile Selassie and was forced to flee Ethiopia to avoid imprisonment. He travelled back to Jerusalem, where he assisted Faitlovitch in supervising the education of young Falasha students sent to Israel to study.

* * * *

Such was the background to Malka's heritage, and the historical setting played an important part in her life of constant uprootings and resettlement. The name "wanderer" could have aptly applied to her.

She was born in the village of Ambober in Gonder Province on August 7, 1945. Her father, recruited at the age of fourteen to be a pupil of Jacques Faitlovitch, was taken to England and France to study in the mid-thirties. But World War II disrupted his education, and he returned to Ethiopia.

"My mother came from a very Orthodox Falasha family, and her father was Abba Towabi, a Kohan Shochet. A legendary figure in the Ethiopian Jewish community, he served as Chief Rabbi and Shochet, founded the village of Ambober and the original synagogue, and was also a renowned defender of Ethiopian Jewish rights.

"The family arranged my mother's marriage to my father, who had come back from Europe with an education and a different outlook on life. My mother was a simple village girl who knew nothing outside of her village existence. There was no common link between them, and they only lived together for two months. My father's intellect was too advanced for any form of communication with her, and he couldn't take that kind of life. He already spoke five or six languages, yet he was unable to converse with her. And so he left, but the war was on, and the Italians picked him up in Asmara and imprisoned him there. They probably thought he was a spy. Perhaps he had criticized the political regime, or his ability with languages could have made the soldiers suspicious. My young and shy mother, two months pregnant, was left in the care of the family, to carry me to full term. Later my parents were divorced."

When Malka was about three, her father returned for her. The war was over, and he had been released. He came to Gonder Province and found work in the municipality's City Hall. Malka was left with a babysitter in Gonder (the city bore the same name as the province), and a year later, he took her with him when he moved to Addis Ababa, where he remained for two years. Once more he was on the move, this time to Harer, where he was to spend six years. Malka was enrolled in a boarding school.

"Every time he came to visit me he inquired about my school-teacher," recalled Malka with a smile. "He was a very handsome man, and finally he married her. My mother had remarried years before and had twelve or thirteen children. I lived with my father and stepmother for a year. He went on to become a very well-known man, and when he died there were many letters and telegrams from prominent people in European countries, as well as from Ethiopia.

"One day my father was accused of writing a letter or making a political comment to someone, and suddenly some men came and took him from Harer to Addis Ababa for questioning. I had an adopted brother by then, and I remember my stepmother coming to school to get me. It was never clear to me why my father had been arrested, but he wasn't imprisoned. The authorities exiled him in Addis, and he was forbidden to leave the city for three years. A friend who had a hotel gave him a room, and my father took care of my step-brother while I was left with another friend in Addis. I was the babysitter for the family's three young children for six months, and then I was placed into the American Mission's boarding school where I remained for eight months."

About this time, a group of Israelis came to visit friends of Malka's family. One of the men said he was preparing a group of children to be sent to Israel for an education. Malka was chosen to go. Before leaving Ethiopia, those who were leaving were given a special audience with Emperor Haile Selassie at the Palace. For Malka it was an exciting event.

On arrival in Israel, children singing songs met the group and presented them with flowers. "I wasn't sure if I was arriving in the Garden of Eden, Heaven or the Holy Land," Malka said with a smile.

The group was taken to Kfar Batya, one of the children's villages, where orphans who had survived the Holocaust had been placed to start new lives. Located at Raanana, near Tel Aviv, the village was to be home for Malka for almost three years.

"It was not as difficult for me to adjust as it was for many of the other children. I had been in boarding school for a number of years and had moved many times during my childhood. I was used to living with other children. And my big dream all my life had been to go to Jerusalem, in the land of my ancestors. We Falasha had repeated this in our prayers for thousands of years. My father had pounded my heritage into my head from as far back as I could remember. 'Don't forget you are Jewish,' he would say. I didn't even know what it meant. So when I arrived in Israel, I felt it was the land of my dreams, my country, my background and that my yearning to see Jerusalem was about to be realized. I was shivering with emotion, and that year was to be the most memorable of my life."

The children studied all the general school subjects such as reading, mathematics and history, as well as religious subjects. They worked—cooking, cleaning, doing farm chores—but managed some time to play. They sang and danced every Friday night after the Sabbath meal.

"Not long after we arrived at Kfar Batya, we had a special guest visit us, a lady from the United States. I was chosen to present her with flowers and welcome her. I hardly knew any English and was very nervous. I didn't even remember her name. Thirty years later, I saw a programme on television and realized that the woman to whom I had been presented was Eleanor Roosevelt. We had many distinguished visitors like her. For many years there was a picture on the wall at Kfar Batya of me with an Israeli lady. Her name was Golda Meir.

"The President of Israel often visited us. So did Yacob Faitlovitch. After spending his entire life helping our people, he had gone into retirement in Israel. He spoke our Amharic language and knew many of our families, especially my father and grandfather. Faitlovitch was like an uncle to us.

"It was an exciting time. But there was one incident that almost cost me my life. I went for a walk alone one Sabbath and without realizing it, I crossed the border. Some Arabs grabbed me and took me to the Police Station. They asked my name and I answered: "Fatima". They wanted to know where I lived, and I told them my parents lived in Jerusalem and had sent me to school in Raanana. With a name like "Fatima", they accepted the story and figured I was a Moslem. They took me back to the border and let me go."

279

In Malka's group there were two other Ethiopian girls from different villages. They found it difficult to adjust. Malka had lived in towns and cities most of her life. The other girls had never seen electric lights or running water. They had never worn shoes, and even though they tried to integrate, it was difficult. They were inseparable, as if they were looking for support from each other. Afraid to make friends, they remained isolated. Malka, on the other hand, moved freely among the groups of other children, organizing all kinds of activities among those from Yemen, Iraq, Iran and Morocco.

"At each table in the dining-hall, there were usually ten children, and you were sure to find they had come from eight to ten different countries. There were even Jewish kids from India, near the Chinese border, and some from Burma. There was some name-calling, but I don't think it was meant to be malicious. We Falashas were called *Kooshi* which means black in Hebrew, but we didn't know this at the time. There was a children's song the kids sang in school about a little black dog. Our language had been Amharic, and when we Falasha children first heard it, we thought it referred to us and we were being called dogs, because the word *Kooshi* was repeated in every verse. The teacher explained it to us. We were learning another language and had not understood. Of course, we were viewed with curiosity because there weren't many black people in Israel in those days. Often we would hear whispers and remarks: 'Look at the Kooshis!'

"An old lady in a shop in Tel Aviv where I was buying something came over to me and tried to rub my skin with a hand-kerchief. 'You are a *Kooshi*', she said in wonder. 'Let me see if the colour is real.'

"I remembered that when white people came to Ethiopia, we called them white in Amharic and after we learned Hebrew, it was *levan*. Some of our Falasha boys were insulted by being called *Kooshi*, but it didn't bother me. There were at least a dozen girls with my name, which is common and means queen. So to distinguish between the other Malkas, I was called Malka Black."

Malka learned many things at Kibbutz Kfar Batya. Her leadership training taught her confidence, something she had lacked before. Now she was being prepared to return home as a grownup ready to help her people. Once back in her country, she was assigned to a primitive village in Gonder Province, where even the langauge was difficult to understand. She had been raised in cities where a modern version of Amharic was used. In Gonder, the ancient tongue was still spoken. At times, her attempts to communicate were met with titters and laughter. Malka became the village storyteller, and day after day, evening after evening, she had to tell of her years in Israel.

"'Were you really in Zion? What was it like? Tell us everything!'" they asked.

"They wanted to know every little detail. They couldn't imagine that I had actually fulfilled what was a dream to them. Because I had been to the Holy Land, they believed everything I said. If I joked about something, they took it literally, and after that, I had to be very careful of what I said, especially with the children."

Malka discovered that it had been easier to adjust to her sojourn in Israel than it was to her return to her homeland. She was not prepared for what she found in this primitive village to which she had been assigned. There was no school, only people sitting on the ground under a tree, waiting to be taught. She realized some kind of structure would have to be built, no matter how simple.

"I organized the villagers to go for timber very far over the mountains, and bring it back. The entire community was involved in the construction of the two rooms we built. One was for me and the other was the classroom. The parents were so happy to have a teacher to instruct their sons and daughters. They looked up to me with such respect, as if I were God. When I realized there was no water nearby, only what could be carried from the river a long distance away, I decided we needed a well. I had noticed a spot about two kilometres from the school where grass continued to grow even in the summer, when it was very hot and dry. I knew there must be water, and told the villagers to dig. Sure enough, there was. From then on it was known as Malka's well, but because we had not reinforced it with cement, it churned into mud when the rains came, and the sides fell in. And then the animals came there to drink. Finally the Israelis, who came out on regular assistance missions to the villages, came in the late fifties and dug us a proper well. In the sixties, they sent a group called Betar, who constructed a proper school. These practical projects, even on a small scale, kept us in touch with our roots.

"In 1958 Taamrat came to visit us. He had been the first Falasha professor in Ethiopia, and he helped me when I decided to go back to Israel to study nursing. He sponsored me. He was an old man by then."

Malka's decision to be a nurse was the result of the horrors she had witnessed in her country. Wherever she went, she saw blind and lame people. Lepers were a common sight, as were people lacking limbs, lying in gutters begging for money. Tuberculosis was rampant, and almost all children suffered from eye disease. Malaria and typhoid raged unchecked, and skin infections, intestinal parasites and fungus growths on children's scalps went untreated. The sight of emaciated people suffering from every form of disease and malnutrition was more than she could bear.

"I saw people dying in the village and other places— mothers, children and babies—and the midwives didn't know why. At the same time I saw little children pass away from what looked like a common cold or childhood fever. My grandfather was sick, and although I wanted to get him to the hospital forty-five kilometres away, he wouldn't go. He refused to eat unkosher food. 'I don't want them to even touch me,' he said. 'I prefer to die. If God wants, he can save me.' Not long after, he died. I couldn't stand it any more. I knew I had to learn to be a nurse so that I could return and help my people."

In 1958 Malka travelled back to Israel to receive her training at Hasharon Hospital in Petach Tikvah, followed by specialized training as a midwife at Kfar Saba Maternity Hospital. She spent three years totally immersed in her studies and acting as a volunteer social worker in her spare time.

"For the first six months, we had classes and then went to work on the wards. My patients liked me. They would give me presents when they were discharged, and my friends became jealous. I never watched the clock and gave a lot of time to my patients. On my days off, I would go and visit them, and even when I slept I would worry about them, especially those in the children's wards. Many times I would wake up dreaming about them, would get up and dress to go to visit them at night to be sure they were all right. I always had a feeling for people and cried when I saw suffering."

Malka met an Israeli doctor at the hospital who had been born in Bulgaria and had emigrated to Italy and thence to Israel. He was much older than she, and her first love, but she was very shy and wouldn't enter into any relationship.

"In the end I couldn't stand it and I left him. I said I had to go back to help my people, and there was no use getting involved if there was no future for us together. I cared, but I had to make the decision, and he understood that helping my people came first.

"And then I met another man in Israel, tall, blond and blue-eyed. He came from a wealthy family. He was in agriculture and would come to visit me on his motorcycle. We kept meeting for about eight months, but again I walked away. I kept thinking, 'What am I doing?' I felt guilty.

"Not long after, I met my future husband who had come to Israel from Ethiopia to study in an ORT (Organization for Rehabilitation through Training) school where trades were taught. I wasn't planning to marry him. He told me he was an Orthodox Falasha, and later I discovered this was untrue. His family had come as refugees to Ethiopia from border areas about one hundred years before and had integrated. I don't think I loved him, but everyone was pushing me to marry.

"Among our people, I felt there was no man I could marry. They were all poor, uneducated village folk. It would have been exactly like my father's situation, and that was why Taamrat, the Falashas' mentor, had never married. With his education, he should have married a European, but he couldn't have returned to live in his village. How would they have communicated with his wife? What kind of life would she have had there? And he had a girlfriend, a very beautiful French girl whose photo I had seen. He was a very handsome and intelligent man, and we both had the same problem. Education had changed us. So, against my better judgment, I married this man and stayed with him, although he was in prison for the last seven years of our marriage."

Malka completed her course of studies and work at the hospital. On her days off she would visit Taamrat and take care of him. She felt he was a great man. One day when she came to visit, he was no longer in his room. All his books, records and belonging had disappeared, and his landlady said he had died and been taken away. It was as if he had vanished without a trace. Later, she discovered he had had a stroke and been removed to a hospital.

In 1963 Malka returned once more to Ethiopia and worked as a nurse, a midwife, and later a hospital administrator at a Swedish clinic. She also trained nurses and participated in public health programmes. During the 1974 drought, she worked with a Swedish health unit in famine-stricken areas, witnessing at first hand the tragic conditions that would take years to be exposed to the world by the media. She also helped establish, with Israeli support, a health clinic in her native village of Ambober, and she participated in many other projects under the supervision of Israeli agronomist Gershon Levy who was serving in Ethiopia with the Jewish Agency.

By 1974, political conditions had worsened, and people were dying of starvation by the thousands. A revolution deposed Haile Selassie, who was blamed for ignoring the state of the country. A Marxist government took over, but it did nothing to stop the drought and famine.

Malka, meanwhile, had continued working, but now was involved in helping people leave the country. Between 1972 and 1974 she managed to get her brother and two sisters safely to Israel.

"I had a babysitter for my three children and was getting a good salary at the Swedish clinic. I also had a part-time job in the evenings which permitted me to earn enough to maintain a nice home. But with the revolution, I was arrested, my home was seized and given to Russian advisers. Released soon after, I was allocated a small house, which I had no choice but to accept. It was a period of insecurity, and I lived in fear.

"At the time I was working as a volunteer in the famine areas. I knew people in the military service and had made contacts there. One of these contacts was very kind and when I had a back problem, he put me in touch with a Russian specialist. In my mind I was hoping he could help me with another problem as well."

Malka had written letters back and forth to a cousin in Montreal, who had contacts and was working on a plan. Malka had also been in touch with a radio station in the Soviet Union after she had filled out one of its questionnaires and sent it away. But with all the mail coming to her address, she was summoned to the police station, where the authorities wanted to know why she was receiving letters from so many places abroad. However, it established that she must be well-known and important enough to receive letters from different parts of the world, including the Soviet Union.

"In 1980 I managed to get my daughters out of Ethiopia. Their names had been entered on a list of children travelling to Communist countries on educational trips, and the papers and exit passes had been processed for them to leave the country. Once they were abroad, they switched destinations and headed for Canada, where they were taken in and cared for by the families of Stan Cytrynbaum, Mark Zarecki and Edit Kuper, my benefactors. These arrangements had been a long time in the planning. I was now scheming to get to Canada myself.

"I knew that the economic and political situation in Ethiopia was deteriorating rapidly. Food was scarce and very expensive. I was exposed to danger because of my background, and my involvement in helping my people leave the country. So when an appointment was made for me to see the Soviet doctor, I went immediately. After X-rays had been taken and he had examined me, we talked about our families. He was married, about fifty-five years old, and had a wife and children in the Soviet Union. His son loved cowboy songs. On my next visit, I brought the doctor a red tie someone had sent me from Paris. He was delighted. Then I brought a record of cowboy songs I had in my collection. I told him about a cousin who lived in Canada. I had to exaggerate a little...that this relative had a restaurant and was very rich, and he would send me papers and tickets so that I could go visit my family. But I needed an exit pass..."

"'Canada is a wonderful country,' the doctor said. 'I have heard it is so big and beautiful and has such kind people.'

"I was trying to get his reaction because I knew he was an important man among the Soviet advisers in my country. And he asked if I went, whether I could bring back some things for himself, his wife and children—things he couldn't get in Russia. I agreed, and asked him to give me a list. I offered to send everything to him a week after I arrived in Canada."

"'No, no, not to me,' he warned. 'Address it to your family or to a friend and I will get it from them.'

"He approved my request to visit Canada, but demanded a great deal of money for the exit papers. I sold everything I had—furniture, clothes, jewellery, to pay him—and everything was arranged for me to leave Addis Ababa on the first Sunday of September, 1982.

"Two days before, the Russian called me after 8 p.m. in the evening to tell me he didn't want to help me. He was afraid. I needed the exit pass or I would not be permitted to leave. I asked for my money back, and he said, 'That you can ask me about next week.' He knew I was supposed to leave in two days. I was desperate. Everything I had was gone, sold to pay him and my plane fare. I rushed madly around approaching people for help. A wealthy Canadian philanthropist advanced the money which the Ethiopian government was demanding—$5,000 for me and for each of my children, despite the fact that they were outside the country. Without this payment of $20,000 I would have been trapped in the country, unable to join my family in Canada."

For nine months after Malka arrived in Montreal, she lived with a family while she waited for her papers to be processed. The Department of Immigration had informed her it would take a few months. When she did not hear from them, she contacted them and was told her papers were in order and a letter would be sent, telling her to come to the Immigration Centre on Dorchester Boulevard. Days went by and still there was no word. Finally Malka went down and asked for an interview with the person in charge of her file.

"The receptionist told me I couldn't see the official without an appointment. I said I would wait and took a chair. Hours went by. Finally a woman came out of an office and again told me that I had no appointment and therefore couldn't see the case-officer. I answered that I would wait anyway, but it must have bothered her because she came out again and invited me into her office. She had my file open in front of her."

"'You have a special Ministerial Permit, which is very difficult to obtain,' she said. 'How did you manage that?'

"And I winked at her and said: 'Maybe he's my cousin.'"

Malka, however, knew how the Ministerial Permit had been arranged.

A few months later in 1983, Malka was at the closing banquet of the Canadian Jewish Congress Convention, and Minister of Immigration Lloyd Axworthy was there as a guest speaker. After dinner he asked to meet "the famous Malka Abraham". He had been personally involved in her case, and Malka was delighted to meet him.

"A photographer took pictures of the Minister with members of my family and myself. But we did determine that he couldn't be my cousin. He's not Jewish," she said with a smile.

"The first nine months in Canada were depressing, and after my papers arrived I began to work. I found some menial part-time jobs here and there, and then finally employment as a nurse's aide at the Maimonides Hospital for the aged. However, I couldn't stay because I hurt my back lifting heavy patients and pushing wheelchairs. The doctor said I had to quit. This added to my depression. I told myself I was lucky to be eating and I had a roof over my head, but I kept thinking of my mother, sister and brothers in Ethiopia. The country was in the throes of a drought and famine, and the newspapers were just beginning to carry reports about how terrible conditions had become. I felt guilty. I kept thinking about the refugee camps in the Sudan, and I couldn't sleep for weeks. I had worked in the area and had seen so many people starving to death. It was such a horrible scene."

The Falashas, as well as other Ethiopians, had been suffering torture, imprisonment and even death, at the hands of the anti-Zionist Marxist regime. There had been reports of incredible brutality inflicted on the Beta Israel. As early as 1975, Falashas had been the objects of increased persecution by the Ethiopian government. Emigration was forbidden, and those attempting to leave were charged with treason. Severe penalties were imposed on those who were caught leaving surreptitiously. All cultural activities of many minority groups were suppressed.

Amnesty International reported in 1982 that many members of the Falasha community were arrested as counter-revolutionaries for practising their religion. Vocational and Hebrew schools were closed; a ban was put on the teaching of Hebrew, and teachers were jailed. Falasha officials were dismissed from local government employment, and medical clinics were shut down. The authorities closed most Falasha villages to visiting foreigners, reserving a few as show-places, to cover up their treatment of the minority group.

A few courageous Falashas had been lucky enough to escape by trekking across the desert and Somalia to the Red Sea, to reach Israel as walking skeletons. Thousands languished in refugee camps in Djibouti, Sudan and Somalia. From 1948 to 1977, only a small number had arrived as immigrants in Israel to join those already in training programmes preparing them to return as teachers to their homeland. Between 1977 and 1983, about 2,700 Falashas had emigrated to Israel. Freedom meant returning to their spiritual homeland, where they could practise their religion and retain their traditions.

Malka knew what conditions in the refugee camps were like. Often guarded by sympathizers of the PLO, the Falashas were denied religious freedom and were exposed to all kinds of diseases in unhygenic conditions. With no medical facilities, sickness spread like wildfire. Twenty to thirty people were housed in rotting tents, and the Falashas' problems were further complicated by the fact that their tenets kept them from eating non-kosher food at the camps. Thus they suffered malnutrition and starvation. Because their culture forbade them being touched by strangers, they refused the meagre medical attention being provided by foreign governments, as news of the situation trickled to the world. Open anti-semitism flourished in the camps, already overcrowded with tens of thousands of other Ethiopian refugees fleeing civil war and drought in Eritrea and Tigre Province.

Malka, in the safety of Canada, was torn between devotion to her people and relatives in Ethiopia and her children in Montreal, as well as trying to adjust to a different lifestyle. It wasn't easy. Because she couldn't find full-time work, she was unable to support her children, and for several years two of her daughters were boarded at the homes of friends who tried to make the family's integration as smooth as possible. But although Malka was grateful for the assistance and community acceptance, it was a blow to her pride.

"A social worker was assigned to me, but my mentality and the Canadian one were different. We didn't think the same way. I felt ashamed that after all I had been through in my life and the way I had supported myself, I had to appear at the agency and ask for my cheque like a beggar. And each time the social worker asked if I was employed, I'd cringe. 'How much are you getting?' she wanted to know when I said yes. I don't want charity. The pride and dignity we have in being able to take care of ourselves is also

288

part of our tradition. If I discuss my problems with someone, it should be kept between the two of us, yet my file is open for others to see, and the social worker calls other people who in turn phone me back. Everyone knows my business. I know they are trying to help and I know I have financial and adjustment problems, and it all depresses me.

"I have three daughters who are totally different in character and I have to solve their problems as well. I don't want others to know that my children had to be looked after by foster-parents because I could not support them. In addition, my girls see things they want everywhere they go, and it drives me crazy not to be able to afford them. I love my children, but I don't want them to see my anguish and guilt because I can't provide for them.

"When my youngest, who had been exposed to colour television, came to visit on the weekends, I didn't have a set for her to watch. She bluntly told me that if I didn't have a colour TV, she wasn't coming home to visit. I felt terrible. I had been working part-time and had put aside a few dollars for more important things, and now I was forced to buy a colour set just to have my daughter with me. She didn't understand at all how much it hurt me to be unable to afford what she saw elsewhere. I didn't have the money. I know it's difficult for the children as well. They get invited to parties and can't afford to buy presents. They're ashamed, and they compare our lifestyle with what they see at their friends' homes. My daughter didn't come right out and say it, but I heard her tell friends she was busy or couldn't accept invitations to various functions. I knew it was because she would have had to invite them back here and she felt ashamed. I tried to make my apartment look comfortable, like a real home.

"The most important thing now is that we're free and are Canadians. My daughters are doing well in school, and one of them was the first Falasha to graduate from high school in Montreal. My eldest is studying biochemistry at university, the middle daughter is in science at CEGEP (junior college) and the youngest is doing very well in high school. They have friends, they're getting a good education, and they speak English, French and Hebrew. We can practise our religion, something we couldn't do in Ethiopia, where I was constantly afraid of what could happen to us.

"To be an immigrant you have to be strong and work hard, and start all over from the beginning. For the youngsters there is nothing special about this, but for older people who come here, it is particularily difficult. When you've worked all your life to have certain material things—a house, furniture, a car, whatever, it's a great hardship to lose it all and start all over in another country with nothing. When you are older like me, it's a time of life when you slow down and should be taking things more easily. Instead you have to work hard physically, mentally and emotionally, and you have to have friends like the Cytrynbaums and Zareckis who have been like family to me.

"But although we have been lucky with our friends, I think there could be so much more help offered, especially in the area of employment. I have been to many agencies and all I do is fill out forms. Nothing happens. I know the agencies are getting grants to find jobs for immigrants and ethnic people, but something is going wrong in the process. If you're lucky, you might get a job for ten days or three weeks, working in the kitchen, housecleaning, washing dishes—things like that. I was head of a nursing clinic and I can't find a job in the profession I was trained in.

"I was offered a job at minimum wage during the Christmas rush at a large gift shop in the Cavendish Mall, through a friend's contacts. Placed behind a counter to wrap parcels, I was working beside women who had worked at this for five or ten years, and knew how to wrap. I found it difficult to work neatly and quickly when I had no experience. And there were people standing in line for more than an hour watching us as we worked. It made me nervous. I had to keep asking what kind of box, what paper, what ribbon should I use. It was like an assembly line. A woman who had bought a gift, dropped it and it broke. Everyone came running. They thought I had been responsible. It was embarrassing, listening to people laughing and making fun of the woman who had dropped the fragile gift. I couldn't stand it and I talked to my social worker, trying to explain how I felt with my lack of experience. I wasn't doing well, and it wasn't fair to the customers. I had to quit."

Suddenly Malka received a notice that her rent would no longer be paid by the social agency. When she spoke to an official, she was told that if she were working, and even if she was making next to nothing, her funding would be cut off. In addition, if she didn't accept any of the positions offered to her, she would not receive any help at all. She wanted to work, but she and her family could not live on the minimum wage she was paid. She didn't want charity, and certainly didn't want to stay home. When the social worker called and asked her to come and discuss the matter, she refused to go.

"Luckily I found work as an assistant teacher at a nursery school. I didn't even ask what it paid, but I hoped it would be enough to support my children and have them all with me. But I get so depressed about it. Here I am, Jewish, black and a woman, fighting to keep my family unit intact while world attention is focusing on the plight of my people in Africa.

"I am torn between the two."

(Malka Abraham is now working at the Jewish Immigrant Aid Society (JIAS) helping new immigrants integrate into Canadian society.)

Editor's note: In mid-December, 1985, while individuals and private Jewish organizations were openly criticizing and condemning Israel for apathy and even racism in failing to deal with the tragic plight of the Falashas in Ethiopia, Sudan and Somalia, the Israeli Government, ever sensitive to the hostility of Moslem nations toward Jews, had been secretly involved in undercover negotiations with officials of the countries bordering Ethiopia, in order to facilitate the exit of the black Jews. A daring clandestine rescue mission planned and executed by the Israelis, was almost aborted by the interference of well-meaning Western Jews, who were unaware of the undercover operation.

Some officials in high places, who had been informed of the mission, had urged news agencies which had picked up information about the secret rescue, not to print the story prematurely before the project had been completed. The resulting publicity would have jeopardized the safety of the Falashas, as pressure from the Moslem Brotherhood in North Africa could have spurred the Sudanese or even the PLO to use violence in preventing this latter-day Exodus to Israel.

Unmarked planes landing at Khartoum after dark, and boats slipping surreptitiously in to land near Port Sudan were highlights of the rescue mission. Diplomatic sources said the United States acted as an intermediary in arranging meetings between the Sudanese officials and Israeli agents, in order to set up the intricate details of the escape.

The news leak, unfortunately, revealed the operation, stranding about 8,000 to 10,000 older men, women and children inside Ethiopia. By May, 1985, about 4,000 Falashas caught in the pipeline were taken to Israel. Those still in Ethiopia are trapped without hope of rescue, unless the Marxist Government can be persuaded to let them go.

Canada has absorbed approximately fifty Falashas to date, the smallest of the eighty-odd ethnic minorities which make up the Canadian pluralistic society.

FROM THE CROSSROADS OF HISTORY

by
George Bonavia and Milly Charon
from the personal memoirs and collected newspaper
and magazine articles of George Bonavia;
historical research, composition and editing by Milly Charon

Within hours of Benito Mussolini's declaration of war against the Allies at midnight on June 10, 1942, Il Duce's planes made two separate raids on Malta.* Falling bombs killed thirty-five civilians and six British soldiers and wounded scores of other residents. This was only the beginning. Malta was to be rocked by 4,000 bombing raids during the war, often undergoing multiple attacks in a day. The island would remain under tight siege for almost two and a half years, while the battle raged for the control of the Mediterranean.

As the bombardment increased, the Royal Navy's Mediterranean fleet was forced to abandon Malta and withdraw to Gibraltar. The arrival of Field-Marshal Erwin Rommel and his Afrika Corps at Tripoli in Libya in February, 1941, had made the Allies realize that his drive on the vital Suez Canal would bring disaster unless he could be halted. For the next eighteen months, the German Field-Marshal's drive pressed irresistibly across Tripolitania, Cyrenaica and into Egypt as he built up his military forces for the final attack on the Canal.

The Allies knew that Rommel's fuel, ammunition and food supply lines, serviced by Italian merchant ships from Italy to North Africa, would have to be cut. Malta, and its little group of small islands at a strategic position in the middle of the Mediterranean—fifty-eight miles south of Sicily, and two hundred and twenty miles north of Libya—provided the ideal base for this operation by

*The following two pages of historical background are drawn from W.L. River's *Malta Story*, American Book-Stratford Press Inc., New York, 1943.

bomber and torpedo squadrons.

In October, 1941, Hitler ordered an air armada of six hundred aircraft to pound Malta into rubble and dust. Caught like a prize nut between the jaws of a nutcracker, the island was locked into a state of siege. Every sea and air route was dominated by the Axis. Mussolini ordered a blockade. All Allied shipping approaching Malta was to be sunk, and the islands to be starved into submission.

Food and medical supplies soon ran out. The bare, rocky soil was hardly able to sustain agricultural attempts to feed the hungry population and local garrison of about a quarter of a million people. Daily air raids disrupted every form of activity, forcing the islanders to seek shelter in cellars, underground caverns and ancient catacombs.

As far as defence was concerned, there were only seven old-fashioned Gladiator fighting planes sitting at an improvised air-field when war was declared. Although two new airfields had been built on the island, they had little value without a strike force of planes. The British had neglected to update the island's security system. It was only too obvious that the islands would have to be defended to the death, since Malta was the only place from which the R.A.F. could operate against Rommel and the Italians. Malta, however, was beyond the range of British Hurricane and Spitfire fighters flying from Gibraltar. The only possible way to get the aircraft to Malta would be through the use of aircraft carriers. With only *H.M.S. Eagle* available, Prime Minister Churchill appealed to President Roosevelt, and within days *U.S.S. Wasp* was ordered to join the operation.

Once the planes were in the air, the pilots would have to find their way to the tiny spot in a hostile sea from six hundred and sixty miles away. To have the necessary range, the planes would have to be stripped of some of their guns and fitted with extra ninety-gallon fuel tanks. From March to October, 1942, three hundred and eighty-five planes flew from carriers to Malta. Four were shot down, and another fourteen were reported missing at sea.

Those heroic flights tipped the balance in favour of the Allies in the struggle for North Africa and the Middle East. But for the courage and determination of British airmen and Maltese soldiers and civilians, the islands would have been lost. On April 15, 1942, King George VI of England awarded the George Cross to the island of Malta for her heroism and devotion.

It had not been the first time that Malta had been under attack. For many centuries, the islands had been in the path of numerous aggressors who had overrun and colonized her. Her position at the crossroads of a vast inland sea had given her a unique place in history.

* * * *

On May 29, 1948, the newspaper *Canada Weekly* in London, Ontario, carried a small news item about Maltese immigrants who were on their way to Halifax, Nova Scotia, as the first group of five hundred from the little Mediterranean island. Their entry had been authorized by the Government of Canada in order to recognize in a tangible way the magnificent wartime accomplishments of Malta. The island had suffered great hardship during the war. The workers accepted by Canada as immigrants were to be given assistance in finding employment by the Department of Labour on arrival in Canada.

On June 9, 1948, *M.V. Vulcania* called at Malta to pick up and transport three hundred immigrants to a new life in Canada. On the ship, which sailed for the New World on June 17, was George Bonavia, a former literary editor of *Il-Berqa*, the only Maltese-language daily newspaper on the island, and his brother-in-law Joe Grech. Bonavia left a wife and child behind, whose emigration he was to arrange in Canada. His wife was expecting their second child in September of that year.

Of the thousands of Maltese immigrants already in Canada and those who would one day make Canada their home, Bonavia was to be most unusual in his dedication to the resettlement and integration of his compatriots. He was to work unceasingly for almost thirty-five years to improve relations among all ethnic groups. His story is one of achievement and honour, and Canada was fortunate to attract such a man, whose humanitarian instincts and devotion earned him the honour of Knight of Grace from the Sovereign Order of St. John of Jerusalem, Knights of Malta in May,

1958. In 1977, he was awarded the Queen's Silver Jubilee Medal and the Canadian Journalists' Award in 1979 for promoting harmony and understanding among different ethnic groups in Canada. He received the Merit Award for services to immigrants by Jewish Immigrant Aid Services (JIAS) in 1980, and the Volunteer Service Award in 1985.

When Bonavia retired in 1982, he did not stop working. This account is a testimonial to a remarkable individual.

* * * *

"My mother was a teacher before she married to become a full-time housewife. My father worked at the Naval Dockyard where most Maltese were employed. He had planned to emigrate to the United States after World War I, but just as he was about to leave, he got sick. Shortly after, I was born in the town of Zabbar, and my birth made him change his mind about emigrating. And then came three brothers, who, when they grew up, became a teacher, a priest and a monk, so my father never did get a chance to emigrate.

"When I was old enough, I was enrolled in the local elementary school, and then went to the Lyceum Secondary School in Valletta. While I was at the Lyceum, a new student from Canada came to our class. Paul Azzopardi and his family had returned to Malta in 1933. We became friends, and he would talk to me about things like the front gardens in Montreal, and, of course, the cold winters and snow.

"During my schooldays I had started freelancing—writing for the literary page of a local Maltese-language daily *Il-Berqa*. This was the beginning of my interest in the media. I had also become involved with a movement to get the Maltese language recognized as an official language in Malta. I had fallen in love with Maltese literature.

"After I finished high school, I took a one-year course in sanitation and medical health, in preparation for a job as a Health Officer with the Maltese Government's Department of Health and Welfare. I began working, but I was there barely a year before war broke out, and I was conscripted into the army. There were no exemptions. Here I was twenty years old in February, 1940, as a private. Five years later I came out of the army a private. For me, this period was a shock because I could never see myself killing anyone. I never liked army life and could never adjust to it, although I felt because of the times we were living in, I had an obligation to do my part, as everyone else did, like it or not. Malta was beseiged, and the daily bombings were a way of life. What could I do?

"I served in an infantry regiment, the King's Own Malta Regiment, and was always dreaming of the day I would be out of the service. After participating in regular guard duties and parades, I finally finished up in Motor Transport, teaching driving and mechanics. All I knew about engines was what was in the book. The expert work was done by the sergeant who knew how to repair cars and trucks. All I knew was the theory of internal combustion engines, and what to look for when there was a malfunction.

"But I'll say one thing for army life. It was an experience mixing with all kinds of people from all walks of life. Perhaps it was this that made it easier for me to adjust to settlement in a new country.

"One of my most memorable experiences was seeing the famous Canadian pilot 'Buzz' Beurling. The army had been assigned the task of providing work-groups to help fill the holes in the runways at the airfields after bombing raids by the Germans. One day I was with a group at Ta Qali (Takali) airdrome, when Beurling had just returned from chasing enemy planes. It seemed that everyone knew about him. He was a top fighter—downing the greatest number of planes during the Malta siege.

"The war finally came to an end, and I was released just before VE-Day on May 8, 1945. Almost immediately, I found a job as news editor with the *Allied Malta Newspapers*. I worked with that daily in Maltese, and on weekends I worked at editing the local news pages for the *Sunday Times of Malta*. I remember that the last story I did for the front page of the *Times of Malta* was a report on the tragic death of Buzz Beurling in Rome while he was acting as a transport pilot flying planes to the new State of Israel in May, 1948.

"In addition to my work on the papers, I was also broadcasting weekly talks on drama and literature on the local broadcasting Rediffusion system.

299

"In 1946 I married my wife Mary, whom I had met while I was in high school. While I was still in the army, I had already made up my mind that I would be emigrating one day. In fact, I had filled out an application registering my desire to go to Canada. When the Maltese Government announced in 1948 that five hundred Maltese would be selected, I was one of the first to be chosen. I figured I had nothing to lose by going to Canada. Ever since I was young, I had dreamed of travelling around the world and had been fascinated by books about other countries. In 1948 I had run into Paul Azzopardi again, and we talked about our school days and about Canada. While I had been serving my four years in the army, Paul had graduated in medicine. Later he would return to Canada and settle in Toronto, where he specialized in children's diseases.

"One of the reasons I chose Canada over Australia—I had toyed with the thought of going Down Under—was that Canada was near the United States, where large Maltese communities were established, with one of the largest in Detroit. So I settled in Windsor, Ontario, right across the border from Detroit. My brother-in-law Joe Grech and I came ahead, but I made arrangements to return, if things didn't work out, and get my old job back in Malta. My wife and daughter Connie stayed with her parents while I was gone. I arrived in June, and by September had decided that I wasn't going back. I wrote my wife to prepare to come in the Spring of 1949, because she had just given birth to our son Joe in September. The delay would give me enough time to find a home for my family.

"Almost immediately, I found a job on the assembly line at Ford Motor Company, but continued to act as a correspondent for the papers back home. Later I contributed to *Migrants* radio programme. And when my family arrived in April, my brother-in-law moved out of the two-room apartment we had shared, and the four of us were cramped for a year in two rooms until we could rent the next-door house owned by a kind English widow, Mrs. Ulch. When she decided to sell her house, we made her an offer of seven hundred dollars down and fifty-dollar-a-month payments until the total cost of $7,500 was paid. Now we had a house of our own, big enough to have two brothers-in-law move in with us.

"It wasn't easy in those early years, but we managed because we didn't have any debts and had not fallen into the bad habit of buying things on easy credit. My wife didn't have to go out to work and could spend time with the children. Although I was laid off several times when I was working at the car plant, I never went on unemployment. Instead, I found odd jobs—clerk in the unemployment office, part-time work at a tomato-canning factory, labourer in a box-manufacturing plant, and a sorter in the Canada Post Office in Windsor during the Christmas rush.

"I'll admit there was a difficult period later on, when I was out of work and couldn't find any kind of job. I *had* to go on unemployment, and we lived on only a thirty-five-dollar weekly cheque—no mean feat for a growing family. I spent this time studying. It was our darkest period, just before I entered government service in the Customs Department and later became an immigration officer in 1953.

"In 1954 I started a monthly newspaper—*The Malta News*—the only Maltese newspaper in North America. I also set up the first Maltese-language radio programme. I was living as a Maltese in Canada; I had not cut my ties with my homeland, and I never stopped being a Maltese within the Canadian sphere of daily living. But what I did was widen my horizons by discovering an unlimited field of Canadian subjects while researching material for a book I wrote in Maltese about Canada in 1951. The book was intended to help prospective immigrants to Canada from Malta. Entitled *Canada—Land of Hope and Prosperity*, the book was followed by others: *Workers in Canada, In Canada Now: Thoughts and Events*, and *Canada: From an Unknown Country to a Great Nation*. All of these were in Maltese. In addition, I was writing weekly columns to the newspapers in Malta. 'Letters from Canada' later became 'George Bonavia's Letter'.

"For many years I was active in the Windsor community, and organized Canadian exhibitions and other programmes in co-operation with the Windsor Public Library and other organizations. I was instrumental in getting the Citizenship Council of Greater Windsor organized in 1962. For several years I had a weekly programme on CBC Radio Network 'International Rendez-vous' directed to ethnic groups.

"In 1965 I transferred to Ottawa to the Information Service of the Immigration Department and was posted for three years in the Canadian Embassy in Rome, Italy. When I returned to Ottawa in 1968, I became active again in the Ottawa Citizenship Council, and was elected their President in 1981 and later also became President of the Canadian Citizenship Federation. In the Department of Immigration in Ottawa, I dealt mainly with ethnic news media and ethnic groups.

"Two years later I developed and edited *Kaleidoscope Canada,* a monthly publication issued by the Department of Employment and Immigration. It was distributed to ethnic news media and organizations interested in immigration and ethnic affairs. I also wrote a monograph on the *Maltese in Canada* as one of the history projects of the Directorate of Multiculturalism, which was put out in English and French.

"Shortly before retirement, I was cooperating in Ottawa with the National Library and Public Archives in collecting and preserving material relating to the Maltese in Canada. I donated newspaper clippings and other documents about Maltese activities, which I had been collecting over the previous twenty-five years. I also helped the Multilingual Biblioservice of the National Library of Canada to acquire books in the Maltese language. Other publications I produced in recent years were the *The Ottawa Ethnic Groups Directory,* the *Directory of Maltese Organizations in Canada and United States* and *Focus on Canadian Immigration.*

"Looking back over my years of service, I realize there has always been an awareness of the presence of immigrants in our Canadian communities. I have no doubt that this subject has been discussed, analysed and considered in depth over the years. It has always been my firm belief that although individual immigrants' problems are essentially the same, the context behind them, and the most effective means to alleviate them, differ from one ethnic group to another. Proper solutions to these problems require a thorough understanding of the immigrants, their personalities, their way of life, their feelings, thoughts and behaviour—in short, of their cultural background and their world view. That is why immigrants' ethnic organizations and their religious groups, be they churches, temples, synagogues or others, have done, and can continue to do a great deal to solve the initial problems of settlement in a new community.

"To go back to my own particular origins, emigration has been looked on in Malta as a solution to alleviate the problems of overpopulation. As far back as the nineteenth century, emigration took the form of spontaneous movement, almost entirely directed toward the coast of North Africa and the Eastern Mediterranean, where opportunities for employment were found in commerce, crafts and general labour. Over eighty-five percent of emigré Maltese returned to Malta between 1840 and 1890. At this time, there was little interest shown in emigration to America, although a few attempts were made, with little success. When a great wave of unemployment hit the island in 1907, a significant number of Maltese left for the United States, Canada and Australia. They were aided by a voluntary body, The Malta Emigration Committee, whose promotional work led the Maltese Government to become involved in emigration. When Malta was faced with the layoff of thousands of workers from the Naval Dockyards in 1918, the government created an Emigration Department to promote and control emigration. Between 1918 and 1920, over ten thousand emigrants left Malta. There was a low level of emigration during the late 1920s and 1930s, because receiving countries had adopted restricted immigration policies during the post-war slump and Depression Years. After the Second World War, there was another wave of exodus, which brought about 17,000 Maltese to Canada, the majority to Ontario.

"Perhaps because the majority of the Maltese speak English, through Malta's association with the British, many people believe that the Maltese who settled in Canada needed little assistance. True, knowing the language is a great help, but it does not eliminate the difficulties all newcomers face in a new community, whether they arrive from abroad or from other Canadian provinces. And often, when an immigrant speaks English, his needs are sometimes ignored or not emphasized enough in the field of social orientation, a process which speeds up integration.

"The two main islands in our group, Malta and Gozo have a surface area of only 122 square miles with a population today of about 335,000 people. For new immigrants to Canada from the islands, there is immediately a feeling or trauma of change—from a small-island community to an enormously larger fairly industrialized country. There is also an environmental change from homogeneous surroundings to a multi-ethnic society, and a lack of understanding by established Canadians of the Maltese personality and background. And what a difference in the climate!

"I can see that two major problems facing any immigrants are knowledge of the language and the need of steady employment, but as long as immigrants feel insecure in adjusting, they will be prone to criticize everything in Canada that is different from their homelands. Because most Canadians are immigrants by choice or necessity, or children of immigrants, the problems they encounter are everybody's business. Therefore, it is everyone's duty to do his share in achieving a better understanding of the situation.

"Immigrants have to realize that if they have chosen to live in Canada, they must make some sacrifices, in order to build a better and happier life. No matter where one lives, one is bound to face some difficulties. It could be a different climate, different customs or different attitudes to life. But even in this context, Canada is still the best country in the world in which to make a living. Canadians, by and large, are kind and friendly people, When I did find some who were indifferent, this apathy was due, I assumed, to a lack of information on the problems of immigrants.

"Because Canada is a country that is made up of many cultures, it has often been called a mosaic. Ideally, this term implies that Canada's different cultural heritages all stand out clearly and are allowed definite individual expression. "Mosaic" is often used as a metaphor for our multi-cultural heritage. However, I don't feel the term is correct as it implies that each cultural tile is set into a colourful but unchanging pattern. A more suitable metaphor would be "Canadian Kaleidoscope" because Canada's pattern is always changing, as new communities and groups are added to our ethnocentric population. Canada is a kaleidoscope which allows immigrants to be proud of their ethnocultural backgrounds, and encourages and assists immigrants to share their culture with others, through multicultural programmes subsidized by the government. And the fact that so many people from different origins can live together harmoniously in an integrated society, is one of the elements contributing to the growth and vitality of Canada.

"Each of us cherishes the right to equal opportunity and freedom of expression and association. All Canadians are free to maintain their values from their own heritages, using their unique talents and skills for the benefit of themselves, their communities and their country.

"As Canadians, our experience with a diversity of cultures

enriches our understanding of many peoples. If our neighbours share with us their traditions, cultures and folklore, each party will broaden its horizons and open the way to a better understanding. Perhaps we should all learn to know our neighbours a little better.

"There is now a more generous acceptance and greater appreciation of the various cultures in our country. This is the time to assert our belief in a unified Canada, still struggling, like the early pioneers, against the elements and wresting a living from a variety of sources. During these restless times of change, perhaps Canadians should look more closely to their separate pasts to help them plan a common future. History is a great teacher.

"As my final words on the subject, I must say I have realized my Canadian dream. All I ever wanted was to work and become involved in activities I enjoyed and excelled in—journalism, print and broadcast. The job came first, then came a home of our own and better opportunities for our children, all five of them—four of whom are now settled with families of their own. The youngest of our children is still single, but among the others, we have eight grandchildren.

"Looking back over the span of thirty-five years, I can say that it was a wise decision to come to Canada. I came, I looked, I liked what I saw, and I stayed. I am proud to be a Canadian and just as proud of my Maltese heritage."

A HYBRID SOCIETY—
THE BEST OF BOTH WORLDS

by
Milly Charon
from an interview with Dan Leeaphon

As children in Bangkok, Thailand, my younger sister and I lived in an unusual establishment owned by my father. It was a kind of hotel—more like a guesthouse—where people could stay through arranged contracts. A business company or conglomerate would contact my father and lease lodgings and board for any number from ten to thirty people. Because the arrangements were for long periods, there was a high occupancy rate. It was a unique type of business because traditionally my father's family had been for generations in rice- exporting, and my father broke with tradition to go off on his own to set himself up in a new occupation.

The land, which the guesthouse and surrounding compound occupied, had been in the family for generations. An old Thai-style mansion formed part of the guesthouse, and to it had been added a new three-storey-high wing and a rather large, one-floor extension. There were about sixteen units, each consisting of a living room, a bedroom and bathroom. A large communal dining room complemented the lodging facilities.

I had a happy childhood, growing up and playing in the huge compound. As friends, I had children from school, a vast number of cousins and second cousins—on my father's side there had been ten siblings—and, of course, the twelve or more servants who ran the guesthouse. My sister and I were never lonely. We talked with the employees, and even helped them with their chores—washing, cleaning and cooking—whenever it was required. We kept busy, but we didn't mix with the other neighbourhood children partly because of our walled-in compound which tended to discourage outside encounters, but also because we weren't in the same social class.

With long-term paying guests around us, we made many good friends among the Japanese, Germans, and Americans who stayed with us. My mother was Japanese, and that was how we were able to persuade Japanese nationals to set up temporary residence at our compound. My mother supervised the menus for the traditional Japanese meals, and was able to negotiate contracts with companies and other groups in Japanese.

She and my father had met in an unusual manner. My mother had come from Japan with my grandmother, and had worked as a nanny for an American couple. The head of the family was a writer for *Reader's Digest*, and my mother learned English in that household, as well as taking English lessons to pick the language up more quickly.

One day my father was driving down a street in Bangkok and noticed an attractive woman turning into the Asian Institute. He admired her but was too bashful to stop. A few days later, a friend of his mentioned that he knew two Japanese women they could both date. My father agreed to go, and who should be his friend's date, but the woman he had admired on the street? In a very short time, she became my father's girlfriend and later his wife. The other pair in the original foursome also married.

My parent's marriage was a good one. I was born in 1960, and three years later I had a sister. At five I started school—a kindergarten run out of the YWCA. Unfortunately, the teacher was sadistic. She had long nails and she used to pinch us with the sharp points. I remember coming home and telling my parents that my teacher had teeth on her fingers. My parents took me out of there immediately and placed me in an old-fashioned Thai school which had a rather forbidding entrance hall—dark wood and perpetual gloom. I was so nervous I threw up the first day.

The business of going to school and returning home each day soon became a daily ritual. Late in the afternoon, the children would all be waiting for parents or family servants to come and pick them up by car. We wore old-fashioned uniforms, and there was corporal punishment, which was savage at times. Once as a penalty for forgetting my pencils at home, I had to hold my hand flat on the desk, while the teacher held down one end of her ruler on the wood, pulled the other end high, and let go. There was a snap as it cracked down on my skin. It hurt.

Learning was by rote, and I studied arithmetic, Thai history and stories such as Aesop's fables. Our parents had to pay under the table to get us into the better schools. Public-school places were not readily available, and those that were, were of very poor quality. Most of the better schools were private ones.

Suddenly there was a new element in the country. We noticed many Americans in our midst. The Vietnam War was on, and the Americans set up bases in Thailand. We were aware of the war, but we were very far removed from it. With the American presence, nightclubs seemed to proliferate, and my parents went out quite often to them and enjoyed the novelty. There were shows, government propaganda against the evils of Communism, and other forms of entertainment. One of our family friends was a lieutenant in the United States Navy, strictly a non-combatant. He was an ophthamologist, and he often took our family to show us around the Navy Base that had been built near Bangkok. For us, the only thing we noticed was the presence of many Americans and the flow of American dollars.

My sister and I were more concerned with school. By the time she entered, I was way ahead of her. One of the local customs was a mandatory afternoon nap. Mats would be rolled out onto the floor, and the pupils had to lie down and sleep for a couple of hours. If the teacher caught you with your eyes open, she'd make you stand with your arms outstretched for hours. School hours were long; we had to stay until four or five o'clock, but not all schooldays were unrelieved misery. We did have fun, going on art and field-trips occasionally.

I didn't finish grade five because a couple of months before the end of the term, my father went into the final stages of his preparation for emigration to Canada. He took us out of the Thai school and sent us to an English school to learn the language, so that we would have less difficulty integrating in Canada. It was total immersion. Administered by a Dutch woman, the school was a tiny, private place of instruction, and most of the kids were foreigners, whose parents had, for various reasons, come to Thailand from elsewhere.

My father's decision wasn't a sudden one. He had always

wanted to live in North America—actually the United States, but he couldn't get in because the yearly quota was already filled. And so, he figured the closest place to the States, where life was similar, had to be Canada. The reason for this great desire for the West was that he had studied business administration at Duke's University in Durham, South Carolina, and had fallen in love with the North American lifestyle. He had waited almost twenty years before he was able to take the steps necessary toward the realization of his dream. My grandfather had also studied in the States, in a military academy in Virginia. He had been planning to be a soldier and had wanted to fight in the civil war in China in the 1930s.

My father had been talking about leaving for a while, and we knew there was all kinds of paper work in process, but he told us to keep quiet about it, so that no one would know we were leaving. It was a precautionary measure, because it would have been bad for his business. He desperately wanted to get out of Thailand. He was fed up with the corruption, the backwardness and disorganization that were common in our country. Everything was a mess. He had had a taste of American efficiency in an organized society. Simple things like domestic plumbing, sewage, electricity and telephones that Westerners take for granted, were not only badly installed in Thailand, but didn't work, or were impossible to obtain without graft.

My father hired a friend, who was in between jobs at the time, to take over management of his guesthouse, as there was no buyer in sight. And when our papers finally came through, we went to Japan first, where we would spend nine months, while my father worried about his investments back home.

Life in Tokyo was an experience for us. We lived in a fairly small apartment in the middle of the city and went to a Catholic missionary school, one of the few English-language schools available. Most of the kids were children of U.S. Air Force servicemen. I found the school interesting, and the people were very warm and friendly. The nuns were Japanese, but spoke English. We had classes in religion, which I found a little strange, because my parents were agnostics, but the nuns didn't indulge in any heavy preaching. They taught it as a subject like history, and made no attempt to force Catholicism down the kids' throats.

I met a lot of American children there, and made one good

friend, Gregory, whose father was a U.S. Air Force sergeant. Gregory invited me to sleep over at the base one night, which was a very unusual experience for me. Here we were in the middle of Japan, and once we passed the front gates onto the base, suddenly I was transported straight into America. There were big houses, duplexes, movie theatres, lawns, ball parks and kids lining up for matinees at the movie house, complete with candy bars and popcorn. I couldn't believe how self-contained a presence the American base represented in Japan.

We also did some travelling and sightseeing while we were there. We went to some resorts, one of which was up in the mountains. We had never seen anything like snow, as it was unknown in Thailand. We were dressed for it, and a good thing, too, because we stayed in an old-fashioned Japanese inn, where everything was made of wood and rice paper with sliding doors and *tatami* floors. It was very cold, but we had huge thick blankets and everything was beautifully arranged. The old, worn pinewood with its warm lustre gave an aura of comfort. We went to Mount Fuji and saw many temples, but they didn't make much of an impression on me. I was more impressed with the snow, but was disappointed in finding it so wet and cold when I touched it.

For my mother, those nine months were a return to her roots, while for us kids, it was like getting acquainted with our heritage. When we arrived in Vancouver, I found it necessary to make much more serious adjustments than during that brief stay in Japan. We were to spend five years in Vancouver.

Compared to Japanese schooling, Canadian education was easy for me. Because the teachers weren't certain of my achievement levels, I was put back a grade after I had already spent some time in school. I lost the friends I had just made and had to make new ones. No sooner had I adjusted there, than they moved me up because I was ahead of the other pupils. And again I lost another group of friends. It was difficult to take, because it isn't easy for a foreigner to make friends in a different country. My English was basic, but not very good.

We had lived in a hotel for two months, but my sister and I didn't go to school for that period until we moved to an apartment and settled in. We didn't stay there long, moved again to another apartment for a few months, and then to a house where we remained for three years. My sister adjusted more easily than I, and became more Canadian than Thai. Deep inside I was still Thai. She learned to handle a knife and fork, but to this day I'm still more comfortable with chopsticks and a bowl. She forgot her Thai language, while I retained it, along with my craving for Thai food, especially rice.

When we had been in Vancouver about six months, my father returned to Thailand to sell the guesthouse. It would take him more than eight months to arrange his affairs. It was a period of stress for us, left alone in a strange country. When my father finally arrived safely in Vancouver, our relief was almost a tangible thing.

He decided to go into real estate, and took the exams which would enable him to get a licence, but what he really wanted was to become the purchaser of some land and an apartment building and get a commission at the same time. It was really funny because he was the worst salesman possible. He tried to sell houses to other people, but what he did actually was sell himself a seventeen-apartment building and some land in Vancouver. In a way it was clever, because his job gave him access to the listings, and it helped him find what he wanted and how to operate.

But he didn't like Vancouver, and when we took a trip to New York City via Montreal, he developed a liking for the Quebec metropolis. He sold off some of his land when he returned to Vancouver, arranged for the income from his apartments to be transferred, and moved to Montreal. However, like a rolling stone, he decided after years that Montreal wasn't all that great and that the people weren't friendly enough, not like Americans. He applied for alien status in the United States after his sister, who lived there, sponsored him, and he received a green card. Burlington, Vermont was his choice of residence, and he's been there since 1980 in semi-retirement, living off his investments.

As for my sister and myself, we decided to stay—my sister to complete her education in chemistry at McGill, and I to finish my degree in Computer Science in 1983 at Concordia University. We had no intention of emigrating to the States; both of us really prefer Canada far, far above the U.S.A. I had no choice about coming here because youngsters are usually dragged where their parents choose to go, but as an adult, I chose to remain in Canada. One of the

reasons for it was my indoctrination into the Canadian Army
Reserve one summer, when I trained as a gunner. By the end of the
season, the army offered me officer training, and I said "Why not?"
I wanted a challenge, and one of the things I learned was patriotism,
a pride of country, which comes more automatically in the services
than it does in civilian life.

It even got through to my sister. I took her to a formal mess
dinner, at the end of which there is a toast to the Queen. Everyone
stands up, the band plays, and the toast begins—to the regiment, to
other regiments, to comrades, and so on and on. At the end of this
impressive ceremony, my sister nudged me and whispered: "I'm
not going to move to the United States. I'm staying here." She was
convinced there was no place like Canada. The entire ceremony of
a mess dinner is designed to instill this esprit-de-corps, a fierce
patriotism and a loyalty to the country, and it works very well.

I continued my officer training the following year, one
night a week, and usually every other weekend. At the same time,
I held down a regular five-day-week job elsewhere. Every other
weekend was spent with my regiment, either in Montreal or in Val
Cartier. Two weeks were set aside in the summer for up-to-date
training. Of course, I'm subject to call-up if anything ever happens,
but I'm not stopping now. I'm planning to go further—become a
captain and probably will go for colonel of the regiment, one day.

In a small way, considering my age, I've definitely contributed something to this country—as an officer in the reserve, adding
to Canada's defence system which is an expression of her sovereignty, and I've worked hard at any jobs I've had, paid my taxes and
developed a great pride in Canada.

Canada has given me a home, a good place to live, probably
one of the better places in the world in terms of standard of living,
safety, freedom and prosperity. I'm very grateful for that. I love
Canada's unique nature, which has a little of everything in it—
British, French, European, American, African, South American—
you name it. I don't know enough about French Canada, but I did
have a French-Canadian girl friend a while back, when I was living
in Quebec City for several weeks, and later shuttled back and forth
from Montreal to Quebec City for four months. I found the French
Canadians extremely open, warm and friendly—real fun people—
and very different from the mainly Anglophones who live in the

west end where I reside. People there appear reserved, even snobbish.

I'm happy to say that I've never been the object of any
racism or prejudice from Quebecers, although one incident here
did give me a few minutes of anger.

I had run out of gas and stalled my car at the corner of
Queen Mary Road and Decarie Boulevard in Montreal. Behind me
an elderly gentlemen was honking his horn incessantly and shaking his fist at me. I told him I was out of gas, and as he pulled out
from behind me and drove off, he cursed me and said: "Why don't
you go back home, you *##+##!* Korean!" He had taken a wild
guess at my nationality. It was the first time I had ever had anything
like that happen to me, and it was the stupidity of it that made me
so angry. As I walked down the street to a gas station, I noticed that
this man was stopped behind another car which was parking, and
again this man was honking at that person, too. So I went over,
knocked on his window and said: "If you keep going this way,
you're going to have a heart attack within two miles of here."

He glared and drove away. To my surprise, I noticed he
had a Florida licence plate. I couldn't believe it, but it made me feel
better that he wasn't a Canadian. But it didn't end there. He must
have been looking for a parking spot and had driven around the
block, because he had stopped and left a note on my windshield,
which I found when I returned. "Fuc yo Bastrd!" it read. He had
misspelled every word. He must have been absolutely crazy.

However, I've heard of others who talk about things of that
sort going on. I live in an area where there are a lot of Vietnamese
and Cambodian families, living among established Canadians.
One day, through my open window, I overheard two men talking
about Vietnamese who are "noisy, dirty, don't keep up their apartments, and their kids run wild all over the place". It was the usual
standard complaint. I was getting ready to go to work at regimental
Headquarters and was in my uniform. When I walked out of the
apartment and they saw me, it just about blew them away. Their
jaws dropped. "Good morning," I said pleasantly. They couldn't
believe it, and continued to stare as I got into the car and drove
away. Some time later I met these same people on the street and
they said, "Hi, how are you doing?" They were very friendly. I
realized that by nature they weren't really prejudiced, but just
tended to generalize, and I felt that if I was an exception, they might

start treating other people of ethnic backgrounds and visible minorities a little better.

Outside of that, I don't remember any time when I was called a name, or my race interfered with my life—not even in the armed forces. They are such a mixture nowadays that racism wouldn't be tolerated.

Our family never lived in any of the ethnic enclaves. We were right in there with the established Canadians, mainstream Canada, so to speak, and it helped us assimilate. That is where many Oriental immigrants have problems, for they tend to become ghettoized. It's the way society works. Any large visible group of people from a certain race or ethnic background will find ways to isolate themselves, but, on an individual basis, there will be less stereotyping. Once society sees visible groups, it tends to become xenophobic, fearful lest its own established little communities be swallowed up by outsiders, who are seen as a threat. Yet, in a strange way, immigrants need the ghettos when they first come to a new land in order to feel secure. They band together, and this very act is what invites criticism and verbal attacks. It isn't the main cause, but it sure is one of them.

I think it would help to have immigrants move into mainstream life rather than joining ghettos, even with the prospect of security amongst their own kind. But not every parent can function the way my father did. He was very determined to become a Canadian, despite some people saying that he would lose his roots and his ethnicity. You really don't. It is something no one can take from you. You can give it away if you wish, but it just cannot be taken. I believe it was good to live the way we did—keeping our traditions and our food preferences, yet living the same way as Canadians.

The process of assimilation should be the task of immigrants themselves, and should not be expected of the government. Community centres, ethnic groups and counsellors could do more to help, although governmental funding is necessary. These centres could introduce different ethnic groups to one another. There should be more publicity to let people know the benefits of enjoying other cultures and events. Half of the problem is the fear of the unknown that keeps people apart.

We were lucky that we weren't raised in a typically Oriental—Thai or Japanese—fashion. It helped us adjust faster. My father had a head start by getting an education in the West, and it helped my mother when she learned English, working as a children's nanny. It did a great deal for us, so we didn't experience that immigrant culture shock to the same degree as those who come here without a knowledge of the two official languages. It was also very useful that we weren't desperately poor. It made it easier for us to get into Canada.

Most people think of immigrants as poor refugees, but there are many who come here with substantial funds. Among these, I find a pattern that is disturbing. These immigrants may have been big shots in their countries of origin, and here become middle- or upper-class Canadian. Yet they seem to alienate themselves from the rest of middle-class Canadian society through their arrogance. They don't realize we have a more egalitarian society here, and there is no such thing as a class system, even if you have money. These monied people often expect others to be subservient to them. They hang on to the old ways, and they can afford to. I know it's good for immigrants who have money to bring it to Canada, and in this way help the economy, but on the other hand, they have to learn to be a little more humble and realize that in Canada money doesn't necessarily mean power, as it does in third-world countries. Canadians will be more receptive to these newcomers, if they act less stuck-up. It's a matter of a whole new orientation, an act of will in understanding.

If there was something bad I could say about Canadians, it would be that they are unappreciative of their country. That's my number one complaint. Canadians take their country for granted. They think what they have is nothing, yet this land is unparalleled anywhere in the world. They don't want to realize that people have given up a lot of themselves, and even their lives, to keep Canada what it is.

Canadians have very short memories, and the reason I say this is that I am in the armed forces, which are extremely neglected. This is a situation which seems to occur after wars—a sort of running-down of services in peace time. I'm not saying that Canada should have a huge continental army like the States or the European countries, but if we are to have a small contingent of armed forces, at least the people of Canada should stand solidly behind them, instead of deriding them for being so puny and ineffective. Let's face it. If the Russians attacked and came over here, we wouldn't stand a chance. Even Mexico and her army could beat us. Things like that seem irrelevant now with no major war on, but one expression of Canada's sovereignty is in her armed forces and their ability to defend her borders in case of attack.

I honestly doubt we could muster an adequate defence system if we had to. We couldn't even play a full role in NATO. We must have a better-equipped defence system. A very small part of the population is in the armed services. As of March, 1986, there was a total of about 84,000. All the equipment is hopelessly out-of-date in this technological age. Just a few years ago, during training, I was riding in trucks built in 1953. They were obsolete. The Canadian Government doesn't consider defence a priority until it's caught with its pants down, the way it was in the last two world wars. People prefer to forget these things, and it's bound to happen again, at the cost of many lives and wasted money.

I don't think the armed forces should be enlarged to mammoth proportions, but at least their efficiency could be upgraded, along with the equipment. Our training is sound, and Canadians should look at the forces as something of which to be proud. Those of us involved are proud of our army, and other countries see us as professional soldiers, sailors or airmen. Unfortunately, our fellow-Canadians make fun of us, because of our outmoded equipment and the fake models on which we train. The soldiers can't change anything, but the Canadian people can. The soldiers' job is to make do with what they have, and they are doing amazingly well with the little they have left to work with.

It is a Canadian attitude to ignore the armed forces. It's part of the national character. We're a sort of "Forgotten Army". I may sound fanatic about it, but it is a passion with me because I'm a part of the services.

Another thing that bothers me is that Canadians are not imaginative or aggressive enough in business. I blame it on the national character again—that quiet, unassuming manner we possess, so unlike the Americans, who are dynamic because they don't care what they do. Criticized or not, they just do it. Canadians are too thoughtful. They worry about the image they'll project, and downplay everything. It's a national apathy. In one way, it's

317

nice to have such modest, unassuming people, but in another way it's like a massive inferiority complex. Perhaps it has to do with our living next door to a huge country. Compared to the United States, everything we do is on such a small scale, and because of this, most of our best people are attracted to the States. We have to find ways of keeping them here.

It's kind of charming, however, that Canada isn't a boastful country. It's rare to find a land like that, where there is such consideration shown to people of other cultures. There is no attempt to shove them into an assimilating melting pot, as is done in the States, where Americanism wipes out everything else. I'm not saying that it's all harmony between cultures here, but they do exist as separate entities. It does add charm and a depth to this country, as it goes along in its own quiet way. It may not grow quickly, but it grows well. It is a part of our history and our character that we didn't have a revolution or civil war like the Americans. We simply separated from Britain, with our own Constitution.

If there was some advice I could give, it would be to tell immigrants not to worry too much about keeping their ethnic backgrounds, which will always remain accessible, and their children will enjoy them too. Look at what Canadian society has to offer in terms of lifestyle, and then merge into it. It doesn't mean losing your sense of identity. You can do both, and have the best of both. It is impossible to expect to live the way you did in your countries of origin. If you don't want to change, why did you come here? You might as well have stayed there. Try the new ways, learn the new things. This is a country that has never had the devastation of war, nor the terrors of disasters and repressive governments like those many of you have come from. It offers a great deal.

Take the best of your society and the best of Canada's, and enjoy the best of two worlds. It may be a hybrid society, but today people have to be hybrids to exist, especially in this country. It really works in Canada.

THE DOLL MAKER

by
Milly Charon
from an interview with Fania Sidline
and from newspaper articles in
The Montreal Star and *The Gazette* (Montreal)

When you visit Fania Sidline's apartment in west-end Montreal, your amazement rapidly turns to disbelief. Everywhere you look are Japanese dolls, many in glass cases, dressed in exquisite silk, georgette and crepe-de-chine costumes with delicate embroidery. The wide *obis* are made of lustrous brocade.

"Oh, do you collect dolls?" is your first question.

"Collect?" asks the tiny, plump, eighty-four-year-old grandmother with a smile. "I make them."

You're not convinced.

Fania Sidline points to what is probably her most impressive creation—a Madame Butterfly doll whose clothing duplicates that of Madame Butterfly in the first staging of Puccini's opera. Dressed in turquoise silk, with soft crimson butterflies, the doll carries a feathered fan, and stands enclosed in a two-foot-high glass case.

The results of Fania Sidline's unique craft fill her home. Every room has dolls, and no two are alike. Each has a story or legend associated with it. A male doll, seated on a piece of polished wood, holds a tiny drum in his lap.

"He represents a folk-tale character who met a mermaid while walking by the seashore, and was enticed to live with her beneath the sea for a hundred years," she explains. "And this one is a flirtatious young girl. That one over there is a Geisha girl, and this very ornate doll is a Princess of the Royal Household. To create a Geisha doll, you have to study the life of a Geisha. The face of the doll should look intelligent, because the Geisha is a graduate of a

321

special school, where she learns not only dancing and singing, but politics, sports and psychology, so that she can converse sensibly. Her hands and figure must be graceful, and her clothes must be subdued in colour so as not to appear cheap and tawdry."

The clothes worn by the dolls are exact miniature replicas of those worn by Japanese women. In Japan, a great deal of care goes into the display of these dolls, which are not everyday toys to be hugged or handled by children, but rather art creations to be displayed and admired. They become heirlooms, which are handed down from generation to generation. They are usually placed in a position of honour in the best room of the house at festival time.

"These dolls are not playthings; they are objects to gladden the eye and not to touch," says Sidline. "The Japanese word for doll is *Ningyo*, which means image of man. When a doll, through some mishap, is damaged, or if a limb is torn beyond repair, each dismembered part is given a beautiful funeral so that the parts will not be mistreated. In Japan there is a day set aside for this purpose, when men, women and children come to a special site with the remains of a doll, and give them an almost human-style burial. It is the Japanese way of saying 'thank you' for the countless joys and memories these dolls have brought them."

When Sidline first started making the dolls in 1955, she was probably the only westerner to have mastered the intricate art. Delicately crafted, her creations measure about eighteen inches to two feet in height. Whether they are warriors, peasant girls, princesses or Geishas, all their bodies are made of cotton cloth, stuffed with wood shavings and threaded with wire, which can be twisted into the required positions. The arms are separately made and are of silk rather than cotton, with the tiny fingers individually wired to express the right gesture when bent into position.

"The head is a half-egg-shaped piece of silk which is stuffed with shavings, and I complete the back of the head with cotton. Once the head has been shaped, the hair, which is made with eight inches or more of silk threads that are ironed smooth and then twisted, must be cut and shaped into the different hair styles appropriate to the various doll characters. In Japan, you can tell the approximate age, work and social position of a woman by her hair-do," says Sidline. "Then the coiffure is stitched and carefully pasted into place."

"This is the most difficult part of the whole process," she says. "It can take eight to ten hours to complete. The hair has to be sewn and ironed to get it right. It is such a meticulous job, that it requires a great deal of patience. And the materials for the entire doll today cost of lot of money—about $250—depending on the size of the doll. Everything is done by hand, and it can take more than four to five days of continuous work to complete the whole thing."

You wonder how someone like Fania Sidline became involved in this type of art. You learn she has been teaching it for the past twenty-five years, and has been asked to speak and demonstrate her work at many women's organizations, at synagogue and church gatherings, as well as at the Ritz-Carlton Hotel, Eaton's Department Store, a Masonic club and on CTV television.

Your curiosity is piqued, and you want to know about her life. Her Russian accent is fascinating, and when you comment, she smiles shyly and admits she also speaks Japanese. But first before she tells you about her early life, she insists on putting the kettle to boil for tea, and lays a plate of assorted European pastries on the table.

Born in Vilna, Lithuania, on Christmas Day in 1902, she was barely four when she moved with her mother and sisters to Harbin in Manchuria. Her father, afraid that he would be inducted into the Czar's Army, had gone there two years earlier to prepare a home for his family.

"At that time, things were really bad in Harbin. My father had arrived at a difficult time. Japan was expanding territorially and had declared war on the Russians, who held territory in Manchuria. We arrived just as the war ended, but there were still many deprivations. The population of Harbin was composed mainly of Manchurians, many Russians, and other foreigners like ourselves. There couldn't have been more than four thousand people there in 1906.

"Of course, there was no electricity then, and my father opened a store, from which he sold oil and kerosene lamps, wicks, candles, as well as kitchenware, such as plates and casseroles. Eventually things improved, and I went to school, learned music and played the piano very well, but when I finished secondary school, I didn't know what to do with myself. I didn't want to work in my father's store. I wanted so badly to go to university and become a doctor."

Without telling her parents, Sidline sent an application to Tomsk University in Siberia, after she had received her teacher's certificate. She was unaware that the Russian Revolution had begun, and one day, when she was out, a letter came from the university. Her father opened it and gave her a tongue-lashing when she came home.

"'Over my dead body do you go!' he yelled.

"He was afraid I would be killed if I went during the Revolution. So instead I became a cashier at a friend's store for about three years, but I wasn't happy. One day a letter came that changed my life. A friend, who had been the most beautiful girl in Harbin, had moved to Shanghai, and she wrote me that if I learned how to type, there would be a job for me. I could stay with her. It took me two months to learn typing, but when I arrived in Shanghai, I discovered the firm had closed down, and there was no work for me."

Sidline decided to give piano lessons, and managed to get four or five pupils, but the fees were not enough to feed her. Her parents couldn't send her anything, but one of her girl friends mailed some money to her. Then she found a job at a beautician's, giving manicures, but that didn't pay enough either.

"I was getting worried. I didn't want to go back to Harbin. A girl friend who lived in Japan wrote to tell me about a divorced man who had lived in Europe and had moved to Japan. He was coming to Shanghai on holiday, and she would send a letter with him so that he could meet me.

"When he arrived, we began to talk. I mentioned my disappointment on coming to Shanghai and explained that I couldn't get a decent job. The next day, a huge bouquet of flowers arrived, and the following day he asked me out to dinner. He told me he had only ten days of his vacation left and had to return to Kobe, where he was working at one of the biggest hotels in the city. We spent every day together and on the last day, he proposed to me. He was eighteen years older than I, but it didn't matter. He returned to Kobe and a month later, I joined him there. I stayed at my girl friend's house on the day I arrived, and the next day we were married.

"It was 1929, and there was no synagogue in Kobe. The

ceremony took place in his home. Four of his friends held up the ceremonial canopy on four sticks, and we were married under it by a rabbi."

Sidline and her husband Boris moved to a larger house, once their two sons were born. Their house, located in a residential district on a mountainside, looked down on Kobe's busy seaport and a magnificent view of the ocean. The air was fresh and clean, and Sidline delighted in taking the narrow path behind their house and following it up into the mountain, where the only sounds she could hear were the hum of insects and the singing of birds.

"My best memories and years were bound up in that place. Down the hill from the house was a big market and many small shops, and the closer you advanced toward the port, the more activity there was. A shopping centre had been built, and there were department stores and government buildings near the port."

Life in this good-sized city was, for Caucasians, similar to living in the country and commuting to work in the busy seaport district. There was a small population of about 1,500 foreigners, and everyone tried to stay within the circle of their racial group.

"We had our own club, and finally a synagogue, churches, and even a mosque. There were quite a number of Moslems in Kobe. All the foreigners had Japanese friends as well, and we never had the feeling that we were segregated. Discrimination because of our race was unheard-of.

"Over the years, we survived a landslide and a tidal wave that hit Kobe, but the worst event was the Second World War. We hadn't been affected by the Russian-Japanese War as much as we were by World War II. We had no inkling that the Japanese were preparing for a war with the Americans. In fact, near us there were factories where armaments were made, and the word was that tubing was the product. It was a well-kept secret.

"The building of underground shelters must have started well before the war broke out, and suddenly more and more were built after December, 1941. I refused to go into them when the air raids on Japan began. I said, 'You can kill me, but I won't go.' We had lived well for twelve years, and suddenly everything had changed.

"I had an amah, a Japanese nanny, whose son was in the army, and one evening he came to visit his mother from the army base where he was stationed. He told her there was going to be a big American air raid the next day. She told me, and I alerted my friends across the street. It was amazing how accurate the Japanese spy networks were. Our friends picked up and left immediately for Ozaki, but my husband refused to go. He wouldn't leave his business. My amah packed a few things in a *tatami* mat, slung it on her shoulder and began hiking up to the mountains. My maid stayed with us.

"At seven in the morning, a strange sound woke me up. I felt something was wrong, but I didn't know what it was that had disturbed my sleep. I went to the window and looked out and on the horizon, I saw the sky was absolutely black, not with smoke, but with airplanes. The droning sound was what had awakened me. I shook my sons and my husband. 'Look, look at that!' I exclaimed excitedly. They woke up and looked out of the window. I could hear the sound of the bombardment coming nearer and nearer.

"'Run!' I yelled. 'We have to go! Run!'"

Near the door Sidline had left two suitcases which had been packed many months before just for this kind of emergency. A box of food, including fruit, was always in the refrigerator, waiting, just in case they had to flee...and the time had come.

"Our house had two stories, and we had prepared a room on the ground floor which we had padded with pillows, but that didn't help. A bomb dropped right through our roof, passed through the floor and landed right near me, bursting into flames. I grabbed one of my sons, while my husband picked up the other, and I jumped over the fire and ran for the door. In the panic, we forgot the suitcases, with everything in them.

"In the middle of the street, I stopped suddenly and looked behind me. I didn't see my husband and son. I began to scream hysterically, and some Japanese people came out of their houses and shouted at me that I was doing a bad thing. They yelled the pilots in the planes would see me and come back and bomb them again. I turned and saw my husband and son running toward me. They had gotten out of the house, but my husband realized he had forgotten the suitcases of clothing and the box of food, and ran back to get them. I thought they had been killed."

The family stood in the middle of the road trying to decide which way to go—right or left for sanctuary—while their house burned steadily, and everything they owned went up in the flames. The street led to the mountains in one direction and to the port in the other. Boris Sidline suggested they go right, to where there was a reservoir, and they could at least have water. His wife said no.

"'We'll go left to the mountains because the pilots will see the water from the air and will bomb the reservoir so we don't get any,' she said.

"So, we headed for the mountains, and from the heights we watched the planes come back and pound the reservoir and surrounding residential area into nothing. Had we gone there, we would have been killed. We remained in the mountains for a whole day, waiting for the raids to stop."

Japan was reeling under the onslaught. The incendiary bombing had started on June 17, 1945, and continued right through to August 15. On August 1, 820 Super Flying Fortresses dropped a record total of 6,632 tonnes of bombs on the cities of Hachioji, Nagaoka, Mito and Toyama. The latter had been obliterated.*

The Sidlines' neighbour across the street had seen them run from the house and flee to the mountains. She followed them at a distance, but could not catch up until they reached the heights. From where they were, they could see nothing but smoke and flames. It appeared as if the entire city was on fire. When their neighbour finally reached them, she told them their house was gone. She wasn't certain about her own.

They came down from the mountains that evening and discovered their neighbour's home was untouched. It was a small house, and she, her daughter, and a boarder shared it. Despite the cramped quarters, she took the Sidline family of four in for a few days. The Sidlines decided to move out to a tourist town, where there was no industry, for safety. They discovered that most of their friends had survived the bombing and had all turned up there.

"We remained there for about two years, while Japan was in ruins. The bombing raids continued, even after the atomic bombs were dropped on Hiroshima and Nagasaki. We moved from there and went to Ozaki for about a year. It wasn't easy rebuilding from nothing."

The years passed, while Japan tried to rebuild after a

*Chronology of World War II, compiled by Christopher Argyle, Marshall Cavendish Books Ltd., London, 1982, p. 190.

disastrous war it had started and lost. The Sidline boys were growing up and wanted to go to university.

"There weren't any places for foreigners, so my oldest wrote to Canada and the United States and said he would take the first offer from any university in either country. As it turned out, McGill was the first one to send an acceptance letter, and my eldest son came to Canada in 1953 as a student, to study engineering. I knew my second son would follow his brother, and we didn't want to be separated from our children. We decided to come to Canada. There were some relatives here I had never met. My parents had told me they had emigrated many years before, and I had my son look them up."

The Sidlines went to the Canadian embassy to apply for emigration. Boris Sidline was by now in the import and export business, and he had travelled a good deal. He had made many contacts and didn't have too much difficulty selling his business when the family was accepted as emigrants.

"It took a year before everything was finalized, and it was during this year that I decided to do something that would give me a craft in Canada. I liked Japan and admired the Japanese people so much. They had always been so nice to us, even during the war. I wanted to bring something from Japan so I could always remember them—something special as my good-will gift to Canada from Japan."

Three times a week, Fania Sidline would be driven by their chauffeur to the train which would take her to Tokyo and the Ozawa School to study doll-making. She also wanted to learn how to make Kabuki Theatre masks, but there was not enough time for this before their departure to Canada. Sidline spent six months at the school and learned more in that time than most students did in a year.

"When I left, the Director of Ozawa School was so surprised that I, an Occidental, could make the dolls all by myself, after such a short learning period. She said she had had many foreigners as pupils over the years, but never one who had picked it up as quickly as I had."

When she arrived in Montreal, Sidline wasted no time in arranging classes to teach others her art. It was not unusual to have twenty-five pupils in a class. Many of Montreal's second-generation Japanese-Canadian women came to her to learn the ancient art of ceremonial doll-making.

"The main purpose of the classes, which I pointed out, was to spread Japanese culture because, before each doll was made, the pupil had to be aware of the legend or history connected with it, and what character the doll represented. Each doll has its own story, which is told in the creation of the figure. I taught all year except from mid-December to mid-Janaury. Once my husband passed away, my students kept me company, so I wasn't so lonely.

"I never thought I would be doing this as an occupation," says Sidline. "It was a work of love. I never charged money for the lessons, only for the material. It was my pleasure to give the classes, and it made me feel good to be able to contribute something beautiful that would last forever and wasn't a temporary fad. It was my link with my adopted countries—Japan and Canada—and it was my way of bringing something beautiful to Canada."

That Fania Sidline succeeded is apparent. Her work has been displayed in craft-and-toy shows as far away as California, and she has a boxful of letters of thanks and appreciation for the classes she gave.

By the time you leave, you are ready to buy a doll, if Fania Sidline is willing to sell you one. You have to persuade her. After all, her beautiful creations are like her children, and what mother would part with her offspring?

A VISIBLE MINORITY

by
Pritam Singh

My parents were married on August 1, 1947, during a period when people on both sides of the border between India and Pakistan were agitated over the creation of the new state of Pakistan carved out of the old territories of the north-western portion of British India. My parents' family had lived in Montgomery (now Sahiwal) Pakistan and about a week after my parents' marriage, their families decided it would not be safe for them to remain where they were. Though it was a difficult choice for them to make, leaving the country would be just as hard, for the only means of exit was by train. There had been reports of entire train loads of passengers being ambushed and butchered. The partition of India and the mass exodus of so many people touched off riots and bloodshed. The Sikhs' way of dressing made them highly visible as a minority, and many of them were singled out and killed by the Moslems on the streets and on the trains.

My parents almost had an encounter with the mobs intent on killing visible minorities. On the day they were to leave, they managed to board the 8 a.m. train to India, under the protection of relatives who had accompanied them to the station. The train service was poor, and no one was certain if the trains would get through. Most of the people were aware of other trains that had been halted and their passengers massacred. My parents were fortunate. The train they were on reached Patiala in the Punjab, but later in the day a news report on the radio announced that the next train, which had been due to depart at 12:00 noon, never reached its destination after leaving the frontier town of Lahore. Everyone on it was killed.

When I was born in 1955, my parents were living in Delhi, India. To this day, I still remember that as a young child I went to the holy precincts of a Sikh Gurdwara, Sis Ganj, in Old Delhi and washed my feet before entering. Other memories revolve around the colourful Independence Day Parade, seen from the rooftop of our house, which, I was told, was acquired in a scramble to find shelter during the time of the partition. I remember the joys associated with visits to a park nearby and surrounding areas, and the companionship of so many relatives, all part of the joint-family system. Two of my uncles, Jagjit and Kartar Singh, had their own three-wheeled motor-scooter business. They serviced the machines when they broke down and would let me play with the spare parts. This curiosity for machinery and gadgets laid the foundations of my interest in electronics when I grew up.

When I was seven years old, I left with my mother Ranjit Kaur and two older sisters, Manjit and Inderjit, by ship for Britain. My father Mohinder Singh had gone on ahead six years before and had settled in England. He had emigrated because he was a machinist and wanted to know about new techniques and practices in use abroad. The memory of the British in India, coupled with a zeal to travel, had persuaded my father to apply for entry into Britain. Because he was impressed by the standard of living in Britain, he thought it would be a good place to bring up his family. We were to spend four years in Britain.

Life in England, as brief as it was, still lingers in my memory. The whole atmosphere—castles and plentiful historic ruins—lent a particular mystique to the imagination of children. At least that's what it did for me. There were school trips I went on, and friends I made, and sunny days spent exploring old ruins with them. Most of the time, however, days of rainy weather and the lack of central heating in our house made me feel that the damp and cold would last forever. But despite it, the gloomy weather gave my sisters and me the opportunity to watch excellent television pro-grammes.

On a number of occasions, our family visited the Sikh Temple Gurdwara in Leeds by taking the local double-decker buses through picturesque old streets and thoroughfares. At other times, we would go to the cinema. Once I started school, my mother did my hair in a knot on top of my head and wrapped a turban around it. For the first few days, I was teased unmercifully by other children. One day, when I was about ten years old, I was accosted by a group of boys about my age as I was walking home from school. They threatened me and out of fear, I was forced to remove my turban. This is forbidden by our religion.

A few days before my family left England for Canada, I was riding my bicycle through some neighbourhood streets and passed one street I had been told was the "Teddy-boys" area. No outsider dared to enter it. Unfortunately, they saw me and made threatening gestures. I kept pedalling, and they followed me on their bikes. I managed to escape to a safe area but heard them yell at me: "We'll get you next time!" I have feared them from that day on.

My parents' decision to emigrate was influenced by the lure of what a great country Canada was, and how much opportunity there was for immigrants. An added inducement was the idea of having central heating, compared to fireplaces in Britain. My father also thought the mild weather in Vancouver would help rid him of arthritic pain. He had read some advertisements early in 1965, where Canada was described as a "paradise, a doorway to Heaven." These ads were placed by the Immigration Department in order to attract skilled workers from abroad. And so one day, my father had dropped in at an Immigration Office in downtown Leeds after finishing his day's work. He picked up some applications and brought them home. In the evening, he and his younger brother Surjit, who had recently arrived from India, filled out the forms and took them to the Immigration Department the next day. An Immigration officer advised my father that he would receive a letter in the mail if he qualified. A few days later a letter arrived, stating that he had been accepted. Then there was a round of medical examinations, and medical forms to complete. The officer called him once more to ask about finances. Eventually, the Immigration Department provided a loan to cover travelling expenses for the whole family, repayable without interest, over a couple of years.

My father travelled ahead by ship to Canada in June, 1965. When he finished his journey by train to the west at the New Westminster railway station in Vancouver, two officers from Canada Manpower were there to meet him. Their job was to help him find accommodation and a job as a skilled machinist. They drove him to a hotel, and the next day picked him up and took him to a company, where he was hired. Later, he found temporary lodging in the home of Giani Mani Singh, who was one of the early Sikh settlers. About eleven months later, he came back to England to bring the rest of the family to Canada.

On April 29, 1966, we arrived by ship at Quebec and then travelled to the west coast by train, a journey that took four days and three nights. But after living in Vancouver for two years, my father was convinced that it was not the best place to raise children. Although he was especially taken by the mountains, Stanley Park and the scenic beauty in a mild climate, he realized, through contacts in the one-hundred-year-old Sikh community, that Toronto was the best place for him. He reasoned that Toronto had more educated Sikhs adhering to Sikh traditions, such as covering the head when entering Sikh Gurdwaras—a practice that had been abandoned by the assimilated community in Vancouver. He felt those in Vancouver had strayed too far from the principles of Sikhism. He was also thinking about the future of his relatives who would be sponsored later on, for there were fewer jobs for skilled people in Vancouver than there were in Toronto.

A week before we left Vancouver, I heard my parents talking about the planned expedition to Toronto by car—an old Volkswagen—along the Trans-Canada Highway. My father, during the short stay of two years, had learned how to rebuild car engines. The Volkswagen had an engine he rebuilt, but it needed attention every now and then. My father, sister Inderjit and I were to come ahead to get things ready for the rest of the family.

When we reached Kamloops, we had trouble with the car, but my father was able to repair it. Along the way, he thought we could all sleep in the car. For me, the night presented a problem with the fear of having the turban come loose during sleep. I had been accustomed to having my mother do the topknot and wrap the turban for me. Anyhow, I slept without having it fall off. After spending a night in the car, we decided to buy a tent. That was in the town of Swift Current. We spent the rest of the trip parking nightly at campsites along the Trans-Canada Highway. It was the first time I experienced black flies. I was never fond of having bugs and insects crawling over me. So, when they went inside the crevices of my turban, I itched and found blood coming out, to my surprise! The first night we put up the tent, we had a funny incident. It was late in the evening, and we were all exhausted. During the night, I knocked out the main tent pole in my sleep. As it came down, my father thought it was an intruder and grabbed a crowbar. We didn't get much sleep, and waking up that way I realized that dew and moisture in the tent was part of my first camping experience.

My job during the journey was important, for I was map guide and lookout scout. But when we left the city of Kenora, Ontario, I fell asleep, and we almost took the wrong way to Sudbury when my sister misread the map. It was about this time, I noticed my turban was all undone. So when we stopped at the nearest campsite, for the first time, I did the topknot and wrapped the turban, all by myself. It took us four days to drive 2693 miles and when we reached Toronto, my father looked up his fellow Sikhs under the name Singh in the phone book, to ask for help. We made contact with a very hospitable family by the name of Mr. Darshan Singh Teji. They were kind and courteous, and invited us to their home, where they answered questions my father had about the city, his job prospects and the way the Sikhs lived. This meeting reassured my father that he had taken the right step in deciding to settle in Toronto.

My father found suitable lodging for us and left us there while he travelled by bus to Vancouver to collect the rest of the family. He used a second car and a U-Haul trailer to move the rest of the family and our belongings, and by 1968 we were established in Toronto, where my youngest sister Jasvinder Kaur was born. I now had five sisters who had been born in three different countries, all of whom later became Canadian.

Initially, growing up as a Sikh didn't appear to me as the root cause for a variety of problems that I experienced—problems such as going through the Canadian educational system, and adjusting to social life. Right from the beginning, as a child, I had had trouble tying a turban. On many occasions, I spent more than a hour, instead of the normal five minutes, trying to wrap the turban neatly, until I felt it was comfortable. My confidence in wearing the turban was undermined by different weights and quality of turban cloth. Some materials were more manageable, while other materials made me more conscious of it coming loose or falling off. I always feared having it fall off in public. Throughout school I never removed it once, not even for gym. Because of this underlying fear, and also the difficulty I had in wrapping a turban, I avoided sports. My parents never thought of providing a Sikh alternative form of turban, called *patka,* for sports purposes. I only became aware of it a few years later. Another reason for my problems was the lack of other Sikh children of my age around me. I lacked role models. As a result, I had an excuse not to participate in gym or swimming because of my "religion". None of the teachers ever questioned me, why I gave this reason.

Throughout my school years, a great feeling of hopelessness, even loneliness, pervaded my being. I never made any friends. Perhaps it was the result of moving too often, new schools and new environments. Socially, dating always remained a mystery. I never dated girls when I went through high school and college. Although the urge to date was there, I shied away from contacts and buried myself in a world of books. When I reached college, I found a world of awareness, which up till then, I had only suspected.

The course material for the Electronic Engineering Technician Programme, combined with the accessibility of re- source materials in the library initiated a "mind explosion". The depth of introspection, coupled with scientific objective analysis of events around me, led me to newer insights within the framework of logic and reasoning, and I developed what I suppose is a kind of scientific outlook.

In my own naive manner, during the second year of college, I was guided through the rituals collectively known as "Arranged Marriage", the implications of which I realized only afterwards. According to Dr. Jarnail Singh, "In every society there is some element of arrangement. The Arranged Marriage is not a religious doctrine but is a product of a socio-cultural environ- ment."* The idea behind this system, was for my parents to arrange an engagement between me and a girl living in India, who was a total stranger. For me it fitted the meaning of the word "unknown". Actually, Unidentified Living Object (ULO) would be more pre- cise. This method of marriage seemed to me to defy explanation or any rationality. My fiancée was known only through verbal reports forwarded by relatives, and images from mailed photo-

* Dr. Jarnail Singh. Personal Interview. February 2, 1985.

graphs. Suddenly, my whole being was obsessed with the thought of the arranged marriage, and I found myself researching and studying the courting behaviour and associated customs of other societies. I concluded from reading a variety of books on the subject, (apart from the physical urges inherent in each of us) that there was a spiritual side to marriage. Although I was influenced to a degree by the mainstream Canadian culture, I sensed intuitively that Manjeet, the girl proposed, would be the right partner for me. My only explanation for this impression was that some inner voice told me so.

At this point I was hard pressed to think about my life and what my parents were doing to me. I felt as if I was in a pressure cooker. As far as they were concerned, their son Pritam was getting married, and a parental responsibility was being fulfilled. Little did they realize what was going on in my mind. I had many encounters with my mother, who was more attentive to my distress. There was a lot ot tension, but now I realize the decision was one I had to make alone. Had I not, I am sure I would have had some kind of breakdown. I still adhere to a discipline of the mind, which provides an inner guide, a voice of the Oversoul, call it what you wish. I believe many major decisions in life can be correctly decided by listening intuitively to the voice within ourselves.

Another essential prerequisite for my acceptance of an arranged marriage came initially from the Sikh Doctrine of *Sanjog*—a union of two souls, and *Vijog*—separation of two souls. In Sikh theology, union and separation take place according to God's Will. The basis for Sikh teachings on marriage rests upon the fact that marriage is a physical as well as spiritual union of two people. There is also the implicit belief that this meeting has been ordained by God. Marriage for me meant what the Sikh Scripture, the Guru Granth Sahib said: "Those are not a husband and wife who have joined purely on the physical level. Only that couple which shares one soul in two bodies, is man and wife."*

After a number of heated discussions with my parents, I agreed to sponsor Manjeet into Canada. Right up to the time she set foot on Canadian soil at Toronto International Airport, I kept asking myself whether this would, indeed, lead to a union of two long-lost souls. Watching her walk toward the exit doors, I breathed

*Adi Granth. Rag Suhi 3, (3), p. 768.

a sigh of relief. Her looks, combined with eye-to-eye contact, provoked a feeling of joy difficult to describe. I felt reassured that I had made the right decision. Our romance, if there was any, lasted through short, peek-a-boo sessions. Glances were exchanged every now and then. We were both chaperoned until the date and time of the wedding, which took place at Stratford, Ontario, within one month of her arrival.

Hard to believe, perhaps, after my total rebellion at the idea of an arranged marriage to an unknown girl living abroad in India, who had been pushed at me. I hadn't been at all pleased with hearing on the family grapevine that my parents were looking for a bride for me. How could any man in his right mind accept and agree to an engagement to a woman unfamiliar to his ways and ten thousand miles away?

However, after a period of eleven years, I now realize other contributing factors that complicate the success of a "mixed marriage"—not in the usual sense, of course, but in the sense that two people had been brought together and blindly betrothed to one another without ever having communicated or been given the opportunity to experience anything through sensory channels.

If children are brought up in an environment foreign to their parents' generation, these children to some extent will be pressured to follow the whims of the parents in practically all spheres of life. As regards my family, attempts were made to keep all the members within the Sikh culture and traditions. To this day, I have accepted a lot of my parents' decisions. I admit this rather grudgingly, because when I followed their regulations I was in no position to foresee the effect of the situation. Once I left their home and got married through their arrangement, I began to realize I was being controlled subconsciously, even though my wife and I live apart from my parents.

Social conditioning is difficult to shake off. The long-term effects of the zeal of Sikh parents in transmitting "heritage" to their offspring are painful, and I realize now the haphazard treatment meted out to youngsters within our community. I am referring to the absence of any Sikh social activities between people my age, and the acute lack of organized support-people or volunteers to initiate educational activities for our children. In the past such activities were non-existent, and the future doesn't look too promising.

The main question now refers to, what is the future of the Sikh community, faith and land? The recent course of events, such as the attack on the Golden Temple in Amritsar on June 6, 1984, and the massacre of thousands of Sikhs in the aftermath of Indira Gandhi's assassination, leads me to say that here in Canada, as well as abroad, the future of the community looks quite dismal.

For the Sikhs, the present situation is no worse than that of the past. Indarjit Singh wrote in an article that "from a traditional disunity, there has always been and is today, a naive lack of political awareness or farsightedness, or the ability to look beyond the immediate and plan constructively for the future. While we can and should draw considerable inspiration from the way of the Sikhs of old, who fought against innumerable odds and created a mighty and democratic empire, I am of the opinion that we cannot afford to rest on our laurels, particularly in today's turbulent times."*

"Disunity is still rife in our community. Comfort, convenience and a despicable lack of sincerity has taken precedence over principles. I fear that if this drift is allowed to continue for a generation or so, Sikhism will forever be lost as a vital force in shaping man's destiny for the common good. Equally, however, I believe that, if Sikhs are prepared to learn from their mistakes and live true to the teachings of our scripture, the Guru Granth Sahib, both as individuals and as a community, Sikhs and Sikhism can and will make a contribution to the world of today, far, far greater, than that achieved by their illustrious forbears."*

Yes, I am aware there is a crisis in the Sikh community and that Sikhs are being discriminated against, beaten and killed in India, and that the communities bicker amongst themselves while this is going on. In my mind there have always been questions about my search for identity. My father, like most fathers, was hypocritical in teaching Sikh values and heritage. What can a person expect if his or her parents have lived outside their country of origin for a period of twenty-eight years? However, in the examples they provided, they were oblivious to their own cultural assimilation of western ideas. Although my father would not admit it, it is painful for him to see his children adopt western ways.

* Indarjit Singh. "The Rise of the Sikh Power," *The Sikh Courier*, Spring/Summer, 1982, Vol. II, No. 1, pp. 11-15.

Even questioning his example on a number of issues has been met with anger.

In truth, my father's fanaticism on the issue of traditions has played a key role in my development. His fanatical adherence to the Sikh religion relegated his family's welfare to a secondary position. This was contrary to Sikh ethics, which clearly state that a man's first and foremost responsibility is to his family.

Raised in an atmosphere drenched with the fear of assimilation into the larger Canadian society, I nonetheless had freedoms which I was never aware of. In comparison, my sisters had no freedoms at all. According to Indian tradition, daughters are a commodity, and only through marriage, can they restore parents' self esteem and respect for the family name. Because of this commodity value, daughters have to stay with their parents until marriageable age. In this sense, commonly accepted freedoms such as socializing at friends' parties, inviting them to sleep over, dating and participation in activities of peer groups, were unknown to my sisters. To put it another way, sex for daughters is a subject best learned after marriage. Boys knew about sex, of course. "But somehow or other, it is expected that daughters carry the *izzat*," the respect of the family, and should behave accordingly.*

But who am I? In my childhood, kids my own age enquired if I was an Arab, Pakistani, Hindu or Moslem or even a genie! No one had ever heard of Sikhs and Sikhism. Sometimes I even received "royal treatment"—being addressed as a "Maharaja."

During the period I attended school and throughout college, Canadian racism against Sikhs as defined through violent attacks, was already brewing. The problem surfaced after the influx of immigrants in the wave of 1973 to 1974. Our family moved from Toronto and bought a home in Cambridge, Ontario, in mid-1974. In the fall I started classes at Conestoga College in Kitchener. During the two years of my studies, I encountered some name-calling, but it was not as serious as the events in larger cities such as Toronto. There was a spate of articles: "Vandals deface Sikh temple: police set up surveillance."**; "The Sikhs get tough"***;

* Philip Marchand. "Strangers in a Strange Land." *Toronto Life*, July, 1982: pp. 48-49, 65-67.
** "Vandals deface Sikh Temple: police set up surveillance." *The Toronto Star*, May 29, 1974, p. B1.
*** Joan Barfoot. "The Sikhs get tough." *The Sunday Sun*, June 2, 1974, p. 21.

"Race—the debate becomes violent—Racism? You can't argue with the facts."*; "We feel like Blacks in Detroit, Sikh says"** and "Riots feared: Sikhs demand police action on race attacks."*** These were a few of the news items detailing the racially motivated assaults. Sikhs were lumped together with the other East Asians when racial abuse was hurled at them. Moreover, Sikhs bore the brunt of this abuse because of their visibility. They were more readily identifiable because of their turbans and beards. In Cambridge, our house was pelted with bad eggs and tomatoes. Our car's paint was scratched, and the walls of our house painted with the words "Paki, go home." Our next door neighbor, Mr. Avtar Singh Bhogel, and my father Mohinder Singh, were featured in an article in the city's newspaper: "East Asians encounter racial discrimination; all people don't find Cambridge friendly."****

My younger sister Surrinder Kaur and Mr. Bhogel's daughter, Balvinder Kaur, faced a lot of abuse at the Preston High School. "You can tell when someone hates you. I try not to judge people if they call us 'Paki'. We ask them why and they say they have to. They can't do anything about it," said Balvinder."****

For me, racial attacks were something I had only read about, but never witnessed. This all changed when I became the victim of an assault in the summer of 1977. At the time, I was living in a flat in Toronto, where I had a job and had already sponsored my fiancée in April. On the night of August 20, at about one o'clock in the morning, I was on my way home from an Indian classical music get-together. My friends gave me a lift, and I got off close to where I lived, in the Riverdale area of Toronto in the vicinity of the Pape Avenue Gurdwara (Shromani Sikh Society). As I passed an intersection where Pape Avenue Public School was

* Angela Ferrante, "Race—The Debate becomes violent; Racism? You can't argue with the facts." *Maclean's*, February 7, 1977, Vol. 90, No. 3, pp. 18-21.
** Ken Becker. "We feel like blacks in Detroit, Sikh says." *The Toronto Sun*, August 30, 1977, p. 16.
*** "Riots feared—Sikhs demand police action on race attacks." *The Toronto Star*, August 29, 1977, p. C1.
**** Daphne Lavers and Anneli Andre Barrett. "All people don't find Cambridge friendly." *The Cambridge Times*, November 16, 1977.

located, I noticed someone following me, and in a split second received a blow to my neck. On that particular day, I had wrapped my turban quite low and my neck was protected. As the blow fell, my turban fell off. My survival instincts came into operation and I found myself drawing my *Kirpan* (a sword, one of the five Sikh religious symbols) while the attacker shouted obscenities, "You f— Paki!" I was lucky because he was frightened when I chased after him with the *Kirpan* in my hand. I was very shaken by this incident, especially because it was the first time my *Kirpan* actually served its purpose, that is to be used as a defensive weapon for the protection of my person. After the attack was over, I kept thinking if that guy was trying to rob me, or assault me because I was a Sikh?

In 1971, when I was sixteen years old, I had taken *Khande-ka-Amrit* (baptism of the double-edged sword). After having taken Amrit, I became one of the Khalsa (The Pure Ones or "Saint-Soldiers"). As a Khalsa, I had to keep the five Sikh symbols (The Five K's) on my person at all times. These symbols include:"*Keshas*— uncut hair. A lot has been written about Keshas, their use and significance. From times immemorial cutting of hair has been associated with renunciation and sometimes with slavery. A Sikh, especially a Khalsa, is a whole, complete person, living in this world, still detached. Keeping uncut hair is renunciation of renunciations, a sign of saintliness in the true sense of the world. *Khanga*—wooden comb. Unlike yogis and ascetics who keep their hair in a matted condition, a Sikh hass to keep his hair clean. The comb is made obligatory to signify this aspect. *Kirpan*—sword. It represents courage and self-respect. The *Kirpan* is for the protection of the weak and the oppressed. Symbolically, it represents a weapon that cuts at the roots of nescience (*avidya*). It is nescience that separates the transient individual self from the abiding, immortal Universal Self. The sword also symbolizes the right of free citizens to wear arms. *Kara*—steel bracelet. The iron bangle on the right wrist is symbolic of Dharma, the Supreme Law. A Sikh must lead a life guided and supported by faith in God. *Kachha*—short drawers. Kachha is the badge and basis of the civilization itself. As the human race marches on the road of civilization, two tendencies show themselves: (a) Renunciation, in extreme going naked, (b) Over-indulgence. Kachha symbolizes the repudiation of both these tendencies. A Sikh is supposed to lead a life of contentment grounded in ethical and social responsibilities."*

According to Dr. John W. Spellman, Professor of Asian Studies at the University of Windsor, "Sikhs who submit to baptism and who assume the obligations of the five K's and the other disciplines are called Khalsa or "Saint-Soldiers." Historically, the *Kirpan* was not an offensive but a defensive weapon; nowadays it symbolizes the obligation to protect the weak and is a source of self-confidence and prestige."**

Observance of the five K's didn't pose any problem until I suffered a back injury in late October, 1978. For therapy, I consulted a chiropractor and received several ultrasonic treatments at the physiotherapy department of Toronto General Hospital. The treatments did little to produce any noticeable change in the severity of the back pain, and eventually I was referred to the Workmen's Compensation Board's Hospital and Rehabilitation Centre, in Downsview, Ontario.

I was registered for out-patient therapy on Friday, April 20, 1979, and three days later attended therapy. On the next day I was scheduled for pool therapy, and my *Kirpan* caught the attention of hospital personnel. I was summoned by the attendance counsellor and in the course of the conversation, made it clear that Orthodox Sikhs who came for treatment in the past had received dispensation from the Sikh "leaders" to wear a jewelled symbol in the form of two double-edged swords miniaturized on the *Khanga* itself. The advice was contrary to the Sikh Code of Conduct*** which states that a person who has taken *Khande-ka-Amrit,* is to wear the *Kirpan* and other symbols at all times. Our conversation ended with my suggestion that the counsellor meet with some resource people from the Sikh community, who would intervene on my behalf. However, my efforts to bring some people from the Sikh community were met with failure.

On May 2, 1979, I lodged a complaint with the Ontario

*Editor's Note. "Retention of the Five (5) K's." *Proceedings of The Sikh Heritage Conference.* Ed. Jarnail Singh and Hardev Singh. The Sikh Social and Educational Society, Willowdale, Ontario, 1981, p. 47.
**The Ontario Human Rights Commission, "Board Rules on Wearing Kirpan," *Affirmation,* December, 1981, Vol. 2, No. 4, p. 1.
*** *Rehat Maryada—A Guide To The Sikh Way of Life,* Amritsar, India: Shromani Gurdwara Parbhandhak Committee (SGPC), 1978.

Human Rights Commission. The issue at stake was the wearing of a reasonable-sized *Kirpan*. The hospital's regulations prohibited anyone from bringing weapons into the premises. They considered a *Kirpan* a weapon. As a settlement could not be reached in conciliation, the commission eventually asked the Minister to appoint a board of inquiry. "Professor Frederick H. Zemans of Osgoode Hall Law School was asked to chair the board. His decision was handed down in mid-summer, 1981. The 29-page document discusses, in detail, the Sikh faith and the responsibility that a believing, baptized member of the religion must assume. In the final analysis, Professor Zemans said the issue was not whether the hospital had a duty toward its other patients to protect them from actual or potentially traumatic situations, or whether Mr. Singh had a basic right to wear his *Kirpan*. In both cases, the answer was a clear, yes. The question, then, was whether the hospital, in preventing Mr. Singh from exercising his religious obligations under these specific circumstances, had acted reasonably. Was it reasonable to hold that Mr. Singh's *Kirpan* qualified as an offensive weapon, and that it was likely to traumatize other patients? Professor Zemans concluded: 'The respondent hospital made no effort to accommodate the legitimate religious practices of the complainant. There was no attempt by the hospital to educate their staff or patients and to integrate the complainant into a therapy programme, which he was entitled to receive. The hospital, in my opinion, took a unilateral, and seemingly arbitrary position, which denied Mr. Singh treatment with their facilities. There was no justification, in my opinion, for the respondent hospital to find Mr. Singh's *Kirpan* to be an offensive weapon within the provisions of their rules and regulations.' The board therefore ordered that Mr. Singh and any prospective Sikh patients of the Workmen's Compensation Board Hospital and Rehabilitation Centre be allowed to wear *Kirpans* of a reasonable length while receiving treatment, and that copies of the Human Rights Code be posted on hospital premises. The judgement has been appealed."* The appeal abandoned on September 22, 1986.

In the Proceedings of the Sikh Heritage Conference in 1981, editors Jarnail Singh and Hardev Singh have included an article I wrote which stated, "...in the last few years, cases alleging

* The Ontario Human Rights Commission, "Board Rules on Wearing Kirpan," *Affirmation*, December 1981, Vol. 2, No. 4, p. 1.

discrimination against Sikhs with respect to their wearing of the five K's have mushroomed across the country. Apparently, it seems that the collective fight for our rights has become individualized to some odd person fighting his battle here and there, with repercussions and headaches [controversies] being flashed on the pages of newspapers...The organization and coordination, so essential to the development of communities, is not evident among our community, in the present circumstances. Belief and strong faith dwell in the heart of many Sikhs. They are dedicated to the upkeep of the five K's. But after some analysis, they stand alone on a crumbling platform of emotions which gives way to apathy. They may stand alone and fight to their last breath...but without the support and backing of reliable sources and authorities, their fight is just an exercise in the art of frustration."*

In my own case, there was no one I could turn to for the resolution of the matter. Gurdwaras were contacted, and the matter was explained to the people in charge. Unfortunately, when the public hearings took place at York University's Osgoode Hall Law School, not one person came from the Executives or the managements of the Gurdwaras, nor did any so-called "leaders" show up. What does this really illustrate? Well, at the present time, no process, mechanism or institution exists whereby information can be obtained about cases being fought for the preservation of Sikhs' rights to wear their religious symbols. Perhaps through my own efforts and that of The Sikh Social and Educational Society, this situation will be changed for the better.

Who am I? Again this question appears. The answer is not comforting. There was a time, given peer pressure and social involvement, when I would have succumbed to the forces of assimilation. That would have changed my destiny, to be something other than a Sikh. Outwardly, I am a Sikh; inwardly, these symbols, forms and colours do not affect my will to survive and to provide an insight from a traveller of two worlds, yet they do.

What am I? As a stranger to the dominant Canadian society, I still don't know how Canadian weddings are held. I've

* Pritam Singh, "Fight For Our Identity—Kirpan." *Proceedings of The Sikh Heritage Conference.* Ed. Jarnail Singh and Hardev Singh. The Sikh Social and Educational Society, Willowdale, Ontario, 1981, p. 50.

never gone to parties, and I never dated. Words have always been my style. It is a very rare occasion when the ideas I express are understood by my people. If I talk in my native Punjabi Language, in which I am now fluent, people don't know who I am. They can't understand it... If I use English, then people don't understand what I say. Much of the community in which I dwell has anchored itself on a base of shifting sands. Priorities have been confused. Quite a lot of emphasis is paid to the country of origin, bypassing issues and concerns affecting the community here in Canada. It is unfortunate that more effort has not been directed to alleviating upcoming issues facing the next generation. Only people like myself can bear witness to some of the problems, as a victim of their experiences of two worlds.

POLONAISE MILITAIRE

by
Jadwiga Krupski
condensed by Milly Charon
from a 300-page work-in-progress

My parents were married in Lwow, Poland in June, 1914, a few weeks before the assassination of Archduke Franz Ferdinand and his wife at Sarajevo—not a very auspicious beginning for a young couple. Although the family residence was in Lwow, in Poland, by the time I was born in Vienna in 1915, the Russians had taken possession of my home town and forced my parents to flee westward. Trying to dodge alien invasions and occupations seemed to become a pattern in our lives from that period on.

World War I broke the even flow of comfortable upper-middle class life as military service took my father to another town. My mother would not leave him and followed him to Lublin where he served as an officer-cadet and apprentice lawyer, finishing his legal studies.

And so, I remained behind, the first and only grandchild, the eldest daughter's first offspring, under the watchful eye of Frau Mathilde, my nurse. Everything seemed to revolve around me in that busy household of grandparents, my young aunt Janka, uncles arriving to visit, cousins, the servants, and even Anna, the young peasant from the mountain country, who periodically arrived from our country house to bring us dried mushrooms, cheeses and other produce.

In 1918, as the Austro-Hungarian Empire split at the seams, the Ukrainian minority in Eastern Poland took the opportunity to carve its own independence out of the general chaos, and occupied Lwow, a predominantly Polish city in a region that was surrounded by Ukrainian rural areas. While the Polish armies were busy regrouping, the city had to defend itself, and women, schoolboys, old men and soldiers on convalescent leave became Lwow's defenders.

Food was so scarce that I danced in delight around the dining-room table one happy day when potato soup was served— the gift of a lawyer friend of my grandfather's, who had picked his way underground, through adjoining cellars and basements, from the Polish side of Lwow, to bring us a bag of potatoes.

We slept on mattresses in grandfather's office—a room with no windows—for a very good reason. A spray of machine-gun bullets had riddled the wall in my nursery, just above the place where my cot usually stood. To this day I treasure a book of translations from English poets, punctured by rifle bullets. I remember my grandfather's ash-grey face as he held me in his arms at the entrance to our apartment, while shouting men in uniforms shoved past him into the living room.

Later I was told that one of grandfather's nephews, who was ten years old and too young to fight, had been firing a gun from an attic window at the Ukrainians in the streets. This, of course, was staunchly denied by grandfather, when a detachment of soldiers came to investigate. No weapon was found, and only because one of the maids had hidden the gun in her bed and had lain down upon it, pretending to be very ill. Had the weapon been found, not only the girl, but all adult males in the family would have been executed on the spot.

After the war, father joined grandfather's law firm as a junior partner, and grandfather, the patriarch, decided that my parents should move into an apartment on the second floor of the family townhouse.

We took our meals downstairs on my grandfather's floor. The arrangement irked my mother, but there was something special in grandfather's tyranny that made rebellion difficult, for it was a tyranny of pure love and benevolence. Any sign of independence hurt him profoundly, and sooner or later we all did rebel. The memory of the hurt we caused remained with us all our lives, and was far more vivid than the recollection of victories we had achieved.

In 1921 my baby brother Juro was born, and I spent hours sitting beside his cradle, humming songs to him and experiencing absolute bliss when my singing put him to sleep. I was at an age now when I was slipping out of the sphere of authority of my nurse,

Frau Mathilde, and a kindergarten teacher was hired to come every afternoon to give me pre-school lessons. And my mother read the most wonderful books to me and taught me to play with paper dolls—a special game—for they were characters of the stories we read together, and their fate had to be re-enacted in endless dramatic games. I had boxes and boxes in which Ivanhoe and Lady Rowena reposed, side by side with characters from *Quo Vadis*, *Little Lord Fauntleroy*, Mary of *The Secret Garden*, *Anne of Green Gables* and all the gallant *Knights of the Round Table*. A whole world of poetry, adventure and dreams lived in those boxes and refused to vanish, even when I was in my teens. Perhaps they were the reason for certain of my stubbornly surviving beliefs in the reality of dreams.

One early spring, mother and father took me to Jaremcze, the mountain village in the Carpathians where our country house was located. A family of neighbouring *hutzuls* (mountaineers of the region) had been taking care of the house and grounds. And now the time had come to restore and reopen the country retreat after the damage wrought by the Russian soldiers, who had used the dining room as a stable for their horses.

It was early spring when the bearded droshky driver pulled up his skinny horse outside the overgrown, weed-choked box hedge. To the right, the brownish ribbon of the river lay unfurled like a scarf. Steep, grey rocks were crowned with the even velvet of mountain firs. A light wind was blowing, combing the firs which appeared like the dark heads of obedient children receiving the ministrations of some giant hand. Above them, soft and delicate, the mountain meadows rolled on from peak to gentle peak, repeating the pattern of the meandering river below. I have seen many landscapes since—the grandeur of the Rockies with their jewel lakes; the autumn flame of the Laurentians, Pacific rollers breaking on a silver beach—I have loved them all, but never with that heartcatching, fierce and wondering love of my lost childhood for a lost country.

There was Anna, the well-remembered messenger of wartime days, grown into a blooming and laughing "baba", with her little Marusia staring at me out of wide, periwinkle-blue eyes. There was Anna's mother and father, and a brood of brothers and sisters, all of them bowing and laughing. They lived in a primitive fashion, sharing their house with newly born livestock, yet the dig-

351

nity, charm and proud freedom of the *hutzuls* placed them beyond the reach of any feeling of superiority a city visitor could experience.

The house and gardens were inspected, and repairs on the house would begin. Father would send a gardener, furniture and building materials, as well as other necessities, from the city. Summer would see us installed in my grandparents' country house.

We spent the night in a hotel in the village, about a mile from the house. The proprietor, an old family friend, toasted our return with iced vodka, and as we ate freshly caught speckled trout, we looked out of the windows at the river winding below, foaming over rocks, tinted with a rosy glow from the setting sun. My parents were laughing and as happy as children, as though the cares, worries and fears of war had fallen from them. I couldn't wait for summer from then on; summer meant going home each year.

Up to then, we had been spending our summer holidays in various seaside or mountain resorts, choosing those untouched by the war. One of these had been an Austrian health spa, in reality a refined and expensive setup for cases of "nervous exhaustion". In fact, some of the patients would have been considered mentally disturbed, if not insane, had they had less money and less exalted physicians. The Indian Rajah, in the pavilion next to ours, had an endearing habit of leaving his rooms, attired only in his turban, and had to be chased by a brace of stalwart attendants. He was harmless, however, and I once had an interesting conversation with him. That day he was wearing a loincloth—perhaps the day was chilly—and he told me in his broken German that he had a little girl of my age, who was far away in India.

He was gentle and beautiful, and I was sorry when his attendants came and coaxed him back to his quarters. And once I went berry-picking with the gardener's daughter without realizing that the whole place was in an uproar. The family thought we were lost, or worse, and when we reappeared hours later, we both were spanked very hard. In those post-war days, the woods, we were told, were full of returning soldiers, but we didn't see the danger in that.

But now we had our summer place to go to, and oh, the magic of the country! I had friends to play with—three boys who lived on the property next to ours—sons of a local Polish farmer.

They were wild, tough and crude, and I learned some colourful language from them, but they were my good friends and let me tag along, and even play soccer on their team.

Because I had a private tutor, I only set foot in a school twice a year—to pass exams and be promoted to the next grade. And so we remained in Jaremcze well into October, when fruit-picking time was a great occasion. Set up in the orchard was a huge cauldron, under which a crackling wood-fire was kept going for several days. Into this went the blue Hungarian prune-plums, which were shaken off the trees and collected in sheets of sacking spread underneath. I climbed up and stood on the thick boughs and bounced up and down, while a storm of golden leaves and sapphire fruit cascaded down under my feet. The plums would be stoned there and then poured into the seething, fragrant cauldron. Any early fallen apples would be cored and added to the brew. One of Anna's brothers stirred the cooking fruit with a large wooden paddle. No sugar or water was added, and the result was a delicious concoction called "powidlo", a thick, brownish-purple jam, pungent and sweet, subtly flavoured with wood smoke, which is used for so many winter desserts of Eastern and Central Europe.

And then came the apples—golden-skinned russets, crimson "Gypsy" apples, perfect for tarts, charlottes and *apfelstrudel* masterpieces, and less noble cooking-apples, masses of them, hand-picked and stored carefully in wooden crates, to be shipped to town.

By then departure was imminent—for me an annual catastrophe—but a few years later an important event took place. My Aunt Janka returned from Mexico, where her husband had invented a new process for recovering oil-production wastes, apparently a significant discovery. Having patented this in the States, he returned to establish himself in Europe, to introduce the process there. They arrived with their three-year-old son Stefan and an English governess, Fraülein Grete, who was really German, but whose knowledge of English qualified her to instruct her charges in the language of affluence, used by Byron and Galsworthy, and deemed the symbol of sophistication.

Aunt Janka had put on a little weight and wore clothes that seemed strange and exciting to me, but shocked my mother deeply.

"That terrible American stuff! How can you?" moaned my

exquisite mother Marysia, who considered herself absolutely devoid of anything to wear if she had run out of Paris originals for the season. Stefan was a picture-book little boy, but he was also a hellion. When he saw himself surrounded by a multitude of clucking aunts, uncles and grandparents, he yelled something in Spanish that translated as "Get the hell out of here!", dismaying and puzzling his admiring audience. My three-year-old brother Juro, opened his velvety brown eyes wide, touched Stefan on the nose with his forefinger and with a deep sigh of satisfaction, said: *"Na, da ist er ja schön"*. The love between the two little boys was extraordinary and moving. They did not associate much with other children. They had each other.

And grandfather celebrated the return of his younger daughter by presenting both Janka and Marysia with identical villas, which were erected on the Jaremcze property and named after the daughters.

And Uncle Dolo, Janka's husband, won my heart by daring to convince my parents that we children had outgrown the tyrannical and crazy-clean Frau Mathilde, and should have a governess. Frau Mathilde was given her walking papers and a month later, Fraülein Gertrud, a friend of Fraülein Grete, made her appearance. Her specialty was French as a second language, as she had studied at the Sorbonne.

It took some time, but she managed to win my heart, and she was the one who became the recipient of my adolescent worries, dilemmas and confidences. Juro adored her from the first day until the last, when he died in her arms.

The years had passed—summer in Jaremcze and winter holidays to enjoy the snow. That particular winter, Juro and I tobogganed to our heart's content. Juro hated leaving and cried bitterly in the car bearing us home. Later, mother called it a premonition.

We were preparing for a visit to Vienna for the Easter holidays, but two days before, Juro developed a temperature. On the day appointed for departure, I was told I was going to Vienna—alone. I was stunned. I had not even been allowed near Juro to kiss him good-bye; however, I did steal into the sickroom and tried to. He only looked at me out of those brown eyes which seemed to be larger than ever, saying nothing; yet, in those tragic eyes I read what, consciously I refused to accept—that I would not see my little brother again.

Two weeks later Juro was dead, carried off by an attack of scarlet fever combined with diphtheria, despite the care of the most renowned children's specialist from Vienna, summoned to his bedside. A year later, immunizations against diphtheria and scarlet fever became common practice.

Gertrud had remained with him day and night, spelled by grandmother, father, and a young boy cousin who contracted the disease, but recovered from it. Mother broke down completely. Juro could not bear the strange nurses that were supposed to take over his care, and it was Gertrud who held him when he died.

And all this time I was in Vienna with Aunt Janka, deliberately closing my mind to what was going on, until finally came a black-bordered envelope addressed in mother's handwriting. Aunt Janka told me. She wept bitterly; I didn't shed a tear. Later, Aunt Janka told me how puzzled everybody was at my strange, withdrawn indifference, even though I had earned the reputation of being sensitive, nervous and easily upset.

Yet after half a century, one of my most sorrowful thoughts is the memory of the little, forgotten, untended grave in the Lwow cemetery—a child so loved, left alone. This, perhaps, is the greatest sorrow of wars and upheavals, for there are such yawning gaps in family histories which even the fondest memory cannot bridge.

Juro's death brought many changes. Mother refused to go back to the old apartment where he had died. Even grandfather would not attempt to change her mind. He bought a beautiful home on a lovely street where the houses had gardens, and which a hilly park divided from the bustle of downtown. The house was completely remodelled for our use.

There were twelve state-supported high schools for boys and only one for girls. It was reserved for the daughters of civil servants, and no fees were payable. I was registered as a day student in one of the more select private schools that was the only one in Lwow to offer a modified classical programme of studies. My Aunt Mina prepared me twice a term for exams at the school, but how I longed to attend classes there with the other children! However, one of the reasons mother had for keeping me home with private tutors was her terror of infectious diseases. Aunt Mina's little son Roman, Aunt Sophie's five-year-old Olga, and our own Juro had all died from childhood diseases.

And so finally I was permitted to join my classmates in my second year of high school, or Gymnasium, as it was called. I was given a seat next to a plump, blond, blue-eyed girl. She was, and remains, my first and dearest friend, Halka, the daughter of a prominent Lwow family. Her grandfather had been a blacksmith by profession and Lord Mayor of the city, as incongruous as it may seem. Her father, a physician, was in charge of the city's public health. Halka and her family lived in a large, cheerful, untidy house, and I was grateful to be admitted into the noisy, ramshackle, good-humoured household. I had been used to my mother's meticulously run menage and Gertrud's German fastidiousness, and I equated Halka's family's casual lifestyle with a delicious freedom and ease. Halka had an elder sister and six older brothers, and one of them, Tadzik, who became a career army officer, was one of my first boyfriends—a truly good friend, who has remained so to this day. Another brother, Stephen (Funek), the best-looking of the lot, became infected in his university years in Warsaw with the bug of anti-Semitism, rampant in the universities of Europe in those pre-war days.

When I lived in Warsaw with my family in 1937, Funek was a regular guest in our house, and squired me to many a dance and party. When I questioned and chided him about his often-expressed prejudices against Jews, he gaped at me in disbelief: "What an idiot you are!" he said. " You people are different. We don't mean people like you! You belong here!"

The incredible naiveté of this outlook became apparent only too soon, when people "like us", completely assimilated, 'Christianized', and Polonized, were forced to wear the Star of David, to live in ghettos, and, eventually, went to their deaths in the gas-ovens. Funek's brother Stach, an eminent professor of veterinary surgery organized and ran an underground Polish University, right under the very noses of the occupying Nazis and evaded capture. Funek, on the other hand, managed to escape and join the rest of his family in Lwow, which was under Russian domination before the German thrust eastward in 1942. He was drafted into the Russian Army, and disappeared forever. But all this was in the future.

356

I was enjoying my school years, and my mother had another baby, her child of consolation. Wanda was a happy, healthy child and was born into the lovely new home, bringing my parents a few years of sunshine, before financial worries and the final catastrophe darkened their lives.

Years went by, and one winter Gertrud left us. My growing up and involvement at school put me out of her educational reach. I had dreaded this event for years, yet when it occurred, I felt only a twinge of regret, as too many other things were absorbing my interest at that time. For one, I was wildly in love with Rudolph Valentino, who had been dead for a good number of years. It was a while before this concern with a cardboard-and-celluloid figure of romance gave way to a healthier interest in live boys. The university students, high school seniors and officer cadets who squired us to dances may have been clumsy on a dance floor, but they were all excellent skiers, tennis players and swimmers. I was no belle, but even I managed to maintain status by producing an acceptable boyfriend, a naval cadet, whose father was one of grandfather's business friends from Warsaw. To appear on the Corso, similar to the Regency promenades in London, with a young man in naval uniform, could only be compared to the triumph of a Regency lady who was seen driving in Hyde Park in a fancy carriage. My relationship with Janek was purely for status, but he was a good friend.

Other things became more important, one of which was the local detachment of the Women's Military Corps in some of the larger schools for girls. In these units, girl students received basic training in auxiliary Army services. With the rise of Hitler in the thirties, European nations were becoming uneasy, and citizens had to be prepared. Although participation in the Women's Services was voluntary, I felt attracted to the service and persuaded my parents to let me change schools, since the one I currently attended did not boast a corps. I settled in very quickly, but my parents vetoed Summer Camp, where a month's training would fit me to lead a squad in drill, to wear an officer's trim uniform, and to train younger girls in subjects that I had mastered. However, something occurred that gave me the independence I so greatly desired.

I had been suffering from frequent bouts of tonsilitis, and my grandfather had vetoed removal of the offending organs. He had a horror of operations. Instead, I was packed off to one of the Frisian Islands in the North Sea to spend two months in a health home for children. To my joy, my governess Gertrud met me *en route* and spent a few days with me until I settled in at the home. In those two months, I not only lost my tendency to sore throats and feverish colds, but I also found I could assert myself and win friends on my own without the family prestige to provide a background.

Back at school in the fall, I became very much aware of poverty and social injustice, and with my schoolmates, formed social-work circles which organized clubs for girls and boys who needed a meeting-place, extra food and help with their homework. I'm sure we must have done some good.

But other worries were beginning to creep in during the year I turned seventeen. I never did find out what actually happened, but words like "debt", "mortgage", "embarrassment", and "bankruptcy" crept into our family conversations. Trips abroad ceased, and the chauffeur-driven car disappeared. Either I was remarkably obtuse and self-centred or my family believed in sheltering children, even those who had outgrown childhood, but I hardly knew or felt the change. Life was still full of magic and excitement for me. The year I matriculated, my parents allowed me to go to Summer Camp.

I adored every moment of it, even the night alarms when a whistle got us tumbling from under our blankets and into our uniforms, complete with laced-up shoes, berets, belts, and accoutrements, mess-kits attached to our belts in the correct manner, and two blankets rolled up and worn bandolier-fashion over the shoulder. To be ready first became a matter of absolute necessity.

It was a Spartan and regimented life, but I found it so rewarding, even if the food was vile. We were told that our diet was what Polish soldiers lived on throughout their year of conscription service, and that female officer cadets were expected to live on the same fare.

Discipline was extremely strict, and minor infractions were punished severely. All the same it was glorious fun—a heady and unforgettable summer. Even though I was looking forward to studies in Paris, I was sad that I would not be able to use my newly acquired officer's status as instructor in some school corps. In this all-female and totally self-sufficient establishment, it was taken for granted that we were capable of performing traditional male tasks with expediency and accuracy—from cleaning and dismantling a rifle or a machine-gun to digging trenches, erecting a tent or surveying terrain for manoeuvres.

The two years I spent in Paris in the late 1930s were a period of studying, growing up and falling in love—twice. My first sentimental episode involved a keenly intelligent young man, who was one of the key figures in the Polish students' political life. While we saw eye-to-eye on politics, our harmony was less pronounced in personal matters. He may have enjoyed my company, but when his former girlfriend arrived late to begin the term, he resumed his former and probably more satisfying relationship. I was heartbroken and took to wandering all over Paris, re-visiting the spots which had had such magical charm before. I did have the sense to seek consolation in the great museums and galleries, becoming a regular habituée of the Louvre.

My next "affaire du coeur" involved Edward, a young Polish athlete with the body of a Greek god, the mind of a nice, twelve-year-old boy, and a faithful and loving heart. This necessary experience, though less platonic in nature than the other, taught me a great deal about love, loyalty and truthfulness, even in a non-permanent relationship.

I tried to line up a job with the Polish consular authorities so that I could continue my residence in France after completing my studies, which were now in their final year. I graduated, summer came, and I returned home, still hopeful of returning to Paris. However, I found my mother very ill, suffering from what turned out to be diabetes. Unfortunately, it was not diagnosed immediately, and only a young doctor's perspicacity resulted in discovery of the disease and a method of control. It must have been a terrible ordeal for this beautiful, fastidious woman to suffer the periodic attacks which rendered her helpless. It was a difficult period in more ways than one, for grandfather's law practice had dropped off, and family finances were in a precarious state. Father had decided to open his own office in Warsaw, and this meant closing down our beautiful home, which was to be sold. We were to move into a small apartment in Warsaw.

While the move was in progress, and furniture was being packed for storage, my little sister Wanda and my mother were living in Vienna, where she still sought a cure for her condition. It would take months. Although I should have been taking charge of mother's treasured possessions, her china and crystal, her rugs, and other beautiful and precious belongings, I was merely going through the motions of helping, leaving father and Wanda's old governess to cope with most of the work and planning.

Poor, loyal Edward kept phoning long distance from Paris, hinting at job possibilities and even entrance to the Sorbonne, in preparation for the offer of marriage he meant to propose in the future. None of these things seemed real, for I had fallen deeply and disastrously in love with somebody else.

We met one autumn evening at a big, public indoor swimming-pool, and we swam about and talked as if we had known each other for ages. He was tall, thin and lanky, and had jet-black hair and an aristocratic profile. His blue-green eyes slanted under their black brows. His name was Voytek, and I thought him the embodiment of all my dreams.

We took walks, talked about our futures, about Warsaw, which we considered inferior to our style-conscious Lwow, and about the many foreign occupations of our country. This general judgment was due to the problems of the unhappy provinces which had suffered under the tyranny of both Russia and Prussia, where there were edicts prohibiting the use of the Polish language, even in schools. In the Prussian West, farmers lost their homes and land for being Polish; in the Russian-dominated central and eastern provinces, people were sent to Siberia for joining secret Polish underground schools, for reading Polish books, or teaching children on Polish estates to read and write their own tongue. Even Polish street-signs were forbidden, let alone the use of Polish in government offices and courts of law. As a result, all of us, already brought up in that portion of Poland that had remained free, felt insulted if anyone wanted to know if we spoke Russian.

However, in lands under the Austrian Crown, beginning in 1870, a Polish school system on all levels had been allowed to flourish, supported by public funds. German was taught as a subject, but treated as a second language. The universities of Lwow and Cracow continued their distinguished work, and Poles could attain to the highest governmental office, as many of them did. Yet there was nothing to prevent the Austrian-occupied provinces from spearheading independence movements and becoming the accepted refuges and organizing training schools for the revolutionaries, who later became the nucleus of the Polish Legions and Army.

I agreed with Voytek wholeheartedly about the charms of Lwow. We danced in cozy little nightclubs and dined in restaurants in the old city, where the walls were covered by poems signed with distinguished names, and every painting was an original by a renowned artist. Those were idyllic days. Voytek told me of his first love, which had ended unhappily, and he wrote a poem dedicated to me. But soon the days grew shorter, and the gold changed to grey.

As the snow began to fall in large, silent flakes, I knew our time was running out. The lamps along the sloping streets where we strolled looked like a string of luminous beads. It was our last evening, for I was leaving the following morning.

Warsaw, although it lacked the charm of Lwow, had all the glamour of a capital city. Tadzik, one of Halka's brothers, who was a career officer, was stationed close to the city, and we attended some wild parties and celebrations in his regimental quarters. It was a good thing I had friends, for my romance was faltering. Voytek replied several times to my frequent letters, first with much passion, then with less, and finally not at all.

I suffered greatly, but plunged into volunteer social work with a working-class youth organization. I found solace in the attentions of old and new friends. I also found work for a year in diplomatic service at the Legation of his Majesty King Fouad of Egypt. When I was admitted to the position of apprentice that I had applied for a year previously at the Social Welfare Ministry, I bade the Legation farewell and began work as an industrial inspector for women and juveniles.

I served under "Auntie K.", a legend in the service, whose name was renowned as a fighter for Poland's independence and for the equality of women. Inspector Kolabinska was tiny, ugly, almost hunchbacked, and possessed of an indomitable spirit and a shining love for everybody who was weak and oppressed. Under her guidance I explored sordid workshops where apprentices were being exploited without pay, and not being taught the trade they were to master. I visited cheap little factories where there were no

361

chairs for the women workers, and it was from "Auntie K." that I learned to argue, fight and invoke the laws protecting women against the greed and selfishness of the small entrepreneur. In larger concerns our task was easier, as major companies were sensitive to publicity, and therefore anxious to project a positive image to the buying public.

My work necessitated periodic trips to outlying districts, where factories and workshops had to be inspected. In the eastern part of my region, near the Russian border, a furniture factory owned by Prince Radziwill, had held out for years against the so-called "Baby-Law". Any factory, which had for at least a month shown an enrollment of 100 women workers, was obliged to provide a day-care centre, with a resident nursing staff and proper medical supervision. As an added bonus, the women were entitled to two daily half-hour breaks without loss of wages, in order to breastfeed their infants. Naturally, there was a great deal of resistance to this legislation, but some of the more far-sighted industrialists accepted it, and found the law's implementation beneficial to output and labour relations.

Not so old Prince Radziwill. He was conducting a protracted legal battle with the Regional Inspectorate, using all kinds of loopholes to evade his obligations. And there I was, all of twenty-one years old, armed with my recently acquired training, on my way to do battle against one of the richest and most powerful men in Poland, in order to convince him that a day-nursery in the Olyka factory was mandatory. I had discovered the Prince made himself unavailable for interviews, and his factory directors refused to discuss the subject. Pressure was mounting from the unions and left-wing political parties to take decisive action.

On the way to Olyka, I stopped in the county capital for a few local inspections and to speak with the wife of the county governor, a noted heroine of the independence struggle in women's political movements. I had a letter of recommendation from Mme. Miedzinska, the Chief Inspector for Women's and Juveniles' Welfare, to smooth my passage. The governor's wife took me under her wing, inviting me to stay at the gubernatorial mansion, and she gave me suggestions on how to handle the difficult situation. She told me to try to get the goodwill of the factory directors, and to speak to the Mayor of Olyka. She said this with a curious smile, but offered no other explanation.

I did exactly as directed, and having taken my leave, boarded the train to Olyka. When I alighted, the noon air smelled of honey and pine, and the wide, slow-moving river gently lapped the bank along which I walked to the Radziwill factory. My inspection passed off as expected. I scored a few points on the subject of some safety precautions that had been ignored, and again reiterated the crèche order. The usual objections were raised, and the topic exhausted.

The factory was outside the village, which was two miles away. I had to walk the distance. I was hungry, hot and thirsty. The village was prosperous-looking, and when I reached the Town Hall, I showed a secretary my credentials and asked to see the Mayor. When I walked into his office, I was amazed to see a staggeringly handsome young man, who rose politely to welcome me. We came immediately to the point, and he agreed with me about the importance of a factory crèche.

"Tell you what we'll do," he said. "Come home with me. I'm sure you won't mind joining my wife and me for lunch. She's very interested in social work and might think of a way to get something done. Besides, I'm sure you must be starved."

I accepted with pleasure, and we walked a short distance through the village until we came to imposing wrought-iron gates opening into a tree-shaded avenue. I followed my guide through a vast park to a palatial house. I had, by now, guessed who the Mayor of Olyka was, though the Governor's lady had neglected to tell me that young Prince Radziwill had been recently elected to that office.

Over drinks inside the mansion, we had a conference with pretty Princess Isabella, who, as her husband assured me, had considerable influence on her formidable papa-in-law. Both were aware of my problem and promised me every help.

Suddenly, official resistance to the crèche law vanished, and plans for the new day-care centre were well under way. But the crèche never materialized. The war came, putting a stop to all progress, class co-operation and love, in Poland and the rest of Europe. Who knows to what heights European civilization might have risen had not Hitler unleashed the forces of barbarism and crushed whatever good there might have been, under blood-stained Nazi jack-boots goose-stepping to the tune of the Horst Wessel Song?

I seem to remember hearing that the Princess and her children were deported to Siberia, which they survived, but I do not know whether the young Mayor of Olyka, inevitably an officer in the Polish Army, was equally lucky. One thing is certain—the friendly village, the palace, the factory where we had hoped to see healthy babies playing in a modern, well-staffed nursery, were lost to them, just as Lwow and my mountain home are lost to me.

But in those days, living in the calm before the storm, I took advantage of my free railway passes to arrange weekends in Lwow, where I stayed with my grandparents. It was an opportunity to renew my old friendships, visit Halka and catch up on the news and gossip. On one of these weekends, I met with Voytek at a small restaurant in old Lwow. The small rooms were furnished like old-fashioned drawing-rooms. Genio, the near-blind pianist, played medley after medley of songs, while Voytek tried to explain his stupid mistakes, his failing his exams, his forgetfulness. I didn't want to hear those everyday things in this nook, removed from time and space.

Into this intimacy erupted a noisy group of friends, who drew up chairs to our table. More wine and food were ordered, and Genio began playing a haunting melody I had not heard before— a song of five sailor boys who all loved one girl, golden-haired Mimi, an innkeeper's daughter. Strangely, each of the young men at the table identified himself with one of the sailors of the good ship Albatross. The melancholy end of the five young mariners when the ship ran aground off a rocky coast could have been a portent of things to come, for a few years and a world catastrophe later, I would hear that song again on a Polish radio programme in England. By then I knew that Henry, the skinny one, had died flying a Spitfire in the Battle of Britain; that red-headed Richard, a Jew, had perished in the Warsaw Ghetto Uprising; that Wladek, the Cavalry officer, had charged German tanks on horseback and so terminated his dashing career; that Staszek, the stubborn one, had been deported to Russia and had disappeared there. And Voytek? His fate was the least glorious and the most tragic. He was shot in the back of the head, with his hands tied, one of the 20,000 Polish officers disposed of by the Russians, or perhaps the Germans, in the infamous Katyn massacre. And for me that silly little song about the five boys of the good ship Albatross became a symbol and a memory of youth, of first loves and a lost world.

A few months after the meeting at the restaurant, I was posted to Lublin, the headquarters of my inspectorial operations. Lublin was a garrison town, and one of my former schoolmates, a very beautiful girl, who had married a doctor and was now living in Lublin, lost no time in launching me into society. In the whirl of dances, picnics and parties, I lost my heart to George, an engineer and workshop manager in the local airplane factory. Because his father worked with the Polish Consulate in Vienna, George had spent most of his life abroad. There was a flavour and allure of international elegance about him, and his ability to speak French and German was one of the sources of my attraction to him.

It was the summer of 1939, and George and I took our holidays in August that year—he to visit friends in Hungary, and I to attend officers' camp—a fact which caused no end of amusement among my Lublin friends. We were not entirely blind to world affairs, and felt that war was imminent, but somehow nobody took it seriously. We knew that in the end Poland would emerge victorious. If Germany attacked, we would fight back with our wonderful army and air force. Even the navy, small as it was, stood ready to defend our cherished Baltic shores. Hadn't our French and British Allies guaranteed us their support?

Camp was engrossing, and we worked and played, preparing ourselves for the coming emergency as if it were a picnic. The British journalists who visited us marvelled at girls handling rifles "as though to the manner born". We sang the same fiery and melancholy songs, sitting around the evening campfires, but with the political situation tense, the camp had to be closed three days ahead of schedule.

The Commander-in-chief spoke to us that last evening. The Germans had just concluded a non-aggression pact with the Russians. We were going to be attacked from both sides. This was the moment we had been training for, and we all knew what we had to do. One day we would all meet there again in a peaceful Poland. It was a wish that was destined not to be realized.

Early the next morning, we left for our various destinations, all of us aware that once the sheltering forest was left behind, the crisis had come. Trains were full of soldiers reporting to their regiments, although a general mobilization had not yet been ordered. Tank columns were rolling in the Western Provinces; regular cavalry regiments were in action; the Germans had already attacked the Baltic ports. These were the rumours already spreading. We heard that there had been an air-raid on Warsaw. We smiled at these horror tales, unaware that at least those concerning the tanks and cavalry were true. There had been no general mobilization, not because the war had not yet begun, but because Chamberlain's umbrella was still open, while he practised his policy of appeasement, afraid to offer Hitler "unnecessary provocation".

The short trip to Lublin took me twenty-four hours, as we had to wait many hours at several minor stations while soldiers and supplies were picked up and rerouted. It was at one of these whistle-stops, where we had slept for a few hours on tables and benches in the waiting-room, that one of the girls returned from stretching her legs outside, with the notice that a general mobilization had been ordered.

We began making appointments to meet again, perhaps in some welfare-and-recreation station in the battle zone. Some of the young men near us were also making plans to meet "in Berlin, a month from now". There was some laughter. The little train puffed in, and we boarded it. The tiny waiting-room was deserted.

The same day as I arrived in Lublin, the city suffered its first air raid at noon. The bombs were all aimed at the aircraft factory. Later, I heard from George and others that the slaughter had been terrible. The Germans had known exactly where important equipment was manufactured. The plant was partly flattened, but the most grievous damage was to personnel. Workers running, as instructed, to outside air-raid shelters had been machine-gunned from the air.

That morning I had reported briefly at the Inspectorate and told my superiors that from then on I could be reached at Women's Auxiliary Army Headquarters. I was no longer a civilian. At Headquarters, my commander looked me up and down and congratulated me on my newly achieved officer's status. She also recommended I lose no time ordering the proper uniform. My camp denims, apart from being the wrong cut for my rank, were shabby and worn. I took time off to visit my tailor, who plied his trade in his small home.

It was the hottest, sunniest September in memory, making it all too easy for German raiders to hit their targets, even when they were as small as women and children scuttling for shelter, as a hail of tracer bullets fell from the skies. We had not realized what Hitler had meant by "Blitzkreig", but we were beginning to discover the reality of that term, as swift tank columns cut most western lines of communication. The regiments, which soldiers had been trying so desperately to reach, were already surrounded, or cut to pieces by fast-moving attacks from tank columns supported by the Luftwaffe. As night went by, we came to recognize some of the young men in uniform, for they had already passed through Lublin before, their journey taking them around the country, wherever trains went, in the forlorn hope of making contact with their units, scattered somewhere in the fog of battle.

The civilians were another story. Their destination was anywhere, just to get away from the German bombs and machine-guns. Women, children, and older men had been under fire in the West.

They had seen their cities in flames, their villages shot up, their woods and fields set afire in order to flush out any lurking military units. Although they had begun their journeys in private cars or on foot, pushing their belongings in pushcarts, they soon discovered that the roads were unhealthy places in daylight. The Nazi flyers were bombing columns of civilian refugees on the roads, and strafing men, women and children as they ran for shelter in ditches or woods. So most of the country's activities were now limited to the night-time. The trains kept moving, with some attempt at regular timetables.

Three shameful days later, after watching Poland's Western front broken for lack of air defences, England finally declared War. This came as a surprise, for Chamberlain was still Prime Minister in Britain, and the day of the man who had the guts to promise his people nothing but blood, toil, sweat and tears, had not yet dawned. So our people went east, to await a certain victory as soon as Allied bombers came to chase away the enemy.

As a military auxiliary, I joined in the work of refugee organization, giving black, unsweetened coffee and loaves of bread to adults, jealously keeping our cans of condensed milk for the babies. Food was getting short in Lublin, for the farmers were not coming in to sell their produce through fear of the daily raids. With the aircraft factory out of operation, George was spending his days driving gasoline from outlying depots to a concealed central reservoir, in preparation for evacuation.

One noon-hour, between raids, I had left Headquarters on an errand. A military jeep was parked in front of a restaurant that had been one of my favourite haunts. A slight figure in uniform jumped out and raised his goggles from his eyes. It was Tadzik, leather-jacketed and armed, dusty and laughing as he introduced me to his driver, a young blond corporal. He persuaded me to have a quick lunch with him in the restaurant—gourmet fare consisting of some vodka, rye bread and a chunk of sausage.

Tadzik tried to convince me to go south with his column as a secretary or nurse, but I refused.

"My assignment is here. I can't just leave for no reason. Besides, my people are in Warsaw and if things crack here, I shall try to join them."

"Warsaw is surrounded," he said. "Soon you'll be on your own. So what about it?"

I shook my head. "Don't you see? I can't be a deserter."

"Well, listen, should you feel you want to get going in a hurry, I'll be following this route..." and he jotted down the names of villages on a scrap of paper he pulled out of his pocket.

We said goodbye on the street.

That evening at George's flat, we listened to the radio. We heard some military music, and the Mayor of Warsaw Stefan Starzynski spoke to the people. I can still hear his final sentence: "We shall fight on, until the last Polish soldier has fallen under the German tanks." A few weeks later, he was shot by the Germans for inciting the city to resistance.

George and I looked at each other. This, then, was the sound of defeat. The game was over. George told me the factory was being moved to the southern border, there to reform and begin production anew, for the southern armies were still intact. I had to stay at my post, even though I knew my real duty lay in Warsaw with my parents and sister.

Next morning, new waves of refugees engulfed the railway station and the city. This was not the orderly evacuation of the first days, but a headlong flight of terrified people. When I reported to Headquarters, our Commander and other senior women officers, pale but calm, issued our orders. The Germans were close, and we were to get rid of our uniforms, identity cards, and any papers which could betray our connection with the Armed Services. Then we should go into hiding, where we could await our call, which would come when "it was all over". This could only mean one thing—German occupation was imminent.

"But the Western Allies...?" somebody asked in a faltering voice.

"The Western Allies will do nothing. They cannot. They are less prepared and worse armed than we are—for the moment. But they will carry on, and we shall be either over there, or here to help them." The Commander's tone was matter-of-fact. No doubt, Churchill would have found her a woman after his own heart. "The war is not over, only the first battle," she said.

The senior officer in command of Lublin asked me what I proposed to do, and I explained my dilemma. "If you want a chance to have a child to shelter one day, go with your George. Don't ask any questions—just go!" she ordered.

I left Headquarters for the last time, but before I made my decision I had an errand to perform. I went to the home of my tailor, Mr. Wachsmann. He and his wife were sitting there, holding hands and sipping tea. Finally, after offering me tea, Mr. Wachsmann asked if I wanted a fitting for the uniform I had ordered.

"I want my uniform, but not for a fitting. Let me have it, please, and all the badges and insignia that are to go on it. And here is the money for it."

"But Miss, it isn't ready yet..." he faltered. Suddenly, despite the heat and scalding tea I had sipped, I felt very cold. How could I tell him that no evidence of having worked for a Polish officer should be left in his workshop. The danger to him and his family was grim enough, without additional provocation. He gave me a steady look and understood.

"All right, Miss. I won't even give it to you. I'll bury it all tonight in the back yard. And thank you."

Mrs. Wachsmann began to sob, and her three little girls clung to her, puzzled and frightened. I said goodbye and left. How many thousands of children's eyes in Poland that day had held, for the first time in their lives, that look of hopeless terror? Not everyone had friends in Hungary or cars to carry them away from the danger. Those who were the most threatened, the Jews, especially the poor ones, were left behind to face a fate that nobody, in those days, would have believed conceivable. But the Jews knew. They had heard what was happening in Germany and Austria, and still they stayed behind, like the three frightened, dark-haired, tiny girls in the tailor's workshop.

And like my own family.

On that sunny day in Lublin, I had to fight my own private battle. To stay involved by joining the Underground, I had only to report to a given address and receive a new identity which would incorporate me in the Great Game. But how could one stand up to torture and Gestapo interrogations? How would it feel to face the firing squad? If I stayed, I would not see George again; with him I might have life and love, and perhaps children of my own. And yet, how could I abandon all those years of training and preparation to take my part in a great tradition?

I went to look for George. He was nowhere to be found and, as a last resort, I went to the garage where his beloved Lancia was kept. The owner begged me to take it away, for he could not be responsible for it anymore. The whole town was hunting for cars in which to flee. I told the garage-owner to wait just a little longer.

Down a side street, I hunted out a fellow-engineer who worked with George. He knew where George was and drove me to him.

The town showed increasing signs of disintegration. Several bombs fell nearby. There was a cloud of dust and smoke hanging in the air. Groups of people with suitcases, children in baby carriages, women pushing handcarts and a string of slow-moving cars with mattresses tied to the roofs, filled the streets.

Outside the town, hidden from the air in a dense grove of trees, was a reservoir of gasoline. George was there, supervising the distribution of gas to trucks—none too healthy an occupation in the middle of a bombardment. A friend relieved him while we hitched a ride back to town in a factory car. We picked up the Lancia, and George told me of his plans to take his brother, a test pilot, and me to Solotvina in the Eastern Carpathians. He intended to travel with factory staff to the South and then detach himself from the group. He had a Hungarian friend, who owned land around Solotvina. George had no intention of becoming a civilian internee in Romania, where his group was heading.

"We could do with a few nights' sleep and some rest in Solotvina, and should there be no Southern Front for us to join, the Hungarian border is close by. I have friends there to help us," he explained.

That settled it. The prospect of joining up with an organized group in the South was the sop to my conscience that I needed, so as not to feel utterly contemptible.

We left a burning Lublin that night, for the Germans had raided after dark. The 13th-century gateway, once part of the medieval walls, stood out starkly and defiantly against the scarlet flames. People tried to stop the car, begging us to take them along, and offering large sums of money as fare. Had George opened the door to the one or two that we could have squeezed in, we would have been mobbed.

Our plans for survival were symbolized by a dinner-jacket and a long evening dress which we had stuffed into our luggage. We had decided that in case of dire need, we could earn a living as dancing host and hostess in some Budapest night club.

As we approached Lwow at dawn, we were stopped by two military policemen, who wanted to know how we had got through the German tank column which had passed by, cutting off Lublin. Incredibly, we had slipped through the gap between the German and Polish units. George and I parted to visit our respective grandparents in the city. Mine were relieved to see me, to say the least. They had had no word from my parents and sister in Warsaw, where the raids had claimed thousands of lives.

I did not stay long. A phone call from George warned me that he was coming to drive us to Solotvina as soon as possible. Grandmother took me aside: "Where are you going with this young man, whom we don't even know?" she asked worriedly.

"To Hungary, and...do you know, Granny...it's just possible that we'll get married..."

Her gentle eyes filled with tears. "God bless you, darling. I would like to see him before you go."

George came in and met us in the once grand entrance-hall. He kissed her hand, and she gave him a long, steady look, then

371

folded me in her arms. I never saw any of my family again.

At Solotvina, George's friend received us with open arms, but had to leave for Hungary a day later. We waited for some kind of contact or news, and three nights later, an agent arrived on horseback in the middle of the night to report that the Russians had crossed the eastern frontier—not very far from where we were.

The next morning the three of us packed knapsacks with the barest necessities, including three hard-boiled eggs and three chocolate bars, and drove the car up the mountain near the local game warden's house. We left him the car, as we knew that finding gasoline would be impossible.

We started our hike through the Carpathians, and as we neared the pass through mountain meadows leading to the frontier, we heard hoarse shouting from a cedar-wood ski hut, the property of a famous skiing club. We could see hands throwing furniture and other articles through wide-open windows. George's brother murmured: "The peasants are looting." The same *hutzuls* whom I had loved all through my childhood, probably relatives of those at Jaremcze, were now wrecking, tearing and destroying every shred of a gracious and happy past. Perhaps, even now, our homes were suffering the same fate. An era of peace and settled order had come to an end, never to return.

We took a detour to avoid being seen and crested the mountain ridge, diving swiftly into the woods on the other side. We never realized when we actually left the soil of Poland.

Close to nightfall, we were accosted by a figure who emerged from a thicket with an infantry rifle pointed at our scared little group. He wore a Polish uniform, and when we identified ourselves, we were invited to join his band in a well-concealed clearing. They were soldiers like ourselves who had waited in vain to join the Southern defence units, but the news of the Russian invasion had made up their minds for them. They shared what they had with us, and we spent the night there, huddled in our blankets under a tree. We left at dawn and finally arrived at a Hungarian mountain hamlet. A welcoming committee of Hungarian policemen led us to the square, where hot soup was being dispensed from a field kitchen. We had no tin plate or cup in which to receive the food, and had to borrow a plate from a soldier who had eaten, which we used in turn. That night we spent on straw in the schoolhouse, where the classrooms had been converted temporarily to accommodate refugees coming over the mountains.

We were well treated, and I was soon moved four miles from the little village to a small house belonging to German immigrants. George came over every day to visit, and we made friends with a group of soldiers from a Polish cavalry unit, whose officers had brought their squadron, horses, weapons and all, over the mountains. Historically, the Poles and Hungarians were the only two neighbouring nations in Eastern Europe who had always lived with each other in friendly fellowship. Now Hungary was neutral, but since the rape of Austria, the country lived in dread of a Nazi invasion. Officially, the government adopted the politics of the Axis Powers; unofficially, the people—soldiers and civil servants—did all they could to help the exiled Poles stranded in their midst. I was the only girl among a large group of young males, and I was respected. I took care to advertise the fact that George and I were betrothed. So we were all good friends, those few days in the mountains, before the winds of war carried us along our separate ways.

The day came when we were told to pack our meagre belongings and board a train to Budapest. A dinner was held for us at the cosy village inn, and everybody toasted me and wished me a happy journey. We already knew, though I have no idea how, that General Sikorski, a great Polish soldier and statesman, had formed a Polish Government in exile, and that Polish troops were reforming within the French Army. Our goal had become obvious.

George came with another group, and we met at the station. He was already on the train, waving and shouting, but there was such a crowd I could not get near the train. Warning lights were flashing, and whistles blowing prior to departure. Suddenly I was lifted into the air by willing hands, and my bearers wedged their way through the crowd. Over the heads of laughing people, I was handed into the train through the window. I had no trouble wriggling through to reach George. The train was already moving. I had made it in the nick of time.

We travelled all that night and stopped in the morning at a station where Hungarians served us hot coffee and rolls. Only a few days before, I had run a similar food station for soldiers and refugees in Lublin. Now our place was gone. We were just part of the great throng of homeless, the helpless, the uprooted, standing in need of the charity of others. The humility of the defeated did not sit too well with us.

The train moved on, puffing across the Great Hungarian Plain, and rolled at sunset into one of the terminals in Budapest. George noticed his friend Dr. Charles on the platform, and as the three of us stepped down from the train, he was there whispering in German: "Quickly, and quietly, take your things and follow me. Don't talk." He then raised his voice and began to address George in voluble Hungarian, while my fiancé nodded his head knowledgeably. Our little group was marched out of the station by the doctor as he carried on this one-sided simulated conversation. This scene was meant to present a normal meeting of Budapest citizens, even if three of them were bedraggled-looking and travel-stained.

We were taken in a chauffeur-driven car to a famous hotel, and suddenly there were lights, flowers, table silver, white napery, and waiters in tails and ties, serving beautiful food and wines. Elegant people sat at tables, and there was music and dancing, while we sat in the middle of this in dusty camp outfits. Yet the looks sent our way were friendly, loving—full of understanding and acceptance—as if those Hungarians were ready to share the threatened, last fragile fragments of peace and happiness with us.

Dr. Charles settled our hotel bill and took us shopping for clothes the next day, and then escorted us to Police Headquarters to have our visitors' visas stamped. An official told us in a loud voice (German secret agents were everywhere, and the Hungarian civil servants had to make a show of impeccable neutrality), that we would have to report every month to have them checked. Exit visas were out of the question, he said.

The uniformed constable outside the Polish Consulate looked resolutely away when we dropped in there later in the day. He appeared blind to the groups of strangely attired gentlemen entering the building in trenchcoats and khaki jackets devoid of all insignia. It was amazing how many soldiers and officers had somehow managed to evade internment and were loose in Budapest. Nor was there any comment made when these same men left the Consulate a few hours later, clad in nondescript civilian clothes, and headed toward the railway station, from which west-bound trains were leaving with peace-time regularity. I can imagine the pressure the Nazi ambassador must have exerted on Hungarian authorities to close down the Embassy and Consulate of a country that had officially ceased to exist as a political entity. Eventually, the Germans did succeed, but only after most of the internees had been passed through to find their way to the Polish Forces in exile in France and Great Britain.

Within a few days, George and his brother had the necessary papers to leave the country; mine, however, were denied. My pleas that I, too, was a member of the armed services had been greeted with smiling disbelief by French consular staff. It was still 1939, and the idea of female military officers was considered a joke. For me, this was the ultimate catastrophe. I was to remain in Hungary, to be parted from George on a continent engulfed in war, while he joined the Polish Army in France. I was too numb to cry, when his train pulled out of the station.

I went to Sunday Mass next day, sung for the Polish community in an ancient underground catacomb church. The words of the closing hymn had been changed to an older version, which implored the restoration of their country and freedom to the Poles, and dated back to the partition of Poland in the late eighteenth century. It was then I experienced an overwhelming feeling of sorrow and despair. The stark facts of oppression, defeat and exile were ours again, as they had been for our parents, grandparents and great-grandparents. Perhaps it was this pain, this twinge of which remains with us for the rest of our days, that shaped our decision to free our children from the burden of these memories and let them grow new roots in a new country, without any bitterness of loss and alienation.

I knew that my efforts would take months, but I was determined to wear the French Consul down by sheer persistence. I went to the Consulate day after day. A passport was wangled out of the Polish authorities, who were sympathetic to the plight of two young lovers, especially when one of them was with General Sikorski's forces in France. And my family connections stood me in good stead, as well.

On arrival in Budapest, I had wired my cousin Bobby, the son of Aunt Janka and Uncle Dolo, who, I remembered, was at St. Lawrence College in Ramsgate in the South of England. I didn't remember my aunt's and uncle's address, except that it was in the

London district of Wimbledon, where they had established themselves after Austria had fallen prey to the Nazis. The cables and messages I had sent to my family in Poland, through the Red Cross, had not been answered. I soon received an exultant telegram from Wimbledon, informing me that my parents had survived the siege of Warsaw and had rejoined my grandparents in Lwow, which was now under Russian occupation. I was told to contact some of my uncle's business friends in Budapest, and they would help me in every way.

Dr. Charles arranged for me to work as a secretary-interpreter to Baroness K. who headed various organizations helping Polish refugees in Poland. This lady and her family received me into their midst as though I were a close relation, and they kept me busy enough to obliterate sorrow and worry. In the endless queue of Polish exiles who had to be housed and fed, I discovered many friends and close acquantances.

One day, I ran into Halka at the consulate. It was a rapturous reunion. She gave me all the news she had. Nothing was known of her brothers, except that Tadzik had crossed into Romania and was now in France. She herself was staying at a camp for Poles, where her husband was an army doctor.

Sadly we said goodbye to each other. We met again years later. Although her husband finally reached France and thence crossed to England, she was trapped in Hungary, when it was occupied by the Nazis. She worked there in the Polish Underground, while studying for a doctorate in German at the University of Budapest, and escaped later to join the Polish Forces in Italy, from where she finally reached England, near the end of the war.

Autumn drew on and when the Baroness and her family moved to the country estate, deep in the plains, they took me with them. It was vintage time, and we all helped gather the bloomy violet and emerald grape clusters. The colours and sounds of the singing harvesters, the lively, happy people, the autumn leaves fluttering about in the warm October air, the breath of the wide, fertile plains stretching in every direction, smelling of rich earth and fresh walnuts, were a kind of festival of happiness. We forgot, savouring it, how fleeting and threatened and doomed it all was. But I couldn't forget for long, for I felt war reaching out slowly, but inexorably, like a dark tide, into this secluded and sheltered corner of Hungary.

The day came when I was summoned back to Budapest. My French visa had arrived, and I was free to go, but my Hungarian exit permit still had to be obtained.

On that cold, blustery autumn day, I observed a police detective at Headquarters, whose job it was to issue or refuse permits to a long line of Poles, get up and give his overcoat away to a thin boy with a distressing cough. I, too, was to experience that quick, heart-warming sympathy, when I approached the counter for my exit permit.

When the officer asked me why I wanted to go to France, I told him I wished to join my fiancé in as helpless-and-lost-in-the-big-world tone as I could muster. I got more than I bargained for.

The detective insisted I sit down and wait for five minutes and then join him for lunch in a café. There wasn't much else I could do. Besides, he really looked dashing, and I was hungry.

Ten minutes later, with plates of steaming goulash and glasses of red wine in front of us, my detective asked in reasonable tones, "What do you want to chase after your fiancé to France for? Why don't you marry me instead? I'm not joking", he added, no doubt in answer to my flabbergasted expression. "Meet my family tonight, and we'll get married next week, if you like. I'll make you happy, you'll see!"

He spoke with total sober commitment. I did not doubt him for a moment. It was a staggering compliment, and despite the sadness in his eyes, he understood. He returned to the subject of the permit and asked me if I spoke any other languages besides Polish and German?

"French and a little Italian," I answered.

"That will do. I'm going ahead, and you come to my wicket in about twenty minutes and listen carefully. I will speak Spanish, which you should understand with your Italian. Goodbye and good luck. I hope you find that fellow in France..." and he was gone.

A little later, standing in front of his wicket, I heard him launch into a loud tirade in German about the foolishness of travelling in wartime and the impossibility of issuing visas to Poles. And then quietly, in slow Spanish: "Wicket number three, tomorrow, eleven o'clock. Your papers will be there, ready and signed."

I thanked him quietly in German, and we looked at one

another. I never stopped hoping that the war and the horrors that followed in Hungary left him unscathed, and I hope he found a girl worthy of his courage, integrity and generosity.

Next day, a fat lady with a dark moustache handed me my papers, and I was finally free to go. All my newly found friends and benefactors came to the station to wish me godspeed.

The trip through Italy was uneventful, but while the Hungarians had offered me love and companionship, our "ally" France showed me a different face. Over and over again I was to hear: "*Cette guerre de malheur—c'est à cause des sales Polonais qu'on s'est foutu la-dedans!*" It was hard to rise above the level of this vocal minority and to make the effort to realize that the real France and her Resistance groups were not speaking in those slimy, hateful voices.

Paris was dark, wet, cold and forbidding. I had very little money, and did not want to wire Aunt Janka for help. George was far away in Brittany. Poland was conquered and occupied, and the newsreels at the cinemas showed each known and beloved street now a smoking heap of rubble, with Nazi soldiers patrolling the ruins. In Lwow, Soviet soldiers stalked about in full possession of the city.

I spent a few miserable days in a filthy little hotel in the Latin Quarter, and then managed to get a room in the American Hostel for Women Students, where I had stayed when last in Paris. It was there I found two old friends, Polish girls, working behind the reception desk, as they had been three years before, when putting themselves through university. Unable to leave Paris after graduation, they had suffered the same fate as many other students, who had become so enchanted with the city that they could not tolerate life elsewhere. For one of these two, Minna, a Jewish girl, this love for Paris proved her salvation. She managed to survive the war in France—the secret of her Jewishness undiscovered by the Nazis. Had she returned to Poland, she would have met the inevitable fate of her family in the ghettos.

A few weeks later, as I stood in line at the Polish Red Cross, applying for a job, I saw a tall, familiar figure. He turned and there was my former "heart-throb" Edward, with his rugged, tanned face. It was a strange and sad meeting. I had to tell him about George. He didn't blame me. All he had to say was: "That's the way things go; it's not your fault." He was waiting to join the army. An old football injury had spoiled his medical record. He finally made it, but I lost touch with him and never knew if he lived through the war.

Because of my fluent French, and ability to type fairly quickly, I soon found a job with the Polish Ministry of Armaments, near the Louvre. George wrote, and we made plans. He was enrolled in an Officers' Training School in Guer, near Quimperlé in Brittany. When he was given a few days leave at the end of the year, we spent Christmas and New Year together, dancing and dining on very little money, yet managing to drain every drop of fun and happiness from those odd few days.

Before George returned to camp, we made plans to get married as soon as possible, for we had no illusions as to what was in store. Nobody who, as George had, watched the French Army at close quarters could harbour any hopes that this corrupt, disorganized, poorly officered military machine could withstand the iron march of the Nazi Juggernaut. After a few bombs were dropped on her outskirts, the "City of Lights" declared herself "an open city" and awaited the entrance of Hitler with passive acceptance.

It was during that dark sad winter that George and I got married. The wedding took some arranging, for I had to get time off from my work, and travel to Guer. I faked illness, and my grey-haired fatherly colonel gave me advice on how to treat myself—rest and plenty of fluids. Half an hour later, the stricken victim was boarding a train to Rennes, whence an unheated, smelly bus conveyed her to Guer, where the flower of Polish youth were remedying the lack of officer-training in their homeland. Caught by the war in France, Belgium and Italy, there were several diplomatic attachés, a famous young painter, a concert pianist, even a former ambassador—people bearing names which echoed back into history, with pedigrees several centuries long. These young men, who could have spend the war cozily installed in Sweden or Switzerland, were here at Guer, wearing stinking French uniforms from World War I, sleeping in icy billets with one blanket each, wearing boots which didn't even match, for any left-over oddments the French Army could no longer use were good enough for "*les sales Polonais*". But the only thing that mattered, even if the uniforms were French, was that the eagle insignia sewn on them and on the ridiculously large army berets, was Polish. The men were officered by Poles, and obeyed the orders of the Polish Minister of War, General Sikorski himself, who was in Paris.

Madame Bignon, whose husband owned a watchmaker's shop in the village and was now in the army, ran the house where George was billeted. Aware of the difficulties attached to marriages in France of non-French, nonresidents, she smoothed our path of true love by inviting the Mayor to share a bottle of wine at the local *estaminet*, of which he was the prosperous landlord, and convinced him of the obvious advantages of marrying us as quickly as possible...it would minimize the likelihood of a few of the local damsels being seduced by at least one less of the untrustworthy but attractive Poles quartered in the district.

And so, the next morning, George and I, escorted by one of his comrades and Madame Bignon, were married in a draughty, gloomy hall, lit by an unshaded bulb. (Much later, in England, we repaired the slight omission of a church wedding, and had our union confirmed by ecclesiastical authority.) Our wedding celebration had to wait until that evening, for George and the other soldiers had to return to their duties immediately after the ceremony. At the Mayor's establishment, where the festivities took place, I was toasted as the first bride in the local Polish colony of exiles. One of the ex-embassy attachés asked if I would stay longer than one night, as he was looking forward to using George's blanket while we were otherwise occupied in our hotel room. Such was the romance of wartime.

Next day George went back to his quarters and his blanket, while a cold and smelly train bore me back to Paris and my typewriter. I heard from my family, who were still together in Lwow. Wanda's postcard sounded as if all was cozily safe, but a month or so later, the Russians started deporting people to Siberia. I did not know that my father had been picked up and was already at the railway station, awaiting transportation, when my grandfather used what influence he still possessed to have him released. Perhaps if he had not been "saved", he might have survived deportation and lived through the war. As it was, he gained just two years of life with his family. Just before the Nazis entered Lwow, he was shot by the rampaging soldiers of some Ukrainian unit of the retreating Russian forces.

In early spring of 1940, George, his training complete, applied for a transfer to the Royal Air Force. A R.A.F. officer who interviewed him bluntly said that the R.A.F. would not recognize any officer-cadet status, and would grant commissions only on its own estimation of merit. In other words, the months of training, with promotion in view, had been wasted. Nevertheless, George persisted in his efforts, and finally after a few snatched days of laughter and happiness in Paris, we said goodbye to each other on the windswept wastes of Le Bourget Airport, from which a R.A.F. Transport plane flew my husband to England. I returned home in the Metro, sniffling dejectedly into my handkerchief.

A few weeks later Norway was invaded, and the German march on France had begun. In beautiful Maytime Paris, it was depressing for me to witness again the same flood of lost-looking refugees—hungry, bewildered children and desperate men and women—trying to find safety from air attack. On the lethal highways, the same cars with mattresses tied to their roofs inched along in a futile attempt at protection against machine-gunning from the air.

Leopold of Belgium had surrendered, betraying not only his own people, but the population of valiant Holland and the British Expeditionary Corps which was now doomed, with its Belgian flank crumbling. The miracle of Dunkirk, that unbelievable effort of civilians who marshalled the "little boats" by their thousands to ferry English soldiers home under relentless attack from the air, is now history. For us Poles stranded in France, it was an act of heroism—an isolated island fortress holding out until the Americans would enter the war and provide some assistance.

I felt that the closer I was to the Channel, the better were my chances of joining George in England. I pulled a few strings and got myself transferred to Quimperlé. My second sojourn in Brittany was different from that brief first stay when I got married. I stayed in a spotless Breton home, in a white-washed attic room filled with the scent of honeysuckle. Our landlady provided me and another girl employee of the Polish factory where we worked with unforgettable meals—freshly caught crab, mussels and fragrant evening soups.

George and I kept in touch by mail, and I was even

planning to spend a week's holiday in England, when I had a rude awakening. Italy entered the war on the side of the Nazis, and then Marshal Pétain made his speech of surrender. It was then that I saw my landlady weep from shame, and she was not the only one. The brave Bretons were shattered and appalled, and later events proved that this part of France never did surrender. Brittany led all the other regions in their staunch support of the Resistance and in the organization of shelter and escape facilities for Allied airmen shot down over France.

As new waves of refugees from the East began to fill little Quimperlé, I realized it was time for our group of homeless Poles to move on. Because of my fluent French, I was dispatched to the Mairie to get us permits to leave for Brest, the nearest major port. But a harassed and desperate Gendarmerie officer confronted me this time.

"To Brest? A bunch of foreigners? Never!" he said with passion.

The Fifth-Column phobia had reached Brittany now, and everyone with a strange accent was a Nazi spy. But I was desperate too.

"Do you really want to be responsible for 200 men, women and children (we had families with us, too), being caught and sent to concentration camps? And do you want us on your hands, on top of all the refugees you have to feed and house? All I ask is to be allowed to leave for England!"

"Ha, England!" he snorted. "How long do you think they will be able to hold out?"

But in mid-snort he signed our permit papers. In the end, however, the 200 of us did not manage to get to Brest.

With an engineer officer to accompany me, I was told to take one of the few available cars to check out transportation to Brest, and then phone the group. Meanwhile a train had to be commandeered, on the strength of our permits, to take the entire party to the coast.

By sheer determination, I had managed to finagle my way as one of the advance party, even threatening to hitchhike to Brest if I was refused. It was a turning point in my life, as it was for all of us, for I had made up my mind that if my bid for England failed, I would go back to Poland, one way or another.

Brest was still and deserted when we arrived. My companion and I set out on our reconnaissance, using different approaches, after arranging a rendez-vous. At the British Consulate, where I asked to see the Consul, I was told that he had cleared out a week before. Disappointed, I made my way to the main square, where I saw a platoon of British naval ratings just breaking ranks. A young British officer seemed to be in command.

Madly waving the document certifying I was the wife of a member of the R.A.F., I accosted the poor man, who showed little doubt or distrust. I could board their ship at once, for special orders had been issued by Winston Churchill that all dependents of Allied personnel serving with British Forces were to be given transportation to Britain whenever possible. But I could not accept that staggering invitation and explained to the young officer I was really concerned with a trainload of people in the same category as myself. He was not sure if accommodation could be found for such a large group, as there was only one destroyer still in Brest. However, he would meet with us in an hour, and we could discuss the case with the ship's captain.

Meanwhile, I met my companion and made a telephone call to Quimperlé, after several maddeningly futile attempts to get through. The situation there was bad, as no trains could be found, and the authorities were getting difficult. We were told that if the party had not arrived by early next morning, we were to proceed to England on our own.

"The captain will not wait for them for so long," said my colleague, as we made our way to the docks to meet the naval officer.

He was wrong. Half an hour later, seated in a boat with my comrade, the officer and a sailor, bound for the destroyer barely visible on the horizon, I could not believe that this was really happening to me. I felt I was watching a movie. Here I was, a girl with shoulder-length brown hair, greenish eyes in a tanned face, clutching an official-looking briefcase. My tanned legs in white ankle-socks and brogues hardly complemented my russet pullover and blue linen skirt. I kept looking at the sea and sky with an incredulous, even puzzled air.

When we reached the ship I went up the ladder, and on the deck found lots of men in khaki, but wearing the familiar short cloak of the Polish mountaineers. They were the Polish Mountain Brigade, diverted from Narvik, which they had recaptured from the Nazis, only to be forced to abandon the city. I was taken to the quarterdeck, where the captain, young, bearded and handsome, interviewed us in fluent French. He frowned when he heard about our party.

"We are carrying a detachment of sappers who are blowing up gun-emplacements and ammunition dumps," he said. "The Germans are expected in Brest tomorrow morning, but I think I may take the risk of waiting, especially since there is still a lot of work left to do."

We were astonished by his willingness to risk a confrontation with the enemy. We had not been prepared for this by the behaviour of our French "allies". I was directed to the captain's cabin, since I was the only woman aboard, and was stunned by this courtesy and generosity. As I glanced around, a steward broke into my reverie: "Come on, Miss, come quick! Come and see 'istory in the making."

Months later, I came to appreciate both the glory of his Cockney accent and the enormity of what he had made me witness. As I followed him on deck, I saw all the Poles excitedly hanging over the rail, watching in breathless silence, the tall soaring silhouette of a great battleship, at fairly close quarters. Then I noticed the guns of our small destroyer trained on it.

"It's the *Richelieu*," whispered the rating beside me. "The bastard wanted to stay here and surrender to *Jerry*. But we're making him take off to North Africa."

And so it was. Like a great bull, intimidated by the barking of a small corgi, the lumbering ship slowly moved out into the ocean—one less prize for the Nazi Navy to commandeer.

That night, lying in my bunk in the captain's cabin, I was grieving over the loss of my brand new swimsuit, two beautiful tweed outfits and a white overcoat with a hood I had bought in Paris, and which I had left behind in Quimperlé, packed into two suitcases to be delivered to me if the group made it to Brest. They didn't, and we sailed without them. Months later I learned they had not been able to get transportation, and the group scattered, finding asylum in many places in unoccupied France, where life was bearable if one was not Jewish. My previous roommate sent me a postcard, which I received later that year in England. She hoped I didn't mind her using my clothes since they were of no use to me and fitted her well.

The journey to England was eventful, with several alerts when German planes were sighted, and the destroyer zigzagged strangely to avoid becoming a target for bombs. On arrival in Plymouth, George's R.A.F. status served me as a passport, sending me speedily through Military Police screenings. A portly lady in a green uniform offered me a steaming mug of tea. Later I learned that "a cuppa tea" is the universal English panacea against fear, loneliness, sorrow, despair, and is the supreme gesture of welcome.

A noisy train bore me inland to Paddington Station, which smelled of coal dust, steam and the subtle effluvium of London— an odour of newly cut grass and frying fish and chips.

I knew Aunt Janka lived in Wimbledon, and thinking of it as a suburb of London, I blithely took a taxi. Almost an hour and eleven shillings later, I stood in front of a semi-detached house on Southey Road. Many months, and the flight from two countries lost in a war that had embroiled the whole of Europe, now lay between me and my old life as a member of a tightly knit family. I felt I had come home. I rang the bell, and a tall young man opened the door. To me he was the black-haired little boy who had swiped his mother's cigarettes for me in Jaremcze—Stefan, the nearest to a brother that I had known since the loss of Juro.

He gasped, and suddenly Aunt Janka appeared. There were tears, hugs, laughter and incoherent questions and explanations. Bobby and Uncle Dolo joined us, and there was a babel of languages—German, Polish and English. There were letters for me from Lwow, via the Red Cross, full of distress: "Poor, Jadzia, lost in conquered France. How will the poor little thing manage all alone?" wrote my mother. And Uncle Dolo kept saying: "Clever girl, I knew she'd get out."

The family had been in touch with George. I had only to wire him and take the train to Blackpool where he was stationed. After two days of shopping and rest in Wimbledon, I took the train to London with Stefan to deposit my papers, containing the names of the personnel of the armament factory where I had worked, in De Gaulle's Free French Headquarters. On my return to Wimbledon, I said goodbye to the family and embarked on the next leg of my journey.

The British trains were full of people, especially refugee children, sent in orderly, carefully labelled groups to areas safe from anticipated air raids. Each child had a label attached to his or her person, in case of straying. I began to understand the strange dialects I heard around me, and then I was at Blackpool Station where George, trim and tanned, looked almost elegant in his blue R.A.F. uniform.

It was wonderful to be together again, and as a married couple we were allowed to have a place of our own—a large clean room in a small semi-detached house, complete with bathroom and kitchen facilities. The large and benign landlady Mrs. P. took me under her wing and taught me to cook, a part of my education that had been previously neglected.

Blackpool itself was a shock for it appeared to be encased in piers and jetties, where nobody swam or sailed, though it was July. On weekends, men, women and noisy children thronged to the white sandy beaches, but all they did was sit and look. A few hardy male souls would roll up their trousers and wade, but I didn't see anyone in a bathing suit. It didn't appear to be a typical seaside English resort. And the hopeless sameness and mediocrity of town streets and houses—row after row of one-storey, semi-detached dwellings, all boarding houses, disturbed me.

Nonetheless, we were blissfully happy, living in our "bed-sitter" and trying to manage on George's meagre pay. I learned to be a housewife, which not only entailed heroic commitments in the face of war and danger, but also the daily and nightly commitment to sharing with another human being the moods—ecstacies, anger, gaiety, sadness, boredom, annoyance and contentment. These were crucial months, and on them our marriage was built.

I had my triumphs, too. At a swimming-pool, when George introduced me to a few other Polish airmen, one of them said: "Unbelievable! People are known to have wives—but to have such a wife, and to have her here—that takes some doing!"

There was an inevitable encounter with Tadzik, a sort of ritual that my path should periodically meet and cross that of my oldest friend. He was stationed with a Signals unit of the newly formed Polish Army Forces in Blackpool. He was a link with my old life, and I regarded him as a brother.

It was August, 1940, and the Battle of Britain was at its height. One Polish squadron after another was formed, and allowed to join in this monumental struggle. Dr. Charles wrote us, via the Red Cross, that this period was the turning-point of the war, and later events proved him right. England was fighting almost single-handedly, for the exiles within her borders still had to be outfitted with British arms and planes, while the Germans were massing invasion forces on the French side of the Channel.

In November, George was moved to Birmingham, and I followed a few weeks later, after having completed my training as a Nursing Auxiliary. The transfer was attached to an important promotion. George had become a sergeant. Our stay in Birmingham was enlivened by the Blitz. Nightly air raids became the rule. We could set our watches by the piercing wails of sirens ushering in the symphony of crashes, roars, whistles of descending bombs and the answering clatter of anti-aircraft guns.

George's first leave was due, and we decided to spend it with the family in Wimbledon. After that week, we were moved to Abingdon, in Berkshire, where George was posted. He had been transferred from Engineering into the Interpreters Corps, and his commission was almost a certainty.

The family were coping with the Blitz with great composure. The children, Evelyn and Bobby, continued at school while Stefan came home from Cambridge for weekends. We spent our days wandering about London, and our evenings in the family's basement, drinking beer and eating sandwiches, laughing and reminiscing.

At Abingdon, George took off every morning for the airfield, while I discovered that my visions of nursing wounded heroes back to life, were just that—visions. Instead I was occupied with looking after children's skin diseases—scabies and impetigo—and whooping cough, as well as a special ward for terminal tuberculosis patients. The children were mainly evacuees or children of bombed-out families. The dirt and poverty of the London slums had accompanied them. They not only suffered from advanced cases of infectious skin diseases, but their hair had to be freed of lice. We would scrub, treat, anoint and clean for two or three weeks and send them home better-fed, better-looking and happy, only to see them back, in the same filthy condition, a few weeks later.

I made some friends among the nurses, but was at constant loggerheads with Matron, to whom my independence and lack of respect for the hospital hierarchy was a constant irritant.

Meanwhile George, unwilling to waste time, enrolled in a correspondence course with London University and earned a second engineering degree, an English one this time.

As for me, being cooped up in a bed-sitting room did nothing to help my failing morale. George came home from the airfield one day to find me in tears. A chance remark from our landlady, who had once been a maid in one of the "big houses" in Oxford, hurt me terribly. When a former employer came to visit her, she remarked: "Reel nice of 'er, i'n'it? Arter all, she's not just anybody like you and me—she's a lady!"

In terms of the English class system, this assessment was justified, for who were we, after all? A couple of foreigners. George, however, didn't probe into the underlying psychological motives, but immediately took steps to remedy the situation. He found us other lodging in Bagley Wood, as paying guests with Mr. and Mrs. Evers, at less money than we had paid for our bed-sitter, and maid service and meals were included. When George tried to expostulate, Mr. Evers, a retired housemaster of Rugby School, put his hands on George's shoulder and said that we were at war, and they felt "our Allies" deserved help and consideration.

The delicacy, kindness and culture of the old couple and the straightforward acceptance by their servants—the maid and cook—created a feeling of belonging, which, probably, few wartime exiles had encountered. It was the turning point of our sojourn in England.

Over a period of time, we met the Evers' children—two sons—both of whom were serving with the Army, and who came on leave with their wives and children, and the youngest daughter Mary, who was a nursing auxiliary in the South of England, visited several times.

Soon great changes overtook us. George had received his commission, and a posting to Bracknell, near London. I discovered I could do more useful wartime work in my own field at the Polish Ministry of Information, where writers fluent in English were in demand. I could earn four times my nurse's wages as a writer, and nursing was not suitable for me just then. I had discovered I was pregnant. And so I had to leave the Bagley Wood retreat. We decided that I should stay in Wimbledon until the arrival of the baby, which was "booked" to be born in Oxford.

We weathered the mounting climax and the aftermath of the Blitz and welcomed with puzzlement and unease Hitler's invasion of Russia, and the subsequent inclusion of the Soviets among "our gallant Allies". At that time, nobody in England had any doubts as to the ultimate outcome of the war. The American entry into the hostilities might have speeded up Hitler's defeat, but to us in beleaguered England, victory was a matter of time and endurance. Roosevelt's generous Lend-Lease strategy showed that America could rise to great heights. The aid made the difference between hope and despair.

My new work in London placed me close to European events and theatres of war. Soon after, I secured a job as translator and newswriter to the Polish Radio Station, which operated in conjunction with the International Service of the BBC. News would come in from various sources in occupied Poland during nightly short-wave transmissions from secret stations in Warsaw. On one of these occasions, we received a flash about the Allied landing in Africa, only seconds before our news was broadcast to the Polish Underground. By the following dawn, the Underground papers were on the streets in Warsaw, spreading the news, before the Germans could present their propaganda version.

Couriers were the second most important source of information, and one of then, Jan Karski, was the first to bring the news of infamies perpetrated in Nazi extermination camps and gaschambers. Disgused as a Latvian, he had witnessed unspeakable scenes. The stories reaching us, safe and prosperous in London, left us incredulous at first. But soon photos began to come in with supporting documentation which could leave no doubt in anyone's mind.

At that time, in London, I still had some hopes that my family was alive. My father had been shot at the very beginning of the occupation, when the Nazis allowed Ukrainian Army units to pillage the town for a few days. Grandfather, happily, had died before the onslaught—a normal death in his own bed. But Mother, Grandmother and Wanda had had to leave their home to be alloted a room in the newly organized Warsaw Ghetto.

I learned later that seventeen-year-old Wanda was given work in a factory making military uniforms. When the Nazis came to take my mother and grandmother away, one of the two was given the choice of leaving or remaining to work with Wanda, whose labour was needed. Grandmother chose to go, thus prolonging the life of her daughter and grandchild. Shortly after, my mother and sister were also removed to a concentration camp. So little Wanda went to her death, never knowing what it meant to be an adult, to love and be a woman.

Meanwhile, in London I was put in charge of a radio-news-and-features programme for the Polish Forces in the Middle East. And then came November, the time for me to go to Bagley Wood where I was to stay with friends while I awaited the birth of my baby. Two days after my arrival, our first daughter Eve-Mary was born with a minimum of fuss and discomfort. George, now resplendent in his Flying Officer's uniform, came to greet her at the Radcliffe Infirmary in Oxford. He stepped into the room warily, expecting to see a bright-red, shrivelled and howling object. Instead he saw a slumbering, pink-and-white little flower of a face, in which two great blue eyes presently opened and looked at him with solemn appraisal. He was overcome.

It was not convenient for us to move in with Aunt Janka in Wimbledon and so, George found us a room as paying guests in an old house in Bracknell, which was owned by the widow and slightly wacky daughter of an English Colonel.

During the lovely, mellow autumn of that late November, I would put Eve into her pram and walk along wooded lanes, golden and rustling with fallen leaves. As I walked, I made up stories about my little girl, and the woman she would grow up to be—lovely, proud, warm and loving.

At Christmas, we went through a period of worry as George contracted a flu which he could not shake off. The removal of his tonsils in a military hospital restored him to his customary health, and we celebrated Eve's first Christmas in our own room with a tiny Christmas tree on the table. We were a family now, and this "bed-sitter" was home.

I had a month's leave from the radio station, and placed an ad for a mother's helper at a local store. It brought wonderful results in the person of Anne, who remains one of our best friends to this day. She was an ideal substitute mother, loving, firm, and intelligent, and Eve flourished.

We soon moved to a former porter's lodge at the gates of a great house. It was tiny, but we turned the kitchen into a nursery for Eve, since we took our meals in the main building, which had been turned into a hotel by the owners for the duration of the war.

Life went on, even though a resumption of the raids on London disturbed our nights by distant noises, and an occasional stray bomb in the vicinity. Many were the nights when Eve was bundled under her bed, which had a wire mattress—a fairly good protection against flying debris and glass splinters.

One day in the following June, I set off with George, now a Squadron Leader with Tactical Air Force Headquarters, on bicycles, with Eve in the rear basket-seat. We cycled the few miles to Bray and had a lovely day at one of the finest restaurants in England. On our way home, we saw an unusual number of planes in the sky. George looked thoughtful, but said nothing. The roar of the planes continued throughout the night, and by morning we knew the invasion of Normandy had begun.

Not only aircraft were on the move. During the following days, I stood by our gateway, from which the iron-work had been removed to be made into armaments, and watched endless columns of troops, jeeps, tanks, lorries, artillery, and guns of every size, pass down the road. One night, the inevitable happened.

The Polish Brigade appeared, and there in the Signals sections was Tadzik, of course, who had made it a habit to pop up regularly on my horizon, whenever great events were taking their course. George was off duty, and we had a wonderful reunion in a neighbouring pub, after which Tadzik departed at top speed in his jeep, to catch up to his unit.

The next day was Sunday, and as I was busy getting breadfast, our ginger cat came into the kitchen, mewing in a very insistent and peculiar fashion, and trying to draw my attention to the door. George and I followed him to the gate, where we saw our baby, whom we thought safely enclosed in her playpen, wandering happily about the highway among the tanks and jeeps, which all slowed down to let her toddle to safety. We whipped her up, and that night I sacrificed my last tin of ration-issue French sardines for a gala meal for the cat.

Hitler was making his last desperate attempt with his rocket weapons, and the V-1 rockets kept buzzing overhead on their way to London, while the beachheads in Europe were being secured by the Allies. We didn't think these surroundings were particularly healthy, and luckily the B.B.C. Polish Section was understanding and released me from my freelance feature-writing contract. Anne, who had looked after Eve, had moved to South Devon with her mother. She invited Eve and me and the cat to stay with them until I could find a place of our own. She came to collect us in a taxi, which she was driving with an official licence, in order to get an extra income and a gas allowance.

That was how Dartmoor became our new home area. It was a new kind of landscape, yet the springy, thyme-scented turf, the grey tors, the swift, foaming rivers and the clear, brown streams, reminded me somehow of the Carpathians.

Two days after our arrival, George and I said goodbye to each other in Plymouth, as he was travelling to an unknown destination, which could only mean the coast of Normandy. He had been under fire before, on airfields which had been strafed from the air, but this time he was actually going to the front. It was lucky that I was busy looking for a home for Eve and myself, otherwise the following weeks would have been very hard to bear.

The house I found was a little, grey-stone, semi-detached cottage with a long, narrow garden in the back, which only a Devon dry-stone wall divided from the open moor. On colder winter nights, the black, shaggy wild moor-cattle would climb over the wall and feast on my Brussels sprouts and broccoli. On one such occasion, I chased them away, armed with a frying pan, the first weapon I could snatch up, while tastefully clad in pyjamas and an old air force great-coat of George's.

I had had some fears of being treated with the insularity and standoffishness which are supposed to be characteristics of English villages, but Crapstone received me with the great warmth of which Devon people are capable. At Christmas, my newly found friends, several girls from the village and from the neighbouring houses, went carolling from house to house, collecting money for the "Save the Children Fund". There was a sprinkling of snow on the moor, and even the stars seemed crisp and crackly. I did not feel an exile, or even a foreigner that night, nor at any other time during my stay in Crapstone.

But when D-Day came and everyone was cheering, and the lights went back on, I stayed at home, put Eve to bed and wept. The Russians were in Lwow and in Warsaw. A puppet government sponsored by Stalin was taking over. My own Lwow was handed over to the Russians. Even Churchill, whom I revered, had yielded to Stalin at Yalta. So victory was not for us Poles in exile, and I knew then that we should never go home. The Underground fighters, the sailors, airmen and soldiers, about whom and for whom I had written radio features, had fought and died for nothing.

This was the end of the strange and brittle stability and shelter that England had offered us during the war. Close to the English earth we had built our illusive permanence of home and family, but now, people were going back to their real homes—those, at least, who were lucky enough to have come from Western Europe. George's career and his feeling of purpose and usefulness died on the day that peace was declared. There seemed little scope for him, and few or no career openings for a foreigner. Millions of Englishmen were returning to civilian life while a large part of British industry had been either reduced to rubble by German bombs, or converted to war production, now no longer necessary.

While he was on duty at R.A.F. Headquarters in Brussels, George had made friends with Jeep, a Canadian. Together they had served through the hostilities, witnessed the liberation of France and Belgium, gone through the setbacks of the final northern counter-offensives, suffered the V-2 bombs, and found time to enjoy some hectic nights out in the staid capital of Belgium, whenever the occasion presented itself. Now this Canadian friend suggested the prospect of emigration to his country.

And so we bid farewell to the little house in Crapstone and set out to stay overnight with friends in Somerset. We continued on to Odiham where we spent a month, George still to undergo the final formalities of discharge at a Demobilization Unit.

When cousin Stefan offered to share his flat in Upminster, near London, Eve and I accepted. His own parents, brother and sister had by then emigrated to the United States and periodically sent us the most glorious food parcels imaginable.

Since we were hoping to receive our permits for Canada in

the near future, I was allowed to teach Eve at home, provided I followed the accredited programme of the Parents' Educational Institute. It was an excellent one, and gave me the basic interest and information which later led to my present career as a university professor. It also enabled Eve to read English quite fluently within three months.

Summer came, without any sign of our emigration permits, and instead there was an outbreak of poliomyelitis, a nightmare to all parents. The friends at whose house we had stayed in Somerset, invited us back to stay in a small summer house, as the manor had been sold. We spent the rest of the summer there, and soon George came to fetch us back to Upminster. Our days in England were coming to an end.

But trouble awaited. A few days after our return, with George back at his Unit, a letter arrived from the owner of the flat we had shared with Stefan. She was on her way back from New Zealand and expected us to vacate the premises within a month. I was sitting with that letter in my hands, wondering what to do, when the bell rang. A telegraph boy brought a wire. It was from George's Canadian friend Jeep, in Quebec, and read as follows: "Order in Council granting permission to come to Canada received. Report to the Canadian Consulate in London."

From then on, the process moved maddeningly through a maze of red tape, and finally we found ourselves on board the *S.S. Aquitania* on our way to Halifax. It was late evening, our good-byes to everyone were behind us, and the English shores were slowly receding. I saw them through a blur, for my eyes were dimmed with tears. This was goodbye to Europe and to England which had restored to us our lives and our human dignity, giving us a chance to build a family and a future.

The five days on board ship were restful and strangely happy. Eve roamed about. We were compelled by a forceful and relentless George not to give in to seasickness, and we withstood it triumphantly, even though many of our fellow-passengers succumbed.

And then came Halifax. A large sign saying "Welcome New Canadians" greeted us as we landed. It became the symbol and the presage of what Canada would come to mean to us, a presage which did not disappoint us.

Freezing in inadequate outfits in a Quebec winter, we made our first purchase of real Canadian snowboots, and then came the move to Montreal, the progression from one room in the servants' quarters of a great home to an apartment, then a duplex and finally our own home in Two Mountains. All are now memories. Eve was there to join us in the joyous arrival of her new brother Andrew and sister Veronica, and she shared the progress, the work, the new friends and careers.

In this account, I have attempted to preserve some fragments of memories of a lost world, all of which live on, and will go on living, in all of those who share our background. And maybe one day my daughter Eve or her daughter in turn will take up the story again and continue it into another generation in Canada, our adopted land.

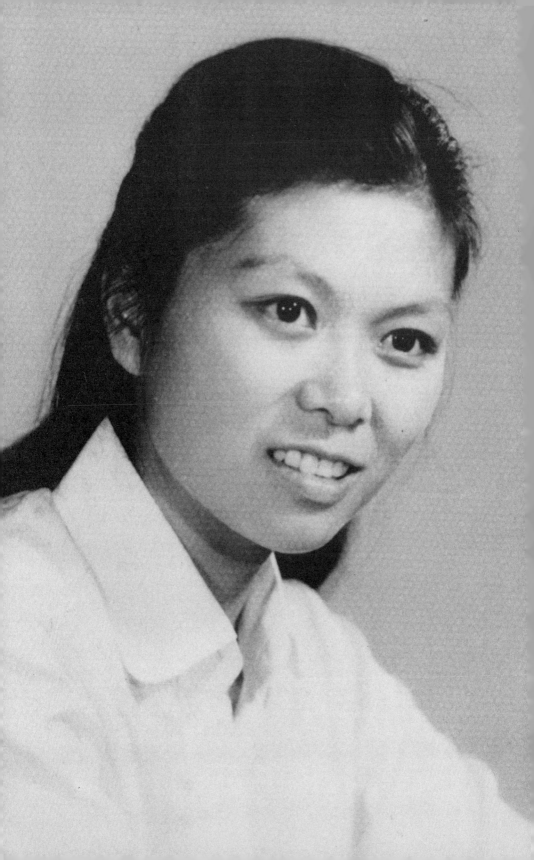

THE DECADE OF MADNESS

by
Milly Charon
from an interview with Nelly Cheng

The beating of the gong could be heard from a distance, and the people in the crowds lining the street craned their necks in an effort to see the spectacle. Many had stones or rotten vegetables in their hands to fling at the approaching dissidents, who had been arrested and detained by the Red Guards.

The parade hove into sight, and the crowd began to jeer and shout as men and women wearing dunce-caps were marched along between Red Guards in olive-green uniforms. Attached to the prisoners' clothes were signs in Chinese characters, identifying them by name as enemies of the State—counter-revolutionaries to be severely punished, if not killed. But first they had to be humiliated—held up as bad examples to the people of China.

From a window of her parents' apartment overlooking the street, thirteen-year-old Nelly Cheng and her younger brother Nigel peered down from behind the curtain, afraid to be seen. Anguished, she watched the denigration of her parents who were in the procession. Her father Doctor Herbert Cheng marched impassively with a dunce-cap on his head, forced to beat a gong while he recited over and over again: "I am an enemy of the State. I am a murderer. My name is Herbert Cheng." His wife, Doctor Stevia Cheng, walked behind him, sharing his disgrace.

Nelly watched dry-eyed, unable to cry. She could only think that her father must be very wicked and had done something terrible to bring such shame on the family. At that moment she hated him for what he had done.

While the parade swept down the Chengchow street, the

crowd shouted insults, and pelted her parents and other dissidents with stones and refuse. Dr. Cheng had not committed what would have been considered a crime by Western standards. Like all professionals in China during the Cultural Revolution, he and tens of thousands of others were the victims of a madness that despised education and professionals, while exalting the role of the labourer and peasant.

It was a period when old traditions were destroyed, and the Communist slogans of Chairman Mao Tse-tung were memorized and shouted from the mouths of millions of Chinese, blindly following, like lemmings, the ideology of a leader whose destructive Red Guards would be responsible for the death and incarceration of millions of Chinese. During those years, the Red Guards would destroy temples, institutions of learning, burn books, disrupt health and economic services, and imprison innocent people whose only crime had been the possession of illustrious ancestors, a good education or to have voiced criticism of the excesses of the regime.

Twenty years would have to elapse from that glimpse of the "parade of shame" before Nelly Cheng could bring herself to speak about those terrible years, and how they had affected her and her family. In Montreal, far from the land of her ancestors, she would seek a new beginning in an attempt to regain the ten years she lost during the decade of madness.

* * * *

Nelly's parents Stevia and Herbert Cheng had graduated from American missionary universities in China, and both had chosen medicine as their profession. Stevia Cheng had started her medical studies in Chungking, but the Japanese invasion of China forced her to leave the military-occupied areas. Before he met his wife, Herbert Cheng had been affected in the same way, finishing his education after moving far from the war zones. Stevia Cheng completed her studies in gynecology and obstetrics in Chengdu, in the interior of China, far from Shanghai where she had been raised.

After the Second World War, she returned to work in Shanghai, and in 1949 was placed in a hospital which treated workers mainly employed in the huge textile factories of Shanghai. Dr. Herbert Cheng who had worked at Chengdu joined the surgical staff at the same hospital as his wife in Shanghai.

"In the 1950s, China began to develop the interior of the country as part of a great plan to improve the lot of the people," Nelly explained. "My parents were ordered to Chengchow in Henan Province, and had no choice but to go. The city was at the junction of the most important railway system in the country, where the main east-to-west and north-to-south lines crossed. Known for its textile factories and tobacco industry, Chengchow needed the railway as a vital link for the transportation of its manufactured products.

"When my parents first arrived, life there wasn't easy. Once travellers alighted from the train, the only transportation was by donkey. The entire city sprawled out over a radius of about two miles and was lit by only fifteen street-lamps. The city was near the Yalu River, and everything was sandy and dusty—very primitive—much like the countryside. My brother and I were left behind to be cared for by our grandmother in Shanghai."

The history of the Cheng family's antecedents was one of the prime factors leading to their disgrace as enemies of the State. They had come from a proud and illustrious family, whose prestigious accomplishments had often been held up by her father as an example to Nelly. "You should always work hard and try to make something of yourself, to bring pride to your ancestors because they achieved something," he would say. He pointed out his grandfather who had been Admiral of the Navy of the South in the government of Sun Yat-sen, the reformer, who had overthrown the tyrannical Emperor and corrupt Empress Dowager in 1911 and changed the Chinese feudal system to a democratic government. Nelly's great-grandfather had come from the same village as Sun Yat-sen, and had held positions of responsibility under the fledgling government, while Sun Yat-sen himself was travelling to other countries in order to raise money for his new democracy.

"My great-grandmother's name was Deng, and she was related to Deng Shi-Chiang who was head of the navy of the North and a great national hero, who had led the battle against the Japanese invaders. My great-grandfather was assassinated by members of the Gui-Xi Army, and his statue in Chengchow was pulled down during the Cultural Revolution by the Red Guards. His family was respected and favoured by the government in return for his services to China, and his sons and grandsons received appointments and titles. One of my grandfather's brothers was sent to England to study naval affairs, and another went to the United States to study chemistry. He married an American-Jewish girl with Communist leanings, and she returned to China with him.

"My great-uncle taught at what was considered the best university in Beijing, while my American great-aunt taught English at the People's University, and published a lot of articles in newspapers. She loved China, its traditions and its people."

However, Nelly's great-aunt's love for China did not help her when she came up against the notorious Red Guard. During the Cultural Revolution, she and her husband were accused of espionage and imprisoned for several years. Nelly met her in Beijing in 1973 after she had been released.

"She had had a nervous breakdown and acted very strangely. She couldn't understand why, despite her love for China and all her hard work, she had been treated this way. She went to the United States for treatment, and died there shortly after. My great-uncle remained in China, but he was a physical and mental wreck after his imprisonment. No one dared to talk about the tortures inflicted in prison, but something must have caused his illness and broken spirit. He died over four years ago.

"On my mother's side, my grandfather received a scholarship to study marine biology in Japan. On his return, he practised his profession in China and later turned to politics. He became the Minister of Finance in the Chiang Kai-shek government.

"And so, it was expected from generation to generation that members of the family do well, not to shame our ancestors. Yet later, it was their accomplishments that caused us great shame during the Revolution.

"Now our family would be held responsible for our antecedents' achievements. My parents continued working after they had established themselves in Chengdu, but they were lonely, and once they found a suitable apartment and a housekeeper, they sent for my brother and me in Shanghai."

By now Dr. Herbert Cheng was head of the Surgical

Department and a Vice-Dean, and his wife was head of Obstetrics and Gynecology at the Chengchow Hospital. Their hours were long and irregular, and the housekeeper became a kind of foster-mother to the children. She looked after the apartment, which consisted of three bedrooms, a kitchen, a storeroom and bathroom.

"It was a tradition that we have someone from my mother's hometown—someone with the same background and cooking style. Our housekeeper was very good to us. She had been well off before 1939. Her husband had been an official in Chiang Kai-shek's government, and when the government fell in 1949, her husband fled with Chiang Kai-shek and the rest of his staff to Taiwan. She never saw or heard from him again. She had been a lady and now was forced to become a housekeeper to support herself. Kind and clean, she cooked well and had good taste. She introduced me to opera, which she loved, and would take me along whenever she went to a performance. I loved to hear her wonderful stories and legends of her home area.

"She would wake me early in the morning, give me break-fast and comb my hair. I would have to be at school about seven, because I was a monitor and had to start the fire to warm up the room. I came home at lunchtime, ate, had a nap or played, and then returned to school. After classes, there would be activities and trips to other schools for recitation, dancing or ping-pong. We would give shows, and my specialty was singing and dancing.

"After school, I would usually run home and play with the neighbourhood children, when there were no trips. I was the only one in the district who went to an outside school, because my parents had wanted me to have a better education and so, they chose a more progressive school in another part of the city. In China there was a strict rule. Children had to attend school in their own neighbourhood, but because my parents had contacts, they were able to bypass the rules."

Nelly kept busy in many activities, not only participating but organizing. She was a born leader and usually would be in charge of directing joint activities with other classes. There was usually some jealousy from the other children.

"But I tried to be nice. If my family sent me fancy candies from Shanghai, I would take them to school and share them with the other children. I was chosen from a large group, on one occasion to participate in a big show at the Children's Palace some distance away, and there was singing, sports and calligraphy displays."

Nelly's need to achieve had been dictated by the example of her family's tradition. She was usually first in class. If not, she would be very unhappy.

"If I received only 99 per cent because of some careless mistake, I would be miserable. I'd cry over that one lousy mark and get upset about it at home. I had to be first."

Suddenly everything changed. The Cultural Revolution began in the summer of 1966, just before Nelly was due to finish primary school.

"Usually political movements in China started in the literary field and then moved to the economic and political sectors. Suddenly all classes in school halted, and we couldn't graduate. We had to remain in primary school because the middle schools weren't admitting any new pupils, and this meant that no young children could begin primary. Our lessons consisted of criticizing capitalism and anything contrary to the doctrines of Chairman Mao. Although my parents had been trying to get me into the best middle school in the district, it was impossible. I stayed in primary.

"The following year, about the beginning of 1967, the attacks against my parents began. First my father was accused of being a murderer. A patient who had been very ill died after an operation, and my father was blamed. He was an outspoken man, which automatically labelled him a counter-revolutionary. In addition, because my grandfather had been in Hong Kong during the years of famine between 1960 and 1963, when millions had died, and had sent us letters and packages of peanut oil, sugar and other staples, this was considered to be 'bourgeois' and was held against us. The fact that we had relatives in the United States was further proof of our perfidy. My father's sister had emigrated to the States after the war, and another aunt had married an American soldier who had been based in South China. When he returned to the U.S.A., she went with him. An uncle, who had married a girl from Hong Kong, had moved there to be with her. All these connections were considered contrary to the best interest of the Communist Government, and we were regarded as public enemies of the highest order.

"My parents' salaries were another cause of criticism. Between them they earned 350 Yuan a month, which by Western standards was next to nothing, yet some people who were jealous denounced them as exploiters of the people. All these issues were enough for charges to be laid against my parents, and finally the authorities, after publicly humiliating him, shut my father up in a small room, which he could not leave, in a compound for political dissidents. All he could do was stare at the four walls, but what was worse was that parade, when he had to march wearing a dunce-cap on which accusations had been painted and he was forced to say out loud: 'I am a murderer. I am an anti-revolutionary, an enemy of the State. My name is Cheng.' And my mother had to follow behind and witness his degradation.

"I didn't understand my feelings at the time. Children can be very cruel, and other kids were coming to me and saying my father was this and that, and I was the daughter of a dog, of a very bad person, and so I felt he was guilty and to blame for the humiliation, and I hated him for it."

And there was more. The Red Guards would come constantly to search the apartment. The family didn't know what they were looking for, and the visits would usually be in the evening. When the sound of the gong, reverberating through the street, was heard, Nelly would begin to shake.

"To this day when I hear a sound like that, I get very nervous. We children were forced to stand outside at the corner of the building, while the Red Guards searched and destroyed our things. We had a lot of records of Western classical music, and they threw them to the floor and stepped on them, smashing them all. My mother had some small pieces of jewellery, many of which were inexpensive pins and necklaces, and the guards would say: 'These were exploited from the working class.' To this day, I don't know what they were hunting for, yet they would return again and again...sometimes twice a week, other times once a week. We never knew on which day it would be.

"One day they came and placed a big poster out in front of the building and told us the housekeeper had to leave, because we were exploiting her. It left us in chaos. My father was in confinement, my mother accused, yet still working long hours at the hospital, and there was no one to take care of us. My brother was only eight years old, and at thirteen I wasn't very good at cooking and cleaning. We had always had help in the house. The poor housekeeper was forced to leave that night, and she had no one to turn to and no place to go. She had never had any children, and we were her family. Not too long after, we heard that she had died of cancer."

The searches continued, and it wasn't long before the soldiers decided that Nelly's mother had too large a stock of lingerie. Her panty-hose, brassieres, slips, and even her dresses and umbrellas, were held up as objects of ridicule. The family had a number of photo albums, for taking pictures had been a hobby, and all of these family mementoes were confiscated, along with personal clothing, to be put on public exhibition, in order to show how the rich Chengs were exploiting the poor.

"When the period of harassment was over, I went and tried to recover whatever I could. My mother was proud and very shy and wouldn't go herself. The clothes and jewelry had all been stolen, and our photographs had been glued in haphazard order onto huge scrolls for hanging and displaying. My mother shrugged and said, 'Who cares?' She was too proud to admit how badly she had been hurt."

Nelly's father, who had been a surgeon and head of a hospital department, was now forced to work as a cleaner, swabbing floors and digging shelters. The regime suffered from a national generalized paranoia. The leaders were suspicious of everyone—imperialists, socialists, Americans and Russians.

"Although my mother was still allowed to work at the hospital, my father was not permitted to come home. Suddenly came an order that we were still living too well, and would have to move to a smaller place. We had to exchange our apartment with a family of cooks and boilermakers, whose place in another building had consisted of two small rooms. We were forced to give away most of our possessions, whatever hadn't already been taken, because we hadn't enough room for them."

What was even worse for Nelly, however, was that former members of her father's staff at the hospital were accusing and deriding her father, saying that he had criticized the Revolution. She had never heard him say anything at home, and she realized that his staff were expecting her to say things against her parents so they could be incriminated even more.

"Luckily I had enough sense to see what was happening, and I didn't cooperate, even though I was young enough to be coerced. If I had, I would be suffering such pangs of guilt today for doing something hurtful to my parents. It was natural for kids who were pressured this way to betray their elders in order to be accepted by peers and government officials.

"The apartment building where we originally lived housed professionals, most of them associated with the hospital where my parents were on staff. All these people were suspects and all were in trouble, though my father was considered the worst of all. Next door to us had lived the Director of the hospital, and he had three daughters, two of whom were older than I. One was in middle school and the other in university, and because they wanted to appear cooperative and be accepted by the revolutionaries, they led the guards to their home to search and ransack the family belongings. On another occasion, the oldest daughter brought home about twenty people to search, and the younger one filled the place with a crowd of forty, all looking for goodness knew what.

"The children of the Director of the Dentistry Department put a poster on the front door, on which was written that they had severed all relations with their father, and denounced him for his crimes. Others on the hospital staff were put into small cells like my father, and three who had been in high positions, committed suicide."

Colour played a significant part in defining the political situation. The Red Guards were 'Red' which was the ideal hue to be, and all those who were accused were 'Black'.

"In school we were considered to be blackened kids. The other students accused us of everything imaginable, and we were told to stand away from the groups of children so we wouldn't blacken them."

In late 1966, when no schools were functioning, the "Socialist Education Campaign" was launched, and it brought millions of students with radical views from all over China to Beijing, where they would parade in review before Chairman Mao, in front of the Gate of Heavenly Peace at the Tiananmen Square. For those under seventeen, born since the Communist takeover of China, the parade represented symbolically the famous Long March of 1934, when 300,000 men and women set out to walk 8,000 miles from Yenan to Beijing, and a year later only 30,000 had successfully completed the journey. In September, permission was granted to all college students, and the more revolutionary-minded teachers and middle-school students, to travel free throughout the country to get an "exchange of experiences".

"I wanted to go, but because I was blacklisted, permission was denied. I was angry and couldn't accept this refusal. I felt like an outcast. Chairman Mao had received the Red Guards for an audience about eight times, and while our class planned the trip to participate, I had to stay home and cook. I couldn't go outside the house, and was afraid to do anything that would indicate how I felt. In front of our apartment was a big poster: 'This is the House of the Traitors'. Everyone and everything had a label to remind us constantly that we were the enemy. It was like what had happened in Nazi Germany. We had to slink along the wall when we did go out, so as not to come into contact with others. Children would throw stones at us as if we were mangy dogs and yell: "There's the daughter of the traitor!"

It was worse for Nelly's younger brother. Because he was smaller and a boy, he was constantly beaten by other children. Many times he would return home with a bleeding nose, cuts on his face or blackened eyes.

"Because I was a girl, I wasn't beaten, but the children would throw stones, insult and curse me. Because I had to go to the market for food, I was exposed to people's malice. Just cooking, shopping, cleaning house and washing clothes without any washing-machine took all my energy. It was barely survival."

Two years passed in this fashion, and the schools finally opened. The students were recalled, and Nelly was ordered to the worst middle school in the district. It was another humiliation. Her brother started primary school, but none of the pupils learned much of anything, for education was in a state of disorganization.

"I tried to apply myself, despite the setbacks, and once the teacher called me aside to speak with me. She said she could see from my school work that I was a good student although my father was an enemy.

"'You must be aware he is the enemy,'" she said, "' and don't be frightened by him.'"

"I tried to be good at everything and became a super-achiever, whether it was digging bomb-shelters, studying or hard, manual labour, wherever I was sent. My early years started to pay off when classes had recommenced, as irregular as they were. We wrote a lot—mainly propaganda about how good and wise Chairman Mao was and how much we loved him. My teacher was quite good, and she herself had suffered during those years. She had been denounced, and so she understood what I was going through. Because I could read well, she allowed me to read the newspapers aloud to the class in the morning. I was like a newscaster, and this one hour every day gave me training in reading and speaking."

Then to Nelly's surprise, her persistence and offers to help others earned her permission to go on a march with other students. Her mother felt she was too young to be marching around the country, but she was willing to torture herself, to do penance to prove that she was worthy and not an enemy of the State. Carrying a knapsack, with a rolled quilt for bedding on her back, she took to the road at the age of fourteen with thousands of others, walking east from Chengchow to different cities. She marched for more than ten hours a day in all kinds of weather. Winter was coming, and it was difficult to stay warm.

"For the cold, I wore padded quilted trousers, but the threads broke from continuous walking and had to be patched. I wore out so many pairs of shoes, marching non-stop. Now when I look back on it, I ask myself why I did something as inane as that, but at the time it was a matter of pride. I had to prove I wasn't bad— that I was a part of the Revolution, and it was the only way I could gain acceptance."

On her return, Nelly was placed in a textile mill, working on different tasks wherever she was needed. She progressed from unrolling cotton thread off wooden sticks to winding it onto spindles, from which it was transferred to larger and larger spools to prepare the thread for weaving on the looms. If there was one error in the threading, the entire machine would come to a halt. It wasn't long before she could operate one of the huge machines herself.

In 1968, Nelly's youngest brother Nelson was born, and in 1969 Chairman Mao issued directives to resettle students in the countryside. He felt that the cadres had been away from their grassroots for too long, and would have to be re-educated. At the same time, they would bring revolutionary wisdom and construction to the most isolated regions of China. There would be a new breed of peasant—educated professionals.

"Mao said the young people would have to study from the peasants instead of from books, but I think he wanted them out of the cities because they were getting wild with nothing to occupy their time. They smashed up so many old buildings and monuments, and burned and destroyed, as an expression of criticism of intellectuals and authority. It was almost impossible to get them back under control. At that point their activities bordered on anarchy. All industrial production had stopped, and perhaps this was the only way Mao could get the situation in hand. Later the Red Guards went wild too, and did even worse. They were also sent to the countryside to be re-educated by the peasants."

When Nelly finished middle school, the graduates were told their turn had come. A huge rally was organized, and the mayor of the city, who had been an army general, gave a speech. "We are sending you out gloriously to the peasants to receive an education and in a year or two, you will return," he said.

One of two graduating classes, Nelly's group was sent to the countryside around Chengchow. It was nothing new for her to work in the fields. The students had already been to communes to learn from the peasants during harvest, and during the school year peasants had been brought to the cities to give an account of their farm lives, and how miserable their lot had been under the landlords.

"About 260 students, divided into two groups, were driven away in trucks. The grouping system used in the army determined the size of the units. We were numbered off into squads, making up a company of about 130. At first we were forced to move in with the peasants because there were no separate lodgings for us. In China, houses usually have three rooms. The middle one is the living room for receiving guests with a bedroom on either side. In these farmhouses there was a bathroom at the back, as well as the pig-sty. Two families would be packed into a house of this type. In the middle room, there was usually a coffin, because it is a Chinese tradition to prepare for death. About six of us students would be crammed into this room with the coffin, sleeping on boards without any mattress. The room was too small to hold six boards, so some of us slept on straw. I was terrified of using straw because I was allergic to it, and it was infested with insects. What was worse was the lack of sanitation. The toilet was a hole in the ground, used by the farmer and his family. It was no problem for them as a family, but for us it was very difficult. And then the farmer refused to use it anymore because we strangers had used it.

"We stayed in that house for a few months, but it wasn't long before the peasants in the area took offence to having noisy, messy students in their village. Soon we had quarrels with the villagers, who had their traditional ways of doing things, and they complained to officials about the 130 strangers who had suddenly come from the outside to disrupt their lives. It really was a disturbance for them to have us there. So, to prevent further arguments, we decided to build our own lodging. A railway ran through the district, and the village was located on one side of the line. The villagers told us to build our residences on the other side of the tracks. They really didn't like us, and it was their way of getting us as far away as possible. At first we built ten units made of mud-bricks, and then ten more. We added to these, and by the time we left there, we had constructed about forty, which accommodated us all in four rows of barrack-type rooms."

Mao's plan was to have the peasants teach the students how to farm, but because the peasants were irritated by the presence of the students, they tended to ignore them and not offer any help. As a result, the young people were left to their own devices and had to experiment on their own, agriculturally. There were no clinics or hospitals, and it was impossible for anyone who was sick or injured to get proper attention. And so a new type of doctor appeared in the fields of China—the barefoot country doctor—to take care of the peasants, villagers and students. It meant a double shift for the doctors, for not only were they supposed to work full-time in the fields, but were on call at all hours of the day or night.

"Because my parents were doctors, the authorities figured I must have learned something from them. How could I? They were never home, and when they were, at rare intervals, they never talked about medicine. I never went to the hospital to watch them at their work. I tried to explain this, but it was useless. 'No, no,' they said. 'You must have the instincts for it, with two doctors in your family.'

"And so, I was sent away to study for three months to the Youth Farm headquarters, where I learned traditional Chinese medicine—the use of herbs, acupuncture, physiology and other subjects, taught by doctors from city hospitals. We read medical books, and it was good for me, because I learned quite a lot. I was getting a better education than the back-breaking work in the fields. I was practising my reading and writing which had been sadly neglected before. I enjoyed listening to the teachers and taking notes.

"From there we were sent to a hospital in Chengchow for practical training. There were about twenty to thirty of us who had been chosen to be barefoot doctors. Girls were segregated from the boys, and the hospital auditorium was turned into a dormitory for the girls.

"As soon as I finished my training, I was sent back to my work company. It was hard labour, for I continued with planting wheat in the winter and corn in the summer, as well as putting in beans and rice. I hated rice planting because we had to stand in mud and water, which ulcerated our feet. We had constant backaches from gathering wheat and corn because there were no agricultural machines, and everything was done by hand.

"My work had increased because I was always on call as a medic, twenty-four hours a day. As far as medical treatment was concerned, there wasn't much of it, because the government had allocated a tiny budget for buying drugs and medicines. I had to prepare my own herbs and keep track of them, but there were emergencies and accidents for which I was totally unprepared."

Shortly after Nelly had returned from medical training, a group from her unit was digging a deep well to be used for drinking water and irrigation. A kind of primitive drill was used, which was rotated by pulling on a hawser. To keep it from unwinding, a girl squatting at the top of the hole, controlled it by pulling on it to keep it taut. As the rope tightened, a bar at right angles to the bore moved round and round. She was careless, and moved into the bar's range. It struck her on the head, and she let go her hold on the rope, which began to unwind at a furious speed, causing the bar to spin and batter her head in piston-like strokes.

"It was at 5 a.m., and I had just come off the night shift and

410

was eating breakfast before going to sleep, when someone came running to tell me I was urgently needed. There had been a serious accident. I ran a kilometre to the site and found that two girls had already been placed on a pair of carts. On one lay the girl who had been hit in the head, and on the other peasants' cart lay the girl who had gone to her rescue, and had been struck on the leg. I immediately noticed that her leg was so swollen it was about to burst from the trouser leg. The girl with the head injury was unconscious, but there was no blood."

Nelly realized the situation was beyond her skills and serious enough to require immediate transportation to the country hospital. The dirt roads were bumpy and full of ruts, and to avoid causing further damage to the injured students, Nelly ordered the wheels removed from the carts, and a group of strong youths raised the carts' platforms to their shoulders and set out for the hospital about seven kilometres away.

"Just outside the village, I noticed that a white fluid was oozing from the ears and nose of the more seriously injured girl. I knew it was hopeless, and she died shortly after. The other girl, whose leg had been badly broken, received treatment and survived. Accidents such as these were common all over the country, and there was no proper way of treating these cases. On one occasion, I was forced to operate on someone with appendicitis. I didn't expect the patient to survive, and I was more amazed than he when he recovered. I knew next to nothing about surgical techniques.

"My work took me just about everywhere. Sometimes I was in the fields, or in the dining hall; at other times, I slaved in the kitchens. If there was a medical emergency, I would drop everything and run. I worked for a period in the animal husbandry group and even was on 'night soil' detail, which meant going to the city and dragging empty carts during the day to load up with human excrement at the public toilets—really just holes in the ground—and travel back to the country by night, dragging the stinking carts. The contents were to be mixed with other compost for fertilizer for the crops. It was a trip that took a day and a night, and there was no sleep for anyone on this detail during that period. The job had to be done with shovels and hand-drawn carts because we had no tractors or trucks to simplify the operation."

It was an impossible existence for Nelly, as she tried to be in many places at the same time. However, she realized that her labour was necessary for her social rehabilitation. She was still trying to be accepted, and now was eyeing privileged membership in a leadership elite, considered to be the highest branch of the Youth League. If she were permitted to join, it would mean instant acceptance into the highest youth cadres.

"I kept applying, and tried to work incredibly hard to please them...to do anything they wanted me to do...to wash away my family's offences with my sweat and even my blood, if necessary. People kept saying I was guilty of crimes, and I believed them. The word really should have been sins, and mine were the sins of my father, so I believed, and the sins of illustrious ancestors. I told the leaders I was willing to suffer and give up all vanities I had indulged in when I was young. Before the Revolution, I had worn pretty clothes. I remember in particular a pair of beautiful red leather shoes from Shanghai that everyone admired. Now I went to the other extreme. I dressed in old shabby clothes, and even took my father's stained and worn hospital whites and donned them. I wanted to look poor like the others. I wouldn't wear a skirt and I kept my hair in an unbecoming fashion. I was doing penance to make myself humble and good.

"The few times my mother saw me on visits, she was shocked at my appearance. It bothered her for she had an innate sense of style and had always dressed nicely. She couldn't understand why her only daughter had no desire to look neat and attractive, and she somehow never realized that I was behaving this way because of what I had been subjected to. In the country, I went to even greater extremes. Many of the students, whose fathers were either labourers or soldiers, used their cast-off work clothes or uniforms to work in. I took my father's old Mao-style suits, so big that they hung on me, and wore them when it would have been ridiculous to appear in his hospital whites.

"I wouldn't wear cream on my face to protect my skin from freezing winter days or the heat of the sun, just to show how tough I was. My skin was red, chapped and blistered, and became infected from neglect. I got a bad case of frostbite from trying to appear tough and hardy. I honestly thought that this way of life was normal in other countries—that one had to work harder and

longer hours and deny oneself the basic comforts and even necessities, to be accepted by one's peers. Although my mother wanted
to give me money to improve my lot, I refused it, afraid that I would
be called a bourgeois."

Yet despite all of this, Nelly was still rejected by the elite
cadre. There would be a meeting, and she would be forced to read
her application aloud, as well as her family history all the way back
to her great-grandparents. And that was what finished her. A
background of high position and social importance was sneered at.
Her ancestry was her downfall. It was considered a black mark on
her record because they were rated as anti-social criminals.

"I was so utterly 'black', and it gave me such pain to read
this list of relatives aloud. When I omitted the American connection, the secretary wanted to know why. I answered that because
I had never known or seen them, I didn't think it was necessary."

"'It shows,' said the leader, 'that you don't have enough
class-consciousness to confess it aloud, and you haven't cut yourself away from them yet.'

"Finally the decision would come down, after an hour of
argument, that I wasn't good enough to be accepted by the League.
I applied at least ten times, and it was always the same result. I was
told to try harder and I would be tested again. It was obvious I was
being deliberately prevented from advancing."

There was a job opening at the Youth Centre for an assistant to two doctors from the city, who had been sent to handle the
more serious medical cases. They needed a young person to take
care of medical accounts and prescriptions. Nelly had been under
their supervision during her training period, and they liked her
work. They submitted an application to get her transferred to their
staff, where conditions and working-hours were better.

Maliciously, the secretary and leaders of the Youth Company sent a letter to the doctors describing Nelly's "bad background". As the daughter of an enemy of the State, she was tainted.
The job offer was withdrawn. It would take four and a half years
of back-breaking labour and constant humiliations and rejections
before she was finally accepted to the Farm Centre's medical facil-
ity.

"What was hard to take," Nelly admitted, her eyes misty
at the recollection, "was the frustration inside that I couldn't

release. I was full of anger, and I couldn't ever tell anyone about it, or I would have been in big trouble. My statement of feeling would have been reported to someone in authority, and I would have been punished. I realize now how ridiculous it was for me to advance to a higher position, only because of a desire for acceptance. To relieve my frustration, I sang constantly. It was better than talking to myself, and without it, I probably would have suffered more. To this day, people still remember me as the girl who sang."

At the end of Nelly's third year in the country, recruiters had come from the city looking for employees to train for the hotel industry, heavy industry, dancing and musical troupes, and even the army. Positions were offered as butchers, cooks, and attendants in public bathhouses. But Nelly had taken none of these because her leaders had said she needed more social training and had not suffered enough.

"My father had been concerned that I had wasted too many years, and he wanted me to return to the city and make something of myself. As it turned out, I was in the last group to leave the countryside, and instead had been given a transfer to the Youth Centre, which I had welcomed. The people there had been older and more reasonable. While I was working there, recruiters came from the Ministry of Education, looking for teachers for the middle schools. There was a big shortage of these, because there had been no flow of graduates during the Cultural Revolution. The recruiters were willing to train the teachers, but many of the young people weren't interested. Teachers, it seemed, weren't paid too well and were looked down on. They had been the first to suffer at the start of the Revolution. After six or seven years on farms, most of those who had used their backs and muscles were afraid to use their brains. For me, it appeared to be the best offer. Nine teachers were required out of the six hundred young people left on the farm. The competition was fierce, but I talked to the Directors, and they said I could give it a try."

That was the turning point in Nelly's life. After long years in the country, she was finally back with her family in the city. She was given the task of teaching first-year mathematics in a middle school, although she had never studied math in her life before. She sought the help of an older graduate in his late forties, named Xiog, who loved the subject. He had foreseen that there would be huge gaps in China's education system because of the excesses of the Cultural Revolution.

"Xiog had suffered a great deal during that period, and was so happy to teach me everything he knew. He spent a lot of time on me, and I was learning and teaching simultaneously. He gave me books to read and exercises to carry out and immediately after a lesson, I would go to the class and teach the students what I had learned. This professor had trouble with his eyes. It could have been a cataract or glaucoma. I was so grateful to him for his help despite his medical problem, that I took him to the hospital where my parents worked and had specialists look at him and try to help. Xiog was determined to teach me everything before he lost his eyesight, pushing me mercilessly to study."

Nelly was assigned sixty students between the ages of thirteen and fourteen, and was appointed Assistant Director of the Artistic Troupe. In addition, she was asked to teach English because no one else was available. Most of the teachers were in their forties and fifties. As the youngest member, she replaced any teacher who was absent.

"It wasn't difficult to teach English because nothing much was required. It was: 'I love Chairman Mao...I love my country...Long live Chairman Mao' and more of this chanting. I was able to teach the English alphabet in a day. By western standards, this type of teaching wasn't very good, but for me it was special because I was finally working at something I enjoyed."

Nine months later, during the summer vacation, an immersion training class was arranged, from 8 a.m. to 5 p.m. Teachers could pick subjects in which to specialize and receive intensive instruction. Nelly was directed to the mathematical section but refused to go. She preferred English although it was considered a subject of secondary importance.

"There were eighty-five teachers in the group, all learning English, and immediately after the two months of training were finished, the city organized a special teachers' college to improve the education of middle-school teachers. They were given a semester's leave of absence, and I was one of those to go."

Shortly after, a male colleague gave Nelly a document issued by the Central Committee, which stated that Deng Xiaoping, the new leader who had replaced Mao after his death, had decided universities should recruit students through selection after rigorous written examinations. Her colleague urged her to apply.

"I didn't think I was good enough, but he insisted I try anyway. He offered to help me and really pushed me hard to study. He had already graduated from university and had been a peasant worker and soldier. So many of my years had already been wasted, and I felt I was getting old, so I decided to do it. I sat for the examinations at the end of 1977, and when I received a notice to appear for a physical examination, I knew I had passed the first hurdle, and had been accepted as a candidate for admission. My parents were so proud. After so many years of hardship and humiliation, their daughter was finally vindicating them."

Nelly was sitting in the teacher's college cafeteria at noon having lunch, when the final admission notices came through. One of the students who had a contact in the Admissions Office came running to report that one of the five applicants from Nelly's class had been accepted. The name of the candidate was Cheng.

"I was delirious. It could only be me. I lost my appetite, but I couldn't show any emotion. It is not the Chinese way, but I was stewing inside. By the end of the day, the tension was too much for me, and I went to the office and asked if there was any information on the results.

"'No, we can't give you any,'" was the response. "'You will receive an official notice telling you if you have been accepted or rejected.'"

When the official letter arrived, Nelly was a little disappointed. She had hoped to go to Chengchow University near her home. Instead she had been placed at Kaifeng University about sixty kilometres away. However, the honour of being chosen out of so many millions of applicants was a special one.

"The Cheng family had come out of a bad situation, and we were regaining our self-respect, our pride, and now people were coming to congratulate us. I resented it, because I felt they were hypocritical. They had condemned us before, and spat on my parents, had stoned us and shouted insults, and now they were congratulating us. It infuriated me. Someone suggested that my parents should throw a banquet in my honour. I said no. Why should we? No one had helped me, and why should we spend money on those who had treated us so savagely? My mother said they wanted to honour us, but I had been too badly hurt. I declined such a two-faced honour."

The university years were, for the most part, happy ones for Nelly. She was determined not to let anything spoil them. At last she was where she felt she belonged. There was so much to learn. Although she specialized in English, she also took courses in psychology, political science, history, philosophy, economy, as well as ancient classical Chinese literature. It was hard work, and university life was not a comfortable one. There were no luxuries. The students slept in dormitories, six to a small room.

"It wasn't bad in our room," recalled Nelly, "because we got along fairly well. In some of the rooms there was a lot of jealousy, and the girls fought bitterly. Five of the six in my room came from families of intellectuals, so we had more in common. One girl's father was a composer, another was a retired editor of a large newspaper, the third girl's father was an engineer, while the fourth student's father was president of a university. The only one we had some trouble with was the last girl whose father was a high-ranking government official. She was a little snobbish. We ignored it, and she finally learned to stop talking about the family chauffeur, the maids and other status symbols of the new China. The rest of us had survived the Cultural Revolution in much the same circumstances, and so our attitudes were different. When this girl finally straightened out, she became rather pleasant. She wasn't mean, and would pass around tickets to all kinds of shows and other events that had been sent to her father, and which he passed on to her for distribution.

"We even pooled our food, putting our ration tickets into a box, so if anyone missed a meal or ran short of tickets, there was always something in the box to help her out. It is to our credit that no one ever took advantage of this, and no tickets were stolen."

The Dean of Kaifeng University had promised at the mass meeting when the students had arrived that those with the best marks would get the best jobs. Keeping this in mind, Nelly tried hard to get to the top of her class, but she was always second. It frustrated her. There was always one man who was one or two marks ahead of her.

"I got along with the foreign teachers and improved my English. However, I had a problem because the Director didn't like me. I was too independent. It is a common thing in China to use gifts to obtain favours. The other students would brown-nose, buying the Director presents, like sacks of rice or doing jobs for him like cleaning out his quarters. I refused to do this, and I wouldn't bow to him. I said I would use my marks and my brains—not bribes—but as it turned out, it lost me a first-class job, good marks notwithstanding.

"On graduation, employment was assigned by the English Department and although the academic staff voted in my favour, they felt I was too proud and too independent. I knew that two positions were open at a good university in Chengchow. Suddenly the offers were cancelled, and the next plum appointment at the Hunan Medical University was given to the student who had swept the Director's quarters and brought him rice.

"The Hunan Province job was a really enviable opening, like getting a position at Radio Quebec, and I know I would have been good at it. I heard from a student who had contacts, that the Director had cancelled the position for the Chengchow jobs because he didn't want me to have one of them. They were assigned to another university. I was sick over this for two days. Instead I ended up in a third-grade college, not even a university, that didn't even have a budget from the Central Committee—as punishment. I remained for four semesters. Everyone knew I was unhappy about it because I had suffered an injustice. Later I saw the Dean at Kaifeng and reminded him of his assurances that graduates with the best marks would get the best appointments. He was rather embarrassed and made excuses for the college. I hated that Director so much.

"What I was now doing was training others to become middle-school teachers, but I wanted to continue my education, to get a Master's degree, and when I applied to Concordia University in Canada, the college tried to talk me out of it. They wanted me to stay and make more of a contribution to China. I wasn't convinced, and so they found ways to make life more difficult for me. The paper-shuffling and bureaucracy were unbearable. Just as I thought I had all the necessary papers, they would come up with a new one I had to have. Suddenly they demanded a certificate of financial sponsorship. I got it. Then they said I had to have two copies, and one had to be witnessed by the Chinese Embassy in Ottawa. To do that it would have to be sent to my relatives in the United States, who would sign it and then forward it to Ottawa. The Chinese Embassy would stamp it and mail it back to China.

"Then I was told that I had to get a special permit from the Higher Educational Commission to leave. I was always snagged on these documents, and there was no end to them. It was the same with the passport and visa. Two years were to elapse before all the papers were assembled."

Finally Nelly was on her way. The trip that had taken two years of paper-shuffling to prepare took a day-and-a-half from Shanghai to Tokyo to Vancouver to Montreal. Nelly's father had made contact with a Montrealer who had visited the hospital in China where he worked. The Montrealer had promised to give Nelly lodging for a few days until she could find a place to stay.

When she registered at Concordia University in early September,1983, she made arrangements for lodging in a home with board in return for babysitting and light housekeeping. The placement didn't work too well because the landlady had just given birth to a child and was nervous and depressed. Nelly found another lodging through the Students' Office at the home of the Dean of Students at Concordia, where she remained for two years.

"This arrangement helped me so very much. It was the ideal thing, living with a Canadian family to learn about the environment, language, Canadian mentality and the way of life, adjustment, and the whole cultural experience. But for this, I would never have gotten over the feeling that I was a stranger. I no longer had to stop and think about what I should do or say in any situation."

Little things, such as grass, which is hardly noticed by Canadians, impressed Nelly. In China, open spaces were either cemented over or consisted of hard-packed earth in which nothing grew. She thought grass and trees in Canada were the most beautiful she had ever seen. To see so much greenery on streets, in gardens and parks was a revelation. She was amazed at the feeling of space, in which each individual could move freely about. China's huge population creates an environment of packed humanity wherever one goes. And people...she was entranced with the Canadian style of social contact.

"I found social contacts so open and direct. People appeared to be so nice, and I enjoyed their behaviour. It is very important for a Chinese person not to show feelings of any kind. The upbringing there emphasizes total self-control, without which you can do nothing in life. Because of this belief, I was considered a misfit in my country, for by nature, I was more open in showing my feelings. My countrymen look down on extroverted behaviour as immature, and criticize it. Canadians, on the other hand, show that they like you or dislike you and if they have an opinion, they express it.

"At first I thought they were nice to me only because I was a stranger, but then I realized it is a unique trait of Canadian personality. I had to discover so much about the new world around me in every-day life, and I learned a great deal from people who helped by getting me to read papers, telling me where to go, whom to see and what do do. By immersing myself in this fashion, I discovered that one thing led to another. Having my type of personality helped, because I like to be occupied with all kinds of activities, even if they are voluntary and I don't get paid.

"If I could offer advice to students or even immigrants coming to a foreign country, I would tell people to get involved in everything, even if the benefit isn't immediately apparent. Exposure to different experiences creates opportunities of making contacts that will broaden the mind and prove helpful later.

"My involvement with the Chinese Programme broadcast on Radio Centreville in Montreal and volunteer work on translation for the Chinese Trade Delegation taught me a great deal, as I gained specialized knowledge. When I realized there was no way for the radio programme or myself to develop any further, and that all I was contributing was my time, I tried another approach.

"The federally-sponsored multicultural programme was broadcast only in Cantonese, and so was reaching a very limited audience. I went to the Director of Programming and pointed out that Mandarin was the language of the majority of Chinese in Quebec, and I gradually convinced him to begin with half an hour of air-time in Mandarin, increasing to one hour. I felt this would help new immigrants who didn't know much about Canadian life when they first arrived here. I prepared a mixture of news, music, literature, and an introduction to the way of life in Quebec and the other provinces. I knew the isolation many Chinese newcomers suffered. Their only outside activity was to shop in Chinatown, and have a meal in a restaurant. They knew nothing of other cultures, and I attempted to introduce these to them, in the hope that they would be encouraged to make more of a contribution to society, rather than remaining isolated.

"I joined the Canada-China Society with the idea of working to bring China and her civilization to westerners who find it difficult to understand the Chinese mentality. There are many ways of access to this huge and ageless civilization—through its art, literature, music and history. I have given lectures at the Learned Societies' Conferences on Chinese ideology, cultural development and use of the media. While working on my Master's Degree at Concordia University, I have worked on translating, not only for Chinese businessmen, but also Canadians seeking trade with my country. I have done this without remuneration, because I feel that cultural and commerical ties are important between the two countries.

"In addition, I take computer courses to assist me with, and improve, my personal efficiency. Each activity brings a new experience. These voluntary jobs and contacts have enabled me to visit business firms, municipal offices and installations, banking and finance houses, as well as giving me insight into economics, commerce and government administration. I am very pleased to have been given the opportunity to learn so much, all of which will be useful for my future.

"When I first learned about the Quebec Translation Service, I became a member, and it opened all kinds of doors and gave me many ideas. One of these was to go to McGill University's Department of East Asian Studies and introduce myself, talk with the Director and submit my curriculum vitae. It turned out that one of the McGill instructors left to take another position, and I was called to teach Chinese for a year to eighteen students. It was an experience teaching Canadians, who are so different from the students in my country. Here they are very lively and joke, treating classes as an enjoyable process. They don't just sit there like zombies.

"I don't think I have learned enough yet to become fully a part of this pluralistic society. No piece of the mosaic is the same as any other. There is so much more I must know, not only to survive, but to go beyond that and achieve something. Because I worked so hard in China and wanted so badly to come to Canada, it would be a terrible anti-climax for me to end up working in a kitchen or a restaurant, like many Chinese who spend their lives doing this. I'm not saying that this is bad, but it isn't my goal. To have a career, I must learn more about systems in the technology which is developing so quickly, and, of course, I need to learn French. All this learning will take a lifetime. I don't want to be a professional student, but you have to keep studying to stay ahead.

"Being an immigrant is a new beginning, and a newcomer is on the same level as a baby. Those born here have had at least a head-start in adjustment, education and building up contacts. An immigrant is handicapped by lack of experience and has to learn everything at an accelerated rate to catch up to the Canadian. And unless an immigrant has money, he has no protection from many difficult situations in his new life. Emigrating is like the first step one takes as a child. It marks a new stage, but it's only the start of a long process.

"Many immigrants come from poor or underdeveloped countries, and for them food and clothing are enough at the beginning. But soon they become dissatisfied, when they look around and see others who have more. They want TVs, cars, furniture, appliances and other things as they advance and become more Canadianized. And some established Canadians get resentful and say immigrants should be satisfied with little and be grateful for the low-paid jobs they hold.

"My own goal is not for material things, but to make a career in Canada and save some money, if I can, and later return to China to open a school where I can teach English and train students in western techniques. They need a sense of responsibility to their work, something which is at present totally lacking in China, especially in office administration. Management skills are important, and because they are absent in China, nothing really gets done, except paper-shuffling and disorganization.

"That is my own plan for the future, and it's my way of sharing what I've learned in Canada with my compatriots in China. Without secretaries and their organizational abilities, commercial companies simply wouldn't function. Because no one is sent abroad by the Chinese to learn these skills, they can't be communicated unless someone like me goes back to teach them.

"But while I'm here, I want to do all the things in my power to promote exchanges between Canada and China in trade, culture, economics, whatever. There's a certain way to deal with the Chinese mentality, and I would like to be part of the liaison between my country and Canada. All my experiences in volunteer work have shown me the way, and I know I can do it. But my plans involve money, and it's up to me to find it. Meanwhile I'll work for others and learn enough to open a company of my own one day."

LAND OF MORNING CALM

by
Mylene Pepin

He traces patience onto a sheet of paper
and presses it into my skin.
The sounds flow from his throat to mine
where they vibrate down my body's tunnel.
I never learned his language.

He remembers Korea, the fishing village
where he was born, the long stalks
of wild plants they raked in for meals.
He loved the white fruit tucked inside
the skin of red heart, the freshness
exploding inside his mouth.

His master taught him to breathe,
open arms, push air into a circle
until the pulse in his chest expanded
like a fish drawing in water.
He learned to smell oranges with his lips
run their red lining over the bumps,
letting the acid escape in streams into his mouth.

The rivers he swam in drew their purple
liquid from his veins.
Shipped to the hard streets of Vancouver,
he defends his corner of Korea,
mouth pounding from thirst,
He rolls his tongue around the new name
they gave him, spits the sounds
like a curse onto the pavement.

At night he forgets where he is,
wakes up, long body shaking,
clinging to Land of Morning Calm.
He murmurs words that fall like a sheet
over his body, locking me out.
I am alone in the dark.
A shadow swims in my eyes.

BIBLIOGRAPHY

Adi Granth, Rag Suhi 3, (3), p. 768.

Affirmation, The Ontario Human Rights Commission, "Board Rules on Wearing Kirpan", December 1981. Vol. 2, No. 4, p. 1.

Archives of Dr. Julius Pfeiffer, 1933-1987.

The Cambridge Times, "All people don't find Cambridge friendly". Lavers, Daphne and Anneli Barrett, November 16, 1977.

Canadian Jewish Historical Society Journal, "A Canadian Footnote to the Holocaust", Rabbi Erwin Schild, Spring 1981.

Canadian Jewish News, "He recalls Canada internment", Janice Arnold, August 14, 1980.

Chronology of World War II, compiled by Christopher Argyle, Marshall Cavendish Book, Ltd., London, 1982, pp. 58-61, 153-156, 190.

Deemed Suspect, Eric Koch, Methuen, Toronto, 1980.

Encyclopaedia Britannica, Micropaedia No. 13, "History of the Ottoman Empire and Turkey", Chicago, 1984, pp. 792-794.

Estate of John Glassco, courtesy of Mrs. John Glassco, used with the permission of William Toye.

The Gazette (Montreal), "An Odd Way to Choose a Country", Julia Maskoulis, July 12, 1980.
"World of Chewing Gum and Death", Patricia Thompson, November 10, 1979.

Jewish Life Publication, "From Amsterdam to Montreal For $1.25", Julius Pfeiffer, New York, July 1973.

JIAS News, "A 'Shofar' is not a Chauffeur", Julius Pfeiffer, Summer 1975.

Malta Story, W. L. River, American Book—Stratford Press, Inc., New York, 1943, pp. 41-46.

Montreal Standard, "Refugees in Camp", Boulkind, February 7, 1942.

Maclean's, "The Welcome Enemies", Barbara Moon, February 10, 1962, pp. 14-15, 36 and 37.
"Race—The Debate becomes violent; Racism? You can't argue with the facts.", Angela Ferrante, February 7, 1977, Vol. 90, No. 3, pp. 18-21.

Problems of Social Policy, History of the Second World War, Richard M. Titmuss, HMSO and Longmans, 1950.

Proceedings of the Sikh Heritage Conference, Ed. Jarnail Singh and Hardev Singh. The Sikh Social and Educational Society, Willowdale, Ontario, 1981, p. 47
"Fight For Our Identity—Kirpan", Pritam Singh, p. 50

Rehat Maryada—A Guide to the Sikh Way of Life, Amritsar, India: Shromani Gurdwara Parbhandhak Committee (SGPC), 1978.

The Sikh Courier, "The Rise of the Sikh Power", Indarjit Singh, Spring/Summer, 1982. Vol. II, No. 1, pp. 11-15.

The Story of the Falashas—Black Jews of Ethiopia, Dr. Simon D. Messing, Hamden, Conn., 1982, pp. 14-15, 16-18, 56-57, 60 and 68.

The Revolution Disarmed, Gabriel Smirnow, Monthly Review Press, New York, 1979, p.6.

The Sunday Sun, "The Sikhs get tough", Joan Barfoot, June 2, 1974, p. 2.

Toronto Life, "Strangers in a Strange Land", Philip Marchand, July 1982, pp. 48-49, 56-67.

The Toronto Star, "Vandals deface Sikh temple; police set up surveillance", May 29, 1974, p. B1.
"Riots feared—Sikhs demand police action on race attacks", August 29, 1977, p. C1.

The Toronto Sun, "We feel like blacks in Detroit, Sikh says", Ken Becker, August 30, 1977, p. 16.

PHOTO CREDITS

—Page 16, March, 1948. The photograph depicts part of a group
of 860 Baltic and Balkan nationals brought in from
camps in the British and American Zones for
resettlement in Canada.
Photo courtesy of the Canapress Photo Service.
—Page 28, Jerry Wexler
—Page 32. Linda Ghan
—Page 44, Glen W. Bradley
—Page 52, 'Aussie' Whiting
—Page 74, Dr. and Mrs. James Hasegawa and family
—Page 104, Nick Auf der Maur
—Page 116, Ray Serwylo
—Page 122, Zaven Degirmen
—Page 140, Carlos Rodriguez
—Page 160, Lempi and Hemming Lauttamaki, 1913
—Page 170, Patricia Thompson
—Page 188, Miodrag Brkic, circa 1950
—Page 198, Anni Sebag Selinger
—Page 206, Dr. Julius Pfeiffer
—Page 228, Anna Torranz
—Page 246, Lena Kraouse
—Page 272, Malka Abraham and family and former Minister of
Employment and Immigration, Lloyd Axworthy.
Photo courtesy of Howard Kay, Montreal.
—Page 294, George Bonavia
—Page 306, Dan Leeaphon
—Page 320, Fania Sidline
—Page 330, Pritam Singh. Photo courtesy of M. Rafelson
Photographics, Toronto.
—Page 348, Jadwiga Krupski, circa 1939
—Page 396, Nelly Cheng

OTHER MULTICULTURAL TITLES FROM CORMORANT
RR 1, Dunvegan, Ontario, Canada K0C 1J0

1. *The Confusion of Stones* by Marwan Hassan. Two novellas about the Lebanese-Canadian experience.

2. *When the Words Burn: An Anthology of Modern Arabic Poetry, 1945-1987* by John Asfour.

3. *Children of Byzantium* by Katherine Vlassie. A novel about growing up Greek in Winnipeg.

4. *Lost Causes* by Leandro Urbina. Stories by Canada's finest Chilean writer.

5. *Souvenirs: New English Fiction form Quebec*, edited by P. Scott Lawrence.

6. *Daniel* by Bruce Rice. Poems of immigration and settlement, from Ireland to Scotland, South Africa to Saskatchewan.

7. *To Samarkand and Back* by Roma Gelblum-Bross. A Jewish-Canadian writer provides a fictionalized account of her childhood experience of being driven from Poland in World War II.

8. *The Lives of the Saints* by Nino Ricci. The first novel of a Proustian trilogy of Italian immigration to Canada (due 1990).

9. *The Guerrilla Is Like A Poet: An Anthology of Filipino Poetry* edited by Robert Majzels.

10. *Burning Bridges* by Nain Nomez. Poems of Canada and Chile.

11. *A Continental Hug.* Canadian poems by Atwood, Layton, Livesay, Lane, di Michele, Crozier, Geddes, and Sagaris read in English by the poets and set to music in Spanish by Amauta.

12. *Bonfire,* an audio-tape magazine of poems, ballads and lively talk of the Scottish folk revival, edited by Alexander Hutchison.

13. *Tears of Chinese Immigrants* by Charlie Jang (Yuen Chung Yip). A novel of Chinese immigration set in Alberta (due 1990).